Gilded Dragons

Silver gilt bodhisattva (cat. no. 104) from the crypt of Famen temple, Fufeng county, Shaanxi province. Tang dynasty.

Gilded Dragons

BURIED TREASURES FROM CHINA'S GOLDEN AGES

CAROL MICHAELSON

Published for The Trustees of

The British Museum by

BRITISH MUSEUM ████████ PRESS

Chinese names and terms are romanized according to the pinyin system, the standard form of transliteration used throughout China today.

$$
\begin{array}{rcl}
\mathbf{c} & = & ts\ (cong = tsoong)\\
\mathbf{q} & = & chi\ (qi = chee)\\
\mathbf{x} & = & sh\ (Xi'an = Shee\text{-}an)\\
\mathbf{zh} & = & j\ (Zhou = Jo)
\end{array}
$$

Chinese place-names are generally given in three parts, ordered from smallest to largest as in normal English usage (site, county, province). Sometimes, however, the Chinese system is used, in which the largest area is given first and the smallest last (province, county, site).

Quotations are reprinted by courtesy of the publishers cited in the relevant notes.

Photographs in the catalogue are reproduced by courtesy of The Administrative Bureau of Museum and Archaeological Data of Shaanxi Province unless otherwise noted, photography by Qiu Zi Yu (cat. nos 1–3, 6, 18, 33–35, 38–39, 44, 46, 48, 50–52, 55, 57–59, 61, 64–94, 97–103), Wang Bao Ping (cat. nos 4–5, 7–17, 19–32, 36–37, 40–43, 45, 47, 49, 53–56, 60, 62, 95–96, 104–120) and Gao Yu Ying (cat. no. 63). Additional photographs © The British Museum, provided by The British Museum Photographic Service (denoted BM OA, Department of Oriental Antiquities, with accession number); exceptions are noted below.
Figure no. **1**: BM OA 1938.5-24.252; **2**: Institute of Archaeology and Cultural Relics Bureau, Sichuan Province; **4**: BM OA 1968.4-22.10, Mrs Walter Sedgwick Bequest; **5**: BM WAA (Western Asiatic Antiquities) 133033; **6**: Hebei Provincial Museum; **8**: photograph H. Espir; **13**: after Beijing 1973b, vol. 1, p. 40, fig. 38; **14**: courtesy of the British Library Board; **17**: courtesy of the Freer Gallery of Art, Smithsonian Institution, Washington, DC, no. F1957.14; **18**: Aurel Stein, *Ruins of Desert Cathay*, Oxford 1921, fig. 281; **20**: photograph H. Espir; **24**: BM OA MAS 876; **25**: BM OA 1919.0101-0.168; **26**: photograph H. Espir.
Catalogue no. **9a**: BM OA 1937.4-16.218; **10a, b**: after Shaanxi 1998a, figs 53, 27; **13b**: after Yang Hong 1992, p. 98, fig. 124; **14a**: after Fu Tianchou 1985, p. 10; **31a**: BM OA 1919.1-1.047 (Ch.lvii.002); **34a**: BM Ch.lii.004; **42a**: after Sun Ji 1986, fig. 16:1; **44a**: after Sun Ji 1994, fig. 6:3; **52a**: BM OA 1983.2-1.03; **53a**: after *Kaogu yu Wenwu* 1983.1, p. 29, fig. 1; **58a**: after Han and Lu 1985, no. 154; **58b**: BM; **59a**: after Han and Lu 1985, no. 246; **60a**: after Han and Lu 1985, no. 261; **80a**: after Han and Lu 1985, no. 81; **86a**: BM OA 1913 Ch.00260; **87a**: after Han and Lu 1985, no. 51; **88a**: after Han Wei 1989, p. 29; **103a**: BM OA 1857.11-18.8.

© 1999 The Trustees of The British Museum
First published in 1999 by British Museum Press
A division of The British Museum Company Ltd
46 Bloomsbury Street, London WC1B 3QQ

Reprinted 1999

A catalogue record for this book is available from the British Library

ISBN 0-7141-1489-8

Designed and set in Perpetua by John Hawkins Book Design

Printed in Italy by Grafiche Milani

CONTENTS

江泽民主席
致《中华人民共和国陕西省文物精华展》的祝词

值此中华人民共和国成立五十周年之际，《中华人民共和国陕西省文物精华展》在大英博物馆展出，我对此表示热烈祝贺。

中国是东方的文明古国，历史悠久。中华民族创造的光辉灿烂的文化，为人类文明作出了举世公认的卓越贡献。

陕西省是中华文明诞生的重要摇篮。中国古代有十一个朝代在此建都，那里曾是驰名中外的汉唐两代的政治、经济、文化中心。陕西的地上和地下文化遗产极为丰富。这次展出的精品，绝大部分选自公元前一至二世纪和公元七至八世纪的文物，显示了中国西汉和唐代文化的辉煌成就。汉唐两代也是中国对外交往相当活跃的时期。这些艺术精品既体现了中华民族文化的历史发展和创新，又体现了对外来文化的吸收和消化。这充分说明，中华民族是勤劳智慧、富有创造精神的伟大民族，具有善于学习和吸取世界优秀文化成果的光荣传统。

中英两国人民有着传统的友谊。我深信，这次展览不但有助于进一步加强两国之间的文化交流，而且有助于增进两国人民的相互了解和友谊，推动两国友好关系的发展。

预祝这次展览取得圆满成功。

中华人民共和国主席

江泽民

一九九九年七月二十九日

I would like to extend my warm congratulations to the exhibition of buried treasures, masterpieces from Shaanxi Province, People's Republic of China, for its opening at the British Museum on the occasion of the fiftieth anniversary of the founding of the People's Republic of China.

China is an ancient oriental civilization with a time-honoured history. It is universally acknowledged that the splendid culture created by the Chinese nation has made outstanding contributions to human civilization.

Shaanxi Province is an important cradle of Chinese civilization. It was home to the imperial capital of eleven dynasties of ancient China and was the political, economic and cultural centre of the world-famous Han (206 BC–AD 220) and Tang (AD 618–906) dynasties. The province boasts an extremely rich array of archaeological and cultural relics, both above and under the ground. Most of the treasures on display in the exhibition date back to the first or second century BC and to the seventh or eighth century AD and represent the brilliant cultural achievements of the Western Han (206 BC–AD 25) and Tang dynasties. As the Han and Tang dynasties were the two periods when China's external exchanges were flourishing, these art treasures are not only a reflection of the historical development and improvement of the traditional culture of the Chinese nation but also a record of China's assimilation and digestion of foreign cultures. They give full evidence of the industry, wisdom and creativity of the great Chinese nation and fully demonstrate the Chinese nation's glorious tradition of learning from other nations and absorbing the excellent cultural heritage of the world.

The Chinese and the British people cherish a traditional friendship. I am convinced that this exhibition will not only help to further strengthen the cultural exchanges between our two countries, but also help to enhance the understanding and friendship between the two peoples and thus promote the development of friendly relations between our two countries.

I wish the exhibition complete success.

Jiang Zemin
President of the People's Republic of China

BUCKINGHAM PALACE

I welcome the initiative which has brought about this exhibition of some of the finest archaeological objects from Shaanxi Province, held at the British Museum on the occasion of the State Visit by President Jiang Zemin, in the year of the fiftieth anniversary of the founding of the People's Republic of China. I am confident that such close cultural co-operation will lead the way to a deeper mutual understanding and will strengthen the existing ties between China and the United Kingdom.

Our two countries share the traditions both of valuing the past and of maintaining careful stewardship of national treasures. We share the belief that museums provide a means by which this past can be preserved and brought to the attention of the broadest public. I am delighted that, through this exhibition, visitors to the British Museum from all over the world will benefit from the opportunity to increase their knowledge of China's ancient and rich heritage and to appreciate her people's outstanding artistic accomplishments and technological skills.

I congratulate the People's Government of Shaanxi Province, the Bureau of Cultural Relics, Shaanxi Province, the State Bureau of Cultural Relics and the British Museum on their remarkable collaboration. I wish the exhibition every possible success.

ELIZABETH R.

Three years ago, *The Times* sponsored the British Museum's enthralling *Mysteries of Ancient China*. The exhibition was a great success and revealed the sophistication of a people who had invented the wheelbarrow centuries before Britons had fallen in love with gardening. The exhibition confirmed our fascination with China – its culture, its technology, and indeed its magnitude.

The Tang dynasty was a time with parallels to our own. New technologies and improved communications created vast wealth and left time for more of the art which forms this exhibition. The Silk Route had the same kind of impact on the Tang as aviation, shipping and the Internet have had on us. The Tang were also fans of those more indulgent pastimes of music, dancing and cuisine. They too liked their drinking games and even revelled in that most luxurious of sports, polo. Their political life was as intriguing and as scheming as ours.

The Times has a long history of being associated with Chinese art. We have unveiled the mysteries of the past two centuries, through our reporting and our sponsorship of the Royal Academy's *The Genius of China* in 1973. It is fitting that *The Times* continues its association in sponsoring this exhibition, which is more than a worthy successor to the magnificence of *Mysteries*. *The Times* is honoured to be associated with *Gilded Dragons*. Such co-operations help to draw our two cultures towards a closer understanding of each other. At this turn of the millennium, that is a powerful virtue in itself.

Peter Stothard
Editor

For Prudential, 1999 will be the most significant year in the development of our relationship with the People's Republic of China. In March, as Chairman of Prudential, I had the singular honour of an audience with President Jiang Zemin during which we exchanged views on the importance of a thriving life insurance industry for China's future. In April, after many years of sustained effort, Prudential was awarded a life insurance licence for China. Since then we have been in constant communication with the Chinese regulatory authorities about the establishment of a joint venture operation to offer our products to the citizens of China.

It is therefore fitting that Prudential should crown our very special year by sponsoring this spectacular exhibition of Chinese archaeological treasures, the major cultural event during the State Visit of President Jiang Zemin. We are convinced that the artefacts on display will delight and impress the people of Britain. We are excited to be helping to enhance understanding and respect between the people of Britain and the people of China.

Prudential has always prided itself on its community spirit. In the UK we support a wide spectrum of welfare and educational activities, and in China we have been true to this tradition. Not only have we supported academic institutions, we have also helped where we could to build up a critical mass of local skills and to upgrade insurance expertise. We have done more than any other UK or European insurer to provide training for short- and long-stay Chinese visitors. We intend to continue this approach. We believe in people. We believe in what they can achieve, whether in financial services or in the arts. We try to improve quality of life wherever we can.

And we express our commitment to China in many ways. As an example, during the visit of Premier Zhu Rongji in 1998, we supported the first ever exhibition of contemporary Chinese ceramics to be held in London, which was opened for us by the Premier's wife. From the most modern last year to some of the most ancient this year, Prudential continues today its association with China's rich and spectacular artistic and cultural traditions. *Gilded Dragons* promises to become one of the most noteworthy and talked-about exhibitions of Chinese treasures ever seen abroad. Prudential's participation in this fine exhibition is true to our commitment to expanding the horizons of understanding and appreciation between peoples.

For us the truth is simple: Prudential and China. Partners for life.

Sir Martin Jacomb
Chairman

I warmly congratulate the British Museum and The Administrative Bureau of Museums and Archaeological Data of Shaanxi Province for working successfully together to produce the exhibition *Gilded Dragons: Buried Treasures from China's Golden Ages*.

Shaanxi province is situated within the middle to lower reaches of the Yellow River. For five thousand years it has benefited from this geographically advantageous position and is one of the most significant cradles of China's ancient civilization. The famous Lantian man (*Sinanthropus Lantianensis*) who lived about a million years ago, the Banpo site of *c.* 5000–3000 BC, and the world-renowned terracotta army of the First Emperor, Qin Shi Huangdi, were all discovered in Shaanxi province. During this time Shaanxi was the cultural and political centre of ancient China. Thus Shaanxi province, with its long and distinguished history and its magnificent culture, is the country's richest archaeological source and is often known as the 'natural museum' of China's history.

Each of the 120 objects in the exhibition is of great historical, artistic or scientific importance, chosen to reflect the brilliance of ancient Chinese civilization. Cultural relics are the crystallization of human wisdom and the witnesses of history. They can build bridges between peoples and nations. I believe that through this exhibition we will increase understanding between the British and Chinese people and will develop firm friendships. I am confident, too, that we will encourage further economic and cultural exchanges between our two countries.

I am grateful to those who support Anglo-Chinese cultural relations and I thank everyone who has been involved with this exhibition for their hard work. I hope *Gilded Dragons: Buried Treasures from China's Golden Ages* will be a great success.

Cheng An Dong
Governor of Shaanxi Province

The British Museum is highly privileged to have the opportunity to display a remarkable group of objects of the highest quality from China's past. For this we offer our warmest thanks to those who have encouraged us in this enterprise: the Ministry of Culture and the State Bureau of Cultural Relics of the People's Republic of China; the Embassy of the People's Republic of China in London, His Excellency the Ambassador Mr Ma Zhengang and his staff in the Cultural Office; and the Administrative Bureau of Museums and Archaeological Data of Shaanxi Province. *The Times* and Prudential have given the essential financial support and have been ideal sponsors. The resulting exhibition is of a nature never before seen in this country, revealing new facets of China's extraordinarily rich cultural history.

The British Museum has had a long fascination with China; Sir Hans Sloane's founding collection of 1753 already contained Chinese prints and ceramics. In the nineteenth century the activities of the remarkable curator Augustus Wollaston Franks provided the Museum with the basis of one of the finest collections in the West. In 1992 the Joseph E. Hotung Gallery of Oriental Antiquities was opened by Her Majesty The Queen, and in 1996 *Mysteries of Ancient China* was seen by the Museum's largest exhibition audience in recent years. Interest in Chinese culture continues at a high level today and collecting activities concentrate largely on products of the twentieth century, although in 1998 a scroll painting of 1321 by Xie Chufang, 'Fascination of Nature', was acquired. It is likely that this had been presented to a member of Lord Macartney's embassy to China of 1792–4; if so, it would be the first Chinese painting to be brought to this country.

What is certain is that *Gilded Dragons* will fascinate the public who come to the British Museum in vast numbers. It is also certain that with a greater appreciation of her past will come a deeper understanding of China's present.

Dr R G W Anderson
Director of The British Museum

ACKNOWLEDGEMENTS

It was just a year ago that the British Museum began to organize an exhibition to mark the fiftieth anniversary of the founding of the People's Republic of China and the first state visit to Britain by a Chinese head of state, President Jiang Zemin. This catalogue has therefore been prepared at great speed in order to accompany the exhibition of which it forms a record. The compressed timetable has imposed enormous demands on everyone involved and I have therefore relied very heavily on many colleagues for help and support, and I am very grateful to all of them. I have drawn upon other catalogues and literature for information about the objects in this exhibition and have tried to ensure that due acknowledgement has been given. It has been impossible within the time available to research all the previous places of publication for every object, some of which have been extensively published elsewhere, but I hope I have given sufficient information for readers to do more research on their own, should they so wish.

I have been helped enormously by three assistants in particular who have given me inestimable support with this project and I especially want to thank them for their enthusiasm, optimism and unremitting hard work: Mary Ginsberg (particularly for the bibliography), YiYi Yin and Harriot Tennant. Christina Kwong and Carol White of the British Museum Department of Oriental Antiquities have done much retyping of the text, Jude Simmons and Rachael Bailey of the Design Office have prepared the maps and plans and Kevin Lovelock and John Williams of the Photographic Service have provided support photography at very short notice.

I thank Emma Way, Head of British Museum Press, for her initial encouragement and I am very grateful to Susan Leiper, whose job as editor went, I am sure, far beyond the normal realms of duty. I also especially thank Nina Shandloff, Senior Editor, for her constant back-up support of the catalogue and her very long hours spent getting the catalogue published on time. The book was designed by John Hawkins, who has worked so well under great pressure, the production was ably managed by Nicola Denny, and the index was prepared by Susanne Atkin.

The exhibition was designed by Paul Tansey with the help of many British Museum Design Office staff, directed by Margaret Hall, and including Jude Simmons and Andrea Easey. Much help both in the Museum and in China was given by the Museum Assistants of the Department of Oriental Antiquities, including Jane Newson, Sophie Sorrondegui and Stephen Ruscoe. I am particularly grateful to Jane Portal for accompanying me to China last December to help select the objects and for a great deal of encouragement and practical help, on both the catalogue and the exhibition.

Many colleagues in various British Museum departments have given their time and expertise on specific entries or offered general support in the administration of the project. These include Silke Ackermann, Anthony Blackstock, Richard Blurton, Sheila Canby, Tim Clark, Michael Cowell, Joe Cribb, Tony Doubleday, Kate Down, Elizabeth Duggal, Anne Farrer, Ian Freestone, Victor Harris, Jessica Harrison-Hall, Catherine Johns, Susan La Niece, Julian Marland, Rita Phillips, Mavis Pilbeam, Jane Portal, Venetia Porter, Maureen Theobald, Helen Wang, Rachel Ward and Michael Willis, as well as Geoffrey House and all his colleagues in the Public Relations Office, John Reeve and Helen Glaister in the Education Service and Marjorie Caygill and her colleagues in the Director's Office. Robert Knox, Keeper of the Department of Oriental Antiquities, has given me encouragement and support on this project at all times and accompanied me to China on the first preliminary visit last October.

Many colleagues outside the British Museum have also given me inestimable help by reading and commenting on various entries and, in some cases, the entire catalogue. I am particularly indebted to Jessica Rawson for her expertise and encouragement and for giving up so much of her time to give me advice. I am also grateful to Robert Brill, Helmut Brinker, Anthony Dicks, Glen Dudbridge, Graham Hutt, Jin Jun, Raymond Keene, Rose Kerr, Stephen Little, Michael Loewe, Hsin-cheung Lovell, Ann Paludan, Laura Rivkin, Roger Sheehy, Jenny So, Yankit So, Wang Tao, Shelagh Vainker, Susan Whitfield, Ming Wilson and Frances Wood. For the Buddhist section I am most indebted to John Huntington, who has given me much new information and a great deal of help particularly pertaining to the subject of Esoteric Buddhism. I am very grateful to Robin Michaelson for help with the maps and for his tolerance and support during this very time-consuming project.

In China, the Administrative Bureau of Museums and Archaeological Data of Shaanxi Province was very helpful at all times and extremely hospitable during my two visits there. I would particularly like to mention Jia Zhibang, First Vice-Governor of Shaanxi Province, Li Bin, and my sometimes daily contact, Zhang Tong, who very patiently passed on so much information. Han Wei was also scrupulous in giving help whenever asked, as were Qin Zao Yuan and Li Kai. In Beijing, I am grateful for the help of Zhang Wenbin and Wang Limei as well as Li Yuanchao of the Ministry of Culture, who were all very supportive of the project. My friends in Hong Kong were also very enthusiastic about the exhibition and were involved from a very early stage in helping me establish contact with the relevant authorities in China. I am most grateful to Chung Wah-Pui, Professor Shang Zhitan and all my jade collector friends there. In London, the Chinese ambassador, His Excellency Ma Zhengang, the Cultural Counsellor, Ding Wei, and the First Secretary, Wu Xun, have all been most helpful and supportive.

Finally I thank the Director of the British Museum, Dr Robert Anderson, the Chairman of the Trustees, Graham C. Greene, and Sir Joseph Hotung, the Trustee responsible for my Department, for their enthusiasm and constant support for this exciting project.

Introduction

Drink each day at Gold Powder Spring
And you should have a thousand years or more:
To soar on an azure phoenix with striped dragons,
And with plumes and tassels attend the Jade Emperor's court.[1]

The famous poet, painter and musician Wang Wei (701–761) wrote these lines in the mid-eighth century, at the height of China's Golden Age, the Tang dynasty (618–906). Woven through these four lines are many of the threads in the present catalogue and exhibition, *Gilded Dragons:* not only gold and dragons themselves, but the ideas of wealth and power, the exotic and the Chinese, the practical and the religious.

Gold endures, It does not corrode: Wang Wei invites us to share these qualities, to seek immortality – a thousand years at least – by swallowing gold, a practice that was indeed carried out by those who could afford it. Gold was used not only as ornament, but also as medicine: it was transformed by alchemists into potions that they hoped would bring long life and even immortality. One could then ride on dragons and phoenixes, symbols of the emperor and the empress, just as the Queen Mother of the West, who resided in one of the immortals' paradises. The land of the immortals was presided over by the Jade Emperor, supreme deity in the Daoist pantheon, himself named after China's most revered mineral, jade, also symbolic of immortality.

This exhibition and catalogue focus on the Golden Age in Chinese history, the Tang dynasty. The name is appropriate for at this time gold and silver were accorded high status and enjoyed great popularity. However gold and silver were used, though much more sparingly, before the Tang and the catalogue has an introductory section

presenting earlier pieces, including those associated with another so-called Golden Age, the Han dynasty (206 BC– AD 220). Both the Han and Tang dynasties were preceded respectively by two short-lived but pivotal dynasties, the Qin and the Sui, and their periods of ruthless unification of a fragmented China were then followed by the stability of long lasting dynasties and stable Golden Ages, eras of great prosperity and unprecedented creativity in the arts.

All the objects in the catalogue have been found in Shaanxi province where the capital of China was situated from the Western Zhou period through the Qin, Western Han, Six Dynasties, Sui and Tang dynasties, a period of over a thousand years. Chang'an (present-day Xi'an) and its neighbouring area in the heart of central Shaanxi province, in northwest China, was always a geographically strategic area, and later formed the eastern end of the Silk Route.

The Western Han dynasty capital, Chang'an, covered an area three times the area of contemporaneous Rome and the magnificence of the Tang capital provided a model for city planners in many neighbouring countries. China during the Han and the Tang periods was characterized by cultural brilliance, territorial expansion and great prosperity. The Silk Route, begun in the Han and revitalized in the Tang, brought, and sent, many exotic treasures along it. The gold and silver and other treasures buried in tombs, hoards and Buddhist crypts, many only discovered in the twentieth century, help us to bring to life the important part that this province and capital have played in Chinese history.

This catalogue has been divided into three major sections. The first, Early Tomb Burials, is an introduction to the use of gold in early China, a period defined here as dating from the Eastern Zhou to the end of the Han dynasty. Here are described early gold and silver objects, many of which have been found in tombs. Many of these are cast, dependent in some ways on the traditional method of making bronzes, yet they also show foreign nomadic influence; gold does not seem a highly regarded material in its own right. Gold and silver were rather used at this time as an adjunct to other metals, such as bronze, for decorative purposes. In the Qin dynasty they were used to embellish the reins of the horses of the terracotta army and for decorating the bronze chariot of the First Emperor (cat. no. 10). However by the Han dynasty gold and silver were becoming more important and the gilding of silver and bronze was also being practised (cat. no. 17).

The second part of the catalogue, Tang Tombs and Hoards, describes pieces found in Tang tombs and hoards, many only recovered in the last thirty years of the twentieth century. The Tang was a period when China was one of the most powerful empires in the world, the dominant power in Asia with whose peoples it was in contact through trade, absorbing new ideas which contributed to the cosmopolitanism of the Tang. Exotic goods that travelled along the Silk Route included the gold and silver that were a relative commonplace for the peoples of Central Asia and which soon became a necessity for the Chinese élite.

The last section, Buddhist Temples and Crypts, covers temple statuary and the gold and silver treasures found in Buddhist crypts, treasures like those buried in the hoards, most likely put away for safe keeping at a time of religious persecution or rebellion and, again, only rediscovered within the last twenty years. The discovery of the treasures at the Famen temple (Famensi) have greatly enlarged our knowledge of Buddhist religion in the Tang period as it is the most important group of Buddhist objects excavated in China in recent years. The temple was one of the very few in Tang dynasty China to own a relic of the Buddha, an object of incalculable spiritual power, and the donations made to it in gold and silver by the emperor and imperial family reflect the importance of objects of gold and silver.

They were at the apex in the hierarchy of valuables in the field of religious patronage. Donations in such highly valued materials must have been regarded as very pious gestures at this time.[2]

THE SYMBOLISM OF GOLD

Jade and bronze were the materials most prized by the Chinese from ancient times and were the ones chosen for their most precious ornaments and sacrificial vessels. The Chinese were highly skilled at working both jade and bronze, but the fact that these techniques are unrelated to those needed for working the soft malleable metals of gold and silver may be one reason why neither gold nor silver played an important role in early Chinese society. Another reason may be that although there were some native deposits, much had to be imported from beyond the Chinese borders.

However, gradually over centuries gold became accepted by Chinese society and its beauty truly appreciated. Like jade it endures: it does not tarnish, rust or fade, qualities that were particularly appreciated. Moreover, unlike jade, it can be easily worked into ornaments for display and can be melted down in times of emergency to make an easily negotiable currency.

By the Tang period gold had acquired associations that were exploited in literature and religion. In the lines of poetry quoted at the beginning of this introduction, Wang Wei alludes to the association of gold with longevity and immortality, and to the use of gold by religious Daoists in potions to confer immortality. Daoist alchemists hoped to transfer the enduring qualities of gold to the human soul, thereby stablizing the soul and lengthening life. Even the immortal sylphs of Daoism were golden. The Buddhist religion also attached enormous importance to gold.[3] All the divine attributes of the Buddha were described as golden, and the Buddha himself was styled the 'Golden Man'. Even today, in many parts of Asia, it is customary to cover images of the Buddha in gold leaf.

On a more prosaic level, gold came to stand for human

virtue, much as jade had always done. Jade was valued for its physical attributes: its extreme toughness which made it so durable, and its incorruptibility in terms of colour, texture and translucence. With such qualities jade came to be seen as a concrete expression of earthly and spiritual power, and it was used as a metaphor to describe the qualities of the ideal man. Confucius wrote: 'Anciently superior men found the likeness of all excellent qualitites in jade…' and he went on to equate various aspects of jade with benevolence, intelligence, righteousness, humility, propriety, virtue, truth and duty.[4] Gold and silver were sometimes used to refer to Paradise, destination of the virtuous: the Han dynasty historian Sima Qian spoke of the sacred sea-island made of gold and silver[5] and tradition had Laozi residing in tall buildings of gold with halls of jade and stairways of silver.[6] However gold and silver were seldom used metaphorically before the Tang dynasty. It was not until the increasing influence of Buddhism and the greater use of gold and silver in this period that gold gradually came to stand for human virtue in China as it did in the West. Emperor Taizong, for example, praised his great minister Wei Zheng as a craftsman who could detect the gold in the raw mineral of the imperial person, extract it, refine it and make it worthy of the good opinion of men.[7]

Such associations of gold with virtue gradually spread beyond the realm of man himself. For example, goldfish symbolize wealth and good fortune for the Chinese because the word for goldfish sounds like 'gold in abundance'. Designs incorporating goldfish are still popular on ceramics and embroidery.[8] In the next major dynasty after the Tang, the Song dynasty, ladies began to bind their feet to make them small and delicate and these were referred to as golden lilies or lotuses. This term originated in the story about Emperor Donghun Hou of the late fifth century, who had water lilies made of gold leaf scattered on the ground for his concubine Pan Fei to dance on.[9] A very popular and well known novel of the eighteenth century, *The Story of the Stone,* describes how Jia Baoyu was born with a piece of lustrous jade in his mouth and Xue Baochai wore around her neck a golden chain of longevity. Both the jade and the gold were inscribed with auspicious phrases concerning longevity and so should have fated them to be joined in a happy marriage of gold and jade;[10] by this time the wearing of gold and jade was a symbol of both wealth and virtue. The twinning of gold and jade as materials of superior value is also illustrated in one of the four-character phrases so popular in China: *'jin yu liang yan',* meaning gold and jade words or valuable advice. In a recent novel, *The Joy Luck Club* by Amy Tan, there is a reference to twin babies being abandoned by their sick mother who was fleeing from the advancing Japanese troops, along with her only treasure, the gold bracelets given to her as a traditional present at her wedding.

SOURCES OF GOLD AND SILVER

Gold is found in a metallic state throughout China. In its natural metallic state gold is easily workable and is usually alloyed with silver in proportions that vary from less than 1 per cent to 80 per cent although sometimes it contains small amounts of copper and traces of other metals, depending on the location of the source.[11] The major sources of gold in ancient China were alluvial placer deposits which exist in every province of China though many are shallow and meagre. Sources in Fujian, Jiangxi, Hubei, Hunan, Guangdong, Sichuan and especially Yunnan and Heilongjiang have been the most productive. There is little evidence for the mining of gold on any scale before the Sui dynasty,[12] and until at least the late Spring and Autumn period there was no specific Chinese character for gold. In ancient literature gold was referred to as *huangjin* or yellow metal. The character *jin* is now used for gold, and is the radical component of characters for metals.

The native sources of gold that were known in Tang times were principally in Sichuan province, where it was found as flakes in alluvial deposits, although gold was also found in Hunan, Jiangxi, Yunnan, Guangdong, Anhui and Shaanxi. There were further gold deposits in Lingnan and Annam, though these were not very accessible as they were in rugged territory. Bai Juyi, the Tang dynasty poet famous for his social comment, wrote about the numbers of people in the south who were drawn to the gold and silver mines in order to try and pay their taxes:

Silver comes from the nooks in the hills of Ch'u
Gold comes from the shores of P'o Stream.
The people of the south no longer till the fields,
But seek gold with great toil and pain.
They clear away the gravel and chisel into the rock.
Hacking and hewing in spring and winter alike.
Their hands and feet are all chafed and swollen;
But they care for profit more than they care for themselves...
Yet after all, what are silver and gold?
They are no more real use than mud or dust.
They are not things one can eat or wear on one's back;
They do not help men who are hungry and cold...[13]

However, although China had its own gold deposits, and Shaanxi proved quite rich, it seems that there was never enough. Gold was therefore imported from beyond China's borders, from Korea, Manchuria, the Nanzhao kingdom, Turkestan and particularly from Tibet whence it was also received as tribute.[14] As Tibet grew more powerful and exported less gold there was a shortage in China and eventually imperial edicts precluded the use of pure gold food vessels to officials of less than first rank and the use of silver to those of less than sixth rank.

By comparison with gold and copper, silver occurs rarely in nature and throughout Chinese history seems to have been relatively scarce compared to gold. What native silver does occur was often, if not abundantly, found in the oxidized zones of metallic deposits. Silver is not as malleable as gold or tin and needs to be annealed after repeated hammering. It is extremely ductile, so one gram of pure silver can be drawn out to produce more than a kilometre of fine wire. This led to its being exploited for use as inlay decoration long before it was used for the form of the vessel itself.[15] The earliest silver objects discovered to date within China's present boundaries are the nose rings unearthed from the Huoshaogou site at Yumen in Gansu dating to *c*. 1600 BC.[16] Silver ornaments were popular with the tribes on China's northwestern borders in the fourth and third centuries BC, and quantities of fine silverwares were found in the King of Zhongshan's tomb dating to the Warring States period.

During the Tang dynasty silver production was concentrated in Lingnan and Annam in the south. By the late eighth and early ninth century silver production centred particularly on the mines of the southeast in Fujian, Zhejiang, southern Jiangxi and Hunan. It has been calculated that yearly production in the middle of the ninth century surpassed the equivalent of fourteen short tonnes. And, probably for the first time, silver enjoyed wider use than gold in Chinese society.[17] At the beginning of the ninth century there were forty silver refineries in operation, producing 123,000 ounces annually and by the middle of the ninth century this production had increased to forty-two refineries producing 150,000 ounces. Until the middle of the ninth century the work of the Tang silversmiths was superb, but after the great religious persecution of 845 and the general political unrest, a period of decline set in.[18]

METALWORKING TECHNOLOGY

Before the Tang dynasty, casting was the most common method used by the Chinese to make both gold and silver objects. As the Chinese were accustomed to using piece moulds for making their ceramics and bronzes, they at first made their gold and silver items in moulds also. The casting was done in the same way as for bronzes, with clay moulds and occasionally the lost wax method. Some examples, such as those in the Shōsōin in Nara, Japan, show the joins from the moulds quite clearly. Cast items gradually become less common, although in the Tang dynasty it remained common practice to cast certain parts of stem cups and cups with handles. The former have the stems cast separately and afterwards soldered to the bowl, and the latter have the handles and attaching plates cast, soldered and riveted.

The Chinese developed during the Tang dynasty many new techniques for working gold and silver, probably influenced by Central Asian silversmiths who took refuge in China in the mid-seventh century fleeing the Arab invaders of their country. During the Sui and the earlier part of the Tang dynasty many pieces of Middle Eastern silver were brought into China along the Silk Route and as tribute. Silver was found in abundance, particularly in Persia. Few other Asiatic countries had such a highly developed technique of gold and silver smithing as Persia during the Parthian and Sasanian periods and many of these wares have been preserved in southern Russia as well as in Iran and China. Hammering was used to shape their objects. They could be raised by hammering the metal sheet against an anvil, or sunk by hammering the sheet into a depression.

The Chinese goldsmiths also became very skilled in such techniques and often raised the sides of objects by hammering from the centre of a circular sheet, a method still practised today. One pointer of this practice is that many bowls and cups are thicker at the mouth than at the base. Another is the almost invisible interior liner fitted to some Chinese bowls and cups to hide the inner workings. In such cases the two layers are so skilfully soldered together at the lip that it is almost impossible to observe the join.

The techniques used by the Chinese to decorate hammered vessels are universal silversmithing methods:

Repoussé Repoussé literally means embossed. The embossing is accomplished by hammering and punching a metal sheet which is held securely against a semi-soft material, like pitch. It is done from the reverse side of the object being worked, to make the pattern stand in relief on the front.

Chasing or **tracing** This is a technique of working metal from the front to indent a pattern in the surface using a hammer and a blunt-ended punch, which displaces the metal but does not remove it. Engraving, on the other hand, removes metal from a groove. Chasing is often used in conjunction with repoussé work, to add fine detail.

Ring matting or **ring punching** This form of matt surface decoration is produced by means of a tool with a concave circular tip, resulting in an overall pattern of small indented circles. Sometimes a tool with more than one ring was used. Ring punching was not widely practised in the West but is known from Hellenistic silver and from provincial Iranian work found in southern Russia.[19]

Filigree Filigree is a decorative pattern made of wires, sometimes soldered to a background but often left as openwork.

Granulation Decoration consisting of minute spherical grains of metal soldered or fused to a background is known as granulation. This technique was practised throughout antiquity with a particularly high degree of skill by the Etruscans. The method was described by both Pliny and Cellini. The technique was known and used in China from the Han dynasty. Many hairpins and fine work show the use of this technique in the Tang (fig. 1).

Gilding Gilding is the application of gold to the surface of an object made of another material, either by mercury-amalgam gilding or by leaf gilding. Mercury-amalgam gilding (also known as fire-gilding) is done by mixing gold or silver with mercury, and applying the resulting amalgam to a metal object: when heated the free mercury boils off and the gold or silver remains on the surface as a matt plating layer, which is then burnished. Mercury gilding was not developed in China until the Warring States period.[20] Leaf gilding involves the application of gold leaf or foil to a roughened surface or

Fig. 1 Detail of granulation on gilt hairpin, Tang dynasty (618–906). Length 17 cm.

sticky size. Gold leaf was attached to objects of wood, bronze and lacquer in the Shang and Western Zhou periods, and applied to paintings by Tang artists, as we know from examples found at Dunhuang.

Gilding of silver was a way of accentuating the patterns on a silver article. This method was used in Persian as well as in Western metalwork. The Chinese had used both gilding and silvering during the Han and earlier periods where objects had a layer of gold or silver applied all over the surface, more like painting. In the Tang dynasty they put the gold only on the pattern itself, the technique known as parcel gilding.

Parcel gilding Parcel gilding means the partial gilding of an object, usually a silver object which has been partly enriched with gilding. Many Tang silver objects have parcel gilding but it is sometimes not expertly done and looks fuzzy. The gilding meant only for an animal, for example, may extend beyond the intended area because the gold amalgam has run onto the background.

Therefore although the Tang dynasty artisans originally adopted many foreign techniques from their Central Asian teachers they became very skilled metalworkers in their own right and produced many masterpieces: two of the most famous ones on display in this exhibition are the parrot pot (cat. no. 82) and the dancing horse flask (cat. no. 81).

As has been noted already, gold does not tarnish and was valued for this property. Silver on the other hand does tarnish, as does bronze. The original appearance of silver and bronze surfaces in antiquity is much debated and there are claims that Greek silver was intended to be black, and 'oxidized' silver was quite popular in post-medieval Europe.[21] For such reasons the cleaning of silver is a controversial issue. In the British Museum it is usual practice to polish Roman silver, for example, which is then lacquered so that it does not tarnish for many years. Cleaning silver inevitably removes a thin layer of silver and is obviously not a practice to be done too often. Some metallurgists recommend leaving the silver in its tarnished state, which accounts for the blackened appearance of some of the Chinese silver in this exhibition.[22]

HISTORY OF GOLD AND SILVER IN CHINA

Before the Tang dynasty gold and silver were not the prestigious materials they were in the West. In ancient China jade and bronze were the most highly valued materials. Gold was used mainly for decorative purposes, as inlay or coating on bronze and lacquer, and only very rarely for vessels: those buried with the Marquis Yi of Zeng in about 433 BC are a rare exception.[23]

However, although gold was not a major force in ancient China it did hold an attraction for the peoples living on the peripheries of China. In an area spanning an arc from Liaoning in the northeast to Sichuan in the southwest were peoples contemporaneous with the Shang dynasty[24] who used gold for personal ornaments such as bracelets, armlets, earrings and head-pieces. This tradition continued into the Eastern Zhou period and many fine gold, silver and gilded bronze pieces shaped as animals in the round have been found in these peripheral areas, together with ornaments for harnesses and belts, used particularly by the inhabitants of Mongolia, the Ordos region and Shaanxi province.

Of great excitement was the discovery in 1986 at Sanxingdui near Guanghan in Sichuan of items belonging to a culture which existed contemporaneously with the Shang.[25] The finds included spectacular life-size bronze heads, their faces partially covered with gold leaf (fig. 2), and a rod completely covered with gold leaf. Other nomadic peoples' burials have yielded items such as the earrings of gold, silver and bronze that were found at the neolithic site of Huoshaogou, in Gansu province.[26]

Archaeological sites in the central plains of China have also yielded gold: for example, several bronze buttons covered with gold foil were found at tomb 1003 at Houjiazhuang, Anyang, the last Shang capital, and a Western Zhou lacquer wine vessel was found at Liulihe, Hebei province, adorned with gold foil and turquoise.[27]

Although the evidence of shared bronze vessel types suggests that societies such as that at Sanxingdui near Guanghan had some contact, probably through trading, with the central Chinese area, the perhipheral societies do not seem to have stimulated a gold industry within China itself. It was not until the early part of the Eastern Zhou period, the Spring and Autumn period, that gold working in China was adopted on any scale. Before then, during the Shang and Western Zhou periods, gold seems to have been regarded as a surface ornament to be applied in the form of leaf or foil to objects of wood, bronze or lacquer.[28] The geographical location of the peoples living in northern Hebei and in the west of China brought them into contact with the gold-using nomadic peoples, and this awareness seems to have encouraged the Chinese to use gold themselves.

From the Eastern Zhou period historical records contain many references to gold. In the *Zhanguo ce*, written

Fig. 2 Human-like head, bronze with applied gold leaf, c.1200–1000 BC. Height 48.5 cm. Excavated in 1986 from ph 2, Sanxingdui, Guanghan county, Sichuan province.

in the Warring States period, more than thirty passages refer to gold in quantities of hundreds of pounds.[29] In the *Shiji*, Sima Qian records that when the rich merchant Lu Buwei of the state of Qin became chief minister he gave five hundred pieces of gold to Zi Chu as an allowance,[30] and when King Xiao of Liang died more than 400,000 catties (240,000 kilograms) of gold remained stored in his treasury.[31] So from the Warring States period gold was beginning to gain a wider use among the Chinese. By the Han dynasty, in AD 23, the Han imperial treasury owned over 6.4 million ounces of gold, supposedly the equivalent of all the gold held by the Roman empire at the same time.[32]

The earliest gold vessels found in China date to the sixth or fifth century BC and include the five gold items buried below the coffin of the Marquis Yi of Zeng, who died about 433 BC, as well as the garment hooks and appliqués in gold found there (fig. 6, p. 24).[33] Solid gold weapon fittings have been found in the late fourth-century BC tombs of the Zhongshan kings at Pingshan in Hebei province.[34] All these golden ornaments were cast, which implies a technical dependence on the bronze-casting methods at which the Chinese of the central plains had long been so skilled. However, these cast gold items were rare for this time, as gold seems still to have been used more as decoration for bronze vessels than as an independent medium. As described in the section on metalworking technology above, from the very beginning of settled living in China artisans had become adept at preparing ceramic moulds, at first for making ceramics and then, from the Shang period, for producing both ceramics and bronzes.[35] This is in contrast to Western Asia where the use of the hammer and anvil, particularly for shaping vessels, was already well established by the beginning of the second millennium BC.

Towards the end of the Warring States period gold was cast into ornaments and weapon accessories, such as the gold hilt from Baoji (cat. no. 9), and these were more common than whole cast vessels. This sword handle is very similar to the one in the British Museum, the handle of which has a conspicuous mould line on its sides, showing that it was probably cast in a two-piece mould. The use of gold and silver on the reins and horse decorations and in the manufacture of the chariots for Qin Shi Huangdi is testimony to the very high standards of technology, as well as organization, that the Qin artisans had achieved by this time.

The period during which such accessories were being manufactured was one in which the various Warring States were vying with each other for hegemony within China and trying to outdo each other in magnificence in the various courts. Bronzes of this period were competing with the more brilliantly coloured lacquers and textiles, which were becoming so popular, and so bronze casters began to inlay bronze weapons, bells, vessels and fittings with gold and silver and semiprecious stones (cat. no. 16). By the end of the Eastern Zhou and during the Qin and Han dynasties the technique of gilding was used more and more extensively as it was realized that this was a less expensive way of achieving a golden surface than by making a solid item or by inlaying with the metal (see cat. no. 17). Complex patterns could be created, as can be seen in a large vessel decorated with dragons from the tomb of Liu Sheng at Mancheng in Hebei province.[36] Granulation was another decorative technique that became increasingly popular in the Han dynasty, but in general Han gold and silver objects followed closely bronze prototypes in shape, form and decoration, although some are more Western Asian in style.

The period from the collapse of the Han dynasty in AD 220 to the reunification of the empire in 589 was a crucial one for the introduction of gold and silver working on an important scale. This was related in part to the decline in status of bronze ritual vessels and also to the invasion of China by foreign peoples for whom gold and silver had played a much more important role. These peoples were also responsible for the introduction and consolidation in China of Buddhism, which placed great emphasis on the use of gold and silver images and utensils. In Central Asia

Fig. 3 Detail of a mural from the tomb of Princess Fangling (d. c. 673), Tang dynasty, showing a maid holding a lobed dish in her hands. Excavated in 1976, Shaanxi province.

and Gandhara (in present-day Afghanistan and Pakistan) images of the Buddha were made from, or covered with, gold and silver. The Buddhist emphasis on gold and silver resulted in an increasing popularity and usage of these two metals in China. During the Six Dynasties period items of silver from the eastern Mediterranean and Iran were brought in by the foreign rulers of northern and northwestern China. Foreign shapes such as stem cups, lobed bowls (fig. 3) and cups with flanged handles, as well as foreign decoration in the form of single and double animals in central positions, often in repoussé, became familiar.

By the beginning of the Tang dynasty, in the early seventh century, China was on the threshold of creating a native gold and silver industry. The three main stimuli were, as described above: the import of pieces of foreign metalwork; the arrival from Persia of highly skilled metalworkers;[37] and the impact of the foreign religion of Buddhism.

Amongst the earliest examples of foreign-inspired goldwork made in China are a number of fine plaques in openwork decorated with animals and birds outlined in granulation.[38] The eating and drinking vessels made in this early period are Chinese interpretations of Iranian and Western classical designs, sometimes combinations of the two sources. Many such items have been found in the provinces of Shaanxi, Gansu and Ningxia in the north and northwest. Some show similarities with vessels from the eastern Mediterranean area, such as a bowl from Gansu Jingyuan which has a figure of Dionysus on a lion in the centre.[39] The decorative border has small heads, vine scrolls and grapes. A shallow dish, more in Iranian style, with a figure hunting a boar in repoussé, has been excavated at Datong, from the fifth-century tomb of Feng Hetu.[40] This dish was found with a cup which was wholly Chinese in shape, with small eared handles (see cat. no. 91 for a similar shape). Another somewhat foreign-looking bowl decorated with a deer was found with silver from the Tang dynasty at Shapocun in Xi'an.[41] These early bowls were to exert a strong influence on later Tang dynasty vessels. The Chinese metalworkers first produced plain versions of them decorated with animals (cat. nos 66, 68, 69 from the Hejiacun hoard), and then went on to make dishes with creatures framed by floral borders.

The foreign ewer shape was one that became particularly popular in China and one of the most striking Chinese ewers is that from a northern Zhou tomb at Guyuan in Ningxia province.[42] It has a tall, slender neck and pear-shaped body and stands on a high foot which is beaded. The beading is similar to that found on Iranian and Roman silver, and the decoration on the body of figures in diaphanous dress, moving or dancing around the surface, is certainly not in Chinese taste but rather more of Central Asian or perhaps Mediterranean origin.

Gold jewellery of the period between the Han and the Tang is rare and that which has been discovered also reflects foreign influence. One of the most spectacular finds is that from the tomb of a Sui dynasty princess, who died at the age of nine, but who was buried with some beautiful jewellery including a necklace of gold beads set with pearls from which hangs a pendant. The necklace is fastened by a clasp decorated with an engraved gem.[43]

Since 1949 more than a thousand pieces of Tang dynasty gold and silver have been unearthed in Shaanxi, Inner Mongolia, Liaoning, Gansu, Jiangsu and Zhejiang. These are mainly vessels or containers for food, drink, medicinal drugs or for use in religious ceremonies, and jewellery. The four major archaeological discoveries are those at Hejiacun, Dingmaoqiao, and the temples of Qingshan and Famen, three of which are represented in this exhibition. The deposits from the crypts of monasteries such as Qingshan and Famen demonstrate the role of gold and silver in the Tang period on Buddhist images, utensils, vessels and reliquaries. However, the relative scarcity of precious metals in tombs, as opposed to those found in hoards, suggests a restriction on the burial of such items.

During the Tang period Chinese metalworkers developed an indigenous style of gold and silver working. This is well illustrated by the Hejiacun hoard which contained some 270 pieces of gold and silver including elaborately decorated cups, dishes and bowls of exceptional quality.[44] Certain of the shapes, such as the faceted cups with ring handles and the lobed bowls, still reflect the foreign influence so prevalent in the earlier period, but others are purely Chinese, such as the eared wine cups made now in gold and decorated with large floral sprays against an undecorated background.

The Dingmaoqiao hoard,[45] which is not represented here, contained about 960 items of jewellery, tableware, chopsticks and a set of inscribed counters used for drinking games. Several of the Dingmaoqiao pieces are decorated with animals and birds in repoussé against a ring punched ground, but many are undecorated, showing that gold and silver were used not only for special pieces, but also for the everyday dinner services of the rich.

The major finds of gold and silver in the foundation deposits and crypts of Buddhist temples are an important source of information on the use of gold and silver in a religious context. The Qingshan find includes two coffin-shaped caskets which fitted one inside the other, and which were fitted into a limestone shrine (cat. nos 99–101). The

Fig. 4 Silver stem cup with design of huntsmen in a landscape. The shape of the cup is Western in origin but the decoration is typically Chinese. Height 9.8 cm.

jewels and appliqués on the stand of the silver coffin-shaped casket replicate a Central Asian form of decoration seen on pre-Tang silverware and also ceramics.[46] Other reliquaries of coffin shape have been found at Jingchuan in Gansu province and at Zhenjiang in Jiangsu province.

The largest hoard of Buddhist items has come from the Famen temple,[47] which dates to the mid- and late Tang period. Here were found four sets of caskets (cat. nos 117–120), one of which held the finger bone believed to have come from the body of the Buddha. Another of these sets (fig. 29, p. 135) was composed of eight caskets which fitted one into the other with a holy relic, or *śarīra*, contained within the smallest, made of pure gold and pagoda-shaped. The many relics in this find included lotus flowers, bodhisattvas, sweetmeat dishes, and sceptres for Buddhist rituals, as well as incense burners. Some of the most interesting pieces within the treasure are items used for preparing tea, such as the wheel and stand for grinding tea and a tea sieve (cat. no. 112).

The decoration on Tang Chinese gold and silver wares shows a gradual development from elements derived from foreign sources to an adaptation of these to Chinese taste, resulting eventually in decorative schemes that are undoubtedly Chinese. Early Tang decoration is characterized by the geometrical and formal rigidity so popular in Near Eastern design. By the middle of the eighth century geometrical rigidity was yielding to the freer flowing linear quality of Chinese design and a fluency of pattern quite different from that favoured in the Middle East (fig. 4).

By the second half of the eighth century decoration on vessels included centrally placed creatures surrounded by flowers, rather than the intricate flower and hunting scenes against a ring punched ground which had been popular earlier (cat. no. 88). Several large dishes with central animals in repoussé have been found at the Karachin banner in Liaoning province;[48] one portrays a crouching deer and is dated to between 787 and 796. A large dish decorated with a pair of phoenixes is dated to between 799 and 802 (cat. no. 58). Of the animals represented on such pieces, five appear more often than the others: dragons, birds, deer, lions and fish. A new departure from earlier Chinese decoration is the single animal often gilded against a plain silver background on metalwork utensils, of which there are a number of examples in the Hejiacun hoard (cat. nos 66, 68, 69, 81). The prototypes would seem to be Sasanian silver, and we know that Iranian bowls, or provincial versions of them, were exported to the Far East (fig. 5). By the mid-ninth century the most popular designs

Fig. 5 Silver bowl decorated with a bird, Iran, Sasanian period or later (4th–6th century AD). Diam. 16.9 cm.

were floral sprays and small birds gilded against a plain silver ground as illustrated by pieces from Yaoxian dated between 849 and 851.[49] By now the patterns are less tightly worked than those of the eighth century.

The Tang dynasty marks the high point in the manufacture and use of gold and silver wares. Although never eclipsing jade which, as indicated by the sumptuary rules, stood at the apex of precious materials, gold and silver were to attain a position of importance that was only possible against the cosmopolitan background of the Tang empire. Because of its easily convertible value much of the gold and silver that existed during the heyday of the empire must have been melted down, which makes it all the more fortunate that the hoards buried at the times of the rebellions and those buried in religious crypts have been found undisturbed in the twentieth century. The purging of the Buddhist church in 845 and the destruction of many of its icons for their metallic content saw the beginning of the decline of the Tang empire and consequently the decline of precious metalwork in China. The Golden Age had shone brilliantly for over two centuries but it was not eternal and was ultimately to tarnish, like silver.

1 Quoted from Pauline Yu, *The Poetry of Wang Wei,* Bloomington 1980, p. 203.
2 Clunas 1997, pp. 106–9.
3 Schafer 1963, p. 253.
4 Rawson 1995a, p. 13.
5 *Shiji,* Zhonghua shuju edn, 1959, chapter 28, p. 1370.
6 Ge Hong, *Baopuzi,* Shanghai guji chubanshe 1990, p. 118; also the immortal paradise of the Daoist Queen Mother of the West is described in gold and jewel-like terms. Cahill 1993.
7 *Jiu Tang shu,* Zhonghua shuju 1975 edn, juan 71, p. 2550.
8 Breeding goldfish is a very popular hobby in China. Goldfish are first mentioned during the Six Dynasties period but it is possible that they were not bred on a popular level until the Song dynasty (960–1279). Lindqvist 1991, p. 73.
9 H S Levy, *Chinese Footbinding,* London 1965, p. 39. Donghun Hou is also referred to as Xiao Baojuan and was one of the Southern Qi rulers, in the period between the Han and the Tang. See also A E Grantham, *Hills of Blue,* London 1927, p. 204.
10 Cao Xueqin (trans. D Hawkes), *The Story of the Stone,* London 1973, vol. 1, pp. 189–90.
11 Bunker 1993, p. 28.
12 Golas 1999, p. 119.
13 A Waley, *The Life and Times of Po Chu-i,* London 1949, pp. 61–2.
14 Schafer 1963, p. 254.
15 Golas 1999, pp. 123–4.
16 Bunker 1994, p. 73.
17 Golas 1999, p. 134.
18 Golas 1999, p.134.
19 Rawson 1982, p. 1.
20 Bunker 1993, p. 29.
21 M Vickers, 'Artful Crafts: the influence of metalwork on Athenian painted pottery', *Journal of Hellenic Studies,* 105, 1985, pp. 108–28.
22 I am very much indebted to Susan La Niece of the British Museum's Scientific Research Department for her help on this section.
23 In this introduction I have much relied on the work of Jessica Rawson for whose help and knowledge I am very grateful. For in-depth information on this subject see Rawson 1982, 1984a, 1984b, 1986a, 1986b, 1989b, 1991, 1995b.
24 Lin Yun, 'A Reexamination of the Relationship between Bronzes of the Shang Culture and of the Northern Zone' in K C Chang (ed.), *Studies of Shang Archaeology,* New Haven and London 1982, pp. 237-73.
25 See Rawson 1996, pp. 60–84, for information on this culture.
26 *Wenwu kaogu gongzuo 30 nian,* Beijing 1979, pp. 142–3.
27 Yin Weizhang, 'Archaeological Discoveries in Beijing', *China Pictorial* 1990.8, p. 34.
28 Examples from the seventh and sixth centuries BC come from Lijialou, near Xinzheng, Henan province (J G Andersson, 'The Goldsmith in Ancient China', *Bulletin of the Museum of Far Eastern Antiquities,* Stockholm, no. 7, 1935, pp. 1–38, pl. XVII) . Other examples come from Shaanxi Houma Shangmacun. These gold appliqués are decorated with striations impressed into the soft metal and are circular or arc-shaped.
29 See, for example, Crump 1970, pp. 77–8.
30 *Shiji,* Zhonghua shuju edn, 1959, vol. 8, chapter 85, p. 2507.
31 *Shiji,* Zhonghua shuju edn,1959, vol. 6, chapter 58, p. 2086.
32 François Louis, 'Gold and Silver from Ancient China: The Pierre Uldry Collection on show at the Museum Rietberg Zurich', *Arts of Asia,* September–October 1994, pp. 88–96.
33 Beijing 1989, vol. 2, colour pl. 18.
34 Paris 1984, nos 27, 32–4.
35 Bagley 1993, 1995.
36 Beijing 1980d, vol. 2, colour pl. V.
37 Gyllensvärd 1953, p. 21.
38 *Wenwu* 1973.3, pp. 10, 16, pl. 1, fig. 47:3.
39 *Wenwu* 1990.5, pp.1–9, colour pl., and Beijing 1997, cat. no. 92.
40 *Wenwu* 1983.8, p. 2, pl. 1.
41 Han and Lu 1985, figs 11 and 12.
42 *Wenwu* 1985.11, p. 11, colour pl.; Luo Feng, 'A Central Asian style gilt-silver ewer', *Orientations,* July–August 1998, pp. 28–33. For information on Central Asian metalwork see Marschak 1986.
43 Beijing 1992a, cat. no. 273, p. 299.
44 Han and Lu 1985; *Wenwu* 1972.1, pp. 30–42.
45 *Wenwu* 1982.11, pp. 15–27.
46 *Wenbo* 1985.5, pp. 12–37, colour pl.
47 *Wenwu* 1988.10, pp. 1–28.
48 *Kaogu* 1977.5, pp. 327–34.
49 *Wenwu* 1966.1, pp. 33 and 46–9.

Early Tomb Burials

This first section consists of objects buried in tombs, dating from the Eastern Zhou period, which began in 770 BC, to the end of the Han dynasty in AD 220.

The Chinese from a very early date were accustomed, like many other peoples, to bury objects in tombs presumably with the idea that these objects should play some part in an afterlife. We cannot be certain as to exactly what kind of afterlife was contemplated but it seems that the Chinese tended to envisage a life very much like the one they were leaving behind on earth. Therefore whatever was needed in this life should be provided for in the next, and objects and treasures would be buried accordingly. Neolithic peoples were buried with ceramics and jades and, from the Shang dynasty (c. 1500 BC), bronzes were also put into tombs. There seems to have been some belief that sacrificial offerings would appease the spirits as well as sustain the dead person, and perhaps the ceramic armies and weapons buried were there to protect the deceased from the spirits the dead person thought he or she might encounter.

So here in this first section we have objects deliberately buried for use in the afterlife. The objects featured are not meant to be a comprehensive picture of what any one tomb contained in these early periods but a focus on the gold and silver and a few other precious objects which the tomb occupant must have wanted with him forever. Many of the tombs have been robbed so that there are relatively few complete tomb contents available to us. The Marquis Yi of Zeng was buried with a gold vessel, of a shape usually made in bronze (fig. 6). We have the soldiers of the terracotta army which the Qin emperor, Qin Shi Huangdi, decided he would need to combat his enemies in the afterlife, as well as a half-size replica of the war chariot he might also need. The succeeding Han emperors also provided themselves with armies, but now they have become miniature rather than the earlier full-size models. Horses, so important to the Chinese in their constant battles against marauding nomadic tribes, were provided for eternity in gold, as witnessed by the Maoling horse. Seals are there for dealing with official business as the Chinese seem to have envisaged that they would have to cope with a bureaucracy similar to the one which they knew on earth. Stoves would provide them with the food they enjoyed. However, many major imperial tombs remain unexcavated at present so we cannot know for sure what Qin Shi Huangdi or the Han emperors took with them to the afterlife, nor what further treasures these tombs will reveal to us at some time in the future.

Fig. 6 *Gold vessel, Eastern Zhou, early Warring States period, 4th–3rd century BC. Height 11 cm. Excavated in 1978 from the tomb of the Marquis Yi of Zeng, Suixian county, Hubei province.*

1

1 Woodpecker

Eastern Zhou, Spring and Autumn period
(770–475 BC)
Gold
Height 1.6 cm; length 1.5 cm; weight 6 g
Excavated 1986, tomb 1 of the Duke of Qin,
Fengxiang county, Shaanxi province
Shaanxi History Museum

This little gold bird stands straight with a
high comb on its head, a long beak, open
wings and a splayed tail. It resembles a
woodpecker. Engraved lines over the body
indicate feathers and its ears are represented
by curved lines. The bird was probably cast
and then the details tooled separately. The
feet are replaced by a flat stem. Although
very small, the bird is beautifully made and
is indicative of the high standard of gold
workmanship that had been achieved in the
Qin state, in western and northwestern
China, at this period.

This woodpecker was found in a very
large tomb thought to have belonged to
Prince Jing, Duke of Qin, who lived from
about 577 to 537 BC. Sets of stone chimes
found in the tomb bear seal inscriptions
providing the tentative identification of the
deceased. The duke was an expansionist and
one of the Qin state's powerful early rulers,
extending Qin influence towards the central
plains.[1] The tomb was 24 metres deep and

had a total area of 5334 square metres,
making it the biggest and grandest earthen
tomb to predate the Qin dynasty. The tomb
also contained the coffins of more than
180 animals and humans including
concubines, ministers and craftsmen,
sacrificed to accompany the duke to the
afterlife.[2]

In this tomb were also found a cast gold
tiger, a gold bird finial and a gold buckle
with a duck-headed beak, some decorated
with turquoise. (Also several iron
implements were found and these are
particularly valuable for the history of cast
iron generally in China. The Chinese were
the first people to cast iron and did so about
650 BC, whereas we in the West did not do
so until about the fourteenth century AD).
The Qin people seem to have used cast gold
quite extensively, possibly because of their
direct contact with the nomadic peoples on
their northwestern borders.[3] At later
Warring States sites cast gold gradually
becomes more plentiful, as illustrated by
the finds at Gaozhuang and Majiazhuang in
Shaanxi province.[4]

Published: Han Wei 1987, p. 15; Yin Shengping
1994; Xi'an 1997, p. 35.

1 Han Wei 1987, p. 16.
2 Han Wei 1987, p. 17.
3 Bunker 1993, p. 33.
4 *Wenwu* 1985.2, pp. 1-29, figs 22-30.

2 Dog

Eastern Zhou, Spring and Autumn period
(770–475 BC)
Gold
Height 2 cm; length 2.9 cm; weight 13.5 g
Excavated 1986, tomb 1 of the Duke of Qin,
Fengxiang county, Shaanxi province
Shaanxi History Museum

This recumbent dog, its head comparatively
big and its two ears pricked up, has its four
legs curling round it. Its tail is also relatively
large and curls upwards. The muscles of the
dog's joints and its feet and tail are all
decorated with a raised cloud design. The
overall shape is somewhat stylized, and the
outline is bold and clearly defined. The piece
is a good example of gold workmanship in
the Qin state in Shaanxi province.

The dog comes from the same tomb as
the woodpecker (cat. no. 1) and they are the
oldest gold items found in Shaanxi province.
Although the tomb had been robbed many
times, a huge quantity of tomb goods,

2

including over 3500 items of gold, bronze, pottery and lacquer, were found by archaeologists.[1]

The Qin people were geographically situated so that they inevitably came in close contact with many of the northern nomadic peoples, including the Xiongnu, who constantly made incursions into China during the Warring States period and later. The Great Wall was later built by the northern Chinese states partly to prevent such people from raiding their lands for the luxuries their pastoral life could not provide.

The use of gold for ornaments and the portrayal of animals on them were both defining characteristics of the art of these nomadic peoples of the steppes. Many different animals are depicted. Dogs, together with pigs, are indigenous to China and dog bones have been found in prehistoric sites. They were used traditionally as guardian animals and for hunting, as well as being a source of food.[2] The *Zhouli* (Rites of Zhou) describes an official rank of 'dog man' whose job was to select dogs for ritual purposes and lead them to the ceremony. In the Han dynasty there was an official charged with rearing the emperor's hunting dogs and the *Feng Su Tongyi* (Penetrating Popular Ways)[3] by Ying Shao (*c.* AD 140–before 205) recounts that the first Qin emperor would kill a dog and smear its blood at the four gates to ward off evil spells.

Published: *Guangming Ribao*, 4 May 1986; Yin Shengping 1994; *Famous Capital*, p. 50, no. 1.

1 Han Wei 1987, p.17; Bunker 1993, p. 33.
2 For animal symbolism see Eberhard 1986, pp. 80–2.
3 For the *Zhouli*, the Rites of the Zhou (dynasty), see Loewe 1993, pp. 24–32; for the *Feng Su Tongyi*, see pp. 105–12.

3 Fantastical beast

Eastern Zhou, Warring States period,
4th–3rd century BC
Gold
Height 11.5 cm; length 11 cm; weight 160 g
Excavated 1957, Nalingaotu village, Shenmu county, Shaanxi province
Shaanxi History Museum

This strange animal with exaggerated horns stands, head bowed, on a base. It has the body of a deer, the beak of an eagle, hoof-like feet, protruding eyes and two huge horns. The body has been hammered out with cloud designs in repoussé. A bowstring pattern decorates the horns, which appear to be made up of long intertwined necks terminating in bird or animal heads. The base on which the animal stands is composed of four petals or leaves and there are three small holes in them, perhaps suggesting that the animal was attached to something. The base also bears marks of rivets.

The village of Nalingaotu, where this animal was found, is located on the southern border of the Mu Us desert, which was inhabited by the Xiongnu people in the

Eastern Zhou period. A storm in 1957 exposed gold and silver objects in the ground and when the area was excavated a tomb was discovered with more than twenty objects of gold and silver, including this strange beast. It is thought that the tomb occupant must have been a high ranking official of the Xiongnu people.

In Inner Mongolia composite beasts with a deer's body and eagle's beak have been found in other Xiongnu tombs although the ten animal heads depicted on the horns of this deer make it unique.[1] Certainly deer-like animals with exaggerated horns or antlers have a long association with the Central Asian regions.[2] The interest in antlers possibly came from the border areas and then gradually infiltrated many areas of the Chinese-speaking regions.[3] An antler decorated with birds was found at Tengxian in Shandong province.

Five silver deer were also found in Nalingaotu.[4] Deer are regarded as auspicious creatures in China as they were believed to have very long lives and were said to be the only animal capable of finding the magic *lingzhi*, the fungus of immortality.

5

The deer therefore became a symbol of longevity as well as an emblem of official rank as the Chinese word for deer, *lu*, and official emolument, *lu*, are homophones. Deer horn has always been an important constituent of the Chinese *materia medica*, with powdered deer horn being taken as a recipe for longevity.

Published: Dai and Sun 1983, pl. 5.4; Osaka 1987, no. 10; Xi'an 1992, p. 23; Yin Shengping 1994; Shanghai 1996, p. 88, no. 15; Xi'an 1997, p. 18; Li Jian 1998, no. 1.

1 *Wenwu* 1983.12, p. 24.
2 See the stag with exaggerated horns in the Sackler Gallery, Washington DC, which dates to the first millennium AD from the Central Asian area. Lawton 1987, no. 19, pp. 46–7; see also *Frozen Tombs: The Culture and Art of the Ancient Tribes of Siberia*, London 1978, no. 52, from Pazyryk.
3 Rawson forthcoming.
4 *Wenwu* 1983.12, pp. 23-30 and fig. 10.

4 Tiger

Eastern Zhou, Spring and Autumn period
(770–475 BC)
Gold
Height 3.3 cm; length 3.3 cm; weight 58.3 g
Excavated 1992, Fengxiang county, Shaanxi province
Xi'an City Cultural Relics Storehouse

This gold tiger has its head turned back towards its tail, its ears pricked up, and its long tail curled back along its body. Its mouth is open to reveal two rows of tightly clenched teeth. Its body is decorated with cloud scrolls and dots; underneath it has square holes. Although it has a small body it is decorated with great skill, in imitation of the granulation technique.[1] This technique was not generally practised by Chinese craftsmen until the first century AD after it had been introduced into China possibly from the ancient Near East where it was used as early as the third millennium BC. It probably came via the sea trade which the eastern Han enjoyed in the first and second centuries AD.[2]

The pre-dynastic Qin peoples used cast gold extensively, undoubtedly due to their contacts with the pastoral tribes on their northwestern borders who were great users of it. This tiger can be compared to the woodpecker found in the Qin tomb of the same period (cat. no. 1).

1 Bunker 1993, p. 33.
2 See, for example, the gold box and cover with areas of granulated surface delimited by soldered gold wire in the Nelson-Atkins Museum of Art, Kansas City, illustrated in Pirazzoli t'Serstevens, 1982, p.165.

4

5 Three belt hooks

Spring and Autumn period, Qin state
(770–475 BC)
Gold
a Height 1.5 cm; length 2.3 cm; weight 25.7 g;
b Height 3 cm; length 2.8 cm; width 2 cm;
weight 30.8 g; *c* Height 1.4 cm; diameter 2.6 cm;
length 2.3 cm; weight 34.7 g
Excavated 1992, Yimen village, Baoji, Shaanxi province
Baoji City Archaeology Institute, Shaanxi province

a This flat belt hook is in the shape of a Chinese duck,[1] head facing backwards. It is hollow, with a square hole, and a small stem underneath. Engraved lines and dots on the surface represent the wings and feathers. On the body are several holes which may have been filled with precious stones. The head of the duck is decorated with a cloud design. It has round eyes and a long wide beak, with symmetrical S-shaped designs, which acts as the hook.

b This belt hook is also in the shape of a duck, its head turned backwards and its long wide beak serving as the hook. The body is engraved with lines representing the feathers, and the tail fans out in an arc shape. The duck's eyes are filled with precious stones which gives them prominence and provides an aesthetically pleasing contrast to the body.

c This flat round belt hook is in the form of a snake-like creature, curled up in a circle with its head looking backwards to create the hook. There are also six smaller snakes, four of them curled along the back of the large snake and the other two head to tail in the centre. The eyes of the large snake are deep set and were probably originally filled with pearls to accentuate them. Such decoration in the pre-Qin dynastic period was quite common.

From an early date in Chinese history men wore girdles, sometimes with a jade ornament to hold up their trousers. During the Eastern Zhou period the various articles of clothing, including belts and hats, were codified into a series of sumptuary rules prescribing the dress for officials and the gentry.[2] At the same time the belt hook became a common male accessory and a large number have been found in Eastern Zhou tombs. Changes in dress may well have stimulated the growing popularity of belt hooks at this time, as well as the more general use of gold, bronze and silver as indicators of status in items of personal adornment. As contacts increased with the nomadic peoples on the Chinese borders, and horse riding became an important way of life for many men, the use of belts to hold up the trousers or to fasten the jacket became common.[3] The three groups of belt hooks, in both gold and jade, unearthed from the tomb of the Marquis Yi of Zeng (died 433 BC) are amongst the earliest found to date.[4] The long, kimono-type robe called the *shenyi*, which became popular at this period, was also secured with a belt which necessitated a belt hook. A bronze lamp bearer from the royal Zhongshan tombs, in Pingshan county, Hebei province, wears such a *shenyi* with a waistband secured by a long narrow belt hook.[5]

During the Eastern Zhou period the Qin state was particularly rich in gold objects for dress ornamentation. It is possible that small gold hooks like the ones here were also used as collar hooks.[6] Others may have been used as sword slings or similar attachments to the belt.[7] Many were very richly inlaid with jade, glass, silver and gold, all markers of status and wealth.

Published: (left and centre) Beijing 1993a, no. 100; Shanghai 1996, p. 85, no. 5.

1 The Chinese refer to this duck as a mandarin duck, which has a long history in China as an emblem of marital bliss, based on the fact that mandarin ducks always swim around in pairs and mate only once and for life.
2 Zhou and Gao 1987, p. 12.
3 Zhou and Gao 1987, p. 19, where it is explained that such belt hooks, besides having a Han Chinese name, also had non-Chinese names, suggesting their foreign origins. Also see Lawton 1982, p. 89, concerning the adoption of a foreign mode of dress by King Wuling of Zhao (reigned 325–299 BC). See also Liu Liang-yu 1996, p. 8.
4 Wang Li, *Wenbo* 1996.1, p. 107.
5 Rawson 1996a, cat. no. 74, p. 157.
6 See Lawton 1982, pp. 90–1 for discussion on how the various sized hooks might have been used.
7 Yetts 1930, vol. 2, pp. 64–5. Some of the small and short hooks may have served for fastening the sheath of the sword to the leather strap by which it was carried rather than for the belt itself. In this case they would have been worn with the hook downwards rather than horizontally across the body when used for doing up a belt. Additionally the hooks may have been worn on a belt to support small knives, pouches or other such items. Some of the very long belt hooks may have been clothes-hooks for joining the lapels of a garment.

6 Belt hook

Spring and Autumn period, Qin state (770–475 BC)
Jade
Height 1.5 cm; length 3.8 cm; width 1.8 cm; weight 9.5 g
Excavated 1971, Gao village, Fengxiang county, Shaanxi province
Shaanxi History Museum

This jade belt hook is flat and very similar to two of the belt hooks in gold in catalogue no. 5. The long beak of the duck-like bird is curved up from the body to form the hook. The head and body are carved with a distorted coiled serpent design, which is very similar to that found on the jade handle for an iron blade from Henan Xichuan Xiasi, tomb M10, dating to the sixth century BC. It

6

is also reminiscent of the iron sword with gold hilt decoration from Shaanxi Baoji Yimen, sixth century BC (cat. no. 9).

It would appear that jade began to be used for belt and dress ornaments in the seventh century BC. From this time onwards states were competing with each other both for hegemony within China and also for supremacy in their general display. For this reason there was extensive use of luxurious and colourful materials such as gold and silver, semiprecious stones and lacquer, to decorate personal dress items as well as chariot fittings, tableware, musical instruments and ritual items.[1]

The tombs at Baoji Yimen yielded many belt hooks in gold (cat. no. 5) as well as in jade, the jade ones apparently imitating the form and decoration of the gold ones. The hooks are of three types. The first is rectangular, in gold, with a slot at the side through which the belt material would have been slotted to attach it by the stud; this is the type replicated here in jade. The second type has a circular gold hook with a similar slot, and the third has a circle in jade with the tube on one side and a duck-head hook on the other. The detailed decoration on the present belt hook would have been much easier to work in gold, a soft material, than in jade. In the jades the slot was often omitted.

A very similar belt hook was excavated in Henan province in 1979.[2]

1 For much interesting information on this topic see Rawson 1995a, pp. 303–7.
2 Hebei 1991–3, vol. 3, no. 117, p. 75.

7 Horse decoration

Spring and Autumn period, Qin state
(770–475 BC)
Gold
Length 4.1 cm; width 3.4 cm; weight 77 g
Excavated 1979, Yongcheng, Fengxiang county,
Shaanxi province
Fengxiang Museum

This gold horse decoration is in the shape of
an animal's head. It is cast and engraved with
complex patterns and the corners are
decorated with a coiled serpent or snake
design. Its back is square and decorated with
a triangular pattern of interlaced hydras. Its
head is round and its eyes are glaring and
decorated with pearls. The edge of the body
of the serpent is in relief and filled with fine
pearl design. The bottom of the fitting is
concave.

The Chinese domesticated the horse
from neolithic times and many cave
paintings dating to both the neolithic and
the Bronze Age, such as in Inner Mongolia,
have depictions of men riding horses. Even
today the 11 million horses in China testify
to the importance this animal has for the
Chinese. The Chinese traditionally did not
use cavalry until they came into contact with
the cavalry of the nomads of the north and
northwest. King Wuling of the state of Zhao
is generally credited as the first to use
cavalry, in 307 BC. Prior to this horses were
employed mainly for pulling carts and
chariots. The Chinese did not have the
breeding grounds for swift horses but

instead bred a more prosaic Mongolian
pony, primarily on the steppes of northwest
China. These Chinese horses were small and
stocky, with large heads, thick necks and
short legs – good enough as pack horses but
not fast enough to be mounted against a
fighting cavalry unit. However, China soon
started bartering silk and other Chinese
specialities for horses bred in Central Asia,
such as in Ferghana, which were so swift and
nimble that the Chinese referred to them as
tianma, heavenly horses or blood-sweating
horses.

During the Shang and early Zhou periods
chariots, both for use in war and in leisure,
were important indicators of status for the
nobility. Archaeological discoveries have
revealed many chariot burials where the
wood has rotted, leaving only traces in the
ground of the shape and size of the chariot,
and the bronze horse fittings. From these it
has been possible to reconstruct details of
the harnessing systems then in use.

The chariots of the Shang and Western
Zhou were drawn by horses harnessed
under a yoke on either side of a single pole.
A Shang dynasty royal chariot and its team
of two horses were probably elaborately
decorated with lacquered wood and bronze
ornaments. During the succeeding Zhou
dynasty chariots were pulled by four rather
than by two horses,[1] and the ornamentation
became more elaborate, with decorations
not only in bronze but also in gold, as in this
example.

1 Toronto 1992, p. 108.

8 Twelve ornaments

Spring and Autumn period, Qin state
(770–475 BC)
Gold
a Each height 0.6 cm; length 3.9 cm; width
3.2 cm *b* Each height 0.9 cm; length 1.9 cm;
diameter 1.3 cm *c* Each diameter 3.1 cm
d Diameters 0.7–3.8 cm. Weights: *a* 38.9 g;
b 33.5 g; *c* 7.5 g; *d* 7.8 g; *e* 33.3 g; *f* 33.7 g;
g 22.8 g; *h* 23.3 g; *i* 9.8 g; *j* 9.6 g; *k* 7.3 g; *l* 6.5 g
Excavated 1992, tomb 2, Yimen village, Baoji,
Shaanxi province
Baoji City Archaeology Institution, Shaanxi
province

a Two harness ornaments of irregular
rectangular shape. On the front is an
animal's face composed of interlaced
serpent designs interspersed with fine lines.
The eyes of the serpent are hollowed out
and filled with a round stone-like material,
possibly glass,[1] and the bulging eyes of the
animal below are also filled with a glassy or
stone material. In the centre of the bottom
edge is a bulging triangular animal's face, its
nose and eyes carved in relief. On the back
of these pieces there is an iron bar.
Altogether seven objects of this shape and
design, but varying in size, were excavated.
The four larger ones were filled with
semiprecious stones. All were cast, a process
in which the Chinese were very skilled due
to their expertise in bronze making.

b Two duck-headed belt fasteners of
pure gold with rings suspended from them.
The ducks' heads are raised, their beaks
extended, and they have short necks. On the
surface of the beaks and behind the ducks'
heads on both sides are S-shaped decorative
devices. Similar objects were excavated in
the tomb of Prince Jing at Fengxiang (see
cat. nos 1 and 2) and at Majiazhuang.[2] This
supplies a reliable dating reference because
the Duke of Qin's tomb was judged to be of
the early stage of the Spring and Autumn
period and the Majiazhuang site was dated
to the middle of the same period. Tomb 2

7

can therefore be dated to the early part of the later stage of the Spring and Autumn period, about the sixth century BC.

c Two faceted pure gold rings. The six objects of this kind were all buried inside a head box between the inner and outer coffins, together with other horse decorations.

d Six bubble-shaped harness ornaments of three different sizes. The centre part is domed and there is a bar across the back of each. There were 56 pieces altogether of this type, in differing sizes. Their diameters range from 0.7 to 3.8 centimetres.

When this Spring and Autumn period tomb at Yimen village, Baoji, was excavated in 1992, there were found not only these gold ornaments but also many pieces in jade, iron, and bronze. The quantities astounded both archaeologists and art historians: there were 104 gold pieces, with a total weight of 3000 grams,[3] a quantity never before encountered in pre-dynastic Qin tombs and suggesting that the owner of the tomb was of extremely high rank within the Qin state. By the Zhou period horse decorations seem

to have been less prevalent than in Shang times but they were larger and predominantly for the horse's head.[4]

Published: *Wenwu* 1993.10; Beijing 1993a, no.101; Shanghai 1996, p. 85, no. 6.

1 Glass was imported from the West from Western Zhou times mainly in the form of eye beads, which have been found in many Zhou period tombs. The Chinese seem to have been making their own glass, in the form of beads and other items, from the Eastern Zhou period onwards. Their glass is distinguishable from the imported material as it contains lead and barium, which were not ingredients of Western glass.
2 *Wenwu* 1985.2, pp. 1–38, figs 22–31.
3 *Wenwu* 1993.10, p. 3.
4 Toronto 1992, p. 108.

9 Sword and hilt

Spring and Autumn period, Qin state (770–475 BC)
Gold and iron
Total length 37.2 cm (sword length 24.5 cm, handle length 12.7 cm); width 4 cm; weight 343.6 g
Excavated 1992, Yimen village, Baoji, Shaanxi province
Baoji City Archaeology Institute, Shaanxi province

The sword's iron blade is in the shape of a willow leaf with a central cylindrical ridge running the length of it. The gold hilt bulges at the top as well as at the junction with the blade. The whole is hollowed out and both sides are decorated with the same design of dragon interlace, inlaid with turquoise. The rounded relief surface and fine detailing reflect the light with great effect. This hilt shape occurs on Central Asian and Bactrian swords and is also characteristic of the steppe region. The combination of turquoise and iron was also Western in origin, from areas such as Bactria.[1] Almost certainly the first people in China to use iron were the people of the Qin area in the seventh or sixth century BC. Therefore both the gold and the iron were foreign materials, their combination in this sword perhaps enhancing its value. The fragility of the gold hilt on an iron blade probably rendered this sword impractical, so its function may have been for taking to the afterlife or for display.[2]

The true sword, as opposed to the dagger or spear, did not develop until late in the Spring and Autumn period. Early swords were designed for piercing and thrusting and not for slashing, and really long swords with slashing power only became common in the late Warring States, Qin and Han periods. Very long swords, though, would have been dangerous and unwieldy for cavalrymen so such swords were probably for the exclusive use of infantrymen or for ceremonial purposes.

A number of jade hilts which appear to be versions of this gold hilt have been found.[3] The Yimen site has produced other items in jade, which seem to be based on gold objects, similar to two of the fittings with monster faces in catalogue no. 8. Some of the designs on these gold and jade examples have clearly been inspired by bronzes. The débris at Houma, capital of the Jin state in the sixth to fifth century BC, included fragments of pattern blocks used to generate multiple sections of decorated moulds for casting bronzes.[4] Some of these designs are very similar to those on this gold hilt from Baoji Yimen. As with bronze, it was possible to cast very fine detail in gold. This may have contributed to the popularity of gold at a time when there was a growing fashion for colourful decoration in the form of bronzes inlaid with gold and silver, and painted lacquers.

The British Museum has a gold dagger handle very similar to the Baoji Yimen example but without the turquoise.[5]

Published: Baoji 1993, p. 4, no. 7; Beijing 1993a, no. 99; Shanghai 1996, p. 84, no. 5; Xi'an 1997, p. 24.

1 White and Bunker 1994, p. 36, where it is suggested that turquoise may have been imported from Xinjiang province or Russia or have come from native deposits in Anhui and Hubei provinces.
2 Rawson 1995a, pp. 290–4 and Rawson 1995b, pp. 28–30. For a report on this tomb see *Wenwu* 1993.10, pp. 1–14. For information on the introduction of gold working into China I am indebted to Jessica Rawson who has written on this subject in many articles. See, for example, Rawson 1995a, pp. 60–6.
3 Hebei 1991–3, vol. 3, no. 88, p. 53, from tomb 10, Xiasi, Xichuan, Henan province, sixth century BC.
4 For a discussion of these moulds used in casting bronzes see Bagley 1993, 1996, and *Orientations,* January 1995, pp. 46–54.
5 British Museum, Hotung Gallery, case 13, OA 1937.4–16.218.

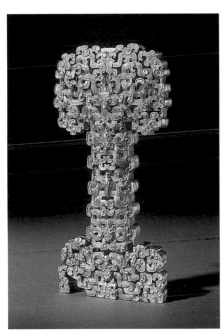

Fig. 9a *Openwork cast gold sword hilt. Eastern Zhou period, 6th–5th century BC. Height 9.8 cm.*

9

QIN SHI HUANGDI AND HIS TERRACOTTA ARMY

The King of Qin swept across the world,
Like cutting through clouds with a flying dagger,
With the majestic glare of a tiger,
Princes and barons all paid homage to the west,
To a wisdom descended from Heaven,
To a mind of great talent and bold vision.[1]

Qin Shi Huangdi was one of the most powerful men in world history. He is renowned for the ruthless manner in which he obliterated the other states of his day. Of all the men who have considered themselves the mightiest in the world in their lifetime he was probably most justified in doing so. He created the largest and most powerful empire in the world, largest both in size and in population. Although his dynasty lasted only fifteen years, the empire he established lasted for more than two millennia and into the twentieth century. The name of his dynasty, Qin, or Cina, China, has long been the name

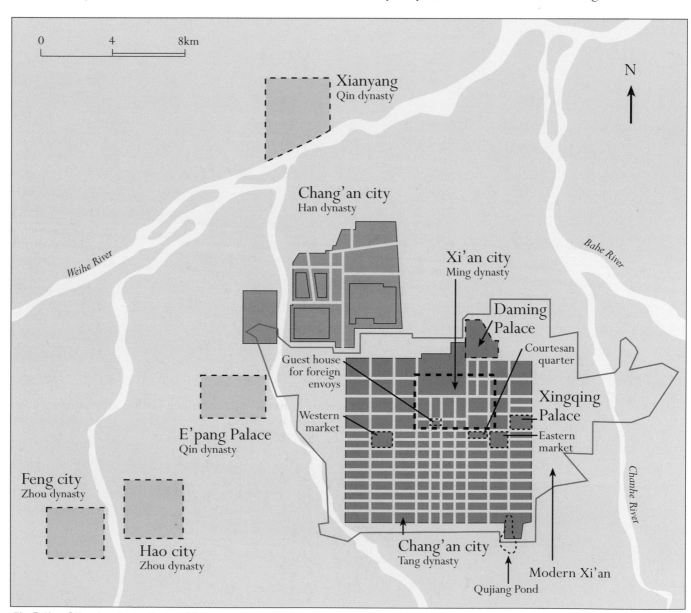

Fig. 7 *Plan of Chang'an, showing the sites of the various dynastic capitals.*

by which the entire country has been known to the West.

The Qin state, although regarded early on in the Warring States period (475–221 BC) by the other states as 'barbarian', gradually became more and more powerful, partly due to its adherence to the policy of Legalism.[2] According to the Legalists man naturally needed harnessing under a very strict code of laws and of rewards which, if applied to all, regardless of rank, would both stimulate and control people's behaviour. This policy was rigidly applied by Qin's capable statesman Shang Yang (died 338 BC).[3] Qin also developed a highly effective army and became renowned for horse breeding.[4] This led to the formation of a cavalry which aided them in their campaigns, from the fourth century BC, aimed at conquering all the other warring states of the period. By 256 BC they had conquered the Zhou, to whom all the other states nominally had owed allegiance. King Zheng of Qin succeeded to the throne at the age of thirteen in 246 BC and by the time he was twenty-one had assumed control of his kingdom and set about conquering all the remaining territories which had formed part of the former Zhou dominion. He defeated the large and powerful Chu state in 223 BC, and in 221 BC, having conquered the remaining state of Qi, the king of Qin proclaimed himself the First August Emperor of the Qin, and united all China under the title of Qin Shi Huangdi.[5]

Qin Shi Huangdi set about unifying the country under his control and making it a cohesive unit by instituting common laws, currency, measurements and script across the whole empire. He brought all the major families from the former independent states by force to live in his new capital at Xianyang to the northwest of today's Xi'an (fig. 7), and built them miniature replicas of their palaces in the grounds of his own.[6] The old feudal system was replaced by a hierarchical local government with many officials directly appointed by the central government and a centralized administrative system of the type which had been so effective in the state of Qin. He greatly improved the communications between all parts of the empire

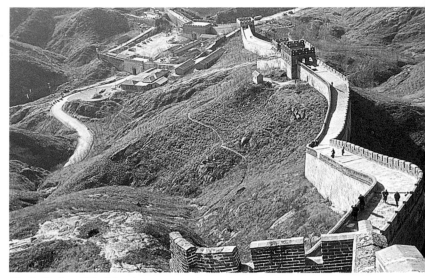

Fig. 8 The Great Wall. Although its origins can be traced to the Qin dynasty (221–206 BC), the wall as it exists today, extending thousands of kilometres from east to west, is primarily a creation of the Ming dynasty (1368–1644).

through his canal and road system, and his postal system, and he joined up large sections of the walls built by the northern states to keep out the marauding nomads, which subsequently became known as the Great Wall (fig. 8).

The Qin emperor, leaning on his sword,
While the vassal lords galloped west to submit;
He pared down their land and pacified the empire,
Unified the script, standardized wheel gauges.
Mount Hua served as his ramparts,
Purple Gulf was his moat.
His breast was filled with ambitious plans,
And he never used his martial might to the full.
He built a bridge of turtles and alligators,
And toured the area right of the sea to escort the sun westward.[7]

The emperor could be said to have been in many ways a 'control freak' and was ruthless and megalomaniacal in his methods of achieving control. However, he was also deeply superstitious, and his desire to achieve immortality for himself and his dynasty, one that would last the 10,000 years he hoped for (rather than the fifteen it actually did), was a fixation. He made journeys to the cardinal directions and ascended the most revered mountains of his empire,

Fig. 9 *One of the two bronze chariots found in an ancillary pit near Qin Shi Huangdi's mausoleum. This one weighs over 1242 kg and is composed of 3462 parts.*

Fig. 10 *View of the mausoleum of Qin Shi Huangdi. Although many burial objects have been found in its vicinity, the tomb itself has not been excavated.*

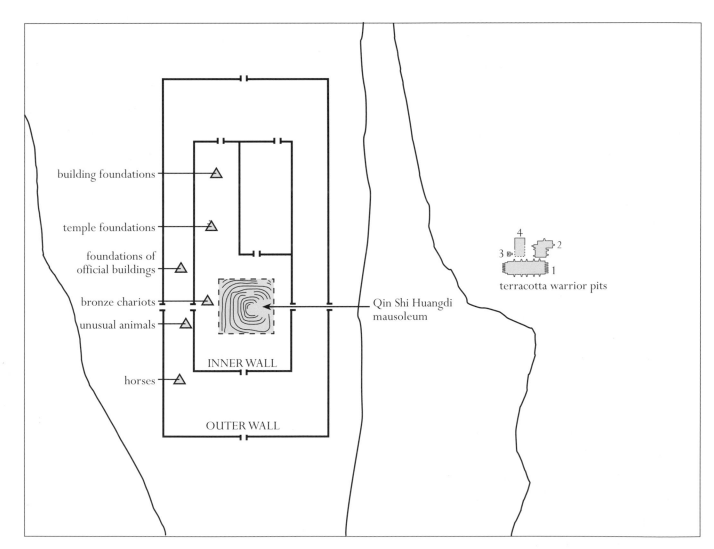

building foundations

temple foundations

foundations of
official buildings

bronze chariots

unusual animals

horses

INNER WALL

OUTER WALL

Qin Shi Huangdi
mausoleum

4

3

2

1

terracotta warrior pits

Fig. 11 *Plan showing the position of Qin Shi Huangdi's mausoleum, the pits of the terracotta warriors and the bronze chariots. The pits containing the soldiers are located almost 1.5 km to the east of the mausoleum. Three pits contain figures, but pit 4 was not completed and is empty.*

such as Mount Tai. Probably the ingestion of various immortality potions, including no doubt the gold that his Daoist alchemists recommended as a longevity medicine, actually killed him during one of his inspection tours, during which he might well have used the full-size equivalent of the *an che* (fig. 9). On these tours he also set up steles broadcasting his achievements.[8] His body was brought back to the capital secretly buried beneath some rotting fish to divert attention from the body while the succession was being arranged.

Qin Shi Huangdi began building his mausoleum as soon as he became king of Qin in 246 BC. This huge area has not yet been excavated by the Chinese (fig. 10), and may well have been looted. We do, however, have an account of it by a Han historian, Sima Qian, written in about 90 BC, which describes the magnificence and huge scale on which it was built,[9] to mirror the empire ruled by the emperor on earth, a microcosm of the world, complete with rivers made of mercury and stars and heavens depicted on the ceiling. The high level of mercury in the area has been verified by scientific measurement so it is possible that the rest of the description is accurate, but this will remain speculative until such time as the excavation actually takes place. Meanwhile, it is the peripheral pits and finds around the tomb area which have been excavated (fig. 11), the existence of which Sima Qian does not mention, and these have of course revealed the huge and magnificent army and the chariots which the emperor thought he would need to fight off his enemies in the afterworld. There are further pits with human and animal sacrifices as well as clay substitutes.[10]

The largest of the army pits, pit 1 (fig. 12), probably held six thousand figures of soldiers aligned in battle array, together with archers and chariots, in eleven parallel corridors. Pit 2 held over 1400 cavalrymen and chariots and the third pit contained what is supposed to have been some kind of command post, with about seventy soldiers and one chariot. The fourth pit was empty and presumably the emperor died before it could be filled. Near the

mausoleum was another small pit in which were buried two exquisite bronze chariots (see cat. no. 10). Their expensive materials, fine workmanship and exquisite detail are indications that they were intended for the emperor's own use in the afterlife, possibly one as a war chariot and one for peacetime travel.

The scale of the enterprise in supplying all these provisions for the emperor's afterlife is astounding and the army is just a part of this complicated depiction. Massive planning would have been needed to achieve it all. Both the planning and the execution of the army, the chariots and the other accompanying buried objects are a great tribute to the organization of the Qin state and to the beliefs and practices that sustained the First Emperor and his subjects. It was obviously a huge undertaking to make such an enormous number of figures and to set them out in such an organized fashion, presumably based on actual battle formations of the time. Although much has been made of the fact that each soldier looks different, it has in fact been established that there are ten basic faces on to which different eyebrows, ears, eyes, beards and moustaches have been individually applied or luted to give the impression of an infinite variety of individuals.[11] The

Fig. 12 *Pit 1 of Qin Shi Huangdi's terracotta warriors.*

variations in facial features suggest soldiers from different parts of China: for example, it is believed that the models with a wide forehead and full lips are soldiers from west Shaanxi province,[12] and those with beards and moustaches are possibly foreigners (the borderland peoples were held in great awe, on account of their strength).[13] Sima Qian indicated that over 700,000 conscripts were brought in to work on the tomb and adjacent projects and many of the terracotta soldiers have stamps on them possibly indicating the name of the foreman in charge of a group of potters.[14]

The mass-production methods utilized in making the terracotta army involved the moulding and fitting together of heads and hands and then the addition by hand of individual details such as armour, robes, belts, facial characteristics, headdresses and shoes. The figures were all brightly painted according to rank and regiment but the colours have disintegrated since the pits were opened.[15]

The bronze chariots buried in a separate pit are no less a testimony to the mass-production and organizational methods utilized by the emperor in his grand plan for the afterlife. The Qin state had, through its geographical proximity to the nomadic states to the west, been influenced by those peoples' use of gold (see cat. nos 1, 2, 3, 4). The workmanship involved in making the parts of each of the chariots, which number over 3000, and the use of gold and silver for the reins and the horses' headdress ornaments bear witness to the superb metallurgical skills of the emperor's artisans and the lavish expense he outlaid on this project.[16]

The emperor also took with him some real sacrifices, for example all his childless concubines and his grooms, as well as animals from his royal zoo. Beliefs about the afterlife were obviously very complex but there is no doubt that Qin Shi Huangdi's megalomaniacal tendencies would have made him many enemies in his lifetime and he must have felt the need for as real and as effective an army as he could produce to protect him against his foes in the afterlife.

1   Poem by Li Bai, *Li Bai Quanji biannian zhushi*, Bashu shushe edn, 1990, vol. 1, p. 839.
2   For a history of Legalism, see L Vandermeersch, *La Formation du Légisme*, Paris 1965.
3   For a biography of Shang Yang, see J Levi, *Le Livre du Prince Shang*, Paris 1981.
4   Ma Fei Bai, *Qin Jishi*, Zhonghua shuju, 1982, p. 701; and cat. no. 12.
5   For further information regarding the emperor see B Watson 1961, 1993a; Cotterell 1981; D Bodde, *China's First Unifier: A Study of the Ch'in Dynasty as seen in the Life of Li Ssu*, Leiden 1939, reprinted Hong Kong 1967; D Bodde, *Statesman, Patriot and General in Ancient China: Three Shih-chi Biographies of the Ch'in Dynasty*, New Haven, Conn. 1940 (Kraus reprint 1967); Chavannes 1969; Twitchett and Loewe 1986; G and Hsien-yi Yang, *Records of the Historian*, Hong Kong 1974. For a discussion on the ideology and uses of writing in early China, and a section on Sima Qian and his history, the *Shiji*, see M E Lewis, *Writing and Authority in Early China*, New York 1999.
6   B Watson 1993a, p. 45.
7   'Rhapsody' by Jiang Yan (444–505): Jiang describes those who died full of 'resentment and frustration' and in this quotation is specifically referring to the First Emperor who enjoyed his reign as ruler of the united empire for only a brief time. Translation quoted from Knechtges 1996, p. 193.
8   Sima Qian, the Han dynasty historian, transcribed many of these steles in his histories. See B Watson 1993a, pp. 46–53.
9   B Watson 1993a, p. 63.
10 For information on the army and the burial pits generally see Shaanxi 1998 a and b; Ledderose and Schlombs 1990; Hearn 1980; Yuan Zhongyi 1990.
11 Fu Tianchou 1985, pp. 12–13; Ledderose 1992.
12 For general accounts of the find and some individual figures see Hearn 1980, pp. 353-73; Ledderose and Schlombs 1990, pp. 35–98, 249–325. See also Yuan Zhongyi 1990. For a discussion of the mass-production of the terracotta figures see Ledderose 1992.
13 Rawson 1998, p. 33.
14 Rawson 1996, p. 167.
15 See cat. no. 13 for details of colouring used.
16 Zhang Wenli, p. 92.

10 Chariot and horses (replica)

Qin dynasty (221–206 BC)
Bronze
Chariot: height 152 cm; length 225 cm; weight 1200 kg. Horses: heights 107.8–110 cm; lengths 91.6–110 cm
Excavated 1980, mausoleum of the First Emperor, Qin Shi Huangdi, Lintong county, Shaanxi province
Museum of the Qin Shi Huang Terracotta Army

Following the discovery of the life-size terracotta army in the area around Qin Shi Huangdi's tomb in 1974, two half life-size bronze chariots and horses were discovered in 1980 to the west of the pits where the

soldiers were found. The chariot pit measured 55 metres north to south and east to west and, when discovered, the chariots were smashed into pieces, requiring several years of restoration. Restoration has revealed the extraordinary richness of decoration and detail on these chariots and horses, all the more remarkable as they are half life-size.[1] They are a supreme example of the Qin artisans' skills in bronze, gold and silver work.

The chariot shown here is chariot no. 1, which is two wheeled and single shafted and drawn by four horses. A terracotta charioteer, 91 centimetres tall, stands under the bronze canopy, holding the reins. His protective bronze shield, long sword, crossbow and bronze arrows indicate that

the chariot is a war chariot. There are rails on either side of the chariot, the inner faces of which are painted with coloured rhombic patterns and the outer with geometric lines. The chariot is open at the back to enable the soldiers access and although there is perhaps room for three people, only the charioteer is depicted, dressed in a long robe and cap. A crossbow is attached to the front of the chariot and a bronze quiver holding fifty-four bronze arrowheads hangs on the inside of the crossbar. A shield case holding a bronze shield is placed on the inside of the left rail. The other chariot found in the pit was marked 'an che' which means comfortable chariot: it had a covered carriage with seating room and windows and was perhaps a replica of the carriage

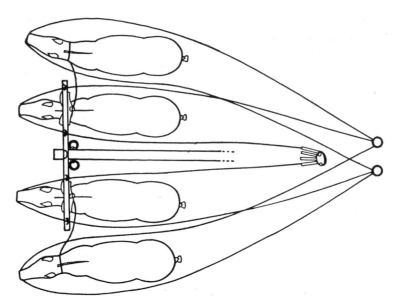

Fig. 10a Drawing illustrating the harnessing system used in the First Emperor's bronze chariot.

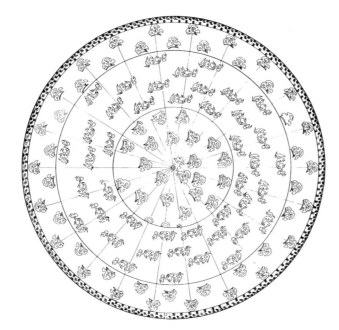

Fig. 10b Drawing illustrating the decoration painted inside the parasol covering the charioteer on the bronze chariot.

used by the emperor on his regular inspection tours of the empire (fig. 9, p. 34).

This war chariot has a bronze canopy with a diameter of 105.5 centimetres, the inner side of which is richly decorated with colourful dragon and phoenix patterns, and the handle is inlaid with silver and gold. All four horses have their manes cut and their tails tied up. Of the four horses, the two in the middle are harnessed with a yoke at the

neck, while the two at each side are tied with a rein around the shoulders, to a block on the frame. The two central horses therefore provide the lead for the two outer horses.[2] The horses are painted white and wear gold and silver head nets with gold plaques on their foreheads and tassels of fine bronze wire hanging from the bottom of the bridles in front of their necks. The bridles, reins and traces are made of bronze with

jointed gold and silver tubes. Altogether the gold and silver pieces on the horses weigh some seven kilograms. The countless metal pieces which make up the reins are still flexible.

The manufacture of both carriages demonstrates the extraordinarily complex production methods achieved in the Qin period. Very efficient organization would have been required to produce so many different components to such a high standard of workmanship. Various technological methods were employed to make the chariots and the horses, including welding, riveting, drilling, engraving, punching, hammering, casting, forging, and polishing. Some of the parts are only 2 to 4 millimetres thick, but the casting is very even. The chariot is composed of more than three thousand parts in gold, silver and bronze. Aesthetically and technologically these chariots are even more remarkable than the terracotta figures showing that the metalworkers of the Qin dynasty were very skilled artists and technicians of their time.

Our knowledge of Bronze Age chariots is based on archaeological finds such as those buried at Baoji in Shaanxi province (see cat. no. 8). Chariots were introduced into China, probably from the Caucasus area, in about 1200 BC in the Shang dynasty, and developed into an important military and status object. Wooden remains of early chariots reveal that they were among the largest two-wheeled vehicles of their time, with wheels up to 150 centimetres in diameter and bodies up to 75 centimetres above the ground.[3] However, because most wooden chariots have deteriorated, it was not until the discovery of these bronze chariots that verification of the details of Qin and Han chariots and their harnessing could be clarified. Now we can see how the outside horses were controlled from moving too near to or too far from the two central horses by a horizontal T-shaped bronze piece with a sharp end at the outer side of each of the central horses.

Histories such as Sima Qian's *Shiji* of about 90 BC describe how the Qin emperor went on inspection tours of his empire accompanied by eighty-one imperial chariots, thirty-six for his retinue and others for high officials. The two bronze chariots discovered near Qin Shi Huangdi's tomb provide a graphic illustration of how impressive such processions must have been.

Published: Osaka 1987, no. 125; *Famous Capital*, p. 57, no. 2.

1 For a detailed examination of these chariots in Chinese (with an English abstract) see Shaanxi 1998a and b. See also Ledderose and Schlombs 1990; Hearn 1980; Yuan Zhongyi 1990; Zhang Wenli 1996. For a list of books and articles on the chariots see *China Archaeology and Art Digest,* vol. 2, nos 3–4, Hong Kong, December 1998, pp. 166–7.
2 See fig. 10a for illustration of how the horses were harnessed. The two outside horses were obviously more vulnerable to enemy attack and there might have been a way of detaching them quickly if necessary and for possibly adding replacement horses. For information on how chariots with several horses were driven in antiquity see M A Littauer and J H Crouwel, 'Assyrian Trigas and Russian Dvoikas', *Iraq,* 1991, pp. 97–9.
3 For an account of early chariots see Lu Liancheng 1993 and Toronto 1992, p. 108.

11 General

Qin dynasty (221–206 BC)
Terracotta
Height 195 cm; weight 250 kg
Excavated 1977, mausoleum of the First Emperor, Qin Shi Huangdi, pit 1, Lintong county, Shaanxi province
Museum of the Qin Shi Huang Terracotta Army

This imposing figure represents a general of Qin Shi Huangdi's army. He is dressed in a double-layered robe, over which is an armoured vest with fish-scale design that hangs below his waist in a V shape. His rank is indicated by decorative tassels on his upper chest. The armour originally had a colourful geometrical design on it but this has largely disappeared. His trousers are buckled around the ankles and his shoes have upturned toes. He stands firmly on a small base. He has a long face with a stern, authoritative expression and his exalted position within the army command is indicated by his military headdress in the form of a double-tailed bird, which ties under the chin. His hair is tied in a bun at the back of his head. His arms hang loosely and one hand is folded over the other in a relaxed fashion. The soldiers in Qin Shi Huangdi's army are of different sizes but the generals are about two metres in height, over life size, to give them a more imposing air. A general in command would order the beating of drums to signal advance and the ringing of bells for retreat.

We have some knowledge of suits of armour of this period as several have been discovered in tombs. In the tomb of the Marquis Yi of Zeng, who died in 433 BC, thirteen lacquered leather suits, as well as helmets and armour for horses, were found and some have been reconstructed.[1] A typical suit of the period consisted of 23 plates for the upper body, collar, chest and back, a skirt of 56 plates and articulated armour for the arms, totalling 131 plates. The armour of the warriors in Qin Shi Huangdi's tomb is of lacquered leather plates, or lamellae, laced together by thongs of leather or cord. The four top rows of plates overlap downwards, the four lower rows overlap upwards and the central rows are covered top and bottom, giving the armour a lightly bulging effect. The plates are connected by thongs, the number of points of attachment being indicated by a knot of the thong as it emerges from the underside. Armour varied according to the soldier's role: a cavalryman wore a short light suit, while a chariot driver was offered the most protection, with articulated lamellar armour for the arms and plates to protect his hands as he held the reins. In the Han dynasty tomb of Liu Sheng, of the royal

11

family, who was buried at Mancheng, Hebei province, about 113 BC, an iron suit of armour with a fish-scale pattern similar to that depicted on this general was found.[2]

All the soldiers would originally have been holding real bronze weapons. However, in the period of civil war following the death of Qin Shi Huangdi in 210 BC, before the establishment of the Han

12

dynasty in 206 BC, the pits were robbed of the weapons and wide destruction of the warriors was carried out.[3]

Published: Osaka 1987, no. 125; *Famous Capital*, p. 57, no. 2. For general information on Qin Shi Huangdi's tomb see Shaanxi 1998a and b; Ledderose and Schlombs 1990; Hearn 1980; Yuan Zhongyi 1990.

1 Tokyo 1992, pl. 65, p. 130; Yang Hong 1992, p. 116.
2 Beijing 1980d, vol. 2, pl. CXV. A recent preliminary report has been filed about the discovery of stone armour from the tomb of Qin Shi Huangdi. Only a few details have been released but a new pit has apparently revealed full suits of armour made out of lozenges of stone which would originally have been sewn together with bronze thread.
3 For general accounts of the terracotta army see Fu Tianchou 1985, pp. 12–13; New York

1980, pp. 353–73; Ledderose and Schlombs 1990, pp. 35–98, 249–325; Yuan Zhongyi 1990. For a discussion of the mass-production process of the terracotta figures see Ledderose 1992.

12 Cavalryman

Qin dynasty (221–206 BC)
Terracotta
Height 186 cm; weight 200 kg
Excavated 1977, mausoleum of the First
Emperor, Qin Shi Huangdi, pit 2, Lintong
county, Shaanxi province
Museum of the Qin Shi Huang Terracotta Army

The cavalryman was found in pit 2 which is sited about twenty metres north of pit 1 and contains about 1400 warriors and horses divided into four mixed groups of archers,

chariots and charioteers, cavalry and infantry in a curved formation.[1] The cavalry was a particularly important component of the Qin army as its speed was greatly superior to that of both the infantry and the chariot forces. It was therefore used as a mobile or reserve unit.

This cavalryman has short tight-fitting armour above the waist, without shoulder plates or sleeves so as to facilitate riding. Beneath the belted waist is a wrap-around, short pleated skirt. The stitched leather shoes are represented in some detail with lacing and ties. He wears a cap tied under his chin and, as with all the warriors, a scarf around his neck, probably both for protection and to prevent his armour from rubbing against his skin. Enough paint remains to indicate that his cap was originally painted a reddish brown, perhaps to suggest leather, and had a decorative pattern of red dots. His hair is plaited into a chequered pattern on the back of his head.

The cavalryman appears to have stood in front of his horse, one hand probably holding the reins and the other a bow. The cavalry was equipped with crossbows and arrows, suitable for medium-range fighting but not for close-quarter fighting for which swords were preferable. One problem for the cavalryman of this period, before the introduction of the stirrup, was how to stay firmly in the saddle and use a weapon at the same time. The warrior was possibly tied to the saddle. Alternatively, the rider, when galloping or jumping, may have hung on tight to the horse's mane.[2] In the Qin dynasty a leather cushion acted as a saddle but by the Western Han this had been replaced by a saddle curved upwards at the front and back. By the time of the Western Jin the front and back ridges of the saddle were more pronounced and a triangular stirrup was hung from the front ridge on the left side. This can be seen in a pottery figurine of a horse excavated from a late Western Jin tomb at Changsha, Hunan province. The Chinese also used very deep pommels in an attempt to provide a firmer seat, but heavy armour could not be used until the problem of stability had been solved. The earliest iron stirrup found in China has been discovered in a Wei-Jin tomb at Nantan, Wuwei, in Gansu province, datable to the late third century AD.[3]

The Qin state in the Warring States period was renowned for its superior horse breeding. Its effective cavalry was an important factor in the Qin state's successful fight for hegemony during the Warring States period and its eventual unification of the empire in 221 BC. The histories speak of the Qin state having fine steeds which could gallop about five metres at one leap.[4] The terracotta horses with slender ankles

and high fetlocks certainly give the impression of being fast movers.

The sculpting of horses in terracotta was an even greater technological challenge than making the soldiers. The horses were fired with an air vent on one side to allow more heat to enter the hollow body and ensure the even firing of both interior and exterior. The kiln temperature had to be carefully controlled because, if it was too high, the horse was liable to break or become distorted.

The horse's head, ears, eyes and mane were formed in complex moulds. The eyes were mould-made but the lids were carved and the irises incised. The body was also moulded in two large sections and, when half dry, removed and the decorative details added. While the horses were drying they had to be supported until the bodies could take the stress of being moved.[5]

The chariot horses were hitched to the chariots by wooden shoulder yokes fixed to a crossbar, but these and the chariots themselves have disintegrated and only traces of the carriages, shafts and wheels remain.

Published: Goepper 1995; Yuan Zhongyi 1990; Hearn 1980. For general information on Qin Shi Huangdi's tomb see Shaanxi 1998a and b; Ledderose and Schlombs 1990; Hearn 1980; Yuan Zhongyi 1990.

1 Zhang Wenli 1996, pp. 30–5; Yuan Zhongyi 1990, p. 65.
2 Temple 1991, pp. 89–90.
3 For a detailed history of Chinese equestrian equipment from the third to the sixth century AD see Wang Wei, *Kaogu* 1997.12, pp. 66–84, and an abbreviated translation of it in English, *China Archaeology and Art Digest*, vol. 2, nos 3–4, Hong Kong, December 1998, pp. 158–61. The earliest complete set of bronze horse harness fittings was discovered in an attendant horse and chariot burial pit at the Shang site of Yinxu (Anyang, the last Shang capital). Harness components have been found at several Western Zhou sites, such as Liulihe, near Beijing, and Fengxi, near Xi'an; for information on saddles see C S Goodrich, 'Riding Astride and the Saddle in Ancient China', *Harvard*

Journal of Asiatic Studies, vol. 44, no. 2, 1984, pp. 279–321.
4 Ma Fei Bai, *Qin Jishi*, Zhonghua shuju edn, 1982, p. 701.
5 For technical details on how the terracotta warriors and horses were made see H J Qu, Z H Cheng and Xiao Jie Wu, 'Research on the Techniques of Making Pottery Figurines of the Qin Army', in P B Vandiver, J Druzik and G S Wheeler (eds), *Materials Issues in Art and Archaeology II*, vol. 185, Materials Research Society Symposium Proceedings, 1991, pp. 459–77.

13 Kneeling archer

Qin dynasty (221–206 BC)
Terracotta
Height 119 cm; weight 110 kg
Excavated 1977, mausoleum of the First Emperor, Qin Shi Huangdi, pit 2, Lintong county, Shaanxi province
Museum of the Qin Shi Huang Terracotta Army

The archer kneels on his right knee with his hands and arms positioned as if he were holding a crossbow and arrows. He wears an armoured, short battle-robe with shoulder pads and short trousers over which he has protective leggings. The lamellar form of the armour is clearly delineated, as is the tread of his square-toed shoes. Despite the fact that potters were making thousands of these figures they still, for example, took the trouble to portray details such as the stippled tread of the archer's shoe (fig. 13a), revealing the difference in tread on the heel, sole and instep. His hair is tied in a bun.

All the soldiers would originally have been painted in bright colours, indicating regiment and rank, but as the pigments were held in a thin coating of lacquer, which has decayed, there remain only traces of colour. It is thought that the warriors' hands and faces were painted pink, the robes green and blue, the rivets in the armour black and the joints red.[1]

The crossbow is first mentioned in a treatise on war, *Master Sun's Art of War*, which

13

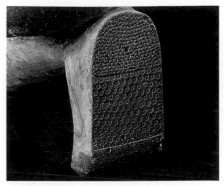

Fig. 13a Detail of the shoe of the kneeling archer. The square-cut shoes show the tread of the sole in great detail.

wood and painted, or possibly lacquered, red. The body of one reconstructed from pit 1 was 71.6 centimetres in length, with a groove at the front for the bolt and a bronze trigger mechanism at the rear. It could reputedly fire a bronze bolt a distance of 200 metres and its effectiveness ensured Chinese military supremacy over the invading nomads from the north and northwest at this time.[4] Stronger crossbows had longer shooting ranges and accuracy was improved by increasing the height of the aiming sight and engraving a scale on it. During the Han dynasty the bow and arrow was made more effective with arrowheads of forged steel. Examples of these have been found in the tomb of Liu Sheng who died in Mancheng, Hebei province, and was buried about 113 BC. Bronze arrowheads have also been found in large numbers probably because the technology of casting them was a well embedded tradition. Sima Qian, the Chinese historian writing in about 90 BC, said that Liang Xiao Wang was in charge of arsenals containing several hundred thousand crossbows, proof that these mechanisms were mass-produced at a very early stage.[5]

Pit 2 lies to the north of pit 1 (fig. 11, p. 34). It has not been fully excavated but archaeologists have postulated that there may be a total of 1400 figures, 450 horses and 89 battle chariots. But whereas pit 1 contains mainly infantry, pit 2 has a greater number of archers, chariots and

cavalrymen. Military specialists speculate that the troops in pit 2 would have been used in an offensive to break up the enemy and the cavalry would have chased an enemy on the run. The archers would have been drawn up in rows so that one row would be firing whilst the next was preparing to shoot as there was a maximum number of arrows that each bow could fire.

Published: Li Jian 1998, no. 17. For general information on Qin Shi Huangdi's tomb see Shaanxi 1998a and b; Ledderose and Schlombs 1990; Hearn 1980; Yuan Zhongyi 1990.

1 For technical information on the paint colours used on the terracotta army, see Thieme 1995 and Herm 1995.
2 Sawyer 1995, pp. 55–61.
3 Yang Hong 1992, pp. 95–7; Needham and Yates 1994, vol. 5, part VI, pp. 135ff.
4 Temple 1991, pp. 218–24.
5 Yang Hong 1992, p. 188.

dates from about 345 BC. In the fourth century BC Sun Bin wrote of the effectiveness of the weapon and that its usage determined the victory of the state of Qi over the Wei at the battle of Maling in 341 BC.[2] The Chinese perfected the bronze trigger mechanism during the Warring States period and the Chu state was among the earliest to equip its armies with this crossbow.[3] Archery was a basic military skill required of every soldier and one on which everyone was tested and rated. The crossbow in the Qin dynasty was made of

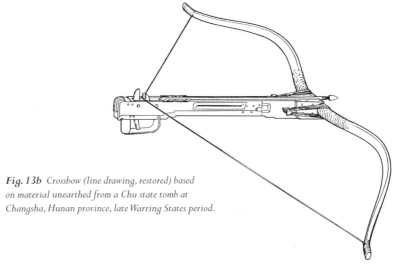

Fig. 13b Crossbow (line drawing, restored) based on material unearthed from a Chu state tomb at Changsha, Hunan province, late Warring States period.

THE HAN DYNASTY

Qin Shi Huangdi died in 210 BC, having ruled for only fifteen years as emperor. His death was followed by a period of civil war which ended when Liu Bang seized the throne and became the first emperor of the Han dynasty. It was during the civil war that the pits containing the terracotta soldiers of Qin Shi Huangdi were raided, the weapons stolen and the pits fired so that the timber-lined ceilings burned and fell on to the soldiers, shattering them and the horses. There they lay until their discovery in 1974.

The Han dynasty endured for four hundred years and built on many of the foundations laid by Qin Shi Huangdi. It proceeded to form one of the greatest and largest empires of its day, contemporaneous with the Roman empire in the West (see map p. 172, top). The Han and the Tang dynasties, and the empires ruled by them, are two of the most glorious periods in Chinese history; many of the characteristics of the Tang empire were already present in the Han.[1]

The capital was moved by the Han from Xianyang to Chang'an (see fig. 7, p. 32) and then in the Eastern or Later Han period (which is separated from the Western or Former Han by a period when Wang Mang ruled from AD 9 to 23) the capital was situated at Luoyang. Both these capitals were also used by the Tang but Chang'an was by then the more important of the two. It was during the Han that Confucianism was accepted as the state ideology, but the idea of a meritocracy created by a formal examination system for entry into the civil service did not begin until the Tang.

Control of the large empire was in the hands of a well trained bureaucracy who shared a common ideology and a similar standard of material life. Highly organized workshops supervised by officials mass-produced the objects for distribution to the official classes (cat. nos 14, 15). The Han period saw significant changes in beliefs about the afterlife. During the Eastern Zhou period there appear to have co-existed two currents of thought: one was the belief in an underworld governed by a bureaucracy similar to life on earth; the other was a belief that there might be some kind of immortal land to which the soul of the deceased might travel.[2] The burying of substitutes in graves, rather than real people and goods, became more common, as did the idea that perhaps the afterlife would not necessarily continue as life itself but might be lived in some paradise. These paradises were seen to lie in the Kunlun Mountains, in the west, or perhaps on the islands of Penglai in the Eastern Sea. Both Qin Shi Huangdi and the Han emperor Wudi anxiously sought to obtain from the islands of Penglai drugs that would confer immortality. Incense burners, which do not become significant until the

Fig. 13 Banner from the tomb of Lady Dai, Han dynasty, 186–168 BC. Length 2.05 m. Excavated in 1972 from Mawangdui, Changsha city, Hunan province.

fourth century BC, are inextricably connected with paradise as they depict mountains where the immortals might be found (see cat. no. 18). Some of the beliefs about the worlds of immortals to which people of this time were beginning to aspire are perhaps depicted on the banner found in the tomb of Lady Dai in the south of China, at Mawangdui,[3] Hunan province, dating from the second century BC (fig. 13). This is one of the most famous early Chinese paintings and, even though the exact iconography is disputed, it shows the tomb occupant, an elderly lady at the centre, leaning on a stick. She appears to be poised between the worlds below and above, where the sun and the moon are clearly depicted. However, it was not until about the third century AD that these universes outside the tomb, to which one might go after death, began to be more clearly defined.

This emphasis on immortality and a new interest in the lands where the immortals might live and where humans might themselves go thus developed gradually and led to the production of replicas for burial in the tomb (cat. nos 14, 15, 17 and 28) rather than the real or life-size objects buried in earlier periods.

The Han dynasty greatly expanded the unified state created by the Qin, particularly under Wudi who ruled from 141 to 87 BC. Korea and parts of Vietnam were brought under control by the Chinese and Wudi sent Zhang Qian to the West to look for the horses (see cat. no.

17) that he needed for his military campaigns and to try to make some military alliances against the Xiongnu nomads. Zhang Qian's journeys (138–126 and 115 BC) and the information he eventually brought back greatly expanded the horizons of the Chinese as well as introducing new and exotic foods such as alfalfa and grapes. It is from this date that the Silk Routes[4] really began, routes which were to play such an important role in Chinese life both in the Han and again in the Tang dynasty (when the monk Xuanzang's accounts of his journey to the West were equally important for the information they contained). But possibly the Han dynasty's main achievement over four hundred years was to sustain the reality of a unified China which had so briefly been achieved by the Qin, an ideal continuously sought during the period of disunity after the fall of the Han and achieved again by the Sui and succeeding Tang dynasties.

1 The main historical texts of the Han dynasty are the *Shiji* (trans. B Watson 1961); *Han Shu*, History of the Former Han dynasty (trans. Dubs 1944) and the *Hou Han shu*, History of the Later Han. For bibliographical information generally about the Han dynasty see Wilkinson 1998, pp. 746–73.
2 A document found at Fangmatan in Gansu province and discussed by Li Xueqin and Donald Harper tells of a man who returned from the underworld to report on the bureaucracy there. Li Xueqin, 'Fangmatan jian zhong de zhiguai gushi', *Wenwu* 1990.4, pp. 43–7; Donald Harper, 'Resurrection in Warring States Popular Religion', *Taoist Resources*, vol. 5, no. 2, 1994, pp. 13–29. I am grateful to Jessica Rawson for this reference.
3 Beijing 1973b; Loewe 1979. It is this tomb complex that contained the great variety of well preserved Han dynasty foods (see cat. no. 28).
4 See the introduction on the Silk Routes, pp. 79–85.

14 Ten miniature soldiers

Western Han dynasty (206 BC–AD 9)
Earthenware with painted decoration
Heights 44.5–48.5 cm
Excavated 1965, Yangjiawan, Xianyang city, Shaanxi province
Xianyang Museum

These miniature soldiers were found in tombs that lay between those of the first and the fourth emperors of the Western Han

(reigned 206–195 BC and 157–141 BC). The graves are at Yangjiawan, a village about 20 kilometres to the northeast of Xianyang, the ancient Qin capital, which itself lies 25 kilometres to the west of present-day Xi'an. It is thought that the tomb may have belonged to the famous Han dynasty general Zhou Bo (died 169 BC) and his son Zhou Yafu (died 143 BC). Both served as senior officials and despite being born into an impoverished family, Zhou Bo was appointed national supreme commander. Both suffered setbacks in their careers and

were gaoled (Zhou Yafu died there), but Zhou Bo was posthumously exonerated. The tomb was obviously on a much smaller scale than that of Qin Shi Huangdi, with miniature rather than life-size soldiers. There were nevertheless 2548 miniature soldiers, comprising 1965 footsoldiers and 583 mounted cavalrymen, as well as musicians, dancers and other attendants.[1]

These ten miniature figures are footsoldiers. They are made of ceramic, brightly painted to show their dress, armour and headdresses, and they stand poised with one arm outstretched, as if to hold a weapon, and one holds a shield. They wear long tunics with collars and cuffs, over tight trousers and socks. One has armour with breastplates and backplates and some have a quiver painted on their back. Several have red turbans wrapped round their heads to keep their hair in position.

The soldiers are valuable evidence of the clothing, armour and weaponry current in the Western Han period. They would originally have carried weapons and some iron clubs have been found. The earliest evidence of armour in China takes the form of protective bronze helmets from the Shang and Zhou dynasties. The earliest remaining leather body armour dates to the Warring States period although leather armour may have been made earlier and perished. Iron armour developed in the Han dynasty, and was made of plates tied together into a suit. The soldiers of Yangjiawan show seven different styles of armour.[2] Most important is evidence of the earliest slip armour in the form of a vest, consisting of only breast and back armour connected by shoulder bands. Some of the soldiers have armour plates to protect their shoulders and flexible plates to cover their waist and hips and some wear armour resembling that of the Qin pottery soldiers.[3]

Shields in the Han dynasty were made of wood, leather and iron. The Yangjiawan soldiers carry the type of shield that first appeared in the Warring States: it has a straight bottom edge and a tapering ridge down the centre. Such shields protect about one third of the height of the soldier.[4]

Similar caches of miniature armies have been found dating to the Han period, such as those in Renjiapo in the eastern suburbs of Xi'an, in Hongqing village, Xi'an, in Langjiagou, Shaanxi, and in Xuzhou.[5] Thousands of soldiers were found at the Yangling Mausoleum of Emperor Jing and his empress (died 126 BC). These Yangling soldiers were naked, having once been clothed with textiles which have since

disintegrated. Some had suits of armour made of wood, and miniature bronze belt hooks and crossbows. Miniature halberds, iron spears, iron swords and bronze arrow heads have also been found. The wooden shields had disintegrated. The Yangling soldiers show a greater variety of facial expression and modelling than the Yangjiawan soldiers.

Published: *Wenwu*, 1966.3, pp. 1–5; *Wenwu* 1977.10, pp. 10–21; *Wenbo* 1993.2, pp. 19–27; Berger 1994, no. 24; *Wenbo* 1996.6, pp. 38–45.

1 Xi'an 1996, p. 55; for Chinese reports on this archaeological find see *Wenwu* 1966.3, pp. 1–5; *Wenwu* 1977.10, pp. 10–21; *Wenbo* 1993.2, pp. 19–27; *Wenbo* 1996.6, pp. 38–45; Brussels 1982, cat. no. 28.
2 Zhou and Gao 1987, p. 49, gives details and drawings of the various types of armour worn by the Yangjiawan soldiers. See also *Wenbo* 1996.6, pp. 38–45, for a topology of the military clothing worn by these soldiers and a comparison with that of the soldiers buried at emperor Huidi's Anling Mausoleum and Shizhishan and Beidongshan, at Xushou. There seems to have been a standardization throughout the Han armies. For a recent article on Han dynasty iron armour found in Inner Mongolia see *Wenwu* 1999.2, pp. 71–9 and Beijing 1998, pp. 288–9.
3 Yang Hong 1992, p. 219.
4 Yang Hong 1992, p. 220; a drawing of the armour of these soldiers can be found on p. 218.
5 Wang Kai 1990, p. 62; Los Angeles 1987, pls 11–15.

14

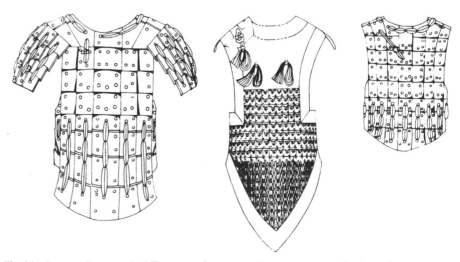

Fig. 14a *Drawings illustrating the different types of armour worn by a warrior, a general and a cavalryman in Qin Shi Huangdi's terracotta army.*

15 Ten miniature soldiers on horseback

Western Han dynasty (206 BC–AD 9)
Earthenware with painted decoration
Heights 68 cm
Excavated 1965, Yangjiawan, Xianyang city,
Shaanxi province
Xianyang Museum

These miniature soldiers were found in the same burial as those in catalogue no. 14. They represent the cavalry. The details of the costumes, with headscarves and red, white, green and purple uniforms, are all painted on, as are the details of the horses' saddles, bridles and whips. With one hand on the reins and the other grasping a weapon, the cavalry figures are in two sizes. The larger ones, representing the heavy cavalry, are 68 centimetres high and some have black armour and halberds. The smaller figurines, the light cavalry, are without armour. Many held bows and arrows and have quivers on their backs. Possibly the larger cavalry unit represented a whole regiment, with the light unit making up a specialized section of it, such as reconnaissance.[1]

The cavalry horses have similar poses and the men are seated astride. The legs and lower garments of the soldiers have been moulded onto the sides of the horses, possibly to prevent breakage. The soldiers' heads and bodies were made separately and then placed on the back of each horse. The horses are painted black, white, red and purple and are furnished with saddle cloths.

Published: *Wenwu* 1977.10, p. 17; W Watson 1973, nos 171–2; Singapore 1990, p. 39; Beijing 1992a, no. 70; Berger 1994, no. 25; Li Jian 1998, nos 26–7.

1 Xi'an 1996, p. 57.

16 Seventeen chariot fittings

Western Han dynasty (206 BC–AD 9)
Bronze inlaid with gold and silver
Lengths 3.1–7.8 cm; heights 2.5–6 cm;
widths 1.9–7.6 cm; weights 21.4–522.1 g
Excavated 1992, tomb of Huo Qubing, Maoling,
Shaanxi province
Shaanxi Archaeological Institute

These bronze chariot fittings are inlaid with gold and silver cloud scrolls, geometrical designs and animal faces. The technique comprised three stages: first, a groove was made in the bronze and this was filled with bands or ribbons of gold and silver, or sometimes red copper, which were hammered in firmly, and finally the whole was smoothed down and polished with a stone. There are many examples of this technique among the bronzes of the Warring States period and the Han dynasty.

Bronze, together with jade, was one of the two materials most prized by the Chinese in their hierarchy of materials. From the time bronze was first made in China, in the early Shang dynasty, about 1500 BC, it was used extensively for ritual vessels with which to worship various deities. The Chinese were not the first to use bronze but they became consummate makers of it. They adapted the cast mould method they had perfected for ceramics, rather than the Near Eastern method of using sheet metal. However, during the Warring States period the popularity of bronze began to wane. This was due in part to changes in ancestral worship practices whereby fewer and less elaborate sets of bronze ritual vessels were necessary, and in part to the increasing popularity of more colourful materials such as lacquer. Such changes appear to have begun in the south of China, south of the Yangzi River, centred on the state of Chu, where the cultural life had always been less austere and more colourful. Finds of lacquer from Chu tombs of the Warring States period have been extensive.[1] Lacquered goods were made in red, black, green and yellow and were often decorated with highly imaginative figures and patterns, many related to the mythology indigenous to the Chu state region. Such ostentation was part of the inter-state competition for supremacy. Decorated chariot fittings were another such item of display. Although the present fittings date from the Han dynasty, the painterly quality of the gold and silver decoration is similar to the decoration on lacquers of the late Warring States period.

Many bronze chariot fittings have been excavated from Warring States and Han period tombs[2] but most sets are not complete. This complete set furnishes us with much useful information on how the pieces fit together and were used. Also valuable in this respect was the discovery of the two bronze half life-size chariots in Qin Shi Huangdi's burial pits (cat. no. 10). Careful study of these two vehicles has revealed that the tubes are part of a coupling device connected with the parasol pole which was mounted from the centre of the chariot box. The smaller tubular fittings were attached to the yoke saddle. The ring was placed to one side of the yoke at the junction with the pole, and the rein guide was bound on to the yoke.[3]

These chariot fittings were found in a tomb adjacent to that of Huo Qubing, a famous general of the Western Han dynasty, the nephew of Queen Wei, wife of the Han emperor Wudi. At eighteen he was already distinguished as a mounted archer of great skill and he became a minor military official. He followed his uncle Wei Qing to fight against the Xiongnu nomads, and after many victories over them he was promoted to a high military position. In 121 BC he became a general and twice more had resounding victories over the Xiongnu, gained control of the western regions of the Yellow River and opened the routes to the West. Because of his extraordinary achievements and his elevated position his funeral ceremony was extremely grand.[4]

1 Rawson 1996a, nos 64, 65, pp. 138–41, both lacquers from the tomb of the Marquis Yi of Zeng (c. 433 BC).
2 See British Museum, Hotung Gallery, case 15: OA 1936.11–18.13; Seligman Bequest: 1937.7–23.76; OA 1932.10–14.45.
3 Toronto 1992, no. 60, p. 109.
4 His tomb is well known for the many stone sculptures outside it, in particular a horse trampling a so-called barbarian, perhaps one of the Xiongnu nomads against whom he was so successful; see Paludan 1991, p. 18, fig. 8.

17 Horse

Western Han dynasty (206 BC–AD 9)
Gilded bronze
Height 62 cm; length 76 cm; weight 25 kg
Excavated 1981, burial pit near tomb 1, Maoling, Xingping county, Shaanxi province
Maoling Museum

This magnificent horse is the largest gilded bronze horse yet discovered in China. It is one third life size and beautifully modelled with its ears pricked, its mouth open to reveal its teeth, and its eyes open. The mane is clearly demarcated on its neck and between the ears, and its muscular body

16

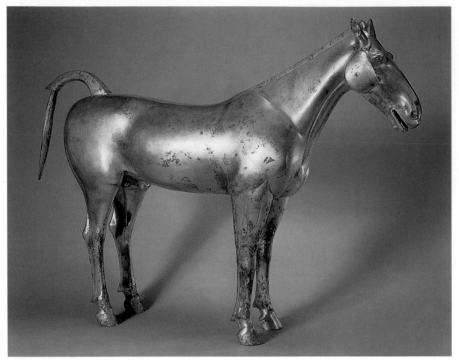

17

exudes strength. The application of pure gold to a bronze surface involved a highly sophisticated technique. In this case it has been done so smoothly and evenly that the horse looks as if it were made of solid gold.

The earliest method of gilding used in ancient China was that of overlaying an object with a thin hammered sheet of gold foil. However during the Warring States period Daoist preoccupations with immortality and scientific experiments in alchemy resulted in the discovery of mercury-amalgam gilding. This form of gilding is a chemical process whereby gold is dissolved in mercury to make a paste that is applied to the object to be gilded. When the object is heated, the mercury is burned off, and the surface of the object is then burnished. [1]

This horse perhaps represents one of the *tianma*, or heavenly horses, which the Han dynasty emperor Wudi (141–87 BC) wanted to import from Dayuan, present-day Ferghana, in the western regions, for use in his battles with the Xiongnu nomads. Zhang Qian was dispatched to explore the western regions and negotiate for these horses. He reached Sogdiana and Ferghana in 128 BC. Wudi is said to have ordered a gilded bronze horse to be presented as a gift to the ruler of the western regions in the hope that he would be presented in return with some of these 'heavenly' swift horses. Because his gift was rejected (and smashed, according to the histories), he sent his general Li Guangli to wage war against Ferghana. Two horse specialists who accompanied him seized more than ten heavenly horses from Ferghana in 101 BC. [2] These horses were much better cavalry horses than the native breeds in China which were stockier, related to the Przewalski horse of the steppes (see cat. no. 12).

The so-called heavenly horses continued to be venerated until well into the Tang dynasty when they were still being bartered in exchange for bolts of silk. At the beginning of the Tang dynasty there were only 5000 horses in Gansu province but within fifty years there were 706,000 horses in the River Wei pasture lands and tributes of up to 50,000 horses were accepted. [3] By the end of the eighth century a Uighur horse cost forty bolts of Chinese silk and early in the ninth century, when the political situation in China was fast deteriorating, a million bolts of taffeta were paid out in one year in exchange for 100,000 decrepit nags. [4]

The Tang dynasty poet Du Fu describes the horses from Ferghana in a poem entitled 'Officer Fang's barbarian horses':

The barbarian horses from the famous Ferghana region
their supple bones and trenchant angles
their ears aligned like tied bamboos
their light legs which fly with the wind.
There where nothing will stop you
I can confide in you about my life as well as my death
Proud cavalier. Our dreams are shared
across a thousand miles of open space... [5]

The present horse was found in one of a row of five tombs to the east of Wudi's own tomb, Maoling, in Xingping county. Many relics were excavated from the tombs and several of the vessels (cat. no. 18) are inscribed to 'Yangxin *jia*', the imperial family, in particular Princess Yangxin who was the elder sister of emperor Wudi. She must have been a favourite of his to have possessed such a rare treasure as this horse.

Published: Beijing 1987, no. 346; Osaka 1987, no. 22; Xi'an 1992, p. 16; Beijing 1992a, no. 190; Berger 1994, no. 16; Li Jian 1998, no. 45; *Connoisseur*, no. 5, March 1997, p. 35.

1 White and Bunker 1994, pp. 47–8.
2 Hulsewe and Loewe, *China in Central Asia, The Early State: 125 BC–AD 23*, Leiden 1979, pp. 131–6; Dubs 1944, vol. 2, appendix V, pp. 132–5.
3 Paludan 1998, p. 94.
4 Schafer 1963, p. 64.
5 From poem by Du Fu, *Du shi xiang zhu*, vol. 1, Zhonghua shuju edn, 1979, p. 18.

18 Censer

Western Han dynasty (206 BC–AD 9)
Bronze, gilded and silvered
Height 58 cm; weight 2.57 kg
Excavated 1981, Maoling, Xingping county,
Shaanxi province
Shaanxi History Museum

This incense burner comes from the same tomb as the gilded horse, catalogue no. 17. It was made for one of the imperial palaces during the reign of Wudi (141–87 BC). Two inscriptions, on the base of the lid and on the edge of the foot, identify and describe the object, giving the dates of manufacture (under official supervision) and of delivery, probably in 137 and 136 BC. The weight of the assemblage is given in Han measurements, corresponding in one case to 2.62 kg and in the other to 2.68 kg. Other inscriptions on other objects associate it with the family of Princess Yangxin, the elder sister of emperor Wudi (r. 141–87 BC).

The incense burner consists of a brazier and a stem shaped like jointed bamboo, which are riveted together and then the whole is plated with gold and silver, a technique which became increasingly popular in the Han dynasty (see cat. no. 27). The base has two coiled open-mouthed dragons, one of which appears to bite the bamboo-like stem with its teeth. Three

18a

coiled dragons are cast near the top of the stem, their heads propping up the brazier on which more dragons are rendered in low relief. Fine lines depict the dragons' scaly bodies. The mountain-shaped brazier is composed of openwork peaks rising one above the other as in a series of mountain ranges. The incense was burned in the bowl, and when the smoke emerged through holes in the lid there would have been an impression of mountain peaks enveloped in cloud. It is justifiably one of the best-known metalwork objects of this period and a consummate piece of workmanship.

Incense burners had been used from at least the fifth century BC, especially in southern China, but mountain-shaped incense burners were not made until the Han dynasty when they became particularly popular. At this time new ideas about where the immortals lived and where one might go to after death were being formulated.[3] Wudi was fanatical in his search for the lands of the immortals and sent out search parties, as had Qin Shi Huangdi, to look for these lands. He venerated the mountains supposedly inhabited by immortals on the islands of Penglai and also on the Kunlun mountains in the west. He performed a special sacrifice on Mount Tai, one of the five sacred peaks governed by the Yellow Emperor, the supreme deity who ruled the spiritual realm, in order to try and access the spirits who he thought might dwell there and would grant him immortality.[4] Decoration of swirling clouds to indicate magical forces or *qi*, the vital forces of the cosmos, was common on Han dynasty objects (see the swirling clouds on the base of the immortal riding the celestial horse, catalogue no.19).

Published: Beijing 1987, nos 225–7; Beijing 1992a, no. 195; Xi'an 1992, p. 115; Li Xiyu 1994, no. 75; Yin Shengping 1994; Li Jian 1998, no. 46.

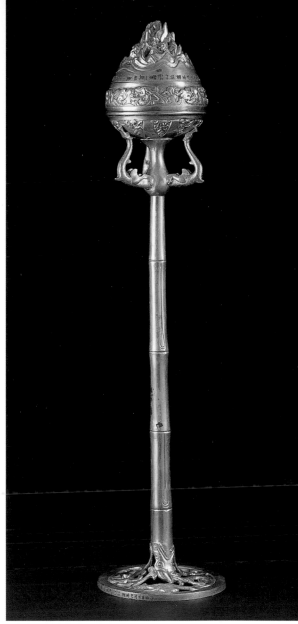

18

1. For the Chinese report on this find see *Wenwu* 1982.9, 'Shaanxi Maoling yi hao wuming zhong yi hao congzangkeng de fajue', pp. 1–17.
2. See *Wenwu* 1982.9, pp. 3, 16; *Wenwu* 1983.6, pp. 62–5; *Kaogu yu Wenwu* 1987.3, p. 84; 1992.1, p. 70. I am much indebted to Michael Loewe for help with this inscription and with many of the Han dynasty entries.
3. Rawson 1996a, p. 172.
4. Erickson 1992, pp. 16–17.

19 Horse with immortal rider

Western Han dynasty (206 BC–AD 9)
Jade
Height 7.0 cm; length 8.9 cm; weight 169.1 g
Excavated 1966, Xinzhuang village, Zhouling
commune, Xianyang city, Shaanxi province
Xianyang Museum

Between 1966 and 1977 a group of Western
Han dynasty jades was excavated at Weiling
in the vicinity of the tumulus of the Han
emperor Yuandi (reigned 49–33 BC). Among
the jades were five three-dimensional
animals: this horse, a bird, a bear and two
bixie (cat. nos 19–23). The horse with rider
was found apparently wrapped in a packet of
cinnabar, together with some eave tiles
dated to the Han dynasty. These five jade
animals are among the best known jades of
this period. They range in size from 2.5 to 9
centimetres and are a testimony to the skill
of the jade workers of the time as jade is
such a difficult material to work: it is too
hard to carve but rather has to be abraded.
The white 'mutton fat' jade, bluish-white in
appearance, used for these animals came
from Khotan in Central Asia, modern
Xinjiang province, and was carried along the
Silk Road to Chang'an. A variety of
techniques were used by the jade artisans,

combining relief working, carving in the
round, and drilling and hollowing out to
achieve a sense of movement and volume.

The figure riding the horse is some kind
of immortal as he has peculiar facial features
with long ears, a pointed mouth and long
flowing hair, and wings protruding from his
shoulders. His dress has a feathery pattern
on it and all these features resemble
depictions of several other winged
immortals of the Han dynasty.[1] The rider
holds the reins in his left hand and with his
right he clasps a magic fungus or *lingzhi* to
the horse's neck.[2] He wears a head scarf, a
short jacket, a shoulder cape and a pair of
wide-bottomed trousers. His clothes appear
to billow in the wind.

The celestial horse is also winged and
perhaps is meant to be one of the heavenly
horses from Ferghana, as idealized in the
Maoling gilded bronze horse (cat. no. 17).
Its base is decorated with a cloud pattern,
suggesting that the animal is flying through
the sky. A cloud-like pillar connects the tail
to the base together with the front legs. The
horse has its head raised and mouth open, its
teeth exposed, and it seems to be neighing.
The upper lip is square and the lower one
round. It has short ears, pointed like split
bamboo, and the two eyes are looking
straight to the front. Its four strong legs are
bent and its two wings are engraved in

relief. Its tail is fluttering and its right
foreleg is raised in the air as if it is galloping.
The mane and the tail are vividly depicted.
The horse's stance is somewhat reminiscent
of the famous flying horse of Gansu which
was one of the most memorable images of
the 1973 Royal Academy exhibition in
London, *Genius of China*.[3]

During the Qin and Han dynasties many
people hoped that after death they would
become immortal. Several of the emperors,
including Qin Shi Huangdi of the Qin and
Wudi of the Han, were obsessed with the
idea of immortality and, as this jade was
found in the vicinity of a Han dynasty tomb,
it may well be a representation of the
imperial desire to be spirited away to the
lands of the immortals.[4]

Three-dimensional jade animals are fairly
rare in both the Zhou and the Han dynasties.
Those produced in the Han dynasty belong
to a different tradition from their
predecessors in terms of function and style
and are more realistically depicted. It has
been suggested that an interest in depicting
powerful creatures in materials as durable as
stone and jade coincided with a growing
interest in miraculous creatures as links with
the spiritual world.[5]

Published: Brinker and Goepper 1980, no. 35;
Hsia Nai 1983, no. 25; Beijing 1984d, p. 87;
Beijing 1992a, no. 29; Hebei 1991–3, vol. 4,
no. 147; Xi'an 1992, p. 45; *Wenbo* 1993.2,
pp. 59–62; Berger 1994, no. 33; Shanghai 1996,
p. 53, no.165; Li and Wang 1997, p. 28;
Xi'an 1997, p. 23.

1 Paris 1994, p. 126; Rawson 1996a, p. 176,
  no. 86; *Wenwu* 1966.4, pp. 7–8; *Kaogu yu
  Wenwu* 1981.4, inside front cover, fig. 2. See
  the jade carving of an imaginary winged
  animal mounted by a feathered spirit, Han
  dynasty or later, from the Sackler Gallery,
  Washington DC, as illustrated in Rawson
  1995a, p. 82, fig. 73; Poo 1998, pp. 161–2.
2 See cat. no. 12, note 3, concerning the
  invention and use of stirrups in China.
3 See the cover image of W Watson 1973.
4 Rawson 1996a, cat. no. 86, p. 176, writes
  about a bronze immortal and Qin Shi
  Huangdi's desire for immortality.
5 Rawson 1995a, p. 351.

20 and 21
Chimera (*bixie*)

Western Han dynasty (206 BC–AD 220)
Jade
20 Height 5.4 cm; length 7 cm, width 4.6 cm;
weight 150 g
21 Height 2.5 cm; length 5.8 cm; weight 50 g
Excavated 1972, Xinzhuang village, Zhouling
commune, Xianyang city, Shaanxi province
Xianyang Museum

These two chimera are fantastical creatures
which are referred to in Chinese by the
generic name *bixie*, meaning to ward off
evil. They possess a mixture of animal
characteristics: a tiger's head, lion's body,
leopard's tail and wings. Their snarling, open
mouths and sharp, bared teeth give the
impression of force and power. The
prowling *bixie* (cat. no. 21) has its wings
lying flat against its body,[1] with bulging
muscles visible on its back legs and breast, a
very short beard and a single horn; it looks
as if it is about to pounce. The jade is very
white, apart from the brown markings
which have been exploited to accentuate the
wings. The other beast (cat. no. 20) has
wings with curling forms raised above the
body. Its front legs rest firmly on the
ground, yet the beast looks up expectantly
as if it were about to jump. The smoothness
of the jade causes it to glisten. The yellow
marking above its hind leg almost gives the
impression of pushing the animal forward.
Both *bixie* have fine lines incised into the jade
suggesting the fur on their bodies.

The beast with its head raised (cat. no.
20) is called a *tianlu*, a heavenly deer,
representing aspirations of riches and

nobility as the Chinese word for an official's
salary, *lu*, sounds the same as that for
deer, *lu*.

Celestial creatures who can ward off evil
are often carved in pairs. One is then called
a *bixie* and the other a *tianlu*, and as these
jade creatures were excavated together it is
possible that this is such a pairing.[2] In the
Han dynasty these two celestial animals
were often placed beside doorways, and
large stone *tianlu* and *bixie* dating to the
Eastern Han period have been excavated in
Henan province. After the Han dynasty such
stone carvings were also found throughout
Shaanxi province. This pair of jade animals of
the Western Han period may be the
precursors of the later stone animals that
began to be used in the Eastern Han dynasty
to line the routes, often known as Spirit
Roads, to major tombs. These stone
creatures brought the forces of the world
before the eyes of those attending the
funeral ceremonies and depicted the
powerful beasts of the unseen spirit world.[3]
They offered both physical and spiritual
protection for the dead whose tomb route
they guarded. Such animals were also
represented in paintings, as on the painting
of the coffin in the tomb of Lady Dai at
Mawangdui of about 168 BC. The materials
of stone and jade had connotations of
immutability and permanence because of
their extreme hardness. These five jade
animals therefore, found in the vicinity of a
royal tomb, perhaps depict the creatures of
the universe, including the creatures of the
spiritual world, and parallel the numerous
representations of animals among Western
Han period bronzes and ceramics. Although

these five jades were not found at the same
time and have no secure dating to the Han
dynasty, it is just possible that they were
meant to be seen as a group. The
workmanship is so similar that they would
appear to have been made by the same
workshop.

20 Published: Hsia Nai 1983, no. 27a; Hebei
1991–3, vol. 4, no. 148; Li and Wang 1997,
p. 29; Li Jian 1998, no. 51.
21 Published: Brinker and Goepper 1980,
no. 38; Hsia Nai 1983, no. 27b; Osaka 1987,
no. 31; Shanghai 1996, p. 54, no.166; Li and
Wang 1997, p. 29; Li Jian 1998, no. 50.

1 *Wenwu* 1979.2, p. 60; *Kaogu yu Wenwu*
1980.1, p. 40; *Wenbo no. 2, Yuqi yanjiu
zhuankan*, 1993.2, pp. 59–62. For a
comparable chimera see Rawson 1995a,
no. 26.7, pp. 363–4 (Hotung Collection).
2 Such a pairing of celestial animals is
mentioned in a text written either in the late
Han dynasty or the succeeding Six Dynasties
period, the *Shi zhou ji* by Dongfang Shuo,
where the author writes of ten islands
inhabited by celestial people, including Xi
Wangmu, the Queen Mother of the West,
who features heavily in Han dynasty
literature and supposedly lived on one of
these islands: *Siku quanshu*, vol. 1042;
Shanghai guji chubanshe, p. 274. See also the
quote from Ouyang Xiu in the *Ci yuan*
dictionary, Shangwu yin shuguan, 1988,
p. 374.
3 Rawson 1995a, p. 352, fig. 3; for surveys of
tomb sculpture see Los Angeles 1987;
Paludan 1991, 1994.

20

21

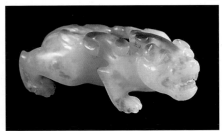

22 Bear

Western Han dynasty (206 BC–AD 9)
Jade
Height 4.8 cm; length 8 cm; weight 135.2 g
Excavated 1975, Xinzhuang village, Zhouling
commune, Xianyang city, Shaanxi province
Xianyang Museum

This bear was found in the same area as the
two *bixie*, the bird and the immortal riding a
celestial horse (cat. nos 19–21, 23). The
jade is pure white and translucent. The bear
is quite small with a large head, tightly
closed mouth, ears flat against its head and
round, expressive eyes, somewhat quizzical,
staring directly ahead. Its four legs are
postured as if it were walking. A few lines
sketchily carved into the cheeks and legs
indicate the pelt, in contrast to the sleek
smooth carving. The sculptor has laid stress
on the characteristics of the round head,
robust body and clumsy stature, with the
rather short limbs and fat front paws with
sharp nails. It is carved with great naturalism
and sensitivity.

Bears were commonly depicted in the
Han dynasty (though rarely in other
periods) by both Chinese and nomadic
tribes such as the Xiongnu on the borders of
China.[1] Bears inhabited the forests of
northern China and ornaments with bears
have been found as far north as Buryatia in
Transbaikalia and as far south as the tomb of
the King of Nanyue of 122 BC in Canton.
Bears were kept in imperial game parks,
used in bear baiting and had an exorcistic
role. A demon impersonator or exorcist 'in
his official function, wears over his head a
bearskin having four eyes of gold and is clad
in a black upper garment and a red lower
garment. Grasping his lance and brandishing
his shield, he leads the many officials to
perform the seasonal Exorcism (*No),*
searching through houses and driving out
pestilences'.[2] The bear-like Chiyou, a god of
war, performed exorcist ceremonies in
times of drought.

The word for bear, *xiong,* sounds the
same as the word for brave or powerful,
xiong. This may be one reason why bears'
paws were eaten, to confer bravery, and they
were certainly considered a culinary
delicacy in Confucius' time and later.[3] For
the same reason this jade bear may have
been a fondling piece or an amulet for use
by someone about to perform some
dangerous feat.

Several Han dynasty jade bears were
made in a seated, upright form, such as the
one in the Hotung Collection.[4] Bears of
similar form were often cast in bronze to act
as supports for *zun* wine vessels. Many
ceramic jars of the period have bears as base
supports.[5] It has been suggested that bears
are found as supports because they were
regarded as some of the mysteriously
powerful inhabitants of the 'spirit
mountain', an intermediary realm of
wilderness between heaven and earth.[6]

Published: Brinker and Goepper 1980, no. 36;
Hsia Nai 1983, no. 27c; Osaka 1987, no. 30;
Hebei 1991–3, vol. 4, no. 151; Xi'an 1992,
p. 143; Berger 1994, no. 32; Li and Wang 1997,
p. 30.

1 Bunker 1997, p. 263, no. 228.
2 Bodde 1975, p. 78.
3 Chang Kwang-chih 1977, p. 67.
4 Rawson 1995a, no. 26.3, p. 359. Also see
comparison between this bear and the British
Museum bear, p. 350.
5 Incense burner, British Museum, Hotung
Gallery, case 17, OA 1909.5–12.29.
6 Munakata 1990, p. 70, no. 16.

23 Bird

Western Han dynasty (206 BC–AD 9)
Jade
Height 2.5 cm; length 5 cm; weight 82.4 g
Excavated 1972, Xinzhuang village, Zhouling
commune, Xianyang city, Shaanxi province
Xianyang Museum

This hawk or owl-like bird was discovered
with the other jades in this group at Weiling
Zhouling commune, Xianyang city.[1] The
jade is white with amber markings. The
bird's head points downwards, its wings are
outstretched and its tail feathers spread out.
It has an aquiline beak, round eyes and the
body is marked with V signs indicating the
feathers. The compact body is elegantly
shaped, the outline is sleek, and the jade
glistens, making it an example of the highly
developed jade carving technique of the Han
dynasty.

Three-dimensional figures of animals are
rare from the Western Zhou dynasty to the
Han. But in neolithic times, in the Hongshan
culture, sited in what is now Inner Mongolia
and in Liaoning province, several three-
dimensional birds carved in jade have been
recorded.[2] Three-dimensional birds were
again portrayed in the Shang period and
many notched birds and animals were found
in the tomb of Fu Hao, a Shang dynasty
consort who died about 1200 BC. Many of
these were for use as pendants, and an
interest in such bird and animal shapes was
perhaps due to a stimulus from Shang
contact with distant areas.[3]

In the Han dynasty birds were often
made in bronze and a few in jade. At this
time the dove or pigeon, supposedly the

22

23

messenger of Xi Wangmu, the Queen Mother of the West, who presided over one of the lands of the immortals, was adopted as a symbol. Images of birds were therefore put on to staffs and bestowed as presents on a person's eightieth birthday, as a wish for continued long life and good digestion, similar to the life of the pigeon.[4]

As Weiling has also been referred to as the tomb of the seven imperial concubines it is possible that these five jades found there may have been buried with the concubines.

Published: Brinker and Goepper 1980, no. 37; Hebei 1991–3, vol. 4, no. 150; Xi'an 1992, p. 45; Li and Wang 1997, p. 31.

1 *Wenwu* 1979.2, p. 60.
2 See the Hongshan bird in the British Museum, Hotung Gallery, case 2, OA 1973.7–26.116, and the Hotung jade bird in Rawson 1995a, no. 1.5, p. 117.
3 Rawson 1995a, pp. 205–8.
4 Ong 1993, p. 276. Also see the bronze bird, British Museum, Hotung Gallery, case 15.

24 Necklace

Western Han dynasty (206 BC–AD 9)
22 various precious stones, including agate, crystal, amber, glass, jade and turquoise
Length of largest 2.8 cm, of smallest 0.5 cm; total weight 42.1 g
Excavated 1975, Huijun tomb, Maquan, Xianyang city, Shaanxi province
Xianyang Museum

This necklace consists of a string of twenty-two decorative stones including agate, crystal, amber and various coloured stones. It is very colourful and the shapes of the stones are varied, being oval, shell shaped, spherical, semi-spherical, tubular and animal shaped. Each one has had a hole pierced through it to string into a necklace.[1]

The necklace was found in the coffin inside the tomb, whose occupant has been tentatively identified as a lady called Huijun, from a seal found in the tomb. We do not know anything about Huijun although she was presumably a lady of some considerable means to have been able to gather together these various stones, some of which would have been quite rare in China at that time. Amber particularly was much prized as an amulet which could protect women from illness, and a legendary relationship between amber and the vital essence of tigers and dragons persisted into medieval times. Amber was imported from Iran and from upper Burma. It was particularly popular in Tang jewellery but was also prized for its medicinal use, being prescribed for 'bad blood' and effusions of blood caused by weapons.[2] This necklace has three pieces of amber in the shapes of little tigers. Glass was also regarded as something quite exotic as originally it was imported from the West and was often made in imitation of jade in the Han dynasty.[3]

24

During the Han dynasty there emerged a distinctive genre of prose-poetry called *fu*, a kind of rhapsodic essay with very evocative poetic language. In these the capital is typically described in terms of precious stones:

Red-black floors, gilt thresholds,
Jade stairs, vermilion courtyards,
Red quartz and axe stone, coloured and fine-grained,
Dark-jade and agate, green and fiery.
Trees of coral and chrysoprase
Grow all around the winding courts…[4]

The Western Han dynasty was one of considerable wealth and one can imagine noble ladies wearing necklaces such as this one at court.

1 *Kaogu* 1979.2, pp. 134–5.
2 Schafer 1963, p. 248.
3 C Michaelson, 'Chinese glass of the Han dynasty', *Transactions of the Oriental Ceramic Society* (forthcoming).
4 *Fu* by Ban Gu (AD 32-92). Translated by David Knechtges in Knechtges 1982, p. 125.

25 Seal

Han dynasty (206 BC–AD 220)
Gold
Length 3 cm; width 1.1 cm; weight 17.1 g
Excavated 1966, Han tomb below brick factory, Xi'an, Shaanxi province
Xi'an City Cultural Relics Storehouse

25

The seal is a cube with a tortoise on the top as the handle.[1] The tortoise is straining its head upwards, mouth open and eyes staring. Its shell has engraved hexagons with raised lotus buds in the centre of each, and its feet are decorated with dots. The stylized decoration contrasts with the realistic attitude of the tortoise. The seal reads 'Wang Jing' in seal character format, probably the name of some high official as only they would have had gold seals, but he is not mentioned in the historical records.

The Chinese dynastic histories, from about 100 BC, contain much material on administration, officials and seals. Seals were essential for all aspects of public and legal

Fig. 25a *Base of the seal showing the inscription.*

affairs and were made from gold, silver, bronze and various stones such as steatite and jade, and were carved with the names and titles of their owners. They perform the function of a signature.

The earliest seals probably date from before the fifth century BC when they were impressed in moist clay, but there is no archaeological evidence for them before the Warring States period. However, with the invention of paper in the Han dynasty and the writing of documents on it, clay was gradually replaced by red seal paste. Seals were, and still are, applied to all official documents but also were frequently applied to books, paintings and calligraphy as a mark of ownership. Seals became more widespread in the third and second centuries BC when a style of script known as small seal script came into general usage. This style, as seen on this seal, has remained

the principal form for the cutting of seals down to the present time.

Qin and Han dynasty seals were used mainly on letters, and the seals were more or less of a standard size, about 2.3 square centimetres, and carved in intaglio. During the Sui and Tang periods the seals were used on paper and they doubled in size. The carving of the characters on the seal changed from being in intaglio into relief, with the result that the printed seal changed from white characters against a red ground to red characters against a white ground.

Many Han dynasty seals have been found, mostly in bronze, but also in crystal, jade, gold and silver. Gold seals are rare. In a commentary to the *Hou Han shu* (History of the Later Han Dynasty),[2] it is stated that princes and nobles should use gold seals, with tortoise handles and red ink.[3] The very mention of such seals indicates their importance in the Han dynasty.

Seals were generally square or rectangular, their distinguishing features being the knob and the material from which they were made. As one handbook of administration quotes: 'The seals of the imperial princes are made of gold, the knob is shaped like a camel, and it is designated as a *xi*. The nobles also bear a golden seal, the knob being shaped like a tortoise, but it is designated as a *yin*. The prime minister and the generals all have golden seals with knobs formed like a tortoise but theirs are called *zhang*.'[4] According to other sources, including archaeological discoveries, the seals of kings and emperors were of jade, with handles of hornless dragons and tigers.

During the Qin dynasty only the emperor's seal was called a *xi*, but by the Han dynasty it was a term commonly used by princes and also by the queen mother. A gold seal was found in the tomb of the King of Nanyue, one of the tributary kings who controlled Guangdong and Guangxi provinces in the Western Han dynasty and who died about 122 BC. He gave himself the title Emperor Wen and had a seal made with a coiled dragon as a knob in imitation of the Han emperor's seal. It shows his desire to be seen as an autonomous and equal power to the Han emperor himself.[5]

The tortoise is regarded by the Chinese as an auspicious animal. In the very earliest references to tortoises in China its shell is compared to the vaulted heaven and its underside to the flat disc of the earth. As it represented the cosmos it was therefore used in oracle bone divination from Shang dynasty times. Its genuine longevity makes it an apt symbol for long life and it also came to symbolize immutability and steadfastness. Epitaph and inscription tablets were commonly supported on stone tortoises.[6] This is allied to the use of the tortoise as support, which had its origin in the belief that the tortoise was at the root of the beginning of things, due to its habit of burying itself under the ground and emerging at regular periods.[7] The assumption that tortoises were only female subsequently led to the belief that in order to mate it had to do so with snakes. The depiction of a tortoise and a snake became the symbol of the North, known as the Dark Warrior of the North, one of the so-called *si ling*, four spirits used by the Daoist astrologers to symbolize the spirits which reside over the Four Directions of the Four Quarters of the Universe.[8] The tortoise design therefore became very popular in ancient China.[9]

1 A silver seal with a tortoise-shaped knob was unearthed in Ankang city, Shaanxi province, possibly dating to slightly later than the Han dynasty, in the Three Kingdoms period. See *Wenwu* 1996.5, p. 86.
2 *Hou Han shu*, the History of the Later or Eastern Han dynasty (AD 25–220), was written by Fan Ye, AD 398–445. The *Yu Fu Zhi: Xu Guang* commentary, Zhonghua shuju edn, Hong Kong 1971, vol. 12, p. 3674.
3 The best quality seal paste is made with pulverized cinnabar (mercuric sulphide) dissolved in a specially prepared seed oil, then soaked into a pad consisting of dried fibres of the moxa plant. T C Lai, *Chinese*

Seals, Seattle and London 1976, p. xviii.
4 *Han Jiuli*, as quoted in Wagner 1997, pp. 209–10.
5 Illustrated in Beijing 1992a, no. 268, pp. 290–1.
6 A notable example of a tablet with a tortoise base is the Nestorian monument in the Beilin in Xi'an.
7 Ball 1927, pp. 41–9.
8 Eberhard 1986, pp. 294–6; Rawson 1984b, pp. 90–1.
9 For two other gold seals with tortoises see Beijing 1993a, nos 115 and 116.

26 Seal

Han dynasty (206 BC–AD 220)
Silver
Height (total) 2.3 cm, (seal) 0.9 cm; length 2.3 cm; weight 74.3 g
Excavated 1983, Liulin Zhendundou village, Fengxiang county, Shaanxi province
Shaanxi Province Fengxiang County Museum

This seal with a tortoise handle is made of pure silver. The seal is carved in intaglio with six characters, '*Wu wei si ming ling jun*', in seal character form of a very high calligraphic standard.[1] This title, which can be translated as 'All Powerful Commander, Lord of Destinies', is not to be found in the Han histories. However, it is possible that this seal was made for Chen Chong, who received the title of Wuwei Siming in AD 9 from Wang Mang, who ruled China between the two Han dynasties.[2] This would have been his official seal.

Official seals were very much hidebound by tradition. Private seals had much more licence but were not in general circulation

Fig. 26a *Base of the seal showing the inscription.*

26

until about the beginning of the Song dynasty. Generally the possessor of an official seal was of high status and social standing. In the Han dynasty Yang Xiong (53 BC–AD 18) wrote in his 'Word of Strong Admonition': 'If I could only wear a red sash and if I could let a golden seal suspend from my girdle, I would feel unlimited joy'.[3] At this time seals were generally small and threaded on to thongs worn at the waist. They were highly valued and often presented to tributary states or to reward officials. Officials in the Chinese bureaucracy were not only very privileged but also sometimes the bearers of too many responsibilities. In the Tang dynasty the poet Du Fu (712–70) wrote:

With grief you look at your large, golden seal, For you longed for the pure and calm life of an eremite.[4]

Official seals were used to move armies when the seals of the emperor, which were the most important, were in general use. At times of rebellion imperial seals were either robbed or forged, the possessor then claiming that as he now had the seal belonging to the emperor he was thus deemed to have received the mandate of heaven to issue commands. In the Tang legal code the sanctions for forging imperial seals are enumerated: 'He who forges the eight seals of the emperor shall be decapitated. He who forges the seal of the emperor's grandmother, the seals of the empress or the heir apparent will be strangled. He who forges the seal of the heir apparent's wife shall be banished 3000 *li* away'.[5]

1 For another silver seal with a tortoise handle see Beijing 1993a, no. 109. 'According to the official system in the Han dynasty, those whose salary adds up to 2000 *dan* (a unit of dry measure for grain, equal to 1 hectolitre) will be granted a silver seal with tortoise-shaped knob, the impression called *zhang*' (see p. 310).
2 For official titles in imperial China, see Hucker 1985. For further information on Chen Chong see M Loewe, *Biographical Dictionary of Qin, Former Han and Xin* (forthcoming); *Hou Han shu*, Zhonghua shuju edn, 1971, vol. 4, p. 901. I am indebted to Michael Loewe for information on this seal and its interpretation.
3 Qin Enfu (ed.), *Yangzi Fayan*, Guji chubanshe, Shanghai 1986, vol. 1, p. 812; quoted in Wagner 1997, p. 212.
4 Quoted in Wagner 1997, p. 212.
5 Quoted in Wagner 1997, p. 212.

27 Hoof-shaped money

Han dynasty (206 BC–AD 220)
Gold
Height 4.0 cm; length 5.2 cm; weight 246 g
Excavated 1974, Xi'an city, Shaanxi province
Xi'an City Cultural Relics Storehouse

During the Warring States period each of the states issued its own currency. This was cast in bronze, usually in the form of agricultural or hunting tools such as spades and knives, or in the form of round coins with a round or square hole in the centre. The state of Chu was unique in issuing gold money. This was in the form of large sheets of gold, stamped with rows of small squares, each of which had an inscription indicating the weight and city of origin. The squares could be cut from the sheet as required.[1]

When the first Qin emperor unified the Warring States in 221 BC, one of his first measures was to standardize the coinage, promoting as China's first national coin the *banliang* coin of the Qin state (a round coin

27

with a square hole in the centre, cast in bronze, with the inscription '*banliang*', or 'half ounce'). *Banliang* coins continued to be issued during the early Han dynasty, but there was great variation in the size and weight of the coins in different parts of the empire. Eventually a series of adjustments was made, and by 118 BC the Han government was able to replace the *banliang* with a new national coin known as the *wuzhu* coin ('five grains' in weight). Some 28 billion *wuzhu* coins were made during the Western Han.

There were two different kinds of money in the Han dynasty. Bronze *wuzhu* coins were used for payments by ordinary people. Gold was used for large-scale transactions and gifts by the aristocracy and the very wealthy. During the Western Han the emperor would reward members of the imperial family and court officials with gifts of gold. Prices were usually calculated in terms of bronze coins, and gold had to be converted into coins before payments could be made.[2]

The shape of Han dynasty gold ingots is unique, and the recent finds of hoof-shaped money serve to confirm the historical texts. The *Han shu* annals for Wudi records that in the (equivalent) Chinese year of 95 BC Wudi promulgated an edict saying:

We captured a white unicorn and used it as an offering in the imperial ancestral temple. The Wuwa River produced a heavenly horse, and actual gold was discovered on Mount Tai [hence] it is proper that [We] should change [some] former appellation. Now [We] change [the shape for ingots of] actual gold to that of unicorns' feet and fine horses' hooves, in order to accord with these auspicious presages and use them to distribute among the vassal kings as grants to them.[3]

This reference indicates that from 95 BC rewards to the nobility may have been made in gold in the shape of the hooves of unicorns or horses, both auspicious animals. The association of the gold rewards with auspicious animals no doubt added a certain mystique. There may also have been a practical reason for the hooves: the fact that such complex shapes could only have been made from pure (about 98 per cent) gold,[4] as they would have been too difficult to plate, assured the purity of the money.[5]

Similar hoof-shaped ingots have been found in Liaoning province and in Inner Mongolia.[6]

Published: Beijing 1987, no. 285; Singapore 1990, p. 31.

1 As illustrated in the British Museum, HSBC Money Gallery, case 1.

2 Peng Xinwei (trans. E H Kaplan), *Zhongguo huobi shi* (A Monetary History of China), Western Washington University, 1994, pp. 134–46. For general information on such hoof-shaped money see *Zhongguo qianbi lunwen ji* (A Collection of Chinese Numismatic Theses), China 1985, pp. 186–92. See also Li Zude, 'A preliminary study of Qin and Han gold', *Zhongguo shi yanjiu* 1997.1, pp. 52–61, for general information on Qin and Han gold currency.
3 Quoted in Dubs 1944, vol. 2, p. 110.
4 Edinburgh 1996, p. 26, cat. no. 8.
5 Private communication from Michael Cowell, Department of Scientific Research, British Museum.
6 Beijing 1987, cat. no. 284. I am indebted to Helen Wang, Department of Coins and Medals, British Museum, for much help with this entry.

28 Stove

Western Han dynasty (206 BC–AD 9)
Gold
Height 1.2 cm; length 3 cm; weight 5.2 g
Excavated 1966, Neihu jiakou, ruins of Chang'an city, northern suburbs of Xi'an, Shaanxi province
Xi'an City Cultural Relics Storehouse

This tiny stove is made of cast gold, with gold wire and granulation. It is equipped with a chimney, a stoking hole and a cooking pot in which the grains of what looks like rice are clearly visible. The chimney consists of very fine gold wires wound round and round, and under a microscope the smoke, made of extra fine gold wires, can be seen spiralling out. The tear-shaped recesses originally contained semiprecious stones but most of these have now disappeared. The stove is decorated with granulation, a technique which had been known for a long time in China through imports from the West (see imitations of it on catalogue no. 4). The genuine granulation on this stove is very similar to that on the gold box in the Nelson-Atkins Museum of Art, Kansas City.[1] The technique had clearly been assimilated by Chinese metalworkers and the workmanship is extremely fine.

Beliefs in an afterlife had gradually been changing throughout the Eastern Zhou and early Han periods. A belief that one ought to continue to enjoy what one had in this world in the tomb or the afterlife seems to have become prevalent and therefore it was necessary for the deceased to be buried with life's necessities. These would inevitably include cooking equipment, and for some people the cook himself,[2] though human sacrifice was rare by the Han dynasty. This stove would have been destined to cook the many delicacies to which the Han élite was accustomed. Ceramic stoves of this shape are common in Han tombs of this period but gold ones are extremely rare.

We have considerable knowledge of the foods available to the rich in the Han dynasty and of the methods for cooking them.[3] A set of three tombs, dating to 186–168 BC and belonging to the Dai family, was excavated in southern China in the 1970s. The tomb belonging to Lady Dai was particularly well preserved because it was lined with clay. Her body was in such a good state of preservation that she still had skin and hair on her body, and an autopsy performed on her revealed she had died at about the age of fifty. Of the three tombs (that of the lady, her husband and her son), tomb 1 contained forty-eight bamboo baskets and ceramic containers of prepared meats, fruit and food laid out on lacquer dishes as well as bamboo slips that identified the foods with much useful information. Tomb 3 had a similar selection of foods. Lists of available foods in this period have therefore been compiled from the evidence in such tombs. There were cereals: rice, wheat, barley and millet; vegetables: soyabeans, kidney beans, bamboo shoots, ginger and garlic; fruits: pears, jujubes, plums, peaches, oranges and water chestnuts; meat: beef, mutton, pork, dog, horse, chicken, wild goose and duck; fish: carp, bream, perch; and seasonings and condiments: salt, sugar, honey, ginger and various alcohols made from cereals as well as many fruit juices. Methods of cooking

28

included roasting, blanching, boiling, frying, braising and steaming. Many foods were preserved by salting, smoking and pickling.

The selection of foods in Lady Dai's grave was obviously more extensive than the range available to more ordinary members of society, but the list provides a good indication of what her class of person was able to choose. From the point of view of regional differences, it is interesting to note that rice was uncommon outside southern China. It was still a luxury to the people of the north who tended to eat wheat and soya. Millet and meat gruel were only eaten on special occasions. From the middle of the Han dynasty onwards, following the expansion of the empire by Wudi, noodles began to become popular.

The rareness both of this gold cooking stove and of rice in western China would suggest that the person buried with this stove was a member of the aristocracy.

Published: Xi'an 1992, p. 21; Shanghai 1996, p. 92, no. 24.

1 See Pirazzoli t'Serstevens 1982, fig. 103, p. 165.
2 One of the Han period kings of the Chu kingdom, buried at Shizishan in Xuzhou, was interred with his cook, identified by the archaeologists from his seal. Presumably the king had favourite dishes which only this chef could prepare (quoted in Rawson forthcoming, note 19).
3 Pirazzoli t'Serstevens 1982, pp. 50–2. For an historical introduction to Chinese cooking and recipes, see Yan-kit So, *Classic Food of China*, London 1992.

29 Lamp in the shape of a ram

Han dynasty (206 BC–AD 220)
Gilded bronze
Height 19 cm; length 23 cm; weight 3.1 kg
Excavated 1984, Baoji, Fengxiang county,
Shaanxi province
Xi'an City Cultural Relics Storehouse

This lamp is modelled on the mountain goat
prevalent in north China. The hinged back
can be swung up to rest on the ram's head as
a receptacle for the wick and some oil.
When it was no longer needed as a light
source the oval dish could be hinged back,
permitting any remaining oil to run into the
ram for storage. A very similar-shaped
lamp, but ungilded, was found in the
Western Han tomb of Liu Sheng, who died
about 113 BC in Mancheng, Hebei province.
The modelling of the ram is a good example
of the new sense of naturalism characteristic
of much Han dynasty art. [1]

During the Han dynasty lamps replaced
candles as the main source of light. Lamps
therefore became important household
items and for the rich some exquisite and
ingenious lamps were made. [2] One of the
best known is that found in the tomb of Dou
Wan, consort of Liu Sheng. Her lamp, which
had previously belonged to the Changxin
palace, is in the shape of a young attendant
and is probably the most prestigious piece to
have been found in her tomb. The attendant
sits back on his or her heels with the lamp in

29

the left hand. The shutters are adjustable so
that the amount and direction of the light
can be controlled and the hollow right arm
forms a chimney through which the smoke
can escape. All parts of the lamp were
movable to facilitate cleaning. [3]

The kneeling ram is a symbol of filial
piety as it kneels to receive nourishment
from its mother. Later, stone rams appeared
on the *shendao*, or spirit way, which was
lined with pairs of animals to guard the
route to the tomb. As symbols of filial piety
and also of incorruptibility, rams on spirit
ways represented senior officials. Rams may
also have been considered auspicious

because the pronunciation of the word for
sheep, *yang*, sounds like the word for
auspiciousness, *xiang*. [4]

Published: Singapore 1990, p. 63; *Imperial China*
1992, no. 32.

1 Lamps in the shape of rams were particularly
 popular in the Han dynasty and several other
 examples are known, such as those in the
 Musée Guimet, Paris, the Rietberg Museum,
 Zurich, and the one in the Nelson-Atkins
 Museum of Art, Kansas City, Missouri.
2 Rawson 1998, p. 32, and Rawson 1989c, *inter
 alia*.
3 Beijing 1980d, vol. 2, colour pl. 10.
4 Paludan 1991, p. 98.

Tang Tombs and Hoards

Just as the Qin laid the foundations for the great Han dynasty, so did the Sui for the Tang. The Sui (589–618)[1] emerged victorious as the rulers of a unified China after a prolonged period of civil war and fragmentation of the country from the end of the Han dynasty in AD 220. Although not successful in holding on to power, the Sui established the political, educational and economic base on which the great Tang and later dynasties were able to build.[2]

During the Tang period China reached its largest physical size yet, with frontiers extending from Korea to Vietnam and across Central Asia to southern Siberia (see map, p.172 below). The Tang rulers felt themselves to be heirs of the Han and for much of the dynasty they held the territory in Central Asia formerly penetrated by Han armies and colonists, although they had to contend, not always successfully, with the armies of three other great empires bordering Central Asia: the Arab caliphate to the west, the Tibetan empire to the south, and Turkic empires, including that of the Uighurs, to the north. The Tang controlled these far-flung possessions by stationing large numbers of troops in the oasis towns under the command of powerful viceroys. They controlled many oasis towns along the Taklamakan desert, and trade flourished, bringing medicines, metals, semiprecious stones, exotic foods, textiles, furs, animals and above all fine horses to the court at Chang'an (present-day Xi'an). As well as the silk sent overland, the Chinese exported ceramics by a maritime route to Southeast Asia, India and Western Asia. The Tang rulers themselves had Turkic ancestry and Tang cities and culture were cosmopolitan and open to outside influences, at least during the first half of the dynasty. Buddhism, which had entered China by the first century AD, was one of the most pervasive foreign influences and became a major religious force in Tang dynasty China. The first half of the dynasty was truly a Golden Age, and was culturally one of the greatest epochs for the arts, architecture and literature – all of which were beneficiaries of Central Asian influences.

The early Tang government was highly centralized and dependent on a complex system of administrative law, much of which was inherited from the Sui. Over the centuries of the Sui and Tang the aristocracy's power and influence gradually declined, and its place in government was to some extent taken by professional bureaucrats who were recruited by examination on the basis of their talents.[3] The intellectual and social effects of this change had important repercussions for China, leading to the widening of the social base of the ruling class by offering greater access to government office to people of non aristocratic birth. These new bureaucrats gradually became the agents of the ruling dynasty, rather than the representatives of their own social group. Such changes took place slowly and were not immediately apparent.

The earlier period of the Tang dynasty was at times dominated by women, particularly Empress Wu Zetian,[4] Empress Wei and the concubine Yang Guifei.[5] Several factors contributed to the relative freedom accorded to women at this time, a freedom which allowed them to ride, hunt and play polo with men and enjoy quite openly the many entertainments at court and elsewhere in mixed society. The development and spread of printing by the late Tang period led to more opportunities for the education of women. Improvements in silk technology also led to more women working in this industry and thereby providing a greater contribution to family income, with a subsequent improvement in their status. Part of the greater freedom allowed women during the Tang might also be ascribed to the non-Chinese origins of many of the great clans – including the imperial clan – which dominated

Tang court life. Such freedom was to be curtailed during the next great dynasty, the Song, with the advent of foot binding and the predominance of neo-Confucian thought with its limitations of women's liberties.

Wu Zetian (reigned 690–705) was the wife of the Tang emperor Gaozong (r. 649–83)[6] and the most formidable of the Tang women (fig. 14). She began as a member of the harem of the Tang emperor Taizong but caught the eye of his son, later Emperor Gaozong, and after a brief banishment to a nunnery returned to court life at the behest of the empress of Gaozong, who thought she might provide a convenient distraction for her husband who was then besotted with a certain Lady Xiao. However, Wu Zetian was absolutely unscrupulous in her ambitions and managed to dispose of both Lady Xiao and the empress. She murdered her own baby daughter by the emperor, creating a scenario whereby the empress was blamed. She had the empress accused of witchcraft and both the empress and Lady Xiao were imprisoned. Wu Zetian then sent an order, supposedly from the emperor, which resulted in the two women first having their limbs cut off and then, whilst still alive, being placed in vats of alcohol until they died – possibly intoxicated but certainly in agony.

Gaozong was a weak emperor who suffered bad health and was very much under the control of his new wife. At first she ruled from behind a screen, advising him in whispers, but she later dispensed with this and ruled openly.[7] After Gaozong's death in 683 she ruled as empress dowager, exiling one legitimate emperor and ruling through another puppet emperor until she felt strong enough to proclaim herself empress in her own right, taking the dynastic name of Zhou. She is the only female in Chinese history to achieve this distinction, as even the formidable empress dowager in the Qing dynasty, Cixi, ruled through puppet emperors. She tried to break the political stranglehold of the aristocrats by employing officials who had passed the state examinations, so men achieved their position purely through merit rather than

Fig. 14 Empress Wu Zetian, the only woman ever to become 'emperor' of China (690–705). Detail of a watercolour from an 18th-century album of imperial portraits.

inherited position. This meritocratic system gradually took hold during the Tang dynasty and slowly began to replace hereditary privilege and personal recommendation as a way of getting into officialdom. However, Wu Zetian was somewhat arbitrary in her methods of government and after reverses abroad, with Khitan tribes invading Hebei and renewed warfare with the Turks, the empress agreed that the throne should revert to the Li family and the Tang dynasty, rather than continue via her own line of Zhou. Her amorous intrigues with various scurrilous individuals after Gaozong's death and her gradual abandonment of active participation in the government of the country eventually led to a coup after which she was deposed in 705 and Zhongzong, her son,[8] was returned to power. Despite her cruelty and scandalous love affairs, Wu Zetian has been judged an effective ruler and certainly she left China a stronger, more united and richer country.

After Wu Zetian's abdication and death, some of her victims were retrieved from their ignominious graves and reburied with great ceremony. Amongst these were Princess Yongtai (died 701), the princes Zhanghuai (Li Xian, died 684) and Yide (Li Zhongrun, died 701), the heir

Fig. 15 *Detail of a mural showing polo players, from the tomb of Prince Zhanghuai (died 684). Excavated in 1971, Shaanxi province.*

Fig. 16 *Detail of a mural showing the towers of Chang'an city, from the tomb of Prince Yide (died 701). Excavated in 1971, Shaanxi province.*

apparent.[9] The excavations of these tombs revealed long frescoed corridors leading to the burial chamber itself, very revealing of aristocratic life of the time. Those of the tomb of Prince Zhanghuai show him as a young man who loved hunting and polo (fig. 15), though he was also an accomplished classical scholar. In the tomb of Prince Yide is a clear depiction of the towers of Chang'an, the only record of the city's outer walls (fig. 16).

Wu Zetian's successor, emperor Zhongzong, was also dominated by his empress Wei, who unleashed a regime of corruption whereby ministers bought and sold offices.[10] The empress poisoned her husband when she feared a loss of power and established a young prince as emperor with herself as regent. However, a counter coup was organized by the future Xuanzong, who eventually overcame both the empress Wei and the daughter of empress Wu Zetian, the formidable Taiping Princess, and in 712 Xuanzong took the throne and inaugurated the most brilliant period in Tang dynasty history; he is commonly known as Minghuang, the Brilliant Emperor.

Xuanzong's reign began in glory and was a high point of Tang power.[11] He was a great patron of the arts, poetry, music and dance as well as a scholar and very knowledgeable about both Daoism and Esoteric Buddhism. His capital was a focal point for the arts and for scholars, and the corruption of the previous few years was brought to an end. He poured resources into the Central Asian garrisons, appointing foreign generals who, he believed, would be

free of political ambition. Several had notable successes against the Tibetans in the Pamirs and the Gansu corridor. The Turks and Tibetans were defeated and a new tax system was inaugurated which was based on a new census, and the more efficient registration of the population helped finance the armies.[12]

However, during the 740s the ageing emperor became infatuated with a concubine, the talented Yang Guifei (fig. 17). She brought her three sisters to court and high positions, and also her cousin, Yang Guozhong. He formed a rival clique to the powerful Li Linfu,[13] the very able administrator who had largely taken over ruling the empire

Fig. 17 Yang Guifei mounting a grey horse, *detail of a handscroll painting by Qian Xuan (c. 1235–1300).*

after the emperor became engrossed first in religious studies and then with Yang Guifei. The border governors also began to exert more power and to intrigue at court, playing off the Yang and Li factions until in 750 one of the generals, An Lushan (Rokhshan), who was half Sogdian and half Turkish, gained control of the whole northeastern frontier. He was reported to be a large, fat and somewhat uncouth character but had somehow gained favour with Yang Guifei, who somewhat incongruously 'adopted' him as her son (although gossip circulated about her more than 'maternal' affections). After Li Linfu died, Yang Guozhong took over power at court and there was much rivalry between him and An Lushan which resulted in open warfare. Eventually the court had to flee Chang'an when An Lushan stormed and occupied the city.[14] It was at this time that many hoards of personal treasures were buried, such as the Hejiacun hoard[15] so prominently featured in this exhibition. On the flight to Sichuan, at Mawei, Xuanzong's troops mutinied and he was forced to hand Yang Guifei over to them. They strangled her in front of him and also executed Yang Guozhong. Yang Guifei's death, and indeed the story of the love affair between her and Xuanzong, have been the subject of many literary works (see cat. no. 31), some of which are extremely poignant.

After this, although An Lushan was defeated and died shortly thereafter, the rebellion continued until 763, with the rebels only being driven from the capital with the help of Uighur forces. Contemporary records report how cartloads of treasures were removed from both Chang'an and Luoyang at the time of the rebels' occupation. The Tang never regained the momentum or prestige of the early part of Xuanzong's reign. During the late eighth and ninth century great economic and social changes took place.[16] Large sections of the population gradually moved southwards to avoid taxation and seek out new land; the Yangzi valley began to replace the great plain of Hebei–Henan as China's most populous and richest area. The focus of wealth and power also moved southwards as new industries and influential groups of merchants emerged

there, and the greater agricultural production of the south meant that Chang'an became dependent on the Yangzi and Huai valleys for grain supplies and revenues. As the commanders on the edges of the empire became increasingly powerful and autonomous, the empire gradually began to disintegrate. The An Lushan rebellion forced the Tang to withdraw their garrisons from the northwest of the empire where the Tibetans seized control, shutting off access to the Silk Road. Peasant rebellions increased, culminating in the activities of Huang Chao, who led a band of bandit gangs which roamed over south China in 878–9 and seized the capital.[17] He was finally defeated in 884 but the rebellion had terminally weakened the government, and though it dragged on until 906 this was in name only; in reality China was divided up among regional regimes. Eunuch generals commanded the best troops and infiltrated many levels of government and finally an army commander deposed the last Tang emperor in 907.[18]

HOARDS

Chang'an and Luoyang were the sites most likely to contain hoards buried at the times of rebellion as the concentration of wealth in the empire was focused on the capitals. Several hoards have been found in the vicinity of Xi'an.

One hoard, found in the pre-First World War period at Beihuangshan, near Xi'an, consisted of fifteen pieces, one of which was dated AD 877, and the entire treasure was acquired by the British Museum in 1925.[19] In May 1957 seven silver cup stands, one inscribed with a date corresponding to 860, were found in the northeast of Chang'an, and a plate decorated with a lion was discovered in the grounds of Daming Palace.[20] The plate was accompanied by inscribed plaques dating from between 743 and 751. A further hoard of fifteen pieces, including four hanging incense burners (see cat. no. 73), was found in Shapocun, a southeastern suburb of Xi'an.

Three of the major finds of the Tang period are those of

Hejiacun, Dingmaoqiao (in Jiangsu province)[21] and the Famen temple (discovered in 1970, 1982 and 1987 respectively).[22] Two of these three were found in Shaanxi province, the province in which the capital Chang'an was situated, and both are well represented in this exhibition.

The largest hoard found to date is that of Tang dynasty treasures found in 1970 at Hejiacun,[23] a village in the southern suburbs of Xi'an.[24] The finds totalled 1023 pieces, including 270 gold and silver items, and were buried in two large pottery jars and one small silver vessel. The silver boxes contained rare medicinal minerals, such as cinnabar and stalactite, and there were also instruments for practising alchemy and making medicines. The vessels represent a cross-section of the repertoire of shapes, and the decorative techniques used, in Tang dynasty metal-work. A few shapes in the hoard feature elements of the foreign forms that provided the original inspiration for the industry, including faceted cups with ring handles and lobed bowls, the lobes outlined by half palmette leaves. But there are also Chinese shapes, such as the wine cups with ear-shaped handles. Beside the many decorated pieces which have been widely published, the undecorated items, including 45 bowls and 51 small dishes, demonstrate that gold and silver were used not only for spectacular individual pieces but also for routine vessels, presumably used for eating and drinking at feasts. Together the treasures represent the glory of the Tang at its height and the gold and silver vessels in particular reflect the extravagant, eclectic tastes of a time when the Tang controlled one of the largest empires in the world.

The hoard was found at the site of what has been identified as the mansion of the Prince of Bin, Li Shouli, who died in 741.[25] Li was a cousin of the emperor Xuanzong. He was succeeded by his son, who continued to live in the mansion until he joined the emperor in flight, and it is possible that some member of his family buried these treasures before fleeing to Sichuan with Xuanzong and his court when An Lushan attacked Chang'an in 755.

The very large numbers and variety of pieces discovered in these hoards show that gold and silver were widely used by both the imperial court and the wealthy lay gentry during the Tang period, truly justifying the description as a Golden Age for this important period of Chinese history.

1 For a history of the Sui dynasty, see A Wright, *The Sui Dynasty: The Unification of China, 581–617,* New York 1978.
2 For Tang dynasty generally see: Berger 1994; Bingham 1941; Dudbridge 1995; *Famous Capital*; Fitzgerald 1933, 1947, 1968; Guisso 1978; Hobson 1926 *re* hoards; Hong Kong 1993; Hong Kong and Shaanxi 1993; Kuhn 1993; London 1955; Louis 1999; Medley 1970; Melikian-Chirvani 1979; Pulleyblank 1955, 1960; Rawson 1977, 1982, 1986b, 1991; des Rotours 1968; Schafer 1963; Scott 1966, 1981; Singapore 1991; Trubner 1957, 1959; Twitchett 1979; W Watson 1984; Weschler 1974; Xi'an 1995; Yen Lei 1959; Zou Zongxu 1991.
3 Twitchett 1979, p. 9.
4 For Wu Zetian generally, see Fitzgerald 1968; Guisso 1978.
5 For the background to the rise of Yang Guifei (also known as Yang Yuhuan), see Pulleyblank 1955; Levy 1957a and b, 1958, 1962.
6 Twitchett 1979, pp. 242–89.
7 Twitchett 1979, pp. 290–321.
8 Twitchett 1979, pp. 321–32.
9 Boston 1976, pp. 90–123.
10 Twitchett 1979, pp. 325–8.
11 For a history of Xuanzong generally, see des Rotours 1981.
12 Twitchett 1979, pp. 359–61.
13 Twitchett 1979, pp. 409–47.
14 Pulleyblank 1955 explains the background and circumstances of this period.
15 Hejiacun 1972.
16 Twitchett 1979, pp. 484–6.
17 Twitchett 1979, p. 745.
18 Twitchett 1979, pp. 682–781.
19 Hobson 1926.
20 See cat. no. 45.
21 Jiangsu 1982.
22 See the final section of this catalogue (pp. 148–62).
23 Beijing 1972b, pp. 44–70; Tokyo 1981; *Wenwu* 1972.1, pp. 30–8.
24 For a list of gold and silver discovered in China, see Rietberg 1996.
25 For a fictionalized account based on fact see Lin Yutang, *Lady Wu,* New York 1965.

30 Hairpins

Sui dynasty (AD 591– 618)
Jade
Lengths 7.1–8.6 cm; weight 12.25 g
Excavated 1988, Xianyang International Airport building site, Xi'an, Shaanxi province
Shaanxi Archaeological Institute

These four hairpins are of the same shape but of differing sizes. There is no surface decoration and each pair of prongs is of equal length, with an almost circular cross-section. The quality of the jade is very fine, the workmanship is good and the pins are well polished. Many similar plain jade hairpins have been found dating to the Tang dynasty.[1]

Hairpins were used by both women and men from the neolithic period. A stone hairpin was discovered at the neolithic site of Taosi, in Shaanxi province, and Fu Hao, the consort of a Shang dynasty king (*c.* 1200 BC), had 527 hairpins of jade, ivory and bone in her tomb, indicating her wealth and high status.[2] Far Eastern women have hair whose properties of straightness, heaviness and round cross-section make hairpins easy to use. This probably accounts for their popularity as a form of hair decoration. Many poems[3] describe the beauty of women in terms of their hair, and hairpins and combs were often highly decorated.[4] In the Warring States period, just as men were initiated into manhood by some kind of capping ceremony, so girls were given various ornaments when they became young women. These ornaments took the form of hairpins for dressing their hair as adults.[5] One of the earliest representations of a hairpin is that worn by the Lady Dai on her funeral banner (see fig. 13, p. 43) dating from the second century BC.

During the Sui dynasty women wore their hair on top of the head, combed flat. Shortly after, from about the middle of the seventh century, it became fashionable for women's hair to be dressed higher and higher, in chignons and false buns, which necessitated the use of hairpins. These piled-up hairstyles continued in vogue throughout the Tang dynasty and evocative names were given to the hair buns: half-turned bun, worried bun, lily bun, obedient bun, lingering bun, alerted swan bun, double-ring fairy-viewing bun. Ponytails were also quite popular amongst a small number of aristocratic women during the reign of Xuanzong.[6] Hairpins were amongst the ornaments listed in the laws of the first Tang emperor: the lower down the social hierarchy one belonged the fewer hairpins one was allowed to wear.[7]

Published: Hebei 1991–3, vol. 5, no. 12.

1 See those published in Hong Kong and Shaanxi 1993, no. 22, p. 61.
2 Rawson 1996a, cat. no. 50, p. 110.
3 'With her cloudy hair, her flower-like face, and twinkling golden headdress', from 'Everlasting Regret' by Bai Juyi in Herdan 1973, p. 146 (reference to Yang Guifei).
4 Tait 1976, p. 140.
5 Hsu and Linduff 1988, p. 374.
6 Zhou and Gao 1987, p. 84.
7 Tsao 1997, p. 79.

31 Nine hairpins

Tang dynasty (AD 618–906)
Gold
Lengths 7–12 cm; total weight 130.9 g
Excavated 1988, Xianyang International Airport building site, Xi'an, Shaanxi province
Shaanxi Archaeological Institute

These hairpins divide into two types: one has two parallel prongs of equal length (seven examples displayed here); the other has only one prong (two examples). The first seven are of varying size but the same shape, undecorated, with a circular cross-section. The two single-sided pins are almost identical in size. They are made in much the same way as the two-pronged ones but one prong is broken off, leaving an obvious mark. The hairpins were made by hammering the gold into shape and the surface has been left undecorated to display to the full the beauty of the pure metal.

The poignant and ill-fated love affair between Xuanzong and Yang Guifei has been immortalized by several poets, among them Bai Juyi, who imagines Xuanzong sending an

30

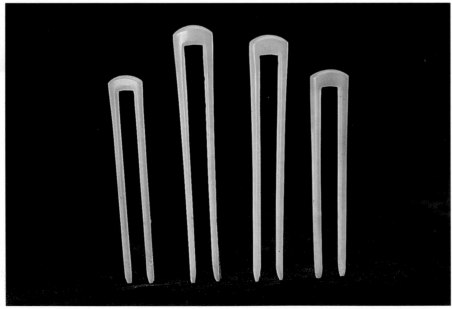

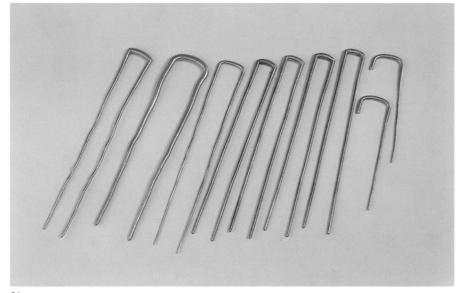

31

Fig. 31a
Detail of donor figure in a Chinese Buddhist donor painting from Dunhuang (late 9th century AD). From her attire, the lady is a noblewoman or a princess; she wears a comb and other hair ornaments.

envoy to the land of the immortals to fetch a memento from Yang Guifei. The envoy returns with a golden hairpin:

With deep emotion she brought the old pledges he had given –
The enamel casket and the golden hairpin, to send with the envoy:
One wing of the hairpin she kept and one side of the casket.
Breaking the gold of the hairpin, splitting the work of the casket,
Bid his heart endure like gold and enamel,
Then in Heaven or on earth we shall meet again![1]

Hairpins seem to have been made of gold from at least the late Han dynasty and this simple kind of gold hairpin changed very little from the Han to the Qing. Several gold hairpins have been excavated in the Tang tombs in the suburbs of Chang'an. These include not only plain hairpins, but also gourd-shaped hairpins and flower hairpins, some of which have gilded tops with moulded and engraved decoration. Decorated hairpins seem to have become particularly fashionable in the Tang dynasty (see cat. nos 32, 33).

Published: Hong Kong and Shaanxi 1993, no. 20.

1 From 'Everlasting Regret' by Bai Juyi in Herdan 1973, pp. 146–57, recounting the love story of Xuanzong and Yang Guifei.

32 Hair ornaments

Tang dynasty (AD 618–906)
Jade
Lengths 10 cm, 11 cm; widths 2.8 cm, 4 cm; weights 13.7 g, 12.6 g
Excavated 1982, Xingqing Palace site, Xi'an Transport University, Shaanxi province
Xi'an City Cultural Relics Storehouse

32

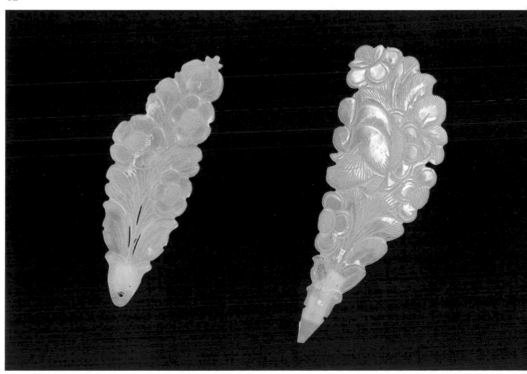

These hair ornaments are of leaf-shaped jade, carved on both sides with luxuriant leaves and bunches of flowers in bloom. Among the leaves on one of the ornaments are Chinese mandarin ducks with their wings flapping in the water. Mandarin ducks symbolize marital bliss since they appear always in couples and mate only once, and for this reason they are a popular element in Chinese design. Wei Ying Wu,[1] a Tang dynasty poet, in his poem about Chang'an, wrote: 'On her head there are two mandarin ducks with green wings', which may possibly be a reference to a hairpin such as this one.

The other ornament is carved with pomegranates. The pomegranate has many seeds, pronounced *zi* in Chinese, the same pronunciation as the Chinese word for children, *zi*. For this reason the pomegranate symbolizes a desire for children, and, along with the peach and the finger citron, suggests abundance and plenty. The carving of both ornaments is very accomplished, the decoration harmoniously organized and the surface well polished.

These two ornaments were excavated from the site of Xingqing Palace,[2] one of the three most important Tang dynasty palaces in Chang'an, the capital (see fig. 7, p.32). The area where the palace stood, to the east of the imperial city near Chunming Gate on the eastern city wall, was originally lived in by commoners, but in the sixteenth year of the Kaiyuan period, AD 728, the Xuanzong emperor moved from Daming Palace to the new Xingqing Palace which then became the centre of political life in the capital.[3] After Xuanzong's time it became a residence for elderly princes and consorts. Both the Xingqing and Daming palace complexes are shown on the oldest known Chinese city plan, the fragmentary stele of Tang Chang'an carved in 1080.[4] Xingqing Palace occupied an area of about 1.3 square kilometres and it was here that some of the famous incidents recorded between Tang Xuanzong and Yang Guifei took place. The high quality of the two ornaments suggests that they belonged to someone of at least the rank of Yang Guifei.

Published: Song Yanyan 1991, no. 31.

1 'Chang'an dao' in *Quan Tang shi*, Zhonghua shuju edn, 1960, vol. 3, p. 1998.
2 Beijing 1983b, p. 463.

3 Zou Zongxu 1991, p. 92.
4 Steinhardt 1990, p. 102.

33 Hairpins

Tang dynasty (AD 618–906)
Silver with parcel gilt
Lengths 35.5 cm, 34.5 cm; weights 34.5 g, 30 g
Provenance unknown
Shaanxi History Museum

These hairpins have been cut out from sheets of silver and soldered to a two-pronged pin for fixing into the hair. The finial decoration is in openwork, on one grass and flowers, on the other five peonies joined one to the other, with intertwining foliage. Details of the design are enhanced with engraving in relief. The flower design is gilded and reveals a high level of workmanship. There are pieces now missing from the broad edges.

Early Tang hairpins were made of cast gold but later Tang ornaments were cut out from sheet metal, rendering them very light and thin but also rather fragile. The technique of combining delicate openwork finials with more solid stems meant that the hairpin quivered slightly when the lady moved, giving the impression that she was floating along in the breeze.

During the Tang dynasty there developed the fashion for very high hairstyles, not dissimilar to those worn by ladies in eighteenth-century Europe. Buns of false hair[1] were decorated with gold and jade hairpins, combs and sometimes flowers. Several examples of these elaborate women's hairstyles can be seen in Tang dynasty paintings, such as the one illustrated in figure 31a, p. 65.

The large number of foreigners in Chang'an in the Tang dynasty stimulated an interest in non-Chinese forms of jewellery and luxury goods. New types of decorative ornament, such as crowns and necklaces, began to appear and hairpins became

33

significantly larger, many of them decorated with Buddhist figures and imagery. This interest in Buddhist imagery was symptomatic of the general fascination for all things foreign and exotic in Tang dynasty China which in turn generated a climate of acquisitiveness not evident in China in earlier periods.[2]

1 For descriptions of the various kinds of buns see Zhou and Gao 1987, p. 84.
2 White and Bunker 1994, p. 24.

34 Face, hair or dress ornament

Tang dynasty (AD 618–906)
Silver
Provenance unknown
Length 7 cm; width 3 cm; weight 2.5 g
Shaanxi History Museum

This silver ornament is in the shape of a cicada with a plump body, outstretched wings and two claw-like feet. The body is hollow, and it and the openwork wings are engraved with fine lines. It is finely made and may well have been one of the ornaments put on a lady's forehead between her eyebrows.

Facial ornamentation played an important part in the lives of fashionable women in the Tang dynasty, at least for those women who had the time and the means to indulge in it. Decorative shapes were sometimes applied to the forehead, either with paint or in the form of gold leaf or paper glued on. Murals and paintings show such beauty marks in red, green and yellow, with red being the prevalent colour.[1] However, decorations such as these were also sometimes sewn on to clothes.[2]

A crowd of girls playing in the dusk,
And a wind-blown fragrance that fills the road!
Golden butterflies are sewn to the hems of their skirts;
Their chignons are pinned with mandarin ducks of jade.[3]

The fashion for forehead decoration is said to have originated in the Liu Song dynasty of the Six Dynasties period, when one day Princess Shou Yang, the daughter of Wudi, was sleeping, drunk, under the shadow of a palace roof and a plum flower fell on to her forehead, staining it irrevocably. It was thought to be so attractive that the palace ladies copied it. Later, in the Tang dynasty, an aristocratic woman masked a spot on her cheek by painting something over it and this also became a fashionable form of makeup.[4]

To achieve the required effect in facial decoration, lead powder was first applied to lighten the complexion generally, then rouge was painted on.[5] Eyebrows played an important role in the Chinese ideal of physical beauty. Chinese women had long tended to shave them off and then paint on decorative ones.[6] Well formed eyebrows were said to resemble a moth, or a butterfly if they were more curved. One of the Tang emperors had a picture painted illustrating ten different kinds of eyebrow, each with a different name. A blue-black pigment made from charred bones was used to draw on the required shape, and finally cheek and forehead decoration was applied. Decoration between the eyebrows was called *hua dian*.[7]

From ancient times the cicada had come to represent immortality because of its strange life cycle whereby it emerges from underground after pupating for about two years. It became customary for the ancient Chinese, of the Eastern Zhou and Han dynasties, to put a jade or glass cicada on the tongue of the deceased in the hope that he or she might be reincarnated. The connotations of immortality of this ornament might explain why it was buried.

Fig. 34a *Detail showing the makeup worn by a female donor in a painting entitled* Fumu enzhong jing, *found by Stein at Dunhuang, dating to c. 970.*

1 Till and Swart 1988, p. 72; *Wenwu* 1984.4, pp. 57–69, for general information on makeup and dress.
2 British Museum, OA+79, silver openwork dress ornament, Hotung Gallery, case 26. Similar ornaments are in the Mengdiexuan collection: D Page Shaver, *Orientations*, November 1994, p. 67.
3 Poem by Han Shan, Tang dynasty poet. Quoted from B Watson (trans.), *Cold Mountain: 100 Poems by the T'ang poet Han-shan*, New York 1970, p. 49.
4 Zhou and Gao 1987, p. 86.
5 For information generally on cosmetics in China see Schafer 1956b, pp. 413–38. Ceruse or white lead had been used as a pigment and cosmetic by the Chinese since Shang times and Tang fashion decreed its application to women's breasts as well as to their faces. Rice powder was stained pink for application as rouge for ladies' cheeks, as it was in ancient Greece and Rome. Vermilion, pomegranates and safflower were also used in the Tang dynasty for rouge.
6 Yellow was at times also fashionable as a colour for adorning the foreheads of Chinese ladies. A monarch of the Northern Zhou dynasty decreed that the women of his court display yellow brows, which might be connected to Buddhist gilded images. Yellow foreheads were extremely popular among the ladies of the Tang dynasty, as attested by the many references to this by Tang dynasty poets. See Schafer 1956b, p. 419.
7 Zhou and Gao 1987, p. 86. For a poem by Du Mu referring to one of these beauty marks, see *Quan Tangshi*, Zhonghua shuju edn, 1960, vol. 8, p. 5971.

34

35 Earrings

Tang dynasty (AD 618–906)
Gold, jade
Length 3.6 cm; weight 12.9 g
Excavated 1988, Xianyang International Airport
building site, Xi'an, Shaanxi province
Shaanxi Archaeological Institute

These earrings have globular gold balls
which were originally inlaid with jade and
other precious stones, some of which are
now missing. They would have had gold wire
to suspend them from the loop. Their gold
U-shaped terminals end in a flower shape
which hangs down from the base of the ball.

Earrings were an accessory worn by both
men and women from neolithic times when
the slit rings, later named *jue*, were probably
worn as such. Examples of these rings have
been found in the northeast of China in the
neolithic Xinglongwa and Chahai cultures,
and it appears that they then spread
southeast to the cultures of Hemudu,
Majiabang and Songze.[1] However, earrings
seem to have been a less common accessory
than hairpins amongst upper-class Chinese
women.

Many different types of hairpin have
been found dating to the Tang dynasty, in a
variety of materials, as can be seen in this
catalogue and in paintings and murals (see
fig. 31a, p. 65). Earrings, on the other hand,
are infrequently depicted or found in tombs,
and they seem gradually to have become
associated with lower-class women and
foreigners. It has been suggested that a
reason for Chinese women not wearing
earrings may be that piercing the ears was
not an acceptable Confucian practice as it
implied violating the body that one had been
given by one's parents.[2]

These earrings bear similarities to
Western Asiatic jewellery, suggesting that
they were either imported along the Silk
Road or were copied by Chinese craftsmen
from Western examples. They were perhaps
in the possession of one of the many foreign
residents of Tang dynasty Chang'an.

35

Published: Hong Kong and Shaanxi 1993, no. 19.

1 Rawson 1995a, p. 119.
2 Tsao 1997, p. 82.

36 Cosmetics box

Tang dynasty (AD 618–906)
Gilded silver
Diameter 2.9–3.4 cm; weight 18.6 g
Excavated 1989, tomb 65, eastern suburbs of
Xi'an, Shaanxi province
Shaanxi Archaeological Institute

The two halves of this shell-shaped box are
made of gilded silver linked by a hinge. It
was probably a lady's powder compact as it
was found together with the mirror,
catalogue no. 37.

One side of the box is decorated with
entwined geese with pomegranates behind
their heads, and the other side with a pair of
mandarin ducks gazing at each other. The
birds are surrounded by flower sprays and
magpies, all against a ring-punched
background.

The imagery is full of significance. The
pomegranates, the geese with necks
entwined and the mandarin ducks are
symbols of riches, nobility and marital bliss,
thereby expressing the maker's or owner's
wish for a rich and happy life.

The box was excavated from a Tang
dynasty tomb dated to the sixth year of the
Kaiyuan period, AD 718. According to the
epitaph the occupant of the tomb was a
female, surnamed Wei, and it is presumed
that she was a descendant of the Wei family
which was renowned in the Tang dynasty,
reaching the peak of its power during the
reign of Zhongzong. Zhongzong's wife was a
member of the Wei family. Zhongzong
himself, a weak son of Wu Zetian, was
totally dominated by his wife and her family
who controlled court politics, sold noble
ranks, and tried to rival the power of Wu
Zetian herself. This was ultimately a futile
manoeuvre and when in 710 they tried to
overthrow the emperor and set up the Wei
dynasty they were unsuccessful and were
killed. (Probably Empress Wei poisoned her
husband before she was herself killed.)[1]
From then onwards the once important Wei
family never again regained its power.
According to the histories the original Wei
family tomb in Chang'an county, Shaanxi,
was destroyed after their defeat and
remaining members of the family had to
move their tombs to other places. This box
was excavated from one of these new tombs
belonging to the Wei family.

The box may have contained face power,
possibly of white lead, which was used from
at least Shang dynasty times. However,
powder was also made from ground rice.[2]

36

although these were probably imports from territories on the northern periphery of ancient China as they were not made in China until the Eastern Zhou period. Fu Hao, the formidable consort of one of the Shang dynasty kings, Wu Ding, had several in her tomb when she died about 1200 BC.[2] As in many cultures, mirrors, on account of their reflective qualities, had cosmological and magical connotations. Even when the use of bronze began to decline towards the end of the Eastern Zhou period, mirrors continued to be made in large numbers. Many Han dynasty mirrors were inscribed with auspicious sayings. The undecorated side was highly polished.[3]

Small mirrors like this one are similar in size to mirrors of the neolithic Qijia culture. They were probably suspended from belts or cords and carried as personal ornaments. Some may have been used as signal mirrors by the military.[4]

Rouge was made from wild safflower or pomegranates,[3] and cheeks were sometimes painted with motifs such as moons or coins.

1 For information on Empress Wei see Twitchett 1979, ch. 6.
2 Yao 1983, p. 62; Zhou and Gao 1987, p. 86.
3 Tang poetry abounds with references to makeup: 'Applying face powder carefully layer upon layer, and putting rouge on the cheeks for a vision of loveliness' and 'A beauty with rouged cheeks and slender waist', quoted from Zhou and Gao 1987, p. 86.

into the centre of each of the six petals and the whole design is set against a ring-matted ground, created by a hammering technique. From the signs of wear, the mirror was obviously much used.

Mirrors have a long history in China.[1] Small polished bronze discs, which probably served as mirrors, have been found at neolithic sites of the Qijia culture, a culture that lived outside mainstream China from the latter part of the third millennium BC to about 2000 BC. A few examples have been excavated from Shang period burials

1 Mirrors are a complex subject and there is much literature on them. For early mirrors see Loewe 1979.
2 For information on Fu Hao see Rawson 1996a, pp. 15 and 90–1.
3 White and Bunker 1994, pp. 42–4; for an example of the back, reflective side of a mirror, see British Museum, Hotung Gallery, case no.16. For general information on mirrors see Needham 1962, pp. 87–97.
4 White and Bunker 1994, p. 25.

37 Mirror

Tang dynasty (AD 618–906)
Bronze with silver backing
Diameter 5.7 cm; weight 59.25 g
Excavated 1989, tomb 65, eastern suburbs of Xi'an, Shaanxi province
Shaanxi Archaeological Institute

This mirror was found in the same tomb as the cosmetics box, catalogue no. 36. It is shaped rather like a six-petalled flower, with a thin silver backing, engraved with flowers, grasses, birds and animals. The central knob is in the shape of a toad which acts as a focus for the lions, monkeys and birds cavorting along a twining tendril. A single leaf grows

37

38 Figure of a lady

Tang dynasty (AD 618–906)
Pottery with *sancai* (three-colour) decoration
Height 44.5 cm
Excavated 1959, Zhongpu village, western
suburbs of Xi'an, Shaanxi province
Shaanxi History Museum

This handsome pottery female figure dates
to the most prosperous period of the Tang
dynasty, AD 713–65. The lady's face is round
and full, she has two small hair buns on her
forehead, her red lips are slightly open and
her eyebrows are immaculate. She is
wearing a collarless blue V-necked bodice
with yellow flowers on it, covered on her
right shoulder by a pale yellow shawl which
is tucked under her left arm and draped
round the back of her dress. The orangey
yellow skirt of her dress is fastened to the
bodice and is so long that it partially covers
her shoes with upturned toes. Her left arm
is slightly raised, her hand hidden inside the
long sleeve. Her right arm makes a gesture
as if she were about to receive something.
This elegantly sculpted lady, at once majestic
and gentle, reflects the dignity of
noblewomen of the Tang dynasty. The three-
colour glaze of yellow, blue and green is
bright and attractive.

Our knowledge of ladies' fashions in the
Tang dynasty is quite considerable as we
have many tomb models such as this one and
representations in stone, and on murals and
paintings.[1] Donor portraits on dated
sculptural monuments[2] show evidence of
dress, as do the small figurines placed in the
Five-storeyed Pagoda of the Horyū-ji in
Japan in 711.[3] Some textiles also survive
from this period, found on tomb figurines
from Chinese Turkestan. From the Sui
period a high-waisted empire style seems to
have become fashionable and the basic outfit
for the Tang dynasty lady was a bodice, a
long flowing skirt and a scarf or stole. This
style did not originate in China and was
probably introduced from Persia by way of
Central Asia. Yang Guifei, the famous
concubine of Xuanzong, was reputedly
'Rubensian' in figure and her plumpness
was admired and copied. The high-waisted
skirt would hide the lack of a waistline and
the scarf would be draped to cover any
other parts of the body to which the
uncorseted lady might not want to draw
attention.

Over such outfits various types of jackets
were worn, including those with very long,
wide sleeves which covered the hands of
dancing girls performing the long sleeve
dance. Many jackets were of brocaded
fabric, showing the influence of Persia and
the town of Kucha on the Chinese Silk
Road. Such fabrics were probably
introduced into China by the Central
Asian musicians and dancers who
came to the Chinese court (cat. no. 39).

Central Asian costumes were current in
China from the late seventh century and
foreign styles were often criticized and
ridiculed by onlookers such as the Tang poet
Bai Juyi:

The fashions of our day
Spread from the City to the four corners of the
world.
At present a custom prevails far and near
Of cheeks unrouged and faces without powder
With muddy grease the ladies smear their lips;
Their eyebrows tilt to the shape of a painted
roof …

Prince, take note! The head-fashions of this period
Yuan-ho-
These heaped tresses and unpowdered cheeks — are
no Chinese way![4]

38

39

Aristocratic and court ladies also liked to dress in men's clothing, sometimes imitating that worn by foreign grooms and merchants such as their tight-fitting coats with turned down collars, with the fastening to the left (cat. no. 47).[5] Such costumes were particularly comfortable for riding and playing polo, activities in which the relatively emancipated Tang dynasty court lady often indulged (see cat. no. 40). At the beginning of the eighth century women exposed their faces and necks when out riding and adopted the hats of their Central Asian maids. The hair was looped over the forehead and around the face, and tied into topknots which often then hung rakishly over the forehead or one eye. Hairstyles were decorated with hairpins and combs (cat. nos 30–33).

The fashionable plumpness was complemented by a full moon face and double chins. As fifty-eight course banquets were not unknown at the Tang court (courses such as 'longevity gruel, fairy meat [slices of chicken in milk]; boiled dragon whiskers')[6] such a vogue was probably inevitable. Yang Guifei was known for her predilection for fresh lichees which were transported by post horse from Lingnan in the south over the whole length of China

specially for her. As the Tang dynasty poet, Du Mu, wrote:

Looking back at Chang'an, an embroidered pile appears;
A thousand gates among mountain peaks open each in turn
A single horseman in the red dust – and the young Consort laughs,
But no one knows if it is the lichees which come.[7]

Published: Montreal 1986, p.109; Wang Renbo 1990, p. 116, no. 5; Beijing 1992a, no. 101; Xi'an 1992, p. 90; Kuhn 1993, no. 31.1; *Empress Wu* 1998, no. 58.

1 Till and Swart 1988, pp. 71ff; Zhou and Gao 1987, pp. 86–7.
2 Sirén 1925, vol. III, pl. 412, in a stele dated AD 726, and vol. IV, pl. 479, a stele dated 734.
3 Mizuno Seiichi, *Asuka Buddhist Art: Horyū-ji*, Heibonsha Survey of Japanese Art, vol. 4), New York and Tokyo, 1974, fig. 139.
4 Quoted in Schafer 1963, p. 214.
5 This left-sided fastening of clothes was invariably regarded by the Chinese as inherently barbarian and foreign (Yao 1983, p. 58).
6 Edwards 1937–8, vol. 1, pp. 192–3.
7 Quoted in Schafer 1963, p. 33.

39 Group of dancers and musicians

Tang dynasty (AD 618–906)
Pottery
Height (standing figures) 27 cm, (sitting figures) 18 cm; total weight 3.25 kg
Excavated 1972, tomb of Zheng Rentai, Liquan county, Shaanxi province
Shaanxi History Museum

This group of seven women comprises two dancers and five musicians seated on cushions. They all wear long skirts and collarless jackets and all but one have double buns. The two standing, dancing figures wear skirts with buttons down the front, and V-necked tops with long sleeves dangling from their raised left arms. They lean over gracefully to the right, their skirts trailing the ground. This would probably have been a typical banquet entertainment scene at the Tang court or at the house of a nobleman. The figures are glazed amber yellow overall.

Tang dynasty female musicians tend to be seated whereas male musicians are mounted on horseback as part of processions and armies. Music and dancing were so much a part of Tang dynasty court life that a special section of the royal palace in Chang'an was set aside for training entertainers and this was attended by both Chinese and foreign girls, such as Indochinese, Koreans and Indians. The cosmopolitan atmosphere of the Tang court at Chang'an was enhanced by the troupes of dancers and female orchestras who were brought as tribute by embassies from Persia and Central Asian countries.

Literary and archaeological evidence attests to the importance of music and entertainment in the daily life of ancient China. Instruments such as musical stones, zithers, panpipes, bells, flutes and drums were often buried in tombs to enable the occupants to listen to the music they had enjoyed during their lifetime. For example, the Marquis Yi of Zeng (died *c.* 433 BC) took with him to the grave not only twenty-two sacrificial musicians, whom he expected to play for him in the afterlife, but also many musical instruments.[1]

Visitors to the Tang royal court enjoyed a variety of entertainment such as wrestling matches, athletics, acrobatics and tumbling. Troupes of entertainers also toured the countryside playing to paying audiences in market towns. Several of the murals in caves such as the Mogao Grottoes at Dunhuang depict music and dance.[2] One of the most evocative dances of the Chinese is the whirling *huxuan* dance which many poets describe so eloquently. Bai Juyi wrote:

Hu-hsüan *girls:* Hu-hsüan *girls!*
Your hearts respond to strings, your hands to drums.
When strings and drums sound, your hands are raised;
You turn, whirl and dance like falling snow –
Turn to the left, pivot to the right, without knowing fatigue,
Make a thousand turns, ten thousand revolutions without stopping.
Nothing in the world is comparable to you.
The wheels of a moving cart, the eddying of the wind are even slower.[3]

Yang Guifei herself was a skilled dancer

who apparently excelled in her performance of the Dance of the Whirling Barbarian. This was a dance introduced, like so many others, from Central Asia. Another well-known dance of the period was the Dance of the Rainbow Skirt and Feather Jacket, also associated with Yang Guifei and quoted by Bai Juyi in his poem 'Everlasting Regret':

War drums at Yu-yang,
Shaking the earth,
startled-broke the song
'Rainbow Skirt and Feather Jacket'.[4]

Published: Wang Renbo 1990, p. 254, no. 10; Xi'an 1997, p. 105; *Famous Capital*, pp. 158–9, no. 4.

1 See Rawson 1996a, p. 132, for the bells found in his tomb and Hubei Provincial Museum, *Lacquerware from the Warring States to the Han Periods excavated in Hubei Province,* Hong Kong 1994, for illustrations of his many instruments.
2 *Dunhuang yanjiu* 1997.4, pp. 26–44.
3 Quoted in Mahler 1959, p. 148. The *huxuan* (hu-hsüan) dance was performed before Emperor Xuanzong by An Lushan who was brought up on the northeast frontier in the region where the Hu people from the West had come to live in numbers. For a history of the distribution of music and dance of Serindia in China during the Sui and Tang dynasties and the origins of the *huxuan* dance see *Shaanxi Shifan Daxue xuebao* 1997.1, pp.105–12. See *China Archaeology and Art Digest,* vol. 2, no. 1, Hong Kong, January–March 1997, pp. 84–5.
4 Levy 1970–8, vol.1, p. 137, where this

reference to the dance implies that Yang Guifei was killed. For another evocative poem about the dancing of the time, see 'The Dancers of Huai-Nan' by Zhang Heng, quoted in A Waley, *The Temple and Other Poems,* London 1923, pp. 85–6.

40 Rider and horse

Tang dynasty (AD 618–906)
Pottery with *sancai* (three-colour) decoration
Height 38 cm; length 52 cm; weight 5.1 kg
Excavated 1975, Medicine Factory building site, western suburbs of Xi'an, Shaanxi province
Xi'an City Cultural Relics Storehouse

The horse leaps, with all four legs outstretched mid-air, a rare pose amongst three-colour (*sancai*) pottery horses of the Tang dynasty. With bound tail outstretched, ears pricked up and eyes staring resolutely forward, the horse possesses a strong sense of dynamics and speed.

Although it is possible that the rider here is a male figure, with merchandise piled up behind him, it is also possible it could be a female. It was fashionable during the Tang dynasty for women to dress as men and this rider could be a woman, dressed as a man. The rider, in contrast to the horse, looks calm and detached, head turned to the side with a smile. Her long hair is parted in the

40

middle and tied back in two buns at the nape of the neck. She sits astride the horse, wearing a long round-collared robe, her sleeves rolled up to her elbows. She is one of the masterpieces of Tang equestrienne sculpture.

During the Tang dynasty women had greater freedom to mix in society than in either earlier or later periods in Chinese history. It was during the Tang dynasty that the only woman who ever attempted to establish her own dynasty came to power, Empress Wu Zetian.[1] The emperors of the Tang dynasty seem to have enjoyed the company of women, who began to lead more active lives.[2] Many women of the palace began to play polo and murals in tombs attest to the popularity of this game amongst both men and women at court. Polo probably originated in Persia, spread to China and from there to Japan and Korea. It was played with sticks, the ends of which were curved like crescent moons, and with net bags as goals. Emperor Xuanzong was known to be a skilled player, his palace having its own polo field, and the game is clearly depicted in the mural in Prince Zhanghuai's tomb.[3]

Han Yu in 799 wrote a diatribe against the playing of polo, trying to persuade his sixty-four-year-old superior Zhang Jianfeng (735–800) to give it up, suggesting that the horses should be kept for doing battle against rebels rather than for play:

Hooves of a hundred horses gather, bright and close together,
The ball leaps up, the stick drives it, as they ride together and apart,
Of red ox hide their straps, of yellow gold their bits.
They lean their bodies and bend their arms around the horses' bellies,
A thunderclap answers hands' movement, the divine bead races.[4]

However, Zhang insisted that polo could only enhance his performance as a military

41

governor and other governors insisted it was good military training. There are extensive descriptions of polo in the notes compiled by Feng Yan (active c. 756–800), including one of a match played at court during the visit by a Tibetan delegation in 709.[5]

Published: Qian, Chen and Ru 1990, no. 236; Xi'an 1992, p. 92; Kuhn 1993, no. 25; Edinburgh 1996, cover, p. 63; Xi'an 1997, p. 109; *Famous Capital*, p. 158, no. 1.

1 There are many books on this redoubtable woman: see references to her in Twitchett 1979 and Fitzgerald 1968.
2 An edict of 671 forbade women to ride horses with their faces unshielded by hats – it was obviously felt that decent women should have been travelling in covered carriages. However, this edict was patently disregarded (Schafer 1963, pp. 28–9).
3 Boston 1976, pp. 100–3, figs 122–5, col. pl. p. 15.
4 Han Yu, 'The Pien and Ssu Flow Together: To Chang Chien-feng' in Stephen Owen (ed.), *The Poetry of Meng Chiao and Han Yu*, New Haven, 1975, p. 88. The divine bead is a reference to the polo ball.
5 See Schafer 1963, p. 67. For an introduction

to polo playing in China see Virginia L. Bower, 'Polo in Tang China: Sport and Art', *Asian Art*, Winter 1991, pp. 23–45. See also James Liu, 'Polo and Cultural Change: From T'ang to Sung China', *Harvard Journal of Asiatic Studies*, 45, no. 1, June 1985, pp. 203–24; People's Sports Publishing House, Beijing, *Sports in Ancient China*, Hong Kong 1986; Wang Yao, 'A New Study on Polo', *Collected Papers on Tibetan History*, Beijing, China Tibetology Publishing House, 1994.

41 Chin strap

Tang dynasty (AD 618–906)
Gold
Height 9 cm; width 5.4 cm; total length 66 cm; weight 71.9 g
Excavated 1979, Hu Mingjun's house, Hong Qingtian, Wangsan village, eastern suburbs of Xi'an, Shaanxi province
Xi'an City Cultural Relics Storehouse

This intriguing object is plain and undecorated, made of very thinly worked gold, with an elliptical bowl possibly for supporting a person's chin. Gold ribbons for securing the object project from both sides of the bowl.

In 1990, in a Tang tomb discovered under the foundations of a meter manufacturing factory in Chang'an county, Shaanxi province, a copper chin strap was found, identical to this gold one. When excavated the strap was still fastened to the dead person's chin, prompting speculation that the strap may have served a medical purpose, perhaps to cure some chin disease or ailment.

In 1988, in the tomb belonging to He Ruo's wife excavated at the site of Xianyang International Airport, Xi'an, another gold chin strap was found.[1] However, this strap was part of a gold ornament set which included a complex arrangement of 109 headdress ornaments and pendent pieces, including gold flower ornaments and other decorations in jade, pearls and precious stones. The whole set must have been particularly impressive. It was certainly a rare combination of so many decorative items. It is possible therefore that the present gold chin strap was an ornament worn in life and taken to the grave.

1 Hong Kong and Shaanxi 1993, p. 56.

42 Belt set

Northern Zhou dynasty (AD 557–581)
Jade, ivory and iron
Total length 150 cm; weight 525 g
Excavated 1988, tomb of Ruogan Yun, Xianyang International Airport building site, Xi'an, Shaanxi province
Shaanxi Archaeological Institute

This is the earliest complete jade belt set discovered in China.[1] It comprises a jade buckle, eight square, plain plaques with rings, one plaque with a design on it and no ring, nine jade rings and one rectangular end plaque. There are also two ivory-handled knives for suspension from the belt which were originally covered in leather and linen

but these have now disintegrated leaving only traces. The buckle, the square plaques and the rings are all carved of a white jade with a gilded copper backing held together with gold studs. Each of the knives is 18 centimetres long, and its sheath is in the shape of a very thin tube, both ends of which are fitted with a golden cap. The cap has a hole in it for suspending the knives from the belt. The knife blades are made of iron, and short but still very sharp. Such knives would have been used for eating and for incising inscriptions. The oval rings attached to the square plaques are very finely worked and may previously have had small ornaments suspended from them.

The ancient Chinese seem to have just tied fabric around themselves as belts or sashes. However from the first millennium BC both Western and Eastern Asian peoples were using belts with attached ornaments and examples of gold belt ornaments have been discovered in the ninth-century BC tombs in Tianma Qucun, Shanxi province,[2] and at Sanmenxia, Henan province.[3] During the Warring States period Chinese contact with the mounted nomadic tribes on their northern borders gradually led to the general adoption of nomadic forms of dress, including the ornamental belt plaques to hold up their clothes.[4] The Ordos tribes made belt plaques in great numbers and Chinese versions of the Ordos animal-style plaques have been found in both gilded bronze and jade.[5] Due to the Achaemenid and later Alexander the Great's disruption of Central Asia there was a migration of nomadic peoples from Central Asia into China. During the latter part of the Warring States period also activities along the Silk Road resulted in the introduction of many new forms of decorative apparel, such as belts and belt sets. The belt plaque from the Heigeda site in Yanqi county, Xinjiang province,[6] is the type that gradually replaced the belt hooks[7] which the Chinese seem to have used from the about the sixth

century BC, although they were of limited practical use and were generally made of luxury materials. (However, they continued to be made and used right to the end of the Chinese empire).

Belt sets comprising a variety of plaques and a rounded buckle, such as that found at Hunan Anxiang Nanchanwan, dating from the third to fourth century AD,[8] began to appear in China in the early centuries AD as descendants of earlier prototypes from the steppe areas. Belt ornament sets had been introduced into Byzantium and Sasanian Iran by the end of the sixth century AD and are depicted on the reliefs of Khosrow II (591–628) in the Sasanian grotto at Taq-i Bustan in western Iran.[9] In the early Tang period the plaques in a belt set were of many different shapes but by the later Tang the majority of belt pieces were approximately square with generally one or two sections of an extended oblong shape, with one rounded and one straight end. The original buckle shape was adapted to a new use to hang behind the belt as one or two tail

Fig. 42a
Drawing showing a man wearing a belt decorated with plaques, from a Tang period wall painting at Dunhuang in Gansu province.

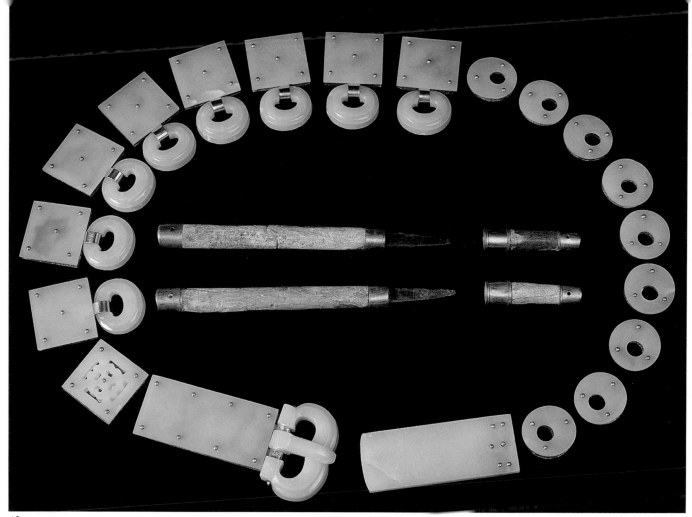

42

pieces. Tang period murals at Dunhuang in Gansu province show how belt sets could be worn[10] and in figure 42a it can be seen how the end piece of the belt is clearly tucked into the belt to point upwards, though it sometimes hung downwards.

In China, belts gradually became a significant accessory indicating a man's rank and status. In the *Xin Tang shu,* a history of the Tang dynasty written in the eleventh century,[11] the section on clothing and chariots lists the regulations on clothing, as do the rules on dress in the *Tang Shi lu:* 'Civil and military officials of the third rank and above wear belts of gold and jade with 13 pieces; those of the fourth rank wear gold belts of 11 pieces; those of the fifth rank have ten pieces; those of the sixth rank have belts of rhinoceros horn, numbering nine pieces; the seventh rank have belts of silver, numbering eight pieces; the eighth and ninth grades have belts of "brass" numbering eight pieces and the common people have belts of bronze or iron with six pieces.'[12]

Published: Hong Kong and Shaanxi 1993, no.17.

1 For a preliminary discussion on the shape and decoration of jade belts see *Wenwu Chunqiu* 1996.1, pp. 40–5; for an abbreviated translation see *China Archaeology and Art Digest,* vol. 1, Hong Kong, April–June 1996, p. 141; for information on the development and types of belt buckles see *Liaohai wenwu xuekan* 1996.1, pp. 34–41; Rawson 1995a, section 25 introduction has a general discussion of belts and belt sets.
2 *Wenwu* 1994.1, p. 17, fig. 20.
3 Beijing 1992b, no. 123.
4 For information on the Chinese adoption of foreign styles of clothing, particularly by men for riding purposes, in the Warring States period see Chavannes 1969, vol. 5, pp. 69–85.
5 Sun Ji 1994 discusses the evolution of these plaques. See also *Wenwu* 1994.1, pp. 50–64. For a jade version of a bronze Ordos plaque, see Rawson 1995a, no. 23.1, p. 311 (Hotung Collection).
6 As illustrated in E Bunker, 'Gold Wire in Ancient China', *Orientations,* March 1997, p. 94.
7 See British Museum, Hotung Gallery, case 16, for a variety of Chinese belt hooks.
8 See Rawson 1995a, p. 324, fig. 2.
9 British Museum, In. BM 134715–33, illustrated in Musée royaux d'Art et d'Histoire, *Splendeur des Sassanides, L'empire perse entre Rome et la Chine [224–642],* exhibition catalogue, Brussels 1993, pp. 180–2. Belt buckle and lappet fittings, seventh century AD, in the Arthur M Sackler Gallery, illustrated in A C Gunter and P Jett, *Ancient Iranian Metalwork in the Arthur M. Sackler Gallery and the Freer Gallery of Art,* Smithsonian Institution, Washington, DC, 1992. Many Sasanians fled to China and Chang'an in the mid-seventh century when their country was invaded by the Arabs.
10 Sun Ji 1994.
11 For this work see Wilkinson 1998, p. 786.
12 *Xin Tang shu,* Zhonghua shuju edn, Shanghai 1975, juan 24, p. 529. *Tang Shi lu,* quoted by Zhou Nanquan, *Gu Yuqi,* Shanghai Guji chubanshe 1993.

43 Belt plaques

Tang dynasty (AD 618–906)
Gilded bronze
Length (of plaques) 3 cm; width 2.7 cm; length
(of tail piece) 4.5 cm; width 2.8 cm; weight 99.5 g
Excavated 1988, tomb of Wei Xun, Nanliwang
village, Chang'an county, Shaanxi province
Shaanxi Archaeological Institute

Seven belt plaques plus one tail piece
make up this belt set. Each piece consists
of two layers, a front and a back, joined by
gilded nails. The fronts are gilded with
repoussé decoration and the backs are
ungilded. The decoration is of a flower
head surrounded by *ruyi*-shaped cloud
heads.[1] The tail piece is similarly decorated
with flowers in the centre surrounded by
ruyi cloud heads.

From studying the dress regulations of
the period (see cat. no. 44) we may be
pretty certain that this belt set is
incomplete. The fact that some plaques seem
to be missing would suggest that dress
regulations were not always strictly adhered
to, or that some of the plaques were stolen
from the tomb.

Wei Xun was the younger brother of
Empress Wei, wife of Emperor Zhongzong
(see p. 61). When Zhongzong became
emperor in 683 he wanted to make his
father-in-law a duke. However, when
Zhongzong was dethroned by Empress Wu
Zetian he became a duke himself and his
father-in-law and all his children were exiled
to Lingnan in southern China. Here the
father-in-law and his children, including Wei
Xun, died.

In 705 Empress Wu Zetian abdicated and
Zhongzong reverted to being emperor. He
decided to posthumously ennoble his
brother-in-law Wei Xun by making him
Duke of Runan. In 708 Zhongzong moved
the deceased members of the Wei family to
Chang'an, to an imposing new tomb.
Following this Zhongzong was poisoned by
his wife Empress Wei, who wanted to be
empress in her own right as Wu Zetian had
been. However, Empress Wei and all her
family were then killed by Li Longji (later
Xuanzong), the grandson of Wu Zetian. Li
Longji's father Ruizong succeeded to the
throne and ordered the Wei family tomb to
be destroyed. It was further mutilated on
the orders of Xuanzong in 750 so it is
fortunate that anything remains in it at all.
The silver cup in catalogue no. 61 also
comes from this tomb.

Published: Hong Kong and Shaanxi 1993, no. 18.

1 The *ruyi* shape is almost always in the form of
a *lingzhi* fungus which has long associations in
Daoism as one of the ingredients in the elixir
of immortality. The *ruyi*, which translated
literally is 'as you wish', therefore combines
the hopeful wishing for good fortune and for
long life. See Taipei 1995, introductory essay
(in Chinese and English), pp. 18–70.

44 Belt set

Tang dynasty (AD 618–906)
Jade, precious stones and gold
Total length 150 cm; buckle: length 2.7 cm,
width 4.8 cm; rings: diameter 3 cm
Excavated 1992, tomb of Dou Jiao, Nanliwang
village, Chang'an county, Shaanxi province
Shaanxi Archaeological Institute

This jade belt set consists of one buckle,
nine circular rings, four rectangular plaques
and one hook fastener plaque in two parts.
All the belt parts, except for the buckle,

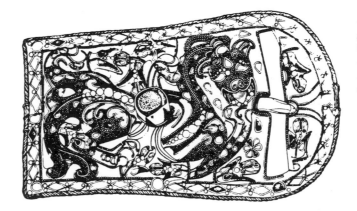

Fig. 44a *Drawing of a
gold belt buckle from the
tomb of Liu Hong at
Hunan Anxiang
Nanchanwan, 3rd–4th
century AD. Length 9 cm.*

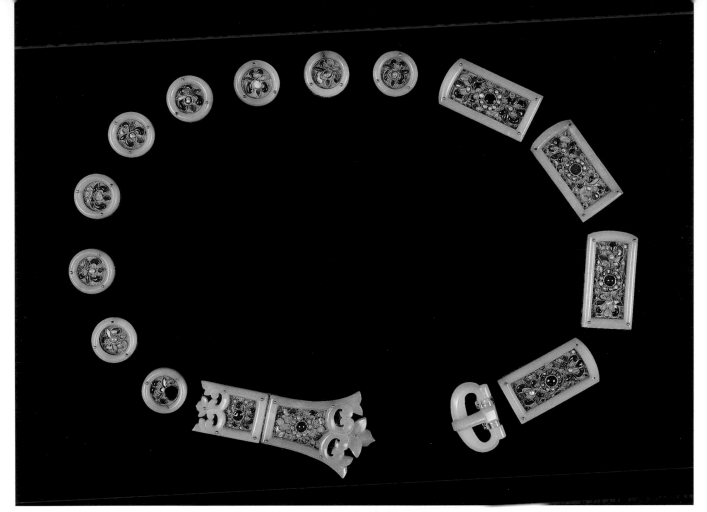

44

have a gold backing. The belt is particularly impressive for its unified and luxurious decoration. Each piece has a jade surround, that of the hook fastener plaque being hollow cut with sprays of acanthus. All the pieces have centres of gold decoration: acanthus sprays on the rings and posies on the plaques and fastener, against a background of ring-punched design and inlaid with pearls and semiprecious stones in red, green and blue. The leather and silk that was attached to the rectangular plaques has disintegrated.

Belt sets and plaques decorated with gold and gilded bronze were of foreign origin, adopted by the Chinese in the third and fourth centuries AD. A spectacular gold buckle (fig. 44a) was found in the tomb of Liu Hong at Hunan Anxiang Nanchanwan, dating to the third or fourth century AD, decorated with granulation, a technique originally foreign to the Chinese, and inlay.[1]

This belt set very effectively combines the fascination for things exotic, gold and foreign with the Chinese appreciation and love of jade.

In ancient China, belts gradually became a significant accessory indicating a man's rank and status. In the *Xin Tang shu*, a history of the Tang dynasty written in the eleventh century,[2] it is stated in the section on clothing and chariots, listing the regulations on clothing: 'The belts with the tip pointing downwards are called *tuowei*; for the first and second grade of officials, square buckles are gold, for the third to the sixth grade they are rhinoceros horn; for the seventh to ninth grade they are silver and the others are iron … purple clothes were for the third grade with gold and jade belts of thirteen plaques; the fourth grade wore deep red clothes and gold belts with eleven plaques; the fifth grade wore light red clothes with gold belts with ten plaques; the sixth grade wore deep

green clothes; the seventh grade wore light green clothes and both grades wore silver belts with nine plaques. The eighth grade wore deep blue-green clothes; the ninth grade wore lighter blue-green clothes and both wore stone belts with eight plaques. The common people wore yellow and copper and iron belts with seven plaques'.[3]

This jade belt set with its beautiful gold floral design, inlaid with semiprecious stones, implies that the owner of the belt was a member of the aristocracy. The tomb in which it was found belonged to Dou Jiao, who may have been a nephew of Empress Wei of the Tang dynasty (see p. 61). His tomb was situated near that of the Wei family but the inscription on his tomb was partly destroyed. What remains of it suggests he was a commander of some sort (*shang zhi guo*) although he is not mentioned in the official histories.[4] The belt set was found near the head of the body and the

unrobbed tomb yielded other fine objects
including a square bronze mirror, glass wine
cups and silver rings. The foreign aspects of
this belt set, particularly the very fine gold
and bejewelled decorative work, were
exactly what appealed to the Chinese
aristocrats of the Tang dynasty.

Published: Hong Kong and Shaanxi 1993, no. 16;
Beijing 1997, no. 37; *Empress Wu* 1998, no. 89.

1 Rawson 1995a, pp. 323–4.
2 For this work see Wilkinson 1998,
  pp. 786–7.
3 *Xin Tang shu*, Zhonghua shuju edn, 1975, juan
  24, p. 529.
4 Liu Yunhwei (Liu Yunhui), 'Dou Jiao: Yuqi
  yudai kao', *Lishi wenwu yuekan*, Bulletin of the
  National Museum of History, 1992.2, Taipei,
  Taiwan, pp. 18–22.

45 Plaque

45

Tang dynasty (AD 618–906)
Jade
Height 4.5 cm; width 5.3 cm; weight 18.1 g
Excavated 1980, Daming Palace site, Sunjiawan,
northern suburbs of Xi'an, Shaanxi province
Xi'an City Cultural Relics Storehouse

This jade plaque takes the form of a scallop-
edged triangle with a straight base and a
small hole at the top. A cloud design is inlaid
in gold over the surface, creating a
particularly effective pattern against the
white jade background. The jade is pure
white, smooth and translucent with no
blemishes. The combination of jade and gold
indicates that the plaque belonged to a high-
ranking aristocrat or member of the
imperial family who lived at Daming Palace.

The Daming Palace was a very large
palace complex in Chang'an (see fig. 7,
p. 32), the capital of the Tang dynasty. It
was begun in the eighth year of Zhenguan,
AD 634, when Emperor Taizong wanted to
prepare for his father Li Yuan a cooler
summer residence. Money for the palace
was given by nobles but in May of the
following year, before the completion of the
palace, Li Yuan fell ill and died. The first
name of the palace was Yong'an Palace but
this was changed to Daming Palace.[1] It was
situated at the highest point of the capital,
with a view down on to the streets and
markets of the town. With an area of about
3.3 square kilometres, the palace was
designed so that the buildings at the front
were occupied by the court and used for
ceremonies, and those at the rear were
domestic quarters. This type of layout was
continued in later dynasties, as can be seen
from the palaces in the Forbidden City in
Beijing. The Daming Palace site has yielded
other objects, also of very high quality.

In the post-Han period jade was widely
used for personal ornaments. This jade
plaque may well have been a pendant or part
of a headdress or belt set. Although the
floral decoration on this plaque is Tang in
style, its combination with the scallop shape
points intriguingly towards the much later
foreign influence of Indian Mughal jades.
This influence was particularly strong
during the Qianlong reign (1736–95) of the
Qing dynasty.[2]

Published: Hebei 1991–3, vol. 5, no. 65.

1 For information on this important palace see
  Kaogu 1961.7, pp. 340–4; *Qingzhu Su Bingqi
  kaogu wushi nian lun wen ji*, Beijing 1989,
  pp. 523–39; Steinhardt 1990, pp. 101–2,
  fig. 87.
2 There are some stylistically similar plaques in
  the Mengdiexuan collection: White and
  Bunker 1994, no. 70, p. 156, where it is
  suggested they were part of pendant sets.

SILK ROUTES

The Tang dynasty was a very cosmopolitan period in Chinese history. It was an age of institutional growth and political consolidation, of new philosophies and religious thought[1] and also one of great creativity in the arts, visual, performing and literary. The Silk Routes played a vital role in this.

The term Silk Route was coined by the German historian von Richthofen in the 1870s to apply to the routes that ran west from China through Central Asia to Syria in the Middle East and onwards to Rome.[2] However, in reality, it was a generic term for many routes, both overland and by sea, and silk was but one of the many commodities carried over it. Shipping routes were also therefore silk routes: the Shandong peninsula linked China with Japan and Korea, and from Canton ships sailed over the South China Sea, the Indian Ocean and on to the Persian Gulf (see fig. 22, pp. 82–3).

The Silk Route began to play a major role in trade during the Han dynasty[3] after General Zhang Qian, a native of Shaanxi province, was sent by the emperor Wudi (141–87 BC) to enlist the support of the Yuezhi against their common enemy the Xiongnu and to seek out the famous horses of Ferghana (see cat. no. 17). By this time the Yuezhi had migrated and settled in Bactria (present-day Afghanistan) and were no longer interested in wars against old enemies. Zhang Qian himself spent many years as a prisoner of the Xiongnu and returned with a detailed knowledge of Central Asian regions and reassurances that their peoples were very happy to trade with China. The highly in-formative and perspicacious accounts of his travels were incorporated into the Han histories.[4] Roman writers were aware of the high value of silk, which was so fashionable in Rome that by AD 14 Tiberius was banning men from wearing it. Pliny and Seneca wrote disapprovingly of silk (the fineness of the fabric 'rendered women naked') and Pliny blamed Roman women for the drain on the nation's economy because of the amount of

silk they bought, which supposedly cost its weight in gold.[5]

From AD 73 to 97 the Chinese general Ban Chao led a large expedition west to the Caspian Sea and brought much of Central Asia under the control of the Han dynasty. Caravans of goods and men travelled west across Chinese Central Asia (present-day Gansu and Xinjiang provinces), and on across the desert, mountains and steppes further west, or south into India. From Dunhuang the main routes divided at the eastern edge of the Taklamakan Desert, skirting the desert on the north and south and then converging at Kashgar, before crossing the Pamirs west to Sogdiana or southwest to Bactria. Another route went north of the Tian Shan (Heavenly Mountains) to Tashkent and Samarkand. From here the routes went west via many exotic cities: Palmyra, Antioch, Damascus, Constantinople, Venice and other cities in the Roman empire, including of course Rome itself. The resilient and cantankerous Bactrian camels plied the eastern parts of these overland routes (figs 18 and 19), carrying up to 120 kilograms of cargo, sniffing out hidden subterranean water, and predicting the terrible and sudden sandstorms[6] (see cat. no. 47). China exported silk, lacquerware, bamboo products, steel, the technology

Fig. 18 *Photograph published in 1912 of Sir Marc Aurel Stein's caravan marching over high sand dunes in the Taklamakan Desert, south of the Tarim River.*

Fig. 19 *Mural of a camel leader from the tomb of Li Feng, Tang dynasty (618–906), Shaanxi province.*

for steel making and well drilling, and advanced farming techniques. China imported aromatics, perfumes and jewels from the Western world, exotic fragrances for baths, bodies and garments, and incense produced from sandalwood resins from Malaysia, camphor from Borneo and frankincense from East Africa. These goods were carried in stages between the many trading posts along the route. At each stage the merchants inevitably took a cut, resulting in great price increases.[7]

The period between the demise of the Han dynasty in AD 220 and the rise of the Sui in 589 was one of disunity, causing disruption to trade. At first China split into the three kingdoms of Shu-Han, Wu and Wei but there was considerable fighting between them. The Jin dynasty unified China again for a short period in the third century but this was disrupted by the pressure of Xiongnu leaders from Central Asia who sacked Luoyang in 311 and captured Chang'an in 317. The Jin court then fled south and established a capital at Jiankang, which is close to present-day Nanjing. From this time until the advent of the Sui, China was divided north and south of the Yangzi River. This period is known as the Northern and Southern dynasties or the Six Dynasties. The north was ruled by non-Chinese peoples, referred to by traditional Chinese historians as 'the sixteen kingdoms of the five barbarians'.

Alien minorities of different racial and geographic origins were dominant at one time or another. The rise of other empires bordering the Silk Route – Turkic, Arabic and Tibetan – meant that any Chinese hold on these areas was precarious. Although China stationed garrisons at strategic points along the routes, many of the oasis cities retained semi-independent status.[8]

By the beginning of the Tang dynasty in the seventh century, its capital Chang'an, at the eastern end of the Silk Route, was a cosmopolitan city with a population including Tocharians, Sogdians, Turks, Uighurs, Mongols, Arabs, Persians and Indians. A general atmosphere of religious tolerance meant that Nestorians, Manichaeans and Zoroastrians from Sogdiana and Persia coexisted with Buddhist students and monks from Kashmir, Japan and Tibet. Chang'an must have seemed like the world in microcosm. Chang'an was the largest city in the world at that time, with an area of eighty square kilometres[9] and a population of one million inside the city and another million in surrounding metropolitan areas (see fig. 7, p. 32). It was six times larger than Constantinople, the capital of the Byzantine empire, and was comparable to Babylon, Alexandria and Rome in their heydays.[10] The main characteristic of Chang'an was its cosmopolitanism, reflected in the large number of foreign residents and the wide range of foreign goods available.

The first major influx of foreigners was in 630 when the Eastern Turks were defeated by the Tang dynasty army and, as a consequence, thousands of Turkish families moved to Chang'an to live.[11] Also during this period rulers of neighbouring empires often sent their children to live in Chang'an as a pledge of their loyalty.[12] These foreigners who took up residence in Chang'an made lasting contributions in political and economic spheres, and marriage alliances were arranged for princesses with Turks, Tibetans and Uighurs. King Peroz of Persia, accompanied by his son Prince Nyas, came to Chang'an to seek help from the Chinese court after the defeat of the Sasanian dynasty by the Dashi.[13] Father and son were appointed right and left

Fig. 20 *Stone statues of 61 headless foreigners at Qianling, the tomb of Gaozong and Wu Zetian, Tang dynasty (618–906). They can be identified from inscriptions on their backs.*

generals of the Tang's defence forces and a model of the king is to be found among the sixty-one stone statues representing envoys (fig. 20) that stand in front of the Qianling tomb complex of the Tang emperor and empress Gaozong and Wu Zetian[14] (see fig. 14, p. 60). It was King Peroz's Sasanian compatriots, in particular the metal-workers who fled with their royal leader, who reputedly introduced to the Chinese the techniques of sheet metal-working. Conversely, Chinese weavers and paper makers, captured in the Battle of Talas River in 751, introduced their skills to the Arab world.

Many of the foreigners who settled in China learned the language and later served their adopted land with distinction. Several Muslims who came to the capital in the middle of the ninth century excelled in the state examinations and were rewarded with important official posts.[15] A Sogdian merchant from Central Asia became Protector of Annam, the same post later held by a Japanese. It was a policy of Xuanzong in the first half of the eighth century to appoint foreigners as generals of the border regions and two of them, a Korean and a Turkic-Sogdian, had notable successes against the Tibetans. Ironically, about the same time, it was a third, a Turkic-Sogdian called An Lushan (Rokhshan), who temporarily destroyed the self-confidence and stability of the Tang empire with his

rebellion in 755 (see p. 62).[16] Troops were recalled from the border garrisons and the cities were then taken by the Tibetans who closed off the direct route between China and the West. The rebellion took eight years to suppress, and in a new climate of retrenchment China began a period of gradually looking inwards for several centuries.[17]

As well as foreign residents, Chang'an welcomed a great number of foreign ambassadors. The early eighth-century tomb of Crown Prince Zhanghuai is decorated with two frescoes showing the reception of foreign ambassadors by officials of the Court of State ceremonial.[18] The eastern wall (fig. 21) depicts ambassadors from the eastern Roman empire and from Korea, as well as a diplomat from the peoples of the northeastern regions. The western wall shows ambassadors from Dashi (now Arabia), Tibet and Gaochang (near Turfan in Xinjiang province). Between 652 and 798 the eastern Roman emperors sent seven diplomats to Chang'an, the Arabian caliph sent thirty-six and Persia twenty-nine.[19]

As a result of all the trade generated by the Silk Route, sizeable foreign communities began to live in the principal trading cities of China. Although the Chinese controlled the distribution of goods and imposed some limits on foreigners within the cities, many did in fact intermingle with the Chinese and were able to go hunting and enjoy

Fig. 21 *Detail of mural showing Tang dynasty officials greeting foreign envoys, one of whom has been identified as a Korean. From the tomb of Prince Zhanghuai, Tang dynasty (618–906). Excavated in 1971, Shaanxi province.*

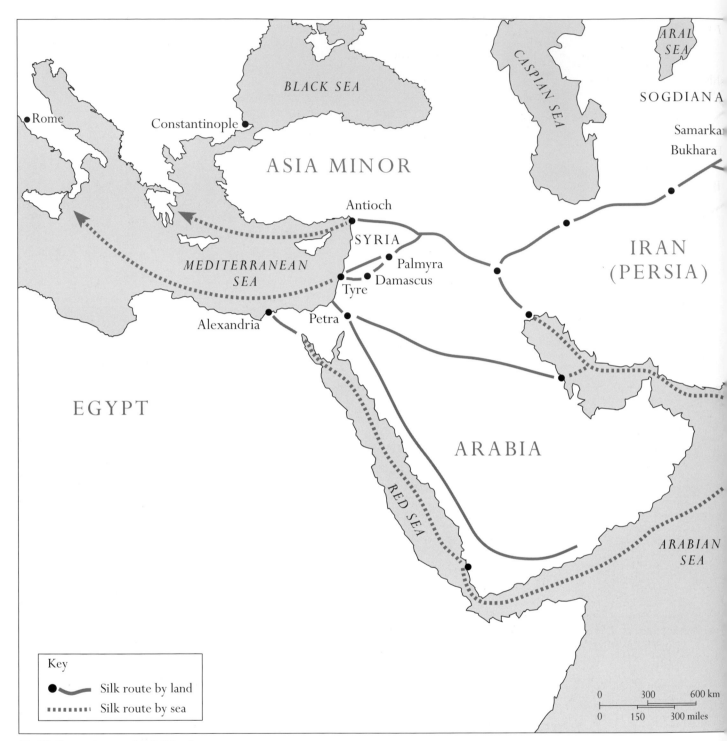

Fig. 22 *Major trade routes of the 'Silk Road'.*

other pleasurable pursuits with their new Chinese acquaintances (see cat. no. 46).

No spectacle within the city of Chang'an (see fig. 7, p. 32) could rival the great imperial Daming Palace in grandeur.[20] Begun by Emperor Taizong in 634, the palace complex occupied an area just outside the northeast city wall, on a site previously used as an imperial hunting park by the Sui dynasty.[21] Covering about 200 hectares, it was larger than medieval London and roughly twice the size of the palace and grounds at Versailles. Among the non-

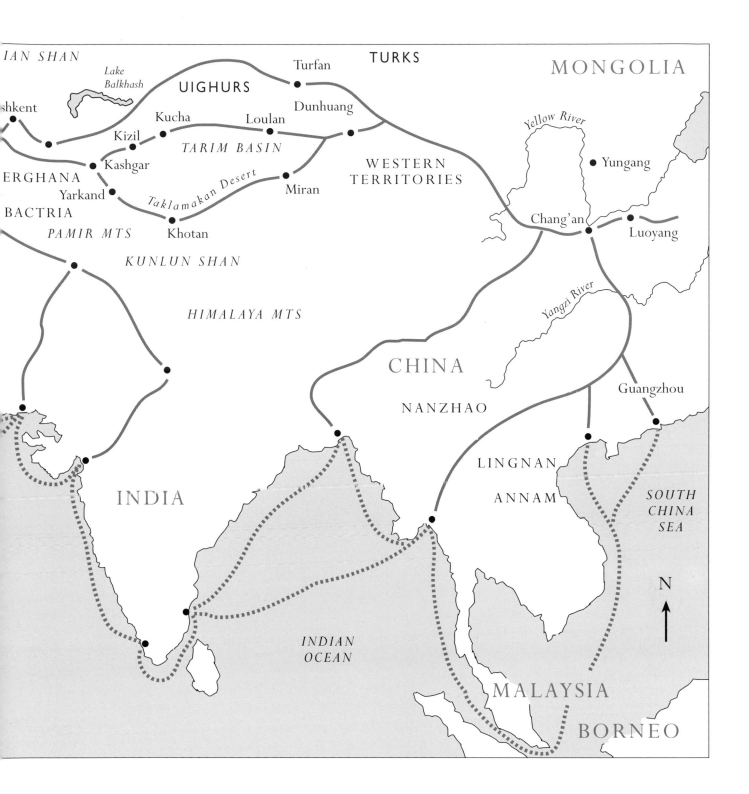

residential buildings was the famous Hanlin Academy of arts and letters as well as an academy of music and dancing where some of the 30,000 or so musicians and dancers of Xuanzong's time were trained.

But the palace was only one of the many attractions of this thriving, cosmopolitan city, with its two great markets selling everything from horses to parrots, with busy tea houses, inns, wards for foreign visitors, courts of law, courtesans' quarters, pleasure lakes, and the public execution ground.[22] For entertainment tea drinking

Fig. 23 *Mural of a dancing girl from the tomb of Zhi Shi Fengjie (d. 658), Tang dynasty (618–906). Excavated in 1957, Shaanxi province.*

Fig. 24 *Printed silk banner from cave 17, Dunhuang. Tang dynasty, 8th or 9th century AD. The outer border of this design is a sinicized version of the pearl roundel motif found on Sasanian metalwork.*

occupied the imperial court and the nobility, while the general populace enjoyed dazzling fireworks displays and festivals, dances and theatrical pageants held in the market places and at the prosperous Buddhist temples. The eastern part of the city had most of the aristocratic mansions, restaurants and many Buddhist establishments including the Greater and Lesser Wild Goose pagodas.[23]

Courtesans inspired poets and beguiled patrons with remarkable skills in music, dance and conversation and western Kuchean women, with light hair and green eyes, were particularly renowned for their dancing. Dressed in gauze trousers and flimsy blouses they danced seductively to the music of Western instruments (fig. 23) while expensive wines were served to clients in fine cups of agate and amber. Dances were categorized as vigorous or gentle,[24] the former including the famous whirling *huxuan* dance (see cat. no. 39). Sylph-like beauties of Cambodia and Thailand were much in demand as dancers or as attendants at court,[25] and the taste for Western music and dances of Indian inspiration that were so popular among the nomadic tribes of Central Asia brought yet more variety and more beauties to the Tang courts. There was a vogue for wearing foreign costumes, particularly Turkish and Persian. Women wore silk pyjamas and a short tunic, convenient for playing polo.[26] The Western-inspired hat and veil were in fashion for a time but the veil was soon abandoned and unveiled women were to be seen riding around the streets of Chang'an. Although an edict tried to ban unveiled women in 671 and ordered women to travel in covered carriages as befitted Confucian ladies, it was ignored.[27] Women wore not only Sasanian-inspired patterned silks (fig. 24), but also jewellery that came from the West, of materials such as jade, crystal, carnelian, malachite and lapis lazuli, ivory from the south and tortoiseshell from Vietnam, amber from Persia and coral from Persia and Ceylon. The air was perfumed with scents from the East, such as sandalwood, camphor, frankincense and myrrh, cloves from Indonesia and cardamom from Malaysia. Drinking games became very popular. Li Bai wrote: 'Tipsy, I snap a twig to make it a wine counter' – and as many as fifty silver counters were excavated in the hoard from Dingmaoqiao, Dantu, Jiangsu province.[28] Each one is incised with the amount of wine to be drunk as the penalty, and words from Confucius's analects. Courtesans were trained in the various drinking games but were also given advice on how to stop themselves becoming drunk: chewing cloves was one suggestion.[29]

All this shows how pivotal the Silk Routes were to much of Han and Tang dynasty life. The trade routes provided channels of communication reaching out beyond the realms of the familiar, native confines.[30] All manner of interactions developed from this, albeit relay trade or short-distance movement of goods and people from one trading community to another. As a result of such trade there was rich cultural cross-fertilization: religious and philosophical beliefs spread across the continents and the visual, performing and literary arts were all stimulated by outside influences. China's Tang dynasty benefited enormously from the material trade and foreign cultural influences, resulting in a period that can truly be called a Golden Age.

1 The Tang period was generally one of religious tolerance. An edict issued by Taizong in 638 stated:
   Truth bears not one name only.
   The sage is not one person only.
   Religions vary with the countries.
   Their influence benefits all beings.
   Quoted from Grantham 1927, p. 249; see Tang Huiyao, Shanghai guji chubanshe 1991, juan 49, p. 1011.
2 For general information on the Silk Route see: Beurdeley 1985; Boulnois 1966; Gray 1959; Hayashi 1975; Herman 1973; Hopkirk 1984; Hsia Nai 1983; Liu Liang-yu 1996; Mahler 1959; Maspero 1953; Pirazzoli t'Serstevens 1991; Schafer 1950, 1951, 1963, 1967; Schloss

1975; Shaanxi 1990; Singapore 1991; Stein 1907–33; S Whitfield 1999; Zou Zongxu 1991.
3 The route was in use in prehistoric times as is attested by excavations of paleolithic and neolithic cultures along it, and even Caucasian remains have been discovered. See Wilkinson 1998 for references. Chinese silk dating from earlier than the Han dynasty has been found in Bactria, showing that trade in silk across this area already existed.
4 See A F P Hulsewe (introduction by M Loewe), China in Central Asia, Leiden 1979, for a translation and commentary on this.
5 'At the lowest estimate, India, China, and Arabia Felix take away from our empire one hundred million sesterces a year: so much do the luxuries of our women cost us' (Hirth 1975, pp. 225–8). Many Roman writers refer to silk, and the expense of importing it. For references to these see S Lieberman, Contact between Rome and China, unpublished PhD thesis, Columbia University 1953.
6 Hong Kong 1993, p. 25; Schafer 1963, pp. 70–2.
7 The Parthians were one of the peoples who controlled the trade in silk between Rome and China and very jealously guarded their section (Hopkirk 1984, pp. 20–2).
8 For an introduction to this period, both historically and art historically, see S Whitfield 1999 and Juliano 1975.
9 Berger 1994, p. 17.
10 Schafer and Krieger 1967, p. 107.
11 Hong Kong 1993, p. 31.
12 Zou Zongxu 1991, p. 136.
13 Zou Zongxu 1991, p. 136.
14 Paludan 1991, pp. 118–19.
15 Schafer and Krieger 1967, p. 171.
16 Pulleyblank 1955 is a very good source on this rebellion.
17 See Schafer 1963, p. 20, for information on the changes in attitude to the foreigners in China after the An Lushan rebellion.
18 Hong Kong 1993, p. 30 and Boston 1976, pp. 94–5.
19 Hong Kong 1993, pp. 30–1.
20 Steinhardt 1990, pp. 101–2.
21 For information on the building and layout of Chang'an generally (and its influence on other East Asian cities) see Steinhardt 1990, pp. 93–121.
22 Berger 1994, p. 17.
23 Schafer 1963, pp. 20–1.
24 Hong Kong 1993, p. 28.
25 Capon and Foreman 1989, p. 102.
26 For information on polo, see cat. no. 40.
27 Schafer 1963, pp. 28–9.
28 See Beijing 1992a, p. 314 for an illustration of this drinking tally; also Jiangsu 1982, Liu and Liu 1982.
29 Schafer 1963, p. 172.
30 S Akiner, in The Significance of the Silk Roads in the History of Human Civilizations, Collection of Papers presented at the International Seminar, Independent Seminar, Osaka, Japan, 1992, pp. 27–30.

46

46 Figure on horseback

Tang dynasty (AD 618–906)
Pottery
Height 30.8 cm; length 21.1 cm
Excavated 1972, tomb of Princess Yongtai, Gan county, Shaanxi province
Shaanxi History Museum

This glazed pottery sculpture of a man on horseback probably depicts a foreigner hunting. The calm attentive stance of the horse contrasts with the dramatic action in the saddle, where the rider appears to have turned abruptly, his right arm raised to ward off a snarling cheetah as it grabs his clothing and the saddle.[1] The saddle is equipped with stirrups, which by now were in common use, but there seems to be no girth to steady them.

The rider's swarthy appearance, his large nose and his thick beard suggest that he was one of the many foreigners, or *hu ren*, from the western regions, living in Chang'an. Other excavated pottery examples of these foreigners indicate that most were engaged in business and transportation, or that they were musicians, craftsmen and servants. At the height of the Tang period there were about four thousand families of foreigners in Chang'an. The book *Tai ping guang ji,*[2] which records numerous strange anecdotes relating to the Tang period, includes many about foreigners from countries such as Persia and Arabia.

During the Tang dynasty Chang'an was a cosmopolitan city of over one million people (see fig. 7, p. 32). It was particularly important as the Asian end of the Silk Road that linked Asia with Europe. The Tang dynasty established friendly relations with over three hundred countries connected with the trade along this route and many foreigners lived and worked in Chang'an. They lived in establishments such as the Hong Lu Si Temple and Li Bin Yuan hostel, both set up by the government. The association of Tang China with foreigners has not been forgotten: even today Overseas Chinese communities are described as living in *Tang ren jie,* street of the Tang people.

In the Tang dynasty foreigners regularly participated in equestrian sports such as hunting and polo. Hunters were often assisted by animals which were brought to China as tribute from the West, from places such as southern India, Bukhara, Samarkand and Persia (see fig. 22, pp. 82–3), mainly in the first half of the eighth century. It was common practice in these places to train animals such as cheetahs, leopards and dogs, and birds such as goshawks and falcons, for hunting. The cheetah and the leopard were particularly adept at hunting antelope and were used by the Sumerians for this purpose. Depictions of cheetahs in hunting scenes appear in Egyptian art of the eighteenth and the nineteenth dynasties. They were also used in India, Persia, Armenia and Abyssinia and more recently in Germany in the seventeenth century and France in the eighteenth.[3] Sun Ji asserts that the cheetah was extensively used for hunting in ancient China.[4] From the Han dynasty he describes some depictions of cheetahs used for hunting, such as on a lacquered pot from a Western Han tomb. There are no depictions of them from the Han to the Tang and they are rarely mentioned in literary texts of Tang dynasty China so their use was probably restricted to court circles. If the animal grabbing the rider in this sculpture is a hunting cheetah it is therefore fairly unusual.

Published: W Watson 1973, no. 275; Osaka 1987, no. 78; Wang Renbo 1990, p. 306, no. 9; Kuhn 1993, no. 23; Xi'an 1997, p. 75; *Daito Bunmei ten* 1998, no. 56.

1 The use of cheetahs in hunting in the Tang dynasty is also clearly depicted in tomb murals: see that from Prince Zhanghuai (Li Xian, AD 654–684) illustrated in Boston 1976, pp. 90–3; and the tomb of Prince Yide, *ibid*. p. 114, fig. 134. See also Schafer 1963, pp. 87–8, who says that trained hunting animals accustomed to hunting with cheetahs were imported from Samarkand and are mentioned in a list of tribute offerings presented by that country in AD 713.
2 This book, 'The Extensive Gleanings of the Reign of Great Tranquility', is a huge compendium compiled during the Taiping reign (976–83) by imperial order. It is important as a compendium of early fiction and widely valued as a source for many non-literary disciplines as well (Nienhauser 1986, p. 744, and Dudbridge 1995).
3 Schafer 1963, p. 88.
4 Sun Ji, *Shoucangjia*, vol. 27, 1998.1, pp. 18–21, and an abbreviated translation in English, *China Archaeology and Art Digest*, vol. 3, no. 1, Hong Kong, April 1999, pp. 145–6.

47 Figure of a foreigner

Tang dynasty (AD 618 –906)
Pottery with *sancai* (three-colour) glaze
Height 56.5 cm; weight 3.4 kg
Excavated 1976, Hongqing village, northern suburbs of Xi'an, Shaanxi province
Xi'an City Cultural Relics Storehouse

This ceramic figure represents one of the many non-Han Chinese of the Tang period, possibly one of the minority peoples living

in the western regions of China at that time. In the Tang dynasty China and the western regions were intimately connected by the Silk Road (see fig. 22, pp. 82–3). Diplomats, merchants and travellers came and went along these routes and one of the principal means of transport was the camel. Many of the pottery figures buried in Tang tombs, particularly those with camels and those shown riding or hunting, have foreign features.[1]

This figure is standing with his head raised, as if turned towards the camel that he would have been leading by the reins once held in his hands. He wears a scarf on his head, has deep-set eyes, a large nose and a full beard. His undergarment has a round neck, and the outer jacket, with short narrow sleeves and green-glazed left lapel, is belted and has a small bottle suspended from it. Wide starched lapels seem to be a speciality of camel drivers. His outer garment is brown glazed and he wears high boots into which would be fitted tight trousers. He stands on a rectangular platform. His features proclaim him to be a Central Asian, possibly a Sogdian. The features of these foreigners seem to be based on recognized ideal models.

Servants featured highly amongst the pottery figures found in the tombs of the Tang dynasty. Among the most evocative are the camel trainers and their mounts,[2] most of whom, as this one, stand with right hand raised to clasp a rope tether (which has disintegrated over time). His full beard and confident stance set him apart from most representations of Chinese native servants, probably suggesting his important associations with exotic animals and trading commodities.

Foreign traders came from many Central Asian countries, but particularly from Persia and Arabia (Dashi), and often took up permanent residence. Many were jewellers or owned food, wine or pawn shops, and some ran banks and even acted as Chinese

47

government emissaries. The growth of foreign trade in the Tang dynasty led to the establishment of special institutions such as a protocol department to receive foreign visitors. This department also provided specially trained interpreters and some travellers were even given expenses for their return journeys. Of the two markets in

Chang'an, the Western Market in particular attracted foreigners.

Published: Edinburgh 1996, cat. no. 88, p. 60.

1 For detailed information about foreigners portrayed in ceramic form during the Tang dynasty see Mahler 1959.
2 W Watson 1984, p. 183.

48

48 Money chest

Tang dynasty (AD 618–906)
Pottery with *sancai* (three-colour) glaze
Height 13 cm; width 16 cm; thickness 12 cm
Excavated 1955, tomb 90, Wangjiafen village, eastern suburbs of Xi'an, Shaanxi province
Shaanxi History Museum

This rectangular money chest has four legs and a lid. It is decorated with a *sancai* (three-colour) glaze in blue, brown and cream. On the front of the chest are two rings which would have held a padlock (see cat. no. 94), and on the edge of the lid is a small hole through which coins could have been inserted. The legs of the chest are decorated with small flower appliqués, and the sides with lion masks. Such chests have prototypes going back to the Han dynasty.[1]

This chest, when excavated,[2] was found placed in front of a *sancai* figure of an elegant woman, whose role may have been to guard the chest. Presumably the inclusion of such an item in a tomb expressed the desire of the occupant to enter the afterlife with the means to acquire all that was needed. The money trees of the Han dynasty fulfilled a similar role (see cat. no. 55).[3]

Published: Venice 1986, no. 98; Wang Renbo 1990, p. 107, no. 7; Xi'an 1992, p. 85; Kuhn 1993, no. 39; Xi'an 1997, p. 92; *Empress Wu* 1998, no. 67.

1 *Kaogu xuebao* 1965.1, p. 142.
2 For a report on this tomb see *Wenwu cankao ziliao*, 8, 1956, p. 31. For a similar example see Christies catalogue, Los Angeles, 4 December 1998, no. 71.
3 For information on money trees see Rawson 1996a, cat. no. 87, p. 177; Erickson 1994b.

49 Byzantine coin

Justin I (AD 518–527)
Gold
Diameter 2 cm; weight 4.1 g
Excavated 1988, Xianyang International Airport building site, Xi'an, Shaanxi province
Shaanxi Archaeological Institute

The obverse of this coin, a gold solidus of the Byzantine empire, depicts a bust of the emperor Justin I, wearing a military helmet decorated with a crest of feathers. Pearls hang from both sides of the helmet by his cheeks. In his right hand is a spear, the end of which appears behind his left cheek, and in his left a shield decorated with a horseman. The emperor is wearing a collar, the edge of which is dotted with strings of pearls, a popular motif at that time. The Latin inscription around the coin starts by his right hand: 'DNIVSTI – NVSPPAVG'. The inscription gives the emperor's name and titles (in Latin the letter U is written V);

some words have been abbreviated:
D: dominus (lord), N: noster (our),
PP: perpetuus (everlasting),
AVG: Augustus (emperor).

The reverse of the coin depicts symbols of Christianity: a winged angel with a cross in his right hand and an orb surmounted by a small cross in his left. The Latin inscription encircling the angel, 'VICTORIAAVGGGB', means 'Victory of the emperors, workshop B'. Under his feet is another line of inscription, 'CONOB' (Constantinopolis Obryziacum), meaning 'pure gold coin of the Constantinople Mint'.

In the economics section of the *Sui shu* (History of the Sui dynasty) it is stated that 'In the Northern Zhou period from 557– 580, in the western regions of the Yellow River, Western money was not forbidden by the government'. The Western money referred to may have included coins such as this one from the Eastern Roman empire and Sasanian silver coins. During the Tang

49 obverse

49 reverse

dynasty Chang'an was one of the main starting points of the Silk Road (see fig. 22, pp. 82–3). The numerous foreign coins found in Tang tombs can be seen as evidence of one of the many exchange systems that existed between China and the West.[1]

There are two holes on this coin to either side of the head of the emperor. The coin was found beside the neck of Henuoshi, the wife of Shuguo, an aristocrat of the Tang dynasty, which would suggest that it was used as a pendant rather than as currency, as some are today.[2]

1 Silk was being traded from China to Rome as early as the first century BC (see note 5, p. 85).
2 The tomb of the little princess, Li Jingxun (600–608), excavated in 1957 outside Xi'an, had two hundred burial goods. One item was a Sasanian silver coin of the ruler Peroz (459–84), also pierced at the rim as if for use as a pendant: *Kaogu* 1959.9, pp. 471–2. I am grateful to Joe Cribb, of the Department of Coins and Medals, British Museum, for his help with all the coin entries.

50 Islamic coin

Dinar AH 83 (AD 702)
Gold
Diameter 2 cm; weight 4.3 g
Excavated 1964, Nitrogen Fertilizer Factory, western suburbs of Xi'an, Shaanxi province
Shaanxi History Museum

This is an Islamic gold dinar struck in AH 83 (AD 702), probably at Damascus during the Umayyad dynasty (AD 661–750).[1]

There are several inscriptions on this coin: on the obverse 'There is no God but Allah, he has no partner', and in the margin 'Muhammad is the Prophet of God sent with guidance and the religion of truth to make it prevail over every other religion, averse although idolaters may be' (Qur'an, *sura* 9 v. 33). On the reverse is 'God is alone, God is eternal, he begets not nor is he begotten, nor is there anyone like unto him' (Qur'an, *sura* 112) and in the margin 'In the name of God, this dinar was struck in the

50 obverse

50 reverse

year 83' (AD 702). The obverse has the additional very interesting feature of scratched graffiti, in the form of Roman letters and numerals, possibly reading 'ANX'.

The Tang dynasty Chinese did not mint gold coins as currency but accepted them from abroad. Serindian (Chinese Turkestan) gold and silver coins, particularly from Kucha, circulated in China in the sixth century and were used in the Chinese protectorates of the West in the seventh and eighth centuries. The contemporary histories relate that Arabs used gold coins in commodity exchanges, and Islamic gold dinars seem to have been so used in Canton.[2]

In 751, Chinese troops led by the famous general Gao Xianzhi, of Korean origin, suffered a huge defeat at the hands of Muslim Arabs at the Battle of Talas River (in modern Afghanistan). This reversed their victories of 747 when General Gao had defeated the Tibetans and taken control of the Tarim Basin. The basin reverted to Tibetan control and shortly afterwards the entire region fell permanently into Muslim hands. (A by-product of the Battle of Talas River was that the Arabs captured many workers in Chinese paper factories at Talas and learnt the art of making paper, which the Chinese had been doing since at least the second century BC. Europeans did not learn how to make paper until more than three

centuries after the Arabs, as the Arabs withheld the secret so as to make money from the sale of the commodity.) Although the Muslims took control in Central Asia they subsequently came to the help of the Chinese government in suppressing the revolt of An Lushan in 755 (see p. 62). On the other hand, Arab pirates were involved in the sacking of Canton in 758.[3]

This coin was found in Xi'an so it may have belonged to one of the foreign missions stationed there. Alternatively it may have been given as a present to a Tang nobleman or woman, as gold coins seem to have been cherished as ornaments by the Chinese of this period.[4]

1 As identified by Xia Nai (Hsia Nai) in *Kaogu xuebao* 1965.8, p. 420.
2 Schafer 1963, p. 257.
3 Schafer 1951, p. 407.
4 I am grateful to Venetia Porter of the Department of Coins and Medals, British Museum, for her help with this entry.

51 Japanese coins

Nara period (AD 710–794)
Silver
Diameter 2.3 cm; weights 6 g, 5.8 g
Excavated 1970, Hejiacun village, southern
suburbs of Xi'an, Shaanxi province
Shaanxi History Museum

51

These are Japanese silver round coins with a central square hole. There are four Chinese characters, '*He tong kaizhen*' (Japanese *Wadō kaichin*, meaning 'opening coin of the Wado period'), around the hole written in *lishu*, or clerical script. This coin dates from the reign of the emperor Gemmei of the Nara period and is one of the first coins issued in Japan. It was based on the Chinese *Kaiyuan tongbao* coins of the Tang dynasty (see cat. no. 92) in shape and weight and in the way the character *kai* was written. Unlike the silver *Kaiyuan tongbao* presentation coins, however, this Japanese silver coin was made for currency use. Japan's rich resources of silver encouraged the import of Japanese coins into China. With this supply of silver from Japan, together with supplies from Sasanian and early Arab Iran, China was able to adopt silver as part of its monetary system. Most of the imported coins were melted and recast into tax ingots.

By the Tang period there were numerous contacts between Japan and China. At the beginning of the dynasty, after a lapse of more than a century, there were two hundred Japanese participating in diplomatic missions and by the end of the Tang dynasty up to six hundred came at one time. The Japanese conceived of these missions as being from one equal to another and never conceded any superiority to the Chinese emperor, which explains why they were such large-scale affairs. The last mission went out in 838 (with the Buddhist monk Ennin who wrote a diary of his visit) and from then until the nineteenth century there was little official contact between the governments of the two countries.[1]

Several Japanese students spent many years in China during the Tang dynasty and returned to make significant contributions to Japanese culture in due course, aware of the benefits to be derived from a greater knowledge and mastery of many of the intellectual aspects of Chinese civilization. The Japanese emperor Kōtoku, when he launched the Taika Reforms in the seventh century, was assisted by Kuromaro Takamuku and others who had studied for many years in China. During this period many skills, including those of metal smelting, ceramic making and silk weaving, were transmitted to Japan, and the Japanese also absorbed much from China, particularly relating to ancient Chinese literature, Buddhist scriptures, the Chinese arts of calligraphy and painting, traditional medicine, architecture, music, dance and poetry. Chang'an itself acted as a model for other cities in the East and both Nara and Kyoto were built according to the same architectural plan. The Japanese came to China primarily on diplomatic visits rather than to trade. However, they certainly purchased medicines and incense which they appear to have paid for with gold dust

that they brought with them and then exchanged for Chinese copper coins.[2] It was not entirely a one-sided relationship though, as China imported from Japan amber, agate, pearls and hemp. However, by the time the last embassy had returned to Japan, the Japanese were in a position to adapt and transform what they had so enthusiastically learnt from the Chinese into something distinctly Japanese.

These coins, imported into China as silver bullion, are therefore an example of the Japanese adoption of a Chinese institution resulting from Japan's cultural contacts with Tang China.

1 In 1401 Yoshimitsu opened negotiations with the Ming dynasty Chinese court about the problem of piracy and received from the Ming emperor the title of King of Japan. Further missions involving large gifts of coins to Japan took place in 1407, 1432, 1434, 1451, 1468, 1476, 1480, 1493, 1511, 1523, 1539, 1550: D M Brown, *Money Economy in Medieval Japan: A Study in the Use of Coins*, New Haven 1951, pp. 19–26.
2 Reischauer 1955, p. 82.

52 Dragon

Tang dynasty (AD 618–906)
Gilded bronze
Height 34 cm; length 28 cm; width 10 cm;
weight 2.78 kg
Excavated 1975, Caochangpo, Xi'an, Shaanxi
province
Shaanxi History Museum

This dragon is made of cast bronze, with an iron core, and it has been gilded. Its body is curved like a bow, thin and sinuous, and its long curling tail balances its bulging breast. Similar echoes can be seen in the S-shaped curve of the neck and of the tongue. The dragon's head is sinuous like its body and tail, and it has piercing eyes, sharp teeth and jagged whiskers. It stands on its front legs, which terminate in sharp talons, while its hind legs stretch up into the air. Rising above the front legs are pointed protuberances which could be wings, and on the neck and tail are two snail-like excrescences. This dragon embodies a virility and majesty which is entirely commensurate with its place in Chinese cosmology. It was excavated in Caochangpo and was probably a guardian animal for the residence above. Even today representations of dragons are buried in the foundations of buildings to ward off evil spirits.

In the histories and chronicles of China the birth of a great sage or an emperor was preceded by the appearance of dragons and phoenixes. When Confucius was born two azure dragons came down from the sky to his mother's house, and the birth of Wudi, the Han dynasty emperor (141–87 BC), was presaged by the appearance of dragons.[1] Han Wudi's dream of riding on six dragons into the sky to become an immortal became a popular image.

The beneficent dragon of the East is in complete contrast to its Western counterpart with its fiery nature and association with evil. In the East the dragon is associated with life and with fertility,

52

Fig. 52a *Rubbing of a dragon on a brick found at Maoling, tomb of the emperor Wudi, Han dynasty, 1st century BC. Length 75.6 cm.*

through its bringing of rain. The dragon is first mentioned in Chinese literature in the *Yijing*, which, though not a homogenous text but rather a series of accretions, took its initial form some time in the early Western Zhou period. According to the earliest

Chinese dictionary, *Shuowen jiezi*,[2] dragons can be visible or invisible, large or small, long or short, and bring clouds and rain. They are generally auspicious. Representations of the dragon appear from at least the Shang dynasty and possibly earlier: the image of a dragon can be seen on a pottery sherd from an Erlitou (*c.* 1700–1500 BC) site in Anshi in Henan province. The dragon is depicted on Shang bronzes and jades, and in written form on oracle bones. The Chinese dragon gradually became an insignia of royalty and dominion.[3] It came to represent the emperor, the son of heaven. The emperor's throne was called the dragon throne and his countenance the dragon's countenance. The dragon is also seen as a male symbol, one of vigour and fertility and therefore *yang*, as opposed to the female *yin*. It is the fifth creature in the Chinese zodiac and represents the East, the region of sunrise, of fertility, of spring rains. It is therefore a force for good. At Chinese New Year dragon dances are a common occurrence.

The image of the dragon changed over time. The dragon of the pre-Qin dynastic period was simple and rugged. It generally had no limbs and looked more like a snake or serpent. Then in the Qin and Han dynasties the dragon became more of an animal, complete with limbs, and looked more like a tiger or a horse. It was often shown walking. Later still, in the Sui and Tang dynasties, it acquired an extremely long mouth and legs and its tail became more like that of a snake.[4]

However, the dragon is often a composite creature combining the powerful characteristics of a number of creatures: the head of a camel, the horns of a deer, the ears of an ox. It may have a bristling beard, tusks, or the scaly body of a serpent, with dorsal spines, a serpent's tail, four legs with tiger's paws and a hawk's talons. It often has flame-like appendages on its shoulders and hips. Its claws vary in number according to its rank, ordinary dragons having four claws and imperial dragons having five, but such rules were not always observed. From the Tang dynasty the auspicious qualities of the dragon meant that its image was often used to ornament buildings, furnishings and the

53

dress not only of the emperor but also of high officials. It was conspicuously displayed on imperial buildings, especially tombs such as that of the emperor Gaozong and his consort Wu Zetian (see fig. 53a).

Published: Osaka 1987, no. 109; Han Wei 1989, front cover; Xi'an 1992, p. 20; Kuhn 1993, no. 53; Li Xiyu 1994, no. 114; Guggenheim 1997, no. 59; Xi'an 1997, p. 19.

1 M W de Visser, *The Dragon in China and Japan*, 1969, reprint of 1913 German edn, p. 43.
2 The *Shuowen jiezi* is the first comprehensive dictionary of Chinese characters, compiled by Xu Shen (*c.* AD 55– *c.* 149). For bibliographic details on this work see Loewe 1993, pp. 429–42.
3 From at least the Han period texts the emperor seems to have been equated with the dragon. For dragons generally see: Werner 1961; Ball 1927; J-P Dieny, *Le Symbolisme du Dragon dans la Chine Antique*, Paris 1987; Eberhard 1986; H Munsterberg, *Symbolism in Ancient Chinese Art*, New York 1986; Rawson 1984a; J Cherry (ed.), *Mythical Beasts*, London 1995.
4 Rawson 1984b, pp. 93–4 for a general introduction to the history of the depiction of the dragon.

53 Dragon

Tang dynasty (AD 618–906)
Gilded bronze
Height 10.8 cm; length 18 cm; weight 245.2 g
Excavated 1979, handed in by the Xi'an Antiques Store
Xi'an City Cultural Relics Storehouse

This gilded bronze dragon is striding along, its head held high on a slender neck, its mouth revealing fangs and a curled tongue. Its pointed snout is matched by a pointed tuft at the back of its head, and it has a single horn and pricked-up ears. Its whiskers curl in the opposite direction to its tongue. Along its spine are zigzag protuberances which break up the sinuous curves of the body, legs and tail. The whole body is engraved with a fish-scale design and the talons have three claws.[1]

In Chinese mythology the dragon was regarded as a celestial animal and as a symbol of the emperor.[2]

Published: Hong Kong 1993, no. 46; Li Xiyu 1994, no. 115; Xi'an 1995, p. 12; *Daito Bunmei ten* 1998, no. 32.

1 For an earlier (Northern Wei, early sixth century AD) but stylistically similar dragon see Juliano 1975, no. 37.
2 See cat. no. 52 for further symbolism regarding Chinese dragons.

54 Dragon's head

Tang dynasty (AD 618–906)
Jade
Height 10.2 cm; length 18 cm; width 7.5 cm;
weight 1.93 kg
Excavated 1976, Tang Qujiang site, Qujiang
village, southern suburbs of Xi'an, Shaanxi
province
Xi'an Antiquities Protection and Archaeological
Institute

54

This large dragon finial has bulging eyes, a
pointed nose, and a wide open mouth baring
ferocious teeth. A pair of ridged horns arch
from behind the eyes, the ears are pinned
close to the head, and beneath them are
three sets of whiskers. The eyebrows curl
upwards. There is a small hole in the top of
the head and a groove under the base,
suggesting that the head was probably made
as a finial to fit into something. The red
around the mouth and eyes is probably the
pigment vermilion, which comes from
cinnabar, a red sulphide of mercury. This was
regarded as a sacred stone to the Daoists, for
whom its conversion into quicksilver
implied it could lead to the transmutation of
metals and the prolongation of life, as well
as being a drug for the treatment of diseases.
In many cultures, vermilion is regarded as
the colour of life and blood and eternity, and
it was applied to the bodies of the dead, and
objects for burial. Many ancient Chinese
jades were smeared with it.[1]

Qujiang Pond[2] was a famous scenic spot
in Chang'an (see fig. 7, p. 32) in the Tang
dynasty. It was originally dug in the reign of
Wudi in the Han dynasty, and had a zigzag
shape (which supposedly diverted evil
spirits), hence its name Qujiang which
means zigzag water. When the new site of
the capital, Chang'an, of the Sui dynasty was
chosen by an astrologer it was sited at the
foot of Longshou (Dragon Head) Mountain.
To balance the geomantic forces of this
northern mountain, Qujiang Pond was dug
again to the southeast of the city.[3] A number
of palaces and offices were built around the
pond, and with the nearby Furong Garden,
Leyou Garden, Ci'en Temple and Xing
Gardens, the area became a tourist
attraction. During the Tang dynasty
successful examination candidates would go
boating on the pond after signing their
names at the Greater Wild Goose Pagoda in
Chang'an and the imperial family would
come on spring outings.[4]

As this finial was excavated from the
bottom of Qujiang Pond it is possible that it
was a decorative fitting from a royal boat.[5] It
is somewhat similar in style to the ceramic
roof tiles commonly used in China not only
to ornament but also to protect a building.
Imperial tombs and palace sites from as
early as the sixth century AD often had ridge
tiles in the shape of water dragons with
serpentine or fish tails. This jade dragon's
head may well have had a protective as well
as a decorative role.[6]

Published: Song Yanyan 1991, no. 24; Yang Boda
1986, no. 44; Li Xiyu 1994, no. 106.

1 Schafer 1967, pp. 156–7.
2 For a map of Chang'an showing Qujiang
Pond see Steinhardt 1990, fig. 81.
3 Steinhardt 1990, p. 94.
4 Zou Zongxu 1991, p. 291.
5 A similar stone dragon's head, dated to the
Tang dynasty, can be seen in Li Xiyu 1994,
fig. 120. A later dragon-head finial for
comparison can be found in Chung Wah-Pui
1996, no. 128, p. 148.
6 Kerr 1999, pp. 15–21.

*Fig. 53a Dragon
incised on a stone
slab from the
Qianling tomb of
Emperor Gaozong
and his consort Wu
Zetian. Tang
dynasty, 7th–8th
century AD.*

55 Two trees

Tang dynasty (AD 618 –906)
Gold
Heights 13.5 cm, 11.5 cm; total weight 8.7 g
Excavated 1971, tomb at Guo Jiatan, Xi'an,
Shaanxi province
Xi'an City Cultural Relics Storehouse

Although these two gold trees are slightly different in shape and height, both are composed of twisting trunks and branches with leaves and blossoms. There are nodules on the trunks and the roots sprout vine tendrils which curl upwards around the trunk. The combination of the strong trunk and the thinner tendrils is particularly attractive. The bases are quite thin and have been hammered into shape. The flowers were originally set with turquoises.[1]

Trees bearing jewels are widely known in other Asian civilizations. The Indian description 'silver trunk, gold branches, emerald leaves, pearls for fruits' was possibly most influential in China and the Tang dynasty poet Guanxiu envisaged jewelled trees with leaves of jade and branches of gold in the garden of his patron the king of Shu.[2] Trees which bear golden pears and peaches have been regarded as examples of the universal gem-tree, which is the tree of wisdom, the tree of life, the world-tree. The *Xijing zaji,*[3] which depicts the brilliance and luxury of the Han dynasty emperor Wudi's court (141–87 BC), describes the imperial hunting park planted with ten trees of white silver and ten of yellow silver. A ruler of the Liang dynasty also described silver trees and jade peaches.

The designing of real and miniature gardens, or *penjing,* was a practice well developed by the Tang dynasty, as can be seen in a mural from the tomb of Li Xian who died in 706.[4] Miniature gardens were arranged in basins, comprising either real plants and trees or artificial ones composed of precious materials such as jade, ivory and coral. The Japanese practice of cultivating bonsai, artificially dwarfed plants, owes its origin to these Chinese miniature gardens.

The idea of burying bronze trees for use in the afterlife dates back at least to the Han dynasty. Typical of Sichuan province and southwest China, the majority date to the late Han period.[5] These so-called money trees of bronze consisted of a trunk from which sprouted many branches, each bearing depictions of Daoist immortals who had associations with the afterlife. On the branches were replicas of the contemporary coinage, the idea presumably being that the deceased person would have access to endless supplies of money in the afterlife. Perhaps these trees, which are of gold rather than bronze and date from the Tang dynasty, had a broader significance than simply providing access to wealth. They may also have embodied the concept of Enlightenment if they were associated with the *bodhi* tree and Buddhism. Trees and plants played a prominent part in Buddhist paintings as the tree was the image most often used to represent the presence of the Buddha before he was shown in human form. (In many narrative scenes he sits enthroned under the *bodhi* tree where he gained Enlightenment). The shape of trees in many Tang paintings is similar to that of these golden trees.[6]

Published: Beijing 1990, no. 122; Wang Renbo 1990, p. 175, no. 18.

1 Beijing 1990, no. 122.
2 E Schafer, 'Mineral Imagery in the Paradise Poems of Kuan-Hsiu' (Guanxiu), *Asia Major*, vol. 10, pp. 85–6.
3 *Xijing zaji*, a miscellany on institutions and events linked to Chang'an. Possibly some material is as old as the purported author, Liu Xin (died AD 23), but some is as late as AD 500. *Xijing zaji*, Shanghai guji chubanshe, 1991, juan 1, p. 6.
4 J Hay, *Kernels of Energy, Bones of Earth:The Rock in Chinese Art*, New York 1986, p. 76; Sullivan 1980, p. 29. For miniature landscapes or *penjing*, see Boston 1976, pl. 123, p. 100; and for images of trees as painted in tomb murals see *ibid.* pls 131, 135, pp. 110, 115.
5 Rawson, 1996a, no. 87, p. 177.
6 For example, see the trees in *Buddha Preaching the Law*, Stein painting 6, in Whitfield 1982–3, vol. 1, pl. 7.

56 Twenty-two inlay decorations

Tang dynasty (AD 618–906)
Silver and gold
Lengths 1.6–10.5 cm; widths 1.1–9 cm; total weight 44.1 g
Excavated 1991, Yuanzitou village, Chengguan town, Long county, Shaanxi province
Shaanxi Long County Museum

One hundred and ninety of these inlay decorations were found in 1991 and twenty-two are displayed here. They would have been hammered into shape and then inlaid into lacquered wooden boxes which have since disintegrated, leaving only fragmentary traces of their existence. The inlays can be divided into three groups. The first group consists of two lions, two tigers, two leopards and two unicorns, all jumping, running or standing, and all with their mouths open and their paws raised. Those that are jumping are biting fiercely and grabbing at something. Their animated eyes are bulbous, their teeth and fangs exposed. It is possible that they are guardian animals of some kind. The second group is

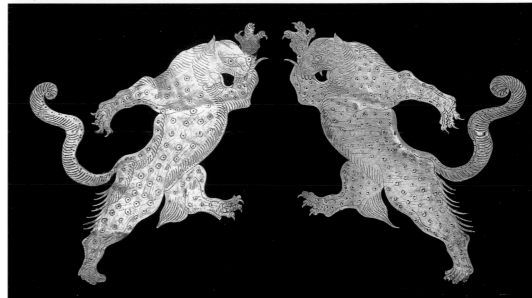

56

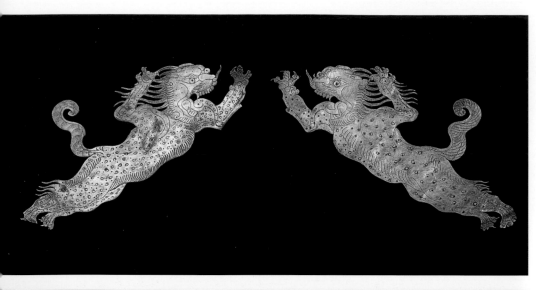

56

more pastoral in character: two are landscape scenes with five flying geese, beneath which are two sunflowers and baskets of flowers. On either side are two pairs of dancing geese. The third group consists of two figures flying with tridents or spears in their hands. There are golden flowers between them. These may also have been guardian figures of some sort.[1]

Similar thinly worked figures[2] in silver have holes in them and may have been sewn on to a textile background. Some were inlaid into the backs of *pingtuo*[3] mirrors, a technique practised from the Six Dynasties period.[4] Precious metals were often set into lacquered boxes, as is evident with these inlays.[5]

There are, for example, several lacquered boxes set with gold and silver inlays of flowers, birds and clouds in the Shōsō-in treasury in Nara, Japan, and Yang Guifei is said to have given An Lushan a lidded box ornamented with precious stones and golden inlays.[6]

1 I am grateful to Professor Glen Dudbridge for this suggestion.
2 See, for example, Singer 1972, no. 52 , p. 44; British Museum, Hotung Gallery, case 26, no. 26; Kelley 1984, pp. 91–3, nos 59–61; and phoenixes: Gyllensvärd 1953, no. 123, p. 19 and no. 43a, p. 100.
3 The *pingtuo* technique consists of cut-outs from thin sheets of gold and silver inlaid into a smooth lacquer surface. It was popular during Xuanzong's reign but Suzong (r. 756–62) forbade its manufacture as too costly after the devastation of the country during the An Lushan rebellion. J Watt, *East Asian Lacquer, The Florence and Herbert Irving Collection*, The Metropolitan Museum of Art, New York 1991, pp. 20–1.
4 A G Bulling, *The Decoration of Mirrors of the Han Period: A Chronology,* Artibus Asiae Supplementum XX, Ascona, Switzerland 1960, pl. 74 and p. 89.
5 For example, a recent archaeological report on the Chen family tomb at Luoyang, Tang dynasty, shows the silver inlays still inset into the remains of the lacquered surface. See *Wenwu* 1999.2, colour pls 4 and pp. 41–51.
6 Cited in Schafer 1963, p. 252.

57

57 Stem cup

Tang dynasty (AD 618 – 906)
Gold
Height 6.3 cm; diameter of mouth 7 cm; weight 170 g
Excavated 1965, White Temple village, southern suburbs of Xi'an, Shaanxi province
Shaanxi History Museum

This unfinished cup has a wide mouth and oval body. There are raised lines dividing the body into two parts, the lower part being slightly bulbous. The stem has a round nodule and a spreading foot. Such small oval-bodied cups were popular in Tang China.[1]

What precisely went wrong with the manufacturing process of this cup is unclear but the surface of the body is coarse and the stem beneath the body is very thin, as is the flat footrim. On the surface of the cup there are marks or drips of the gold liquid from the casting, indicating that technological errors were responsible for the failed casting.

This cup should perhaps be viewed in the same light as the block of jade buried in the Hejiacun hoard (cat. no. 93). Both were probably hidden because of their inherent value, the intention being to work on them at a later date when the owner was in a position to do so. Presumably there was insufficient time to melt down the cup

before the impending emergency, perhaps the An Lushan rebellion of 755. It was therefore buried in this unfinished state.

Published: Xi'an 1995, p. 3; *Daito Bunmei ten* 1998, no. 83.

1 This cup is similar in shape to the gold stem cup found in the tomb of the Sui princess, Li Jingxun (AD 600–608), *Kaogu* 1959 9, p. 472, pl. 3, fig. 9.

58

58 Dish

Tang dynasty (AD 618–906)
Silver
Diameter 55 cm; weight 3.35 kg
Excavated 1962, Kengdi village, northern suburbs of Xi'an, Shaanxi province
Shaanxi History Museum

This large six-petalled, lobed dish has a wide flared mouth and rim and a flat base. It has been hammered into shape and engraved with gilded designs. The central roundel of floral sprays with two flying phoenix, their heads and tails symmetrically arranged, is surrounded by six clusters of alternating flowers and leaves. The lobed rim of the dish is outlined with two bands, within which are twelve alternating groups of decoration, made up of two birds with either butterflies or flowers in their mouths, and flower medallions.

The phoenix was the symbol of the empress in China, the dragon being that of the emperor. The Western legend of the phoenix reborn from ashes was unknown to

the Chinese and our use of the word phoenix refers to two different Chinese birds, the Red Bird of the South,[1] the *zhu niao*, and the *fenghuang*, a mythical bird with lavish plumage which came to be paired with the dragon. The Red Bird of the South may have been associated with the good omens that the appearance of red birds was thought to signify.[2] Chinese buildings were traditionally aligned on a north–south axis with their doors facing south and the Red Bird represented this direction.

On the base of the dish is a forty-one-character inscription. This tells us that the gilded silver plate was a gift to Tang Dezong from Pei Su, an official of Zhedong province (near modern Shanghai), between 799 and 802.[3] It is recorded in the *Xin Tang shu* (new Tang history) that Pei Su had such an outstanding record for fighting crime in his area that he was rewarded by the emperor with an important official post in Zhedong province.[4]

Gold and silver items were considered very prestigious and acceptable gifts to be given to the emperor or received from him. Officials would present gifts of this kind as a means of gaining favour and this dish, of such exceptional size and beauty, would have been an appropriate offering to someone in a high position. Several such inscriptions on gifts of dishes and ingots from high officials to the emperor are recorded in the eighth and ninth centuries. These indicate that the imperial household led the fashion for using silver vessels for eating and drinking.[5]

Published: Tokyo 1981, no. 179; Han and Lu 1985, no. 153; Wang Renbo, 1990, p.168, no. 4; Hong Kong 1993, no. 43; Xi'an 1995, p. 12; Shanghai 1996, p. 112, no. 77.

1 See cat. no. 25, p. 55 for reference to the animals of the four directions.
2 Rawson 1984b, p. 99 and fig. 80.
3 Lu Zhaoyin, *Kaogu* 1983.2, p. 174.
4 *Xin Tang shu*, Zhonghua shuju edn, 1975, juan 182, p. 5371. He is also mentioned in a Qing

dynasty compilation: *Siku quanshu*, Shanghai guji chubanshe, vol. 396, p. 224 and vol. 546, p. 555.
5 Rawson 1986b, pp. 48–50 lists the hoards that contain silver vessels with *jinfeng* (dedication) inscriptions. Such inscriptions, which end with the character *jin*, record the presentation of silver vessels or silver ingots by high officials, presumably in return for favours received. These offerings went to the palace for the emperor's use and two special storehouses were established in 784 to receive them. Many such pieces were perhaps presented to the emperor who then gave them to other officials and courtiers. The inscribed piece given by Pei Su is noted on p. 50.

59 Cup

Tang dynasty (AD 618–906)
Gold
Height 3.5 cm; diameter (of mouth) 13.1 cm, diameter (of foot) 7 cm; weight 174 g
Excavated 1983, Tai yi road building site, Xi'an, Shaanxi province
Shaanxi History Museum

This shallow oval cup has four lobes and a footrim. It has been cast and hammered into shape and is decorated with engraved designs against a ring-punched ground. Two of the inner surfaces of the lobes are decorated with a floral bouquet flanked by floral and leaf sprays, and the other two with a more layered floral and leaf design also flanked by leafy sprays. The lobes are separated by a chain of petals, and the rim of the cup and the ring foot are both decorated with overlapping lotus petals.

The central motif of the cup is a *mojie* or *makara* chasing a flaming pearl. It is set against engraved waves and surrounded by one ring of pearls and another of overlapping lotus leaves. The *mojie* or *makara* is a monster with the head of a dragon and the body of a fish. It has its origins in Asian and Indian mythology where it is considered to be a spirit of river water and the origin of life.[1] The appearance of a *mojie* on a Chinese object shows the influence of Buddhism. *Mojie* appear in China around the end of the

Fig. 58a Drawing of the decoration.

Fig. 58b Rubbing of the Red Bird of the South from a brick found at the Maoling tomb of the emperor Wudi, Han dynasty, 1st century BC. Length 1.6 m.

59

fourth century AD and, according to the *sūtras*[2] brought to China at that time, particularly during the Eastern Jin period, the *mojie* was a vicious creature that would destroy ships and harm humans. The *mojie* on this object is very different from the early versions brought from India, as the gradual sinicization of Buddhism caused the *mojie* to adopt the characteristics of a Chinese sturgeon. This *mojie* seems to be fairly benign, and to have acquired a flaming pearl, more usually associated with the Chinese dragon. Many Buddhist examples of the *mojie* were known to Tang craftsmen and

a number of Tang dynasty silver dishes have been found with it depicted on them, such as a late eighth-century dish excavated in the Karachin banner, Liaoning province,[3] and one from the hoard at Dingmaoqiao in Dantu, Jiangsu province.

The cup is related in shape to the lacquered oval eared cups of the Han dynasty (see cat. no. 91), many of which were used for drinking wine. Before Zhang Qian introduced grapes to China from the western regions in the second century BC, Chinese wine had been made first from fermented cereals and then from rice which

became the staple source of alcohol.[4] Grape seeds were sown in China and the resulting grapes were at first considered a great delicacy. It was not until the Tang dynasty that they were used on any important scale for making wine, and even then grape wine was probably restricted to the wealthy and to the court. It is known that Yang Guifei drank grape wine, and clusters of grapes were familiar enough to become a common decoration on bronze mirrors and later on ceramics. This cup made of gold and decorated so beautifully must have belonged to a member of the court or the aristocracy, and it may have been for wine.

Published: Beijing 1987, no. 308; Wang Renbo 1990, p. 159, no.11; Kuhn 1993, no.61; Shanghai 1996, p. 109, no. 67; *Daito Bunmei ten* 1998, no. 21.

1 *Makara* are carved in early Buddhist caves at Ajanta in India; a Gupta example from Sarnarth is in the British Museum, and is illustrated in M Archer, 'Benares and British Art' in *Chhavi*, Golden Jubilee Volume, Benares 1971, pp. 43–7, fig. 186. Also see Soothill and Hodous 1975, p. 436; *Kaogu* 1980.1, pp. 59–65, fig. 3.
2 Literally a thread and refers to Hindu or Buddhist scriptures strung together as a sermon.
3 *Kaogu* 1977.5, pp. 327–34, fig. 3.
4 Schafer 1963, pp. 141–5.

60 Ewer and cover

Tang dynasty (AD 618–906)
Gold
Height 21.3 cm; diameter (of mouth) 6.6 cm, (of foot) 6.6 cm; weight 800 g
Excavated 1969, North West Medical Instruments Factory building site, Xianyang, Shaanxi province
Xianyang Museum

This is the only gold ewer of such a shape to be found so far and so it is unique. It has a deep body with round shoulders, and a straight neck with lid. Its squat straight-mouthed spout contrasts with the thin,

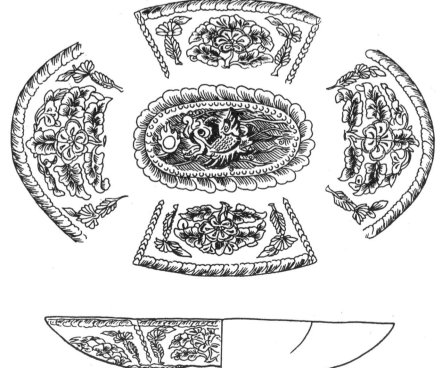

Fig. 59a *Details of the decoration.*

60

pairs of mandarin ducks; the third has interlocking plants and a continuous cloud pattern; and the fourth has three layers of lotus petals facing upwards, standing out in relief. The decoration is dense, the whole a masterpiece of goldworking techniques, and oddly reminiscent of later Song and even Ming ceramics with their layered decoration.[1]

Pouring vessels in the Tang dynasty tended gradually to become less squat and more elongated in shape.[2] Such vessels were often used for wine and continued to be popular into the Song and Yuan dynasties for this purpose.[3]

The Tang dynasty poet Li Bai, in a poem entitled 'Hard is the Journey' which is a melancholy harking back to happier times in the empire, talks of:

Gold vessels of fine wines,
Thousands a gallon,
Jade dishes of rare meats,
Costing more thousands...[4]

Published: Han and Lu 1985, no. 259; Beijing 1992a, no. 296; Xi'an 1995, p. 25; Shanghai 1996, p. 104, no. 54.

1 The decoration is organized somewhat similarly to that of the tenth-century phoenix-headed ewer in the British Museum, Hotung Gallery, case 27, OA 1936.10-12.206.
2 M Beurdeley, *A Connoisseur's Guide to Chinese Ceramics*, New York 1974, p. 102.
3 See the porcelain wine ewer and warming basin in the British Museum, Hotung Gallery, case 28, OA 1936.10-12.153.
4 Quoted in Cooper 1973, p. 136.

elegant, *ruyi*-shaped handle, each end of which is joined to the body with three rivets. A small tortoise at the top of the handle holds a chain made of gold wire that extends to the knob on the lid which is in the shape of a lotus bud.

The entire body of the ewer has exuberant decoration against a ring-punched background with creepers and vinescrolls. The knob is decorated with an eight-petalled flower under which are two layers of lotus petals. The decoration on the body of the ewer is divided into four horizontal bands: the first has interlocking plants aligned around four lotus flowers; the second has interlocking plants with four

61 Cup

Tang dynasty (AD 618–906)
Silver
Height 4.5 cm; diameter of mouth 5.2 cm
Excavated 1988, tomb of Wei Xun, Nanliwang village, Chang'an county, Shaanxi province
Shaanxi Archaeological Institute

This cylindrical wine cup has concave sides, flares widely at the mouth and stands on an everted footrim. The body of the cup has a

Fig. 60a *Detail of the decoration.*

62

pattern of flying geese and flowers, and above and below the main decoration are *ruyi*-shaped cloud decorations. The inside of the cup and the footrim are undecorated. Similarly shaped cups, but with a ring handle, are to be found in several collections including that of Carl Kempe[1] and the Metropolitan Museum of Art[2] and from the finds of Shapocun, in Xi'an, Shaanxi province.[3]

The handleless goblet was the favoured shape for a Chinese drinking vessel, although the foreign-inspired cup with a handle made a brief foray into the Chinese repertoire[4] (cat. nos 88–90). Cups with handles do not seem to have been made after the An Lushan rebellion in the mid-eighth century.

By the end of the seventh century

61

Chinese artists had adapted and sinicized many imports and decorative motifs of foreign origin. Both the shape and decoration of this cup are distinctly Chinese in character. The more naturalistic treatment of clouds and flowers and the looser, less symmetrical composition of the design all point to a Chinese idiom.

This cup was found in the grave of Wei Xun, the younger brother of Empress Wei of the powerful Wei family (see p. 61 and cat. no. 43). The cup shows considerable signs of wear.

Published: Hong Kong and Shaanxi 1993, no. 35.

1 Gyllensvärd 1953, cat. no. 90, p. 143.
2 Metropolitan Museum of Art, 1974.274.1, gift of John M Crawford Jr in memory of Joseph H Heil.
3 *Wenwu* 1964.6, p. 31 and pls 1:1–2.
4 Willetts 1965, p. 272.

62 *Guan*-marked white dish

Tang dynasty (AD 618–906)
Porcelain
Diameter of mouth 13.5 cm; height 3 cm; weight 99.8 g
Excavated 1985, Huoshaobi, northern suburbs of Xi'an, Shaanxi province
Xi'an City Cultural Relics Storehouse

These shallow petal-shaped dishes have thin rims and are finely potted. They are covered

inside and out with a white glaze which has a greenish tinge and is shiny and lustrous. The ringed foot on each dish was cut with a knife and the bases are engraved with the character *guan* (official). This character would have been incised after the glaze was applied but before firing. The elegant shape of the dishes is derived from a lacquer or silver prototype. Such high-fired ceramics made for daily use are in contrast to the thickly potted, highly colourful *sancai* (three-colour) pottery made for burial which is more commonly associated with the Tang dynasty. It seems very likely that the influence of lightweight lacquerware and the thin-walled silver dishes of the Tang, made from sheet metal rather than cast in moulds, influenced the much thinner late Tang and Song dynasty ceramics. Ceramic copies of metal prototypes were of course made for economic reasons as it was standard practice to make cheaper imitations of expensive fashionable vessels. It was also forbidden by law, although the law was not strictly adhered to, to bury items made of silver and gold and the Tang emperors tried several times to restrict the burial of precious materials. This was another reason why it was practicable to manufacture similar items in ceramic.

Fig. 62a *Detail of the inscription 'guan'.*

White wares were first used for ceremonial purposes in China in the Shang dynasty but from the end of that period (*c.* 1050 BC) until the late sixth century AD[1] they seem to have been made only rarely. During the Sui and Tang dynasties, however, white wares became the most technologically advanced ceramics and, when economic reasons caused ceramics to supersede bronze wares, their popularity increased even more. The two main white wares[2] of the time were made either at the Xing kilns in Neiqiu and Lincheng counties in Hebei province or at the Gongxian kilns in Henan province. In the Tang dynasty some white wares marked with the character *guan*, from the Xing kilns in Hebei province, became tribute items for the court.[3] Excavations at Daming Palace at Beimenwai, Xi'an, have revealed white sherds of the type produced at the Gongxian kilns in Henan, which corroborates the textual evidence of the period.[4] The hoard at Huoshaobi from where these two dishes came had thirty-three white *guan*-marked pieces and there are fewer than a hundred recorded such pieces from all sources.[5]

These white wares were much admired in their time and various Tang poems mention fine ceramics and their place in the tea ceremony.[6] The Tang poet Du Fu wrote: 'The fine white bowls surpass hoarfrost and snow', and they were doubtless used at court.[7] They are arguably the world's earliest porcelains, if the qualities of hardness, whiteness and translucence are taken as the defining characteristics of porcelain.[8]

Published: Song Yanyan 1991, no. 34; Guggenheim 1997, no. 126; *Daito Bunmei ten* 1998, no. 24.2; *Empress Wu* 1998, no. 106.

1 Li Jiazhi *et al.*, 'A study of Gongxian white porcelain of the Sui–Tang period', in Shanghai Institute of Ceramics, Academica Sinica, Scientific and Technological Insights on Ancient Chinese Pottery and Porcelain, Proceedings of the International Conference on Ancient Chinese Pottery and Porcelain, Beijing 1986, pp. 129–33.

2 J Harrison-Hall, 'Ding and Other White Wares of Northern China', in I Freestone and D Gaimster (eds), *Pottery in the Making*, London 1997, pp. 182–7. I am much indebted to Jessica Harrison-Hall for information regarding this entry.
3 This was a system under which foreign states submitted to Chinese suzerainty in exchange for gifts and trading privileges in China. From the Han dynasty the Chinese allowed non-Chinese states to retain their autonomy if they agreed to the symbolic sovereignty of the Han, through exchanges of gifts such as silk and intermarriages. However, even Chinese provinces were involved in a tributary system, which involved presenting gifts to the capital.
4 The provincial gazetteer *Yuanhe junxian zhi* states that in the Kaiyuan period (AD 713–42) Henan province offered white porcelain as tribute. Quoted from Vainker 1991, p. 64.
5 Berger 1994, fig. 57.
6 There is a whole chapter on the merits of various types of ceramic wares in the *Chajing* (Classic of Tea), by Lu Yü, AD 760. For further information on white wares see Kai-Yin Lo (ed.), *Bright as Silver, White as Snow: Chinese White Ceramics from Late Tang to Yuan Dynasty*, Hong Kong 1998.
7 Quoted in Paludan 1998, p. 105.
8 Vainker 1991, p. 66.

63 Set of twelve zodiacal animals

Tang dynasty (AD 618–906)
Pottery
Heights 22.2–30 cm
Excavated 1950, Ba Qiao, western suburbs of Xi'an, Shaanxi province
Shaanxi Beilin Museum

This set of twelve figurines with human bodies and animal heads represents the Chinese twelve-year cycle in which each year is associated with a specific animal: the rat, ox, tiger, hare (or rabbit), dragon, snake, horse, ram, monkey, rooster, dog and pig. In Chinese they are called *shengxiao*, meaning birth and resemblance, as it came to be believed that a person's character was influenced by the animal that symbolized the year of his or her birth. The belief also developed that through the Chinese zodiacal

system it was possible to gain insights into relationships with other people and the universe and therefore some understanding of one's fate.

Probably as early as the Western Zhou the zodiacal animals were associated with the Twelve Earthly Branches[1] which, in combination with the Ten Heavenly Stems, form a numbering system used to calculate the sixty-year cycle which is as important in Chinese history as the century is in the West. The earliest known reference that links the animals with the Twelve Earthly Branches dates from the early Eastern Zhou when in the *Shijing* (Book of Odes) and then in the *Zuo Zhuan*, a commentary appended to the Spring and Autumn annals, a historical work, a zodiacal animal and an Earthly Branch are mentioned together. A work of fortune telling, the *Ri Shu*, was discovered in 1975 in Shuihudi, Yunmeng prefecture, in a Qin dynasty tomb and the bamboo strips found there listed the first known systematic record of the twelve animals of the Chinese zodiac. Certainly by the Han dynasty they were well enough known[2] for a Confucian scholar of the time, Wang Chong, to criticize the geomancers for telling people's fortunes and making people rearrange their lives according to theories based on the combinations of the five elements and the resulting harmony or conflict between the animals of the zodiac.[3]

The earliest known pictorial representation of the cycle is in a Northern Wei tomb in Shandong province dating to 524.[4] By the Northern Zhou dynasty the custom of relating a person's year of birth to one of the twelve cyclical animals was established and by the Tang dynasty the calendrical animals were frequently used on epitaphs and engraved on funerary steles. Before the Tang the animal-represented duodenary cycle of nature was becoming common but the animal-headed human figures seem to have been a Tang invention. The practice was adopted in Chinese Buddhism as a fifth-century Buddhist text

63

found near Dunhuang in Gansu province refers to the animal cycle which was linked to the animals living in caves previously occupied by bodhisattvas.[5]

These Twelve Earthly Branches and the animals of the zodiac are also associated with the twelve two-hour intervals into which the Chinese traditionally divided the day and with the five elements – wood, fire, earth, metal and water – out of which all physical matter is supposed to originate. The animals are also associated with certain colours and directions. Each of the twelve animals also represents a specific hour, day, month and year of the cycle. To get a full understanding, therefore, of how a person is ruled by one of the twelve animals and to use the almanacs it is important to know details such as the animal of the year of birth, the lunar sign that ruled the hour of birth, and the element related to the year of birth. All of these are taken into consideration when the Chinese investigate their almanacs for divination purposes.[6]

There are several stories about the origin of the order in which the animals are placed. Popular ones include those that relate how the Jade Emperor asked to see Earth's twelve most interesting animals on the first day of the first lunar month,[7] and one of the gods meeting the rat asked him to pass the invitation on to the other eleven, saying that the first to arrive would be made king of the animals. The invitations were duly accepted by the twelve animals chosen. The ox set off very early on the appointed day but the rat jumped on to his back without his knowing, and when the door was opened the rat jumped in first and so ranks first in the sequence of the zodiacal animals. The cat was afraid of sleeping late on the day and asked the rat to call her at the appointed hour but he deliberately did not do so and, needless to say, the two were doomed to become sworn enemies. Because the cat did not arrive there were only eleven animals. The emperor therefore sent a servant racing back to earth to bring back the first animal he saw, which just happened to be a pig, and this is how the pig became number twelve in the zodiacal list.

There is of course no relationship between the Chinese lunar calendar system and the Western millennium; the current sixty-year cycle began in 1996 and the year 2000 will supposedly be the 4698th year since the time of the legendary Yellow Emperor.[8]

Published: Osaka 1987, nos 89–100; Hong Kong 1993, no. 87.

1 The Twelve Earthly Branches were used to designate the hours at least as early as the Shang dynasty. For a background to their history and usage and for a list of articles on them, see *Huaxia Kaogu* 1997.3, pp. 68–75, 79.

2 The depiction of cyclical animals is found on Han mirrors and tomb tiles also. See Pirazzoli-t'Serstevens 1982, p.182, fig. 139.

3 See Willow Weilan Hai, *Animals of the Chinese Zodiac*, exhibition catalogue, China Institute Gallery, New York 1995. A classic study of the history of these animals can be found in E Chavannes, 'Le cycle Turc des douze animaux', *T'oung Pao* 1906.7, pp. 51–122.

4 Paludan 1994, p. 49. During the Northern Wei the mother of Yu Wen Hu wrote a letter to her son saying that her children were born under the sign of a rat and a rabbit and that she herself was a snake.

5 Paludan 1994, p. 49.

6 For information concerning the Chinese cyclical systems see Theodora Lau, *The Handbook of Chinese Horoscopes*, 1979, pp. 9–30 and Wilkinson 1998, pp. 179–86.

7 In the lunar calendar the day is divided into twelve sections of two hours each, beginning at 11 pm, with each section ruled over by one of the animals. (The lunar year is divided into twelve months of 29½ days to which every two and a half years an intercalary month is added for adjustment.)

8 Taking the dates of the Yellow Emperor from *Mathews' Chinese-English Dictionary*, Cambridge, Mass. 1939.

64 Pair of bracelets

Tang dynasty (AD 618–906)
Jade and gold
Outer diameter 8.5 cm
Excavated 1970, Hejiacun, southern suburbs of
Xi'an, Shaanxi province
Shaanxi History Museum

Each of these bracelets consists of three arcs of white fluted jade joined by three gold hinges. The hinges are fashioned in the shape of dragons' faces whose bulging eyes and prominent teeth are reminiscent of the *taotie* masks on archaic Chinese bronzes.

The use of jade bracelets in China seems to have originated in the neolithic Hongshan culture of northeastern China and they became a relatively common feature of many other neolithic cultures including the slightly later southeastern Liangzhu. Bone and ceramic bracelets have been excavated from neolithic sites belonging to the Dawenkou and Longshan cultures in eastern China, as well as from the Shang dynasty tomb of Fu Hao (*c.* 1200 BC). However, from the Shang dynasty right down to about the seventh century AD, the wearing of

bracelets seems not to have been general practice.[1]

In 1957, in Liangjiazhuang, west of Xi'an, a Sui dynasty tomb was discovered and identified as that of Li Jingxun, a granddaughter of the eldest sister of Emperor Yang. She had died at the age of nine and had been accorded a particularly sumptuous burial with more than two hundred items. These included a pair of gem-studded gold bracelets and a jewelled gold necklace, both of extraordinary craftsmanship.

The reemergence of the bracelet in China may have owed something to Indian influence. When the Chinese Buddhist monk Xuanzang travelled to India in the seventh century to collect the Buddhist *sūtras* for translation into Chinese, he was particularly struck by the lavishness of Indian jewellery. Examples of such jewellery can be seen in Gandharan art of the second century AD, in the reliefs from the *stūpa* at Amaravati in eastern India of the second and third centuries, and in the Ajanta caves in central India, where bejewelled bodhisattvas are depicted dating from the fifth and sixth centuries. Sources such as these, or Indian jewellery itself, may have provided

inspiration for the Chinese craftsmen.[2]

Devotion to Buddhism, current in the Tang dynasty, may have encouraged fashionable Tang ladies to replicate the bejewelled images of the bodhisattvas they would have known from murals or images in temples. Jade was one of the preferred stones for bracelets, which would later be buried with their owner in her tomb. The durability of jade made it synonymous with immortality, and its purity made it an allegory of the Daoist paradise.[3] Such associations would have been comforting reminders to the deceased if they had items of jade in their tomb.

Although women were not subject to the sumptuary laws which regulated men's wearing of certain materials and ornaments, the jewellery worn by Chinese women, as in any society, indicated status. The use of precious materials in jewellery not only enhanced the beauty of the wearer but also announced to the world the owner's wealth. The combination of jade and gold in these bracelets is an interesting one: jade is the traditional Chinese material and gold the newer foreign material. But it is the gold which bears the familiar Chinese animal mask. The juxtaposition of the traditional

64

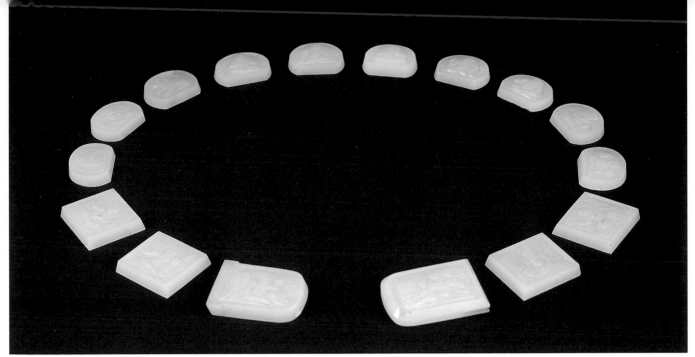

65

and the exotic perhaps conferred some special value to these bracelets.

Published: *Wenwu* 1972.1, p. 32; Beijing 1972b, p. 61; Tokyo 1981, no. 195; Hebei 1991–3, vol. 5, no. 21; Hong Kong 1993, no. 45; Berger 1994, no. 60; Yin Shengping 1994; Shanghai 1996, p. 63, no. 192; Xi'an 1997, p. 89; *Empress Wu* 1998, no. 92; *Daito Bunmei ten* 1998, no. 16.

1 Rawson 1995a, pp. 146–9.
2 Xiong and Laing 1991, pp. 163–4.
3 Rawson 1995a, pp. 84–5.

65 Belt set

Tang dynasty (AD 618–906)
Jade
Lengths 3.5–5.4 cm; total weight 335 g
Excavated 1970, Hejiacun, southern suburbs of Xi'an, Shaanxi province
Shaanxi History Museum

This belt is made up of sixteen pieces of flat white jade with a greenish hue. There are two tail pieces, four square plaques, and ten semi-oval plaques. The decoration on the front of each plaque consists of Western musicians playing various instruments. The figures have scarves over their shoulders, short jackets and pointed boots. Some are kneeling and some are sitting. The backs of the plaques are plain and undecorated, with holes for attachment to a leather underbelt.

From the quality and design of this jade belt set, and the number of plaques, it must have belonged to a member of the nobility.[1] This is one of several jade belt sets in the Hejiacun hoard, possibly gifts from the emperor.

At the beginning of the Tang dynasty General Li Jing (571–649) conquered Shaoxian, for which the Tang emperor Taizong rewarded him with jade from Yutian in the form of plaques. One of the most common decorative themes on jade belt sets was that of foreign musicians and entertainers. Some of the longer plaques display dancers and the shorter ones musicians of Central Asian origin. The idea of combining a foreign decorative image with a traditional Chinese material seems to have been particularly appealing and can be seen on many plaques that have become detached from their sets and are in private collections and museums.[2] The decorative images provide us with useful information on the variety of costumes worn by foreign musicians and the instruments played by them in the Tang period.[3] It is also possible that, as well as providing evidence of the foreign contacts that were so prolific in the Tang, these foreign figures may have had a Daoist significance. The West was the home

of the Daoist deity Xi Wang Mu, the Queen Mother of the West, whose palatial residences were known for their fine music. The musicians and dancers on these jade plaques may display a desire to make contact with the Daoist paradises.[4]

A vogue for Western-style music was already popular under the Sui emperors and was enthusiastically embraced by the Tang court. As areas to the west of China were brought under some form of political control by the Chinese so too was their music incorporated within the empire, and entertainers were often demanded as tribute from such regions. Foreign

Fig. 65a *Belt plaque decorated with the figure of a Western entertainer.*

66

orchestras were commanded to perform at court. There were two bureaucratic agencies in Chang'an where both foreign and native music and dance were professionally taught, not only to high-class courtesans, many of whom then performed at court, but also to lesser ranking artists who performed for the general populace. Xuanzong, in the eighth century, is said to have employed 30,000 musicians and is irrevocably associated with the famous song 'Rainbow Skirt and Feather Jacket' at which Yang Guifei, the emperor's favourite consort, was said to be particularly proficient (see cat. no. 39). Musical styles and elements from places as diverse as Kucha and Qoco, Kashgar, Bukhara and Samarkand, India and Korea were all gradually assimilated into the Chinese repertoire. Magicians, conjurors, tightrope dancers, contortionists, all performed for the Chinese court and in the market places of the major cities. Dancers were amongst the favourite entertainers and the twirling, whirling *huxuan* dance was particularly popular. Yang Guifei again was supposedly adept at this type of dance, as performed by the Sogdian girls on top of a ball rolling about on the dance platform, dressed in crimson robes with brocaded sleeves, green damask trousers and red deerskin boots.[5]

Published: *Wenwu* 1972.1, p. 31; Shanghai 1996, p. 63, no. 193.

1 For other comparable belt ornaments and the regulations regarding the wearing of jade belts in the Tang dynasty, see cat. nos 42–45.
2 Rawson 1995a, cat. no. 25.2, p. 329 (Hotung Collection); Yang Boda 1986, nos 219–20, 225–6; see also Hebei 1991–3, vol. 5, nos 49–64; Guang Qing 1993; Tait 1976, no. 214; Cheng Te K'un 1954; Forsyth and McElney 1994, nos 189–93.
3 See British Museum, Hotung Gallery, case 26, for an agate belt set (OA 1937.4-16. 129–37), similarly decorated.
4 Rawson 1995b, p. 35.
5 See Schafer 1963, pp. 50–7 for details of entertainers generally.

66 Dish with bear

Tang dynasty (AD 618–906)
Silver with gilding
Height 1 cm; diameter 13.4 cm; weight 139.5 g
Excavated 1970, Hejiacun, southern suburbs of
Xi'an, Shaanxi province
Shaanxi History Museum

This six-lobed, shallow dish has a narrow rim and a flat base. The centre of the dish is decorated with a realistic, gilded bear. The bear is very big and fat, with its head raised and its mouth open, growling. It has strong, muscular legs and paws with sharp talons. Its cheeks are engraved with dense lines to indicate the thickness of its fur.

Both the black bear and the panda bear were fairly common in China. The bear is the Chinese representation of the Great Bear constellation, Ursa Major. As the bear symbolized man, there was a common belief that if a woman dreamt of a bear she would have a male child: bears were thus a common form of decoration on Chinese ceramic pillows.[1] Bears are auspicious creatures as they are regarded as a symbol of bravery and strength.[2] However, apart from their appearance in Han dynasty art, bears are rare in Chinese art. Silver dishes with animals in the centre are of Central or Western Asian origin.

Published: *Wenwu* 1972.1, p. 30; Beijing 1972b, p. 53; Brinker and Goepper 1980, no. 93; Qian, Chen and Ru 1981, no. 249; Tokyo 1981, no. 190; Han and Lu 1985, no. 35; Montreal 1986, no. 100; Beijing 1992a, no. 286; Yin Shengping 1994; Shanghai 1996, p. 112, no. 76; Guggenheim 1997, no. 61.

1 BM OA 1936.10-12.169, width 31.5 cm, Cizhou-type ware, Northern Song dynasty, late eleventh to twelfth century AD, illustrated in Vainker 1991, no. 85, p. 115.
2 Eberhard 1986, pp. 34–5; Ong 1993, pp. 120–2; Ball 1927, pp. 146–8. See also cat. no. 22.

67 Dish with two fish

Tang dynasty (AD 618–906)
Silver with gilding
Height 2.7 cm; diameter 11.6 cm; weight 122.5 g
Excavated 1970, Hejiacun, southern suburbs of
Xi'an, Shaanxi province
Shaanxi History Museum

This shallow bowl with wide mouth and everted rim is flat bottomed but has a footrim. The outer surface is completely undecorated. The centre of the dish has two gilded fish entwined within a roundel. One fish is viewed from above, so that both its eyes and the curling whiskers on each side of its head are visible. The other is a more conventional side view. Both fish have uneven shapes outlined on their backs, suggesting patches of colour.

In ancient Chinese legends, the carp, *li*, was regarded as magical and could transform itself into a dragon after leaping over the Dragon Gate in the upper course of the Yellow River. Many carp never get through but those that do, according to folklore, cause a scorching flame to descend from the heavens, which burns off their tails and transforms them into dragons. As the Chinese word for benefit or profit is pronounced *li*, similar to the word for carp, the carp came to symbolize good fortune. For this reason depictions of carp were, and still are, often put on New Year cards as a sign of good luck. This was particularly the case in the days of imperial examinations, success in which would almost automatically have brought family fortune for at least a generation or two. As preparing for the examinations required much time and patience, similar to the carp's journey up the Yellow River, the carp came to be seen as a symbol of patience. Its beard is a sign of its supernatural powers. There is a legend that when the wife of Confucius (551– 479 BC) gave birth to a boy, the king of Lu was so happy for him that he sent a carp to congratulate him. Confucius, in order to express his gratitude for the reward, gave his newborn son the name Li, meaning carp. Thus began the custom of sending carp to congratulate couples on the birth of a son, which continues today in Japan.

During the Tang dynasty the family surname of the ruling royal family was Li, so the carp became a royal symbol. For this reason, the present bowl may have belonged to the royal collection. When foreign officials entered or left the palace they wore a fish tally as an official credential.[1] One of the gifts sought by a foreign ambassador when coming to do obeisance to the Tang court was an embroidered wallet in which he might carry this official token. These tokens were generally bronze and in the shape of a fish, fashioned in two halves: the 'male' half remained in the Chinese palace and the 'female' half was sent to the tributary country.[2]

As fish swimming in pairs also signify marital harmony, pairs of fish are often incorporated into gifts given on marriage. Another auspicious connotation regarding fish is related to the Chinese pronunciation of the general word for fish, *yu*, which is the same as the word for abundance, *yu*. In Buddhism fish are regarded as a holy emblem symbolizing the unrestricted freedom of the fully emancipated person.[3] All these associations attached to carp, and to fish in general, make them a popular decorative motif.

In China there was a taboo on writing or mentioning certain personal names, especially those of the older generation of one's family, those of widely venerated personalities such as Confucius and Mencius, and that of the current emperor. Such a taboo system was already in effect in the Qin and Han dynasties.[4] The taboo required the omission of the character or an orthographic change, either the omission of a stroke in the character or an alternative form of it. Because of this taboo system[5] people could not say 'eat carp', as it sounded

Fig. 67a *Detail of the two carp inside the bowl.*

the same as 'eat the emperor'. To avoid this, alternative words for carp had to be introduced and so people would say eat '*huan gong*' (another species of carp-like fish) instead.[6]

Published: *Wenwu* 1972.1, p. 30.

1 Schafer 1963, p. 26 and des Rotours 1952, pp. 62–5.
2 Schafer 1963, p. 26.
3 For symbolism generally see Eberhard 1986, pp. 57–8; Ong 1993, pp. 244–8; Ball 1927, pp. 189–204.
4 Wilkinson 1998, p. 107.
5 Reischauer 1955, p. 135; Wilkinson 1998, p. 107. For an article on Chinese language taboos see B Lundahl, 'Tehui: A special kind of Chinese language taboo', *Outstretched leaves on his Bamboo Staff, Studies in Honour of Göran Malmqvist*, The Association of Oriental Studies, Stockholm 1994, pp. 177–88.
6 For more information on carp see Lindqvist 1991, pp. 72–4. This book presents a very interesting background to the construction of Chinese characters generally.

68 Dish with two foxes

Tang dynasty (AD 618–906)
Silver with gilding
Height 1.5 cm; diameter 22.5 cm; weight 322.5g
Excavated 1970, Hejiacun, southern suburbs of Xi'an, Shaanxi province
Shaanxi History Museum

This bowl, in the shape of a cut-open peach, has a shallow belly and flat base. In each section the image of a fox with a long bushy

67

2 Wang Chi-chen, *Traditional Chinese Tales*, New York 1968, p. 220.
3 Wang Chi-chen, op. cit., *Jenshih* (The Fox Lady), pp. 24–34.
4 A popular account of this episode in history is recounted in *Fangshen yan yi* (The Investiture of the Gods) written in the Ming dynasty and generally attributed to Xu Zhonglin (died *c.* 1566), which recounts the Shang dynasty king's indulgence of his concubine Danji and his brutal treatment of loyal ministers which led to his downfall.
5 The *Shanhaijing* is a *descriptio mundi,* written down in the Han dynasty but based partly on older oral tradition. For information on the text see Loewe 1993, pp. 357–67. For references in English about the *Shanhaijing,* see Schiffler 1978; Birrell 1999.

68

tail has been hammered out and gilded. Both the foxes twist their heads, one up and one down, to look at one another.

Foxes are regarded by the Chinese as not only cunning but also nimble and auspicious and there are many legends about them.[1] In fact fox legends outnumber all other animal legends in popular Chinese mythology, including those about dragons.[2] One such story, *Renshi*, written by Shen Zhiji (active 750–800), concerns an official who falls in love with a woman who is really a fox. However, when he refuses to listen to her pleas not to accompany him on a journey she is killed by dogs, whereupon she is transformed back into a fox.[3] It was thought that a fox could turn itself into a woman when it was fifty years old, a young girl when it was a hundred, and after a thousand years it became a celestial fox. The thousand-year-old fox had nine tails, one of which assumed the form of a beautiful woman who led the last king of the Shang dynasty into evil ways, ending with his losing his throne.[4]

In China there are black, yellow and white foxes. As the white ones are rarest, legends about them are the most magical. One legend concerns a man by the name of Great Yu, of mythical times, who, when he

was thirty and unmarried, was trying to control the floods. When he passed by Tu Mountain he became suddenly afraid that he was becoming too old to have offspring. He stopped to pray to the gods and, as soon as he had finished, there appeared a white fox with nine tails. Thinking that this was some sort of response from the gods, Yu married a girl from the area. According to the *Shanhaijing* (Classic of the mountains and seas)[5] there is a fox with nine tails which will emerge when virtue reigns. The appearance of a nine-tailed white fox was therefore a sign that a virtuous king was about to appear. The image of two foxes on this dish possibly implies flattery of the royal family, praising their virtue.

Published: *Wenwu* 1972.1, p. 30; Beijing 1972b, p. 53; Qian, Chen and Ru 1981, no. 250; Han and Lu 1985, no. 33; Montreal 1986, no. 101; Wang Renbo 1990, p. 168, no. 5; Beijing 1992a, no. 281; Kuhn 1993, no. 58; Yin Shengping 1994; Xi'an 1995, p. 20; Shanghai 1996, p. 111, no. 73; Guggenheim 1997, no. 62; Xi'an 1997, p. 87.

1 Ideas about the fox, interestingly, vary from place to place. The Germans regard it as sly, but other cultures consider it easily victimized and the English have always hunted it. For the Chinese it has supernatural powers of transformation (Burckhardt 1958, vol. III, pp. 47–56).

69 Dish with a mythical creature

Tang dynasty (AD 618–906)
Silver with gilding
Height 1.4 cm; diameter 15.3 cm; weight 211 g
Excavated 1970, Hejiacun, southern suburbs of Xi'an, Shaanxi province
Shaanxi History Museum

This shallow dish has a narrow, six-petalled rim and a flat base. In the centre of the dish is a strange mythical creature with open wings, bushy upstretching tail and two hooves. It has an ox's head and hooves, a unicorn's horn, a phoenix-like tail and a horse's mane. Such an exaggeratedly strange animal is very rare in silver and gold objects of the Tang dynasty. Even today there is a Chinese saying that a combination of the phoenix, the horse and the ox, '*feng, ma, niu*', is an irrelevancy, like trying to connect an apple to an oyster!

Perhaps the creature has its origins in ancient Chinese mythology. It may be the celestial creature *fei lian,* a wind god.[1] This creature is mentioned in the *Li Sao* (Encountering Sorrows), a narrative poem by Qu Yuan (*c.* 340–278 BC) which is also a remonstrance against his ruler.[2] The Han dynasty Mawangdui coffins (dating from about 186–168 BC) were painted with all

69

kinds of strange, hybrid animals, including sheep with human bodies.[3] However, bearing in mind all the foreign contacts prevalent in the Tang dynasty, it is also possible that this strange creature is a combination of Western and Asian mythical creatures, including the winged gods of victory. The religious iconography of many ancient cultures has examples of hybrid figures which combine human, animal and other motifs. There are many winged demons amongst ancient Near Eastern figures and there were winged protectresses of the dead in ancient Egypt. The influence of Buddhism in China also led to the combination of Chinese and Indian mythical creatures.

Published: *Wenwu* 1972.1, p. 30; Beijing 1972b, p. 54; Qian, Chen and Ru 1981, no. 249; Han and Lu 1985, no. 41; Han Wei 1989, plates, p. 2; Wang Renbo 1990, p. 158, no.9; Beijing 1992a, no. 279; Xi'an 1995, p. 21; Guggenheim 1997, no. 60; Xi'an 1997, p. 87.

1 The *fei lian* was a spiritual bird, somewhat akin to the garuda of Indian mythology which was half man, half eagle. It is mentioned in the *Li Sao*, a long allegorical and narrative poem supposedly written by Qu Yuan. There are two images of it , one having an animal's body with a bird's head and the other a bird's body with an animal's head (Werner 1961, p. 125).
2 Hawkes 1985, p. 28, line 100 and note 9. See also Knechtges 1982, p. 136, note to line

330, for the reference in the Wen Xuan, *Western Capital Rhapsody,* dating to the Han dynasty, by Ban Gu.
3 Beijing 1973b, vol. 2, figs 47–57.

70 Cup

Tang dynasty (AD 618–906)
Jade
Height 3.5 cm; diameter (of mouth) 10 cm, (of foot) 5.5 cm
Excavated 1970, Hejiacun, southern suburbs of Xi'an, Shaanxi province
Shaanxi History Museum

This oval cup has eight petal-shaped lobes and a splayed foot rim. The petals suggest an opening lotus flower, possibly derived from Central Asian designs, and each is decorated with faint linear patterns of grass and

clouds. There are many Tang period gold and silver vessels of similar form and decoration. The patterns are related to the acanthus leaves and half palmettes of the art of Western Asia. The body is thin, the carved lines smooth and the craftsmanship very skilful.[1] The quality of the Hetian jade is high, Hetian jade being regarded as particularly precious.[2] The colour is almost white, with a hint of yellowish brown at the mouth and the footrim.

A jade bowl was found in the tomb of Fu Hao, a Shang dynasty consort who died about 1200 BC.[3] This was a fairly large bowl, with a diameter of 20.5 centimetres, decorated very much in the fashion of contemporary bronzes. However, it was a great rarity because at that time the tools necessary to hollow out the centre of the bowl and make the sloping walls would have been primitive. Moreover the time, expense and wastage of jade involved in making such a vessel would have been prohibitive except for someone of a very high status. From the Shang dynasty until the late Eastern Zhou jade vessels were unknown. By the Han period, however, eared cups were occasionally made in jade, presumably only for rich patrons. Eared cups[4] had been in use in China since the Warring States period, and by the Han period many were made in lacquer and ceramic. From both textual and archaeological evidence in the Mawangdui tombs of the mid-second century BC we

70

know that such cups were used for drinking both wine and soup.[5] The oval shape (but not the lobes) of the present jade bowl is therefore quite traditional.[6]

From the end of the Han dynasty there is again a dearth of jade vessels. By the Tang dynasty gold and silver wares had become fashionable for food and drink, and it may have been these which inspired the making of similar vessels in jade. The ownership of such vessels of jade would have implied great wealth and status and it is possible that their use was restricted to the court and the royal family. This cup is very highly polished and would presumably have been used for drinking wine.[7]

People of the Tang dynasty enjoyed drinking and contemporary poetry contains many references to wine. All educated Chinese of this period were trained in the writing of poetry and it was acknowledged that wine often acted as an inspiration. Li Bai (701–62), one of the best known and loved Tang dynasty poets, was renowned for his love of wine:

Best wine of Lan-ling, with yü *gold aromatic –*
Comes in brimful cups of jade, amber shining.[8]

Published: *Wenwu* 1972.1, p. 31; Tokyo 1981, no. 197; Shanghai 1996, p. 62, no. 189.

1 For a similar example see Rawson 1995a, cat. no. 29.1, p. 391, Hotung Collection. Also see the general introduction to that section, pp. 385–90.
2 A nephrite jade from Khotan in Xinjiang province, Chinese Turkestan. Jade from Khotan was listed in the imperial pharmacopoeia as a drug which lightened the corporeal frame and prolonged life. It was reduced to a liquid or ingested as a powder or small grains. It was thought it could cleanse the inner organs of impurities. Schafer 1963, p. 227.
3 Rawson 1995a, p. 385, fig. 1.
4 See the Han dynasty lacquered and ceramic eared cups in the British Museum, Hotung Gallery, case 14.
5 See Mawangdui report where eared cups are illustrated with inscriptions on them saying 'May his lordship enjoy his wine' (Beijing 1973b, vol. 1, pp. 83–4, figs 77–8).
6 Willets 1965, p. 267.

7 Grapes were introduced into China in the Han dynasty by the traveller Zhang Qian, but more as food than for making into wine at that period. The main wine drunk then and until the Tang dynasty was rice wine (Schafer 1963, pp. 141–5).
8 Li Bai, *Quan Tangshi*, Zhonghua shuju edn 1960, vol. 181, p. 1842. As with certain Roman wines, some Tang wines were flavoured and coloured with saffron. *Yü* gold refers to saffron and to exotic odours.

71 Cup

Tang dynasty (AD 618–906)
Agate
Width 7.1 cm; diameter of mouth 11.5 cm; weight 176 g
Excavated 1970, Hejiacun, southern suburb of Xi'an, Shaanxi province
Shaanxi History Museum

This agate cup appears to have been used as a mortar in which to grind medicines as several jade pestles were excavated nearby in the same hoard. The cup is oval, with a deep belly, and so highly polished that the natural streaks and patches of yellow, white and amber gleam against the darker brown ground colour.

It was fashionable among the royal family and nobility of the Sui and Tang courts to take various medicines, or elixirs, containing substances such as gold powder and alluvial gold, the function of which was to strengthen the qi, the rarefied form of energy pumped by the lungs throughout the body. By strengthening the qi,[1] a person hoped to enjoy a longer and healthier life.[2]

Several of the vessels in the Hejiacun hoard were connected with medicine (cat. nos 76–77, 79–80). There were both deep and shallow dishes, pots for refining elixirs, medicine boxes and bowls and cups for the storing and taking of medicine. Various elixirs were also found in the hoard. These included cinnabar (mercuric sulphide), calcium carbonate and gold filings. The Chinese at this time ingested powders made from grinding together five different substances: stalactite, sulphur, quartz (white and purple) and hallogsite. Daoists had long believed in the efficacy of swallowing elixirs to prolong life, despite much evidence to the contrary. As the Tang royal family traced its origins back to Laozi, the progenitor of Daoism, many of its members were followers of the religion.[3] Some of the Tang emperors of the ninth century, including Xianzong, Jingzong, Wuzong and Xuanzong, were believed to have died from the highly poisonous elixirs they had been swallowing in their desire for immortality or at least longevity. Wuzong in particular was addicted to immortality potions which affected his sanity and killed him at the age of thirty-three.

Published: *Wenwu* 1972.1, p. 31; Hejiacun 1972, p. 41, no. 31; Tokyo 1981, no. 198; Shanghai 1996, p. 62, no. 190.

1 Han Wei 1994a, p. 33.
2 Temple 1986, p. 123.
3 Han Wei 1994a.

71

72 Incense burner

Tang dynasty (AD 618–906)
Gilded silver
Height 31.7 cm; diameter (upper) 16 cm,
(lower) 21.3 cm; weight 4.15 kg
Excavated 1970, Hejiacun, southern suburbs of
Xi'an, Shaanxi province
Shaanxi History Museum

This incense burner has three sections: a shallow dish with legs, a waisted upper section, and a lid. The deep lower dish is supported by five outward-curving legs with hoof-like feet. Five chains hang down between the legs. Connected to the lower part by a tight-fitting join is an upper section with a bulging body and narrow waist. The domed lid has a knob shaped like a lotus bud riveted to it. The body of the burner has five cloud-shaped perforations partly filled with decorations in the shape of a peach or a *ruyi*. These are reflected at the top of the lid, where there are also trefoils within perforations. The incense would be dispersed through all of these perforations. Where the two parts of the body meet there are four horizontal *ruyi*-shaped catches. Under the base is an inscription stating: 'Three tiers holding five and a half *jin*'.[1] This indicates the number of parts to the vessel and its capacity, a measure taken to prevent theft or substitution.

Incense burning was a custom favoured by the Chinese literati.[2] Incense has the function of purifying the atmosphere and generally refreshing the spirits, giving one a 'high' in today's parlance (see also cat. nos 18, 73). According to archaeological and literary evidence Chinese people knew about incense as early as pre-dynastic times (third century BC) and by the Han dynasty incense seems to have been universally used. By the Northern and Southern dynasties perfuming clothes had also become an established habit of the literati. In ancient China incense was sometimes processed

72

with wood into a cake and put on the fire to burn. Some incense such as vanilla and aloeswood needed to be burnt, whereas other, flower-based incenses were usually placed in perfumers and left to dissipate their aromas naturally. As Buddhism began to take root in China between the fall of the Han and the beginning of the Tang dynasty, so incense burners were more commonly used in religious ceremonies as one of the chief altar vessels.

Published: *Wenwu* 1972.1 p. 31; Hejiacun 1972, p. 41, no. 28; Beijing 1972b, p. 59; Han and Lu 1985, no. 97; Montreal 1986, p. 124; Yang Boda 1987, no. 58; Beijing 1992a, no. 285; White 1995, p. 119; Shaanxi 1997, p. 43.

1 A *jin*, or catty, is approximately 600 grams or 1.5 lb, avoirdupois.
2 *A Special Exhibition of Incense Burners and Perfumers throughout the Dynasties,* exhibition catalogue, Taipei 1994, is a good reference for incense burners generally.

73 Perfumer

Tang dynasty (AD 618–906)
Silver
Diameter 4.5 cm; height 4.5 cm; weight 35 g
Excavated 1970, Hejiacun, southern suburbs of
Xi'an, Shaanxi province
Shaanxi History Museum

This censer is made up of two hemispheres joined by a hinge, with a bolt on either side. It hangs from a short chain. The bowl inside is suspended from two concentric rings, called gimbals, which turn on their own axis, rather like a ship's compass, on gyroscopic principles. Thus the bowl maintains an upright position and, regardless of how much the censer is swung, the incense will not spill.[1]

The censer is made of silver which has been hammered and tooled to produce the openwork decoration. This decoration consists of birds in flight, vine tendrils and grapes against a scrolling leafy background, common motifs on such vessels. Censers were seemingly very popular in the Tang

73

myrrh.[4] Those who could afford such things 'lived in clouds of incense and mists of perfume'. Such clouds would be emitted from censers held by ladies' maids or hung on chariots and sedan chairs. Court ladies were profusely scented, as described by the Tang poet Han Shan:

Once for a short while I went down the mountain
I ran into a flock of young ladies,
Upright and proper, beautiful in countenance and
face.
With rouge on cheeks, smooth and glossy powder
Bracelets of gold — chased with silver blossoms,
Robes of thin silk, purple and scarlet red.
Peachy complexions — akin to goddesses and
sylphs;
Their perfumed sashes — richly fuming vapours.[5]

A story concerning one of these censers relates to the concubine Yang Guifei (see pp. 61–2). During the An Lushan rebellion the Tang emperor Xuanzong and his concubine had to flee the capital Chang'an and eventually the emperor had to submit to watching his lover being strangled by his angry troops. When he returned to the capital he ordered her reburial and it was reported in the texts that, though her body had rotted, her remains smelled sweet because of the scent bag buried with her. This had always puzzled historians because it was thought that such bags would be made of textile[6] and therefore would have rotted along with the corpse. However, when the Famen temple hoard was discovered it contained four of these balls which were identified from an inventory list. It was then realized that the scent bag was in fact a censer such as this, made of metal and not textile.

Published: *Wenwu* 1972.1, p. 32; Hejiacun 1972, p. 41, no. 29; Beijing 1972b, p. 60; Brinker and Goepper 1980, no. 90; Yang Boda 1987, no. 54; Wang Renbo 1990, p. 172, nos 11–12, no. 13; Beijing 1992a, no. 278; Kuhn 1993, no. 52; Xi'an 1995, p. 22; Shanghai 1996, p. 119, no. 97; Xi'an 1997, p. 86.

dynasty but although four were found in one of the other Tang hoards near Xi'an, the Famen temple hoard, only this one was found in the Hejiacun hoard.[2] All the excavated examples are of similar construction.

Censers such as this were used for both religious and secular purposes.[3] Incense could be burned in them, or they could be filled with aromatic herbs and perfumes for freshening clothes and homes and for repelling insects. Native Chinese perfumes and incenses included cassia, camphor, sweet basil and citronella, civet and musk, and imported ones comprised sandalwood, aloeswood, camphor, frankincense and

1 Such a method of suspension was apparently in use in the Western Han period (Needham 1965, vol. 4:2, pp. 228–36, figs 477–80).
2 For Chinese report on Shapocun in the southeastern suburbs of Xi'an, which included four silver censers, see *Wenwu* 1964.6, pp. 30–2. For a discussion of the Shapocun find see Han Wei 1982.
3 The Chinese had used long-handled censers since Han times. These are depicted in Tang tomb murals and examples are preserved in the Shōsō-in, in Nara, Japan.
4 Schafer 1963, p. 158; for general information on this subject see pp. 155–75.
5 Han Shan (a sobriquet rather than a name, and meaning Cold Mountain) was a Tang dynasty recluse whose dates are uncertain. *Quan Tang shi* (Ch'uan T'ang shih), Taiwan 1971, vol. 12, p. 9084. For translation see R Henricks, *The Poetry of Han Shan*, New York 1990, poem no. 169.
6 Usually these sachets were made of textile such as fine gauze and there are several in the Shōsō-in, of gauze net and linen.

74 Part of a lamp

Tang dynasty (AD 618–906)
Gilded silver
Height 1.5 cm; diameter of mouth 3.5 cm; weight 73.5 g
Excavated 1970, Hejiacun, southern suburbs of Xi'an, Shaanxi province
Shaanxi History Museum

This eight-lobed lamp part has a wide mouth, flat ribbed rim and straight sides, a round base, and is in the shape of a lotus flower. The whole body is gilded but undecorated. Along one side a handle has been soldered to the body. The handle top is flat and hollow and it looks as if it were at one time joined to a lamp assemblage.

The practice of using lamps possibly came to China from the West, and they were widely utilized by the Han dynasty. The lamp was therefore an everyday object (see cat. no. 29).[1] As this lamp was part of the Hejiacun hoard and found in a royal palace, it may have had a special role in some religious ceremony, probably a Buddhist one. Lighting was highly significant in Buddhist ceremonies: lights were placed in

74

front of the image of the Buddha to signify his power and that of Buddhism generally.

In the Tang dynasty lamp wheels and lamp trees were popular at Buddhist fasts and festivals. Two agate lamp trees were brought to the court in the middle of the seventh century by the son of the king of Tukhara and such artificial trees were used during the most brilliant of all Tang festivals, the New Year, which lasted about three days. During festivals curfews were lifted and celebrants tried to outshine each other with their artificial lights. The *Tang Huiyao* mentions the presentation of a one-metre-high agate lamp tree for a Buddhist ceremony in Tang Gaozong's time in AD 665.[2] The description of a large lamp tree in Chang'an states that it was decorated with embroideries and precious metals and held fifty thousand bowl lamps.[3] The Japanese monk Ennin, who visited Yangzhou in 839, described the splendour of a New Year festival.[4] The Tang poet Zhang Yue praised the lamp trees of the western regions:

In the dragon's mouth the fire tree with thousands of lamps shining, ... in the western regions, the lamp wheels cast a thousand shadows...[5]

Published: *Wenwu* 1972.1, p. 32.

1 See Rawson 1996a, cat. no. 97, p. 190, for a Han dynasty lamp tree which may have been similar to the Tang dynasty lamp trees.
2 The *Tang Huiyao* (Collection of important documents pertaining to the Tang dynasty) traces the history of institutions of a given dynasty using excerpts from contemporary documents. The first such compilation was made during the Tang dynasty by Wang Pu (922–82) (see Wilkinson 1998, pp. 521–3). *Tang Huiyao,* Shanghai guji chubanshe 1991, vol. 99, p. 2103.
3 Schafer 1963, pp. 259–60.
4 Reischauer 1955, pp. 128–9.
5 *Quan Tangshi*, Zhonghua shuju edn 1960, vol. 89, p. 982.

75 Basin

Tang dynasty (AD 618–906)
Gold
Height 6.5 cm; diameter of mouth 28.6 cm; weight 2.15 kg
Excavated 1970, Hejiacun, southern suburbs of Xi'an, Shaanxi province
Shaanxi History Museum

This basin has a wide mouth and an everted rim, slanting sides and a flat base. It has been hammered into shape and its undecorated surface shows off the sheer beauty of the gold.

This basin is the only surviving Tang example of its kind in gold. Presumably others were made but were either stolen or melted down. It was probably used for washing the hands and face. The poet Wang Jian (*c.* 767–830) described entertainers using a golden flower basin in which to wash their faces before putting on their makeup for a performance.[1]

However, such basins would also undoubtedly have been used for ceremonial ablutions and those made of gold probably belonged in royal households. When the child of an emperor's wife or concubine was three days old, it was given a ceremonial washing, *xisan*, in a golden basin. The poet Zhang E (active *c.*707) wrote:

The imperial concubine had a baby girl who started to cry. She was washed in a gold basin, she was wrapped in an embroidered sheet.[2]

Published: *Wenwu* 1972.1, p. 32; Hejiacun 1972, p. 41, no. 33; Hong Kong 1993, no. 34; Xi'an 1995, p. 14.

1 *Quan Tangshi*, Zhonghua shuju edn 1960, vol. 302, p. 3444.
2 *Quan Tangshi*, Zhonghua shuju edn 1960, vol. 110, p. 1129.

75

76 Jar and cover

Tang dynasty (AD 618–906)
Silver
Height 4.4 cm; diameter of mouth 2.6 cm;
weight 56.5 g
Excavated 1970, Hejiacun, southern suburbs of
Xi'an, Shaanxi province
Shaanxi History Museum

This lidded jar has a narrow mouth, short, straight neck, bulging body and a flat base. The lid fits tightly and its knob is shaped like a small bud. The body is undecorated. The interior of the pot is clean and shiny but tool marks are evident in places.

This jar was a container for medicine. Jars of exactly this shape were still in use for medicines at the pharmacies of the Qing dynasty royal court.

The oldest Chinese medical texts in existence today were compiled about two thousand years ago. Traditional Chinese medicine had four diagnostic techniques: looking at a patient's face, listening to his voice, asking about his diet and feeling the twenty-eight recognized pulses. Meridian therapies included acupuncture and moxibustion (the burning of mugwort on the surface of the body) as well as drug therapy. In the tomb of Liu Sheng, a king buried in a jade suit in Hebei province about 113 BC, some gold and silver needles used for acupuncture were recovered.[1] The earliest known Chinese pharmacopoeia, or list of drugs, called the *Shennong baicao jing* (The Divine Husbandman's Pharmacopoeia), compiled in the first or second century AD, lists 365 drugs.[2] The Daoists seem to have been the leaders in the testing, application and cataloguing of drugs, the main focus of their work being the pursuit of longevity and eternal life.[3]

Following Buddhist custom, in the Tang dynasty charities were set up to look after the poor, the sick, the aged and the orphaned and many hospitals were also established. Sun Simiao was an example of the best medieval physician, devoted to the Buddhist principle of compassion, but also a Daoist. He came to the court of the Tang emperor Taizong and wrote a collection of remedies called *Recipes Worth A Thousand Metal Coins*.[4] A wealth of pharmacological literature was available to Tang dynasty druggists, including the *Shennong bencao jing* which was a revision in 659 by Su Jing (or Su Gong) of the earlier, similarly named, *Shennong baicao jing*.[5] This work put special emphasis on the drugs recommended by Daoists for longevity, and graded them according to three categories.[6] There were superior drugs: cinnabar, azurite, mica, ginseng, musk and oysters for lightening the body and lengthening life; middle-range drugs: orpiment, realgar, sulphur, ginger and rhinoceros horn for use as tonics; and inferior drugs: ochre, ceruse, frogs and peach seeds to cure sickness. We know that Epsom salts (magnesium sulphate) were used in Tang dynasty China.[7]

As might be expected, our greatest body of knowledge concerns the royal pharmacy. A large area in the capital was set aside for the imperial herb garden supervised by a master who also had responsibility for general medicine, acupuncture, massage and magic. In the palace there was a pharmacist responsible for the diagnosis, prescription and compounding of drugs.

Several drugs were found in the Hejiacun hoard, such as gold powder, alluvial gold, *guangming sha* and *guangming suihongsha* (different qualities of cinnabar), crystal, amethyst, and *shang ru* (types of ointment). These drugs, some in the form of ointments, pills and powders, were stored in large undecorated silver boxes and jars such as this one.[8] Drugs have also been found in Nara, Japan, in the Shōsō-in, the storehouse of the Buddhist temple Tōdaiji. When Emperor Shōmu died in 756 his empress Kōmyō presented the contents of the Shōsō-in repository to the Tōdaiji temple and they have been preserved intact since that date. Most of the items there were presented by visiting foreigners and a very large number of the drugs were of Chinese origin.

Published: *Wenwu* 1972.1, p. 31; Beijing 1972b, p. 60; Han and Lu 1985, no. 84.

1 Beijing 1980d, vol. 2, colour pl. 14. See also Rawson 1996a, cat. no. 81 for information on Liu Sheng himself.
2 See Wilkinson 1998, p. 649 and Xia Leiming, 'The Eastward spread of herbs and medicines of the Western Region and the development of Chinese medicine', *Xiyu yanjiu* 1998.1, pp. 28–38 and abbreviated translation in *China Archaeology and Art Digest*, vol. 3, no. 1, Hong Kong, April 1999, pp. 152–3.
3 The Mawangdui tombs, dating to 186–168 BC, contained fragments of medical manuscripts which included theoretical as well as practical drugs, information on gymnastics and petty surgery, as well as demonological rituals. See D J Harper, *Early Chinese Medical Literature: The Mawangdui Medical Manuscripts*, Kegan Paul International, 1998.
4 He died in 682 and his official biography says that he was over a hundred years old.
5 Xia Leiming, see note 2.
6 For details on Chinese alchemical practices see Needham 1974 and 1976, vols 5:2, 5:3.
7 For general information on Chinese medicine see Temple 1991, pp. 123–37; Schafer 1963, pp. 176–94.
8 Han Wei 1994a, p. 33.

77 Box with cinnabar and jade belts

Tang dynasty (AD 618–906)
Silver
Height 6.5 cm; diameter 17.5 cm
Excavated 1970, Hejiacun, southern suburbs of
Xi'an, Shaanxi province
Shaanxi History Museum

The body and lid of this round silver box are
both slightly bevelled with a flat centre. The
box is undecorated but some scars of the
working process can be seen. On both the
outside and the inside of the lid is the same
inscription in black ink: 'Four *liang* [approx.
160 grams], bright powdered cinnabar one
large *jin* [one catty, approx. 600 grams],

fifteen square white jade plaques missing the
penannular ring, one set of Guduo jade, one
set of jade with deep and variegated colour,
separately fifteen pieces with penannular
ring'. The contents of the box matched this
description.[1]

The Hejiacun hoard revealed great
quantities of minerals and other ingredients
connected with medicine (see cat. no. 76).
The cinnabar contained in this box is just
one of these. In the *Shennong bencao jing*, the
first Chinese pharmacopoeia compiled
under a slightly different name in the first or
second century AD, cinnabar, *dansha*
(mercuric sulphide), was named as the
premier elixir. Several grades were used but
dansha was supposed to be useful for
calming the heartbeat and nerves and
removing poisons from the body. Another

form, but more expensive, was *guangming
sha* (bright powdered cinnabar) which was
often presented to the emperor on his
birthday by rich officials. Another elixir,
shizhongru (calcium carbonate), was thought
to improve the function of the five organs
(heart, liver, kidney, pancreas, lungs) and
the soul and to act as a general panacea as
well as improving the chances of longevity.
Some of these materials were rare and
expensive but it was believed they could
calm the spirit, brighten the eyes and make
one feel better generally.[2]

Published: *Wenwu* 1972.1, p. 31; Beijing 1972b,
p. 65; Xi'an 1995, p. 5; *Empress Wu* 1998, no. 78.

1 For the Guduo jade belt see cat. no. 78. The
   other jades are not included in this catalogue.
2 See catalogue no. 76 for more information on
   medicine in the Tang dynasty. Also Xi'an
   1995, pp. 5–8.

78 Belt set

Tang dynasty (AD 618–906)
Jade
Length of plaques 3.7 cm; widths 2.6–4.2 cm;
total weight 246.8 g
Excavated 1970, Hejiacun, southern suburbs of
Xi'an, Shaanxi province
Shaanxi History Museum

These belt plaques were found inside the
silver box, catalogue no. 77. They are made
of variegated coloured jade, yellowish green

79

in colour, with some black spots. There are sixteen pieces altogether, comprising two tail pieces, four square plaques, and nine U-shaped plaques, one penannular jade ring, and one pin. The upper surfaces of the plaques are polished but the backs are rough. There are no holes pierced in them, as there would normally be to secure them to a backing, so it would appear that the belt was never completed.

As jade of this colour and quality is rare, it is particularly useful that the inscription on the lid of the silver box in which the plaques were found states the source of the jade (see cat. no. 77). The jade is described as Guduo jade, Guduo being a small state in the region of the Pamirs, near what is today Afghanistan and Tadjikestan, inhabited by a Turkish people related to the Xiongnu nomads. At the beginning of the Tang dynasty these Turks often made incursions over the Chinese borders, and during the reign of Emperor Xuanzong, in 729, the prince of Guduo, Gu Dushi, came to pay court to the emperor as his suzerain. In 752 the emperor rewarded the ruler, Luo Quanjie, with the title of Yehu (a high rank).[1]

Published: *Wenwu* 1972.1, p. 32.

1 *Xin Tang shu*, Zhonghua shuju edn, 1975, juan 221, p. 6257.

79 Box

Tang dynasty (AD 618–906)
Gold
Height 3.4 cm; diameter 8.2 cm; weight 258.5 g
Excavated 1970, Hejiacun, southern suburbs of Xi'an, Shaanxi province
Shaanxi History Museum

This gold box is round with a slightly domed, tight-fitting lid. The whole piece has been hammered into shape and the absence of decoration allows the gold to gleam in its unadulterated state.

The box was a container for Chinese medicinal powder or pills. Gold filings[1] were found in the Hejiacun hoard and gold was an important ingredient in Tang dynasty Daoist recipes for longevity. It was consumed in both powder and liquid form to 'stabilize the soul and prolong life'. Meng Shen, an eighteenth-century pharmacologist, reported that burning medicinal gold produced a five-coloured aura which he himself had verified.[2] The alchemists believed moreover that by heating a mixture of mercury and sulphur to produce cinnabar they could make immortality pills from the compound, but the mercury content poisoned many patients.[3] The bright red colour of cinnabar was associated with the metal gold and,

since gold was a stable substance which did not tarnish or decay, it therefore became associated with immortality.[4]

Boxes seem to have been the favoured container for longevity medicines. Gold boxes often have the weight of gold stamped on their base, probably to prevent palace staff from exchanging lighter boxes for heavier ones.

Published: *Wenwu* 1972.1, p. 31; Xi'an 1995, p. 14.

1 *Fujin*, gold filings, was refined from gold sand and looked like wheat bran. Several emperors ingested gold filings. Restaurants in Guangzhou used gold in some of their dishes: Xi'an 1995, p. 8.
2 *Xin Tang shu*, Zhonghua shuju edn, 1975, juan 121, p. 5599.
3 For general information on alchemy in China see Beijing 1983b, pp. 213–28.
4 The best quality seal paste is made with pulverized cinnabar (mercuric sulphide) dissolved in a specially prepared seed oil, then soaked into a pad consisting of dried fibres of the moxa plant. This suggests the permanence of the seal.

80 Wine warmer

Tang dynasty (AD 618–906)
Gold
Height 3.4 cm; diameter of mouth 9.2 cm; weight 269 g
Excavated 1970, Hejiacun, southern suburbs of Xi'an, Shaanxi province
Shaanxi History Museum

This vessel has a wide flared mouth with an everted rim and a shallow body with slanting walls resting on three animal legs. Riveted to one side is a handle in the shape of a sprouting leaf. The outer surface is designed as a lotus leaf with the veins of the leaf undulating across the surface, dividing it into nine sections, against a ring-punched background. The sections contain engraved designs of pearls, birds carrying ribbons, other birds holding talismans, a lion and flowers interspersed with floral and grass patterns.

In the centre of the base of the warmer are two lions in high relief surrounded by a circular design of curled leaves. This vessel is beautifully made and the decoration of flowers, birds and animals is naturalistic and lively.

Vessels for warming wine, liquids, including perhaps tea, and medicines were generally made of silver in the Tang dynasty, and several silver examples have been excavated. This is the only gold warmer known.

The heating of substances was an important element in ancient Chinese alchemical practices. The first substance to be studied by Chinese alchemists was *dansha*, cinnabar, a bright red mercuric sulphide. Experimentation began in the Han dynasty or earlier and there are Han texts describing various experiments. It was discovered that when cinnabar was burned it decomposed into sulphur dioxide and mercury, but that the mercury would combine again with sulphur to form mercuric sulphide. These could then be sublimed into the original state, cinnabar, when heated once again. Mercury is the only common metal which is liquid at room temperature and it could be heated again and again into *huandan*, a cyclically transformed regenerative elixir. This was referred to as *shendan*, the miraculous elixir, 'which not only ensures longevity but is also capable of turning other substances into gold'.[1]

The property of mercury to dissolve other metals and form amalgams was exploited in the gilding of metal objects from the Warring States period but it does not seem to have been utilized for alchemical purposes until the Eastern Han dynasty. Chinese alchemists then discovered that gold and mercury would merge completely into a homogeneous silver white paste which may be yellowish with a high gold content. From this paste alchemists succeeded in making very fine gold and silver dust as the mercury evaporated or the mixture was cooled. As alchemists began to discover that gold was uncorrodable, so gold came to be regarded as the most precious of all things. Alchemists hoped that these properties could somehow be transferred into humans. They successfully produced several alloys similar to gold and silver in appearance, including fifteen kinds of pharmaceutical golds and thirteen kinds of pharmaceutical silvers.

More than ten kinds of apparatus and equipment are mentioned in the alchemical classics including water basins, mortars, grinders, and distilleries for the extraction of mercury. Vessels were made of metal (gold, silver or copper) and sometimes ceramic. For the extraction of mercury from cinnabar several vessels are mentioned, including a simple device in two parts. The upper part was in the shape of a round-bottomed flask and called the pomegranate pot and the lower part was a

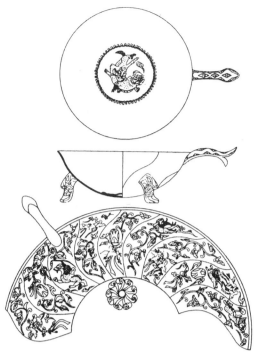

Fig. 80a *Details of the decoration.*

tub-shaped crucible. When in use this crucible was filled with cold water and buried in earth. Cinnabar and charcoal were then loaded into the pomegranate pot and its mouth covered with a small tile, secured with iron wire. The pot was then placed, mouth down, on the crucible and heated. The vaporized mercury thus produced went into the pot and was condensed to liquid mercury by the cooling effect of the water. Four such silver pomegranate pots were discovered among the mass of pharmaceutical and alchemical items in the Hejiacun hoard.[2]

Published: *Wenwu* 1972.1, p. 31; Beijing 1972b, p. 62; Montreal 1986, no. 104; Han and Lu 1989, no. 80; Wang Renbo 1990, p.156, no. 7; Beijing 1992a, no. 276; Hong Kong 1993, no. 38; White 1995, p. 117; Shanghai 1996, p. 105, no. 56; *Empress Wu* 1998, no. 73.

1 This is stated in the chapter on the Metallous Enchymoma of the *Bao Pu* (Book of Master Bao Pu) by Ge Hong (AD 284–364) (Beijing 1983b, p. 217).
2 For a concise study of Chinese alchemical practices see the essay on alchemy, Beijing 1983b, pp. 213–28. I am grateful to Michael Cowell, Department of Scientific Research, British Museum, for help with this entry.

80

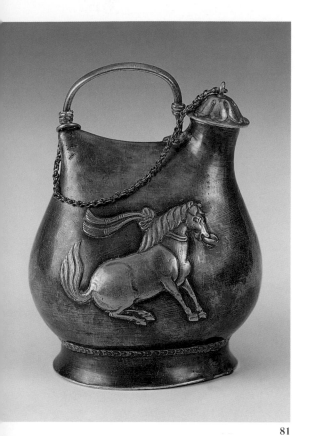

81

81 Flask

Tang dynasty (AD 618–906)
Silver with gilding
Height 14.3 cm; diameter (of foot) 8.9 cm;
weight 549 g
Excavated 1970, Hejiacun, southern suburbs of
Xi'an, Shaanxi province
Shaanxi History Museum

This wine flask is an imitation in silver of the
leather bottles used by the nomads on the
northern borders of the Chinese empire.
The number of ceramic copies of such
bottles testifies to the popularity of the
shape at the time.[1] It is roughly symmetrical
with, at one side of the top, a small straight
opening with a stopper and, on the other,
the start of the bow-shaped handle. The
handle is welded on and a chain connects it
to the stopper which has a lotus leaf design
on it. Both handle and stopper are gilded, as
is the band of braided chain above the
footrim. Inside the footrim is a line of
writing in black with the weight 'thirteen

liang' (approximately 400 grams) clearly
marked.

Each side of the flask is decorated with a
dancing horse holding a cup in its mouth.
These horses have been hammered out in
gilded repoussé. The contrast between the
silver background of the flask and the gold
of the horse contributes to the three-
dimensional effect of the horse, whose
general outline mirrors almost exactly the
shape of the flask. This is achieved by the
ribbon or scarf that flutters from the horse's
neck, following the curve of the top of the
flask, and by the bushy tail which curls up
and round like the body of the flask. The
horse's head, with luxurious mane, balances
the ribbon, and the outstretched front legs
balance the tail.

In the Tang dynasty the nomadic habits of
riding, hunting and fighting on horseback
were very popular. At court people
especially enjoyed polo, horse circuses, and
shooting from horses while riding. The Tang
emperor Zhongzong had dancing horses at
the beginning of the eighth century,[2] but
those belonging to Xuanzong several
decades later were even more famous. At
court Xuanzong had four hundred dancing
horses, each with a pet name, and divided
into left and right divisions just as in an
army. At that time, in the nomadic areas
under the control of the Chinese empire
beyond the Great Wall, people often gave
tribute in the form of horses, and Xuanzong
always kept them and had people train them
to dance. The horses also performed a type
of dressage to music and when it stopped
they were trained to kneel and hold wine
vessels in their mouths, to wish the emperor
a long life, particularly on his birthday, on 5
August.[3] The horses could even apparently
dance on three-tiered benches and would
stop when the benches were lifted up by
athletes. On such occasions the horses were
beautifully decorated, draped in silk, with
trappings of gold and silver and ornaments
of jade and pearls in their manes. The

musicians surrounding them wore yellow
clothing, with jade belts. Xuanzong's prime
minister, one of the most influential writers
and statesmen of the first decades of the
eighth century, Zhang Yue, describes such
performances:

Heavenly horses came from
west of the sea.
They advance slowly and bow
their two knees, ...
With hair standing up, manes
flying, they stamp their feet,
Angered by the drum, they raise
their heads and suddenly rise up.
With banquet's end, a tune sounds
and they hold cups in their mouths...[4]

The horses on this flask mirror this
description exactly.

Xuanzong's dancing horses had an
unfortunate end. At the onset of the
rebellion of An Lushan (see p. 62) Xuanzong
fled, without time to prepare anything,
leaving the horses to scatter. As An Lushan
admired these dancing horses he rescued a
few dozen. However, at An Lushan's defeat
the horses were captured by a warlord who,
unaware of their dancing skills, corralled
them with war horses. One day, when the
military were celebrating a triumph, music
was played and all the dancing horses began
to dance. The horse master, thinking that
these horses were bewitched, ordered them
beaten to death.[5]

Published: *Wenwu* 1972.1, p. 31; Beijing 1972b,
p. 49; Brinker and Goepper 1980, no. 91; Qian,
Chen and Ru 1981, no. 248; Tokyo 1981,
no. 194; Han and Lu 1985, no. 70; Yang Boda
1987, no. 56; Osaka 1987, no. 106; Beijing
1992a, no. 274; Kuhn 1993, no. 59; Berger
1994, no. 42; Yin Shengping 1994; Shanghai
1996, p. 103, no. 52; Xi'an 1997, p. 84.

1 British Museum, Hotung Gallery, case 25,
OA 1959.4-21.1; 1938.5-24.3 . The taste for
exotic shapes, particularly those related to
nomadic ways of life, is typical of the period.
One of the sons of Taizong, Li Chengqian,
adopted Turkish habits to the extent of living
in a complete Turkish camp in the palace

grounds, in a tent, wearing Turkish dress and attended by servants in Turkish dress (Schafer 1963, p. 29).

2 Schafer 1963, p. 67.

3 Xi'an 1995, p. 21. Such horses perhaps resemble the Lipizzaner horses in Austria today.

4 *Quan Tangshi,* Zhonghua shuju edn 1960, vol. 89, p. 981. Translation quoted from Beijing 1992a, cat. no. 274, p. 300. A ceramic dancing horse has been unearthed from the tomb of Zhang Shigui (Hong Kong 1993, no. 79, p. 208).

5 Quoted in *Tangdai congshu,* 1806 edn, Ming Huang zaji, vol. 6, pp. 8–9. See also Waley 1952, pp. 181–3, for a translation of this account by Zheng Chuhui (*c.* AD 850).

82 Pot

Tang dynasty (AD 618–906)
Silver with gilding
Height 24.2 cm; diameter (of mouth) 12.4,
(of foot) 14.3 cm; weight 1.95 kg
Excavated 1970, Hejiacun, southern suburbs of
Xi'an, Shaanxi province
Shaanxi History Museum

This pot is one of the great silver treasures of the Tang dynasty. It has a wide, lidded mouth, short neck, broad shoulders, globular body and a spreading ring foot. Soldered to both sides of the shoulder are two gourd-shaped supports for the flexible handle. The pot has been hammered into shape and decorated with engraved designs against a ring-punched ground. The entire pot is covered with flowers, leafy sprays and grasses, with vivacious parrots at the centre. The neck and the foot are both decorated with a ring of continuous waterchestnut flowers. Inside the ring of the lid is a decoration of *baoxianghua*,[1] surrounded by a ring of grape[2] and acanthus designs. The handle is decorated with rhomboid designs. Inside the lid is a contemporary inscription in black: '50 *liang* of *ziying* and 12 *liang* of *shiying*' (2 kilos of purple quartz and 480 grams of quartz).

This pot is beautifully worked and the decoration is of a particularly high standard.

82

When this pot was excavated it was full of water, and when the archaeologists opened the lid the first thing they saw inside was a floating golden leaf, on which were twelve tiny gold dragons (cat. no. 83). Putting their hands under the dragons they discovered rubies, sapphires and topaz (cat. no. 84).

The parrot is native to southern China but new breeds had been imported from further south, such as Vietnam, from the

83

second century AD. Even more colourful and greatly prized in the Tang dynasty were those imported from Indochina and Indonesia. Taizong ordered a rhapsody to be written in favour of one, and another, which could talk, became the pet of the emperor Xuanzong. Yang Guifei had a white cockatoo which, it was said, she flew at the gaming board when Xuanzong was about to lose, thereby disconcerting the other players and allowing Xuanzong to win![3]

Published: *Wenwu* 1972.1, p. 32; Hejiacun 1972, p. 39, no. 18; Beijing 1972b, p. 57; Melbourne 1977, no.181; Qian, Chen and Ru 1981, no. 254; Tokyo 1981, no. 189; Han and Lu 1985, no. 91; Wang Renbo 1990, p. 173, no. 13; Xi'an 1995, p. 5; Shanghai 1996, p. 115, no. 84; Xi'an 1997, p. 43.

1 Imaginary, idealized lotus-like flowers associated with Buddhism.
2 Grape patterns were popular in the Tang dynasty. Grape wine became more common during this period and bunches of grapes were used as decorative devices on bronze mirrors (British Museum, Hotung Gallery, case 21, OA 1910.4-18.10) and on perfume and incense burners (cat. no. 73).
3 Schafer 1963, p. 101.

83 Dragons

Tang dynasty (AD 618–906)
Gold
Height 2.8 cm; length 4 cm; weight 4.7 g
Excavated 1970, Hejiacun, southern suburbs of Xi'an, Shaanxi province
Shaanxi History Museum

These tiny skeletal dragons, each only 4 centimetres long, are made of pure gold. Curves undulate through their necks, bodies, legs and tails, the upward curl at the end of the tail mirroring that of the horns. They are exquisitely made, with eyebrows and beard clearly delineated and the bodies covered in minute scales.

Dragons are the first of the four spirits, *si ling*,[1] and they are the symbol of the emperor.[2] These dragons belong to the set of twelve discovered in the gilded silver pot with parrot design (cat. no. 82). They were found placed on a gold leaf, on an internal beam within the pot, and under them were many precious stones (cat. no. 84). Because of the association of dragons with the emperor this pot and its contents probably belonged to the imperial household.

The Chinese dragon is a dynastic symbol representing the royal house and the power of the emperor, in the way that the phoenix represents the empress and the head of the female line. Literary references indicate that dragon robes were given to Chinese officials above the third rank by the Tang empress Wu Zetian as early as 694.[3]

During the Tang dynasty paintings of dragons became very popular. In the sixth century Zhang Sengyu painted a mural with four dragons. When viewers pointed out that he had left out the eyes, the painter resumed his work, adding eyes to two of the painted figures whereupon the air was filled with thunder and lightning, walls cracked

and the dragons ascended to heaven, while the two which had not received eyes remained on the wall. The famous eighth-century painter Wu Daozi painted dragons on the palace walls from which smoke and mist emanated whenever it was going to rain.[4]

Published: *Wenwu* 1972.1, p. 32; Hejiacun 1972, p. 40, no. 38; Beijing 1972b, p. 61; Tokyo 1981, no. 196; Han and Lu 1985, no. 109; Yang Boda 1987, nos 50-1; Kuhn 1993, no. 54; Li Xiyu 1994, no. 112; Yin Shengping 1994; Xi'an 1995, p. 3; *Daito Bunmei ten* 1998, no. 31.

1 The four spirits are the dragon, unicorn, phoenix and tortoise, which represent to the Chinese longevity and rarity, hence they are seen as superior spirits. See *Zhongguo shenhua chuanshuo cidian*, Shanghai 1985, p. 126.
2 For information on dragons generally see catalogue no. 52.
3 Munsterberg 1972, pp. 11–12.
4 Sirén 1956–8, colour pl. 1 and p. 110; for dragons generally see Munsterberg 1972.

84 Precious stones

Tang dynasty (AD 618–906)
Diameter 2.5 cm; weight: sapphires 19.5 g, 10 g, 7 g, 3.5 g; topaz 119 g; ruby 12.5 g; 2.5 g
Excavated 1970, Hejiacun, southern suburbs of Xi'an, Shaanxi province
Shaanxi History Museum

These stones were found hidden at the bottom of the magnificent silver pot containing miniature dragons and a golden leaf (cat. no. 82). They had probably been bought to make something of in the future

84

but buried before there was time to work on them.

The sapphires have a high transparency and vary in colour from dark to light blue.[1] Sapphires are not easily identifiable in historical sources, but lapis lazuli is frequently mentioned and seems to have been called sapphire on many occasions. Li Jingxun[2] had sapphires in her jewellery but in general blue stones are referred to as lapis. Lapis came from Badakhshan where it was very common. It was thought of as the Persian gem from which many Sasanian jewels were cut. Emperor Dezong sent an official named Zhu Ruan to Anxi and he obtained there a hundred *jin* of jade, including white jade and blue beads, and some other treasure. Anxi is in Xinjiang province which also produces diamonds, rubies, aquamarines, tourmalines, amethyst and citrines.[3]

The rubies have a high transparency also and vary in colour from a rose to a ruby red.[4] Again, rubies are not easily identifiable in literary and historical sources though it is known that red spinels, called 'balas rubies', were popular in the medieval Orient and were found in the area now known as Tashkent.[5]

The topaz is transparent and of various yellow hues. Its weight is 119.2186 grams or 596.093 carats.[6]

The fourth stone, the chalcedony, is in soyabean-shaped pieces of various sizes, as if they had been partially worked. One may be

an unfinished ring ornament.[7] This mineral was imported from the West and there are various historical references to carnelian (a reddish variety of chalcedony) being received by the Tang court. Some came from Samarkand, some from Tukhāra, and a Persian embassy of the eighth century presented a couch of carnelian.[8]

Published: *Wenwu* 1972.1, p. 32.

1 They have a refractive index of 1.76 and a specific gravity of >3.33.
2 The blue stones in Li Jingxun's jewellery have been labelled both sapphires and lapis.
3 *Xinjiang's Gems and Jades*, Hong Kong 1986, pp. 22–3.
4 They have a refractive index of 1.76 and the specific gravity is >3.33.
5 The difference between rubies and spinel rubies is described in *Xinjiang's Gems and Jades*, Hong Kong 1986, p. 57.
6 Its refractive index is 1.63 and its specific gravity is >3.33.
7 They have a refractive index of 1.52 and a specific gravity >0.5753.
8 Schafer 1963, p. 229.

85 Box

Tang dynasty (AD 618–906)
Silver with gilding
Height 4.8 cm; diameter 12.4; weight 425 g
Excavated 1970, Hejiacun, southern suburbs of Xi'an, Shaanxi province
Shaanxi History Museum

This beautiful round box has a gently curved base and a very tight-fitting domed lid. It has been hammered into shape, and the design is engraved and gilded against a ring-punched ground. The central roundel of the lid contains a winged and horned mythical beast standing, with one leg raised, on clouds; its mouth is wide open, its head raised, its hair stands on end and its wings are outspread. It is framed by a beaded band of lozenges. On the outer ring of the lid are six alternating flowerheads, joined by buds, leaves and tendrils. The lower part of the lid and the sides of the box are decorated with flowers, flying birds and running beasts. On the edge of the lid, where the lid and the box meet, is a decorative border of willow leaf and geometric patterns. The base of the box has a centralized design of six identical flowerheads surrounding a six-petalled design of intertwined pomegranate flowers and knots and six *baoxianghua*,[1] with an open flower at the centre.

Gold and silver wares were the most popular gifts from the emperor to his courtiers, officials and concubines, and he

85

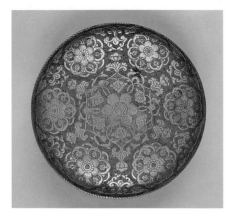

Fig. 85a *Base of the box.*

also received gifts of such objects from his wealthier subordinates. The emperor customarily gave silver boxes containing makeup to his maids on the Winter Solstice. This silver box may well have been a gift, or it may have been a container for medicine (see cat. nos 77 and 79).

Published: *Wenwu* 1972.1, p. 30; Beijing 1972b, p. 46; Tokyo 1981, no. 194; Han and Lu 1985, no. 76; Wang Renbo 1990, p. 157, no. 8; Beijing 1992a, no. 280.

1 Imaginary, idealized lotus-like flowers associated with Buddhism.

Fig. 86a *Detail showing one of a pair of lions guarding the Buddha, from an embroidery of the Buddha Śākyamuni preaching on the Vulture Peak, found at Dunhuang. Tang dynasty, 8th century AD.*

86 Bowl

Tang dynasty (AD 618–906)
Silver with gilding
Height 3.5 cm; diameter of mouth 12.5;
weight 200 g
Excavated 1970, Hejiacun, southern suburbs of Xi'an, Shaanxi province
Shaanxi History Museum

This bowl with rounded sides and everted rim has been hammered into shape. The inner walls of the bowl are decorated with ten *ruyi* cloud designs and in the centre of the base of the bowl there are two gilded lions looking at each other with laurel leaves in their mouths. Encircling them are two rings of gilded decoration surrounded by an outer ring of acanthus design.

The Chinese word for lion, *shizi*, is probably derived from the Persian *šīr* and it was only through contact with the West that China became acquainted with the animal.[1] The lion was frequently depicted in the Near East and Mesopotamia where it was treated as a symbol of power and authority, and in the ninth century BC lion hunts were held to glorify the Assyrian kings.[2] Stone and clay lions were used to guard the front of sacred buildings from the second millennium BC in Babylon and then in many parts of the Near East. During the late Zhou and Han periods crouching and pacing lions may have been introduced to China from Iran and the Near East and stone guardian figures of what are possibly meant to represent lions are found at tombs in Sichuan province from the second century

86

AD. After the fall of the Han dynasty and the gradual introduction of Buddhism into China, lions are more often encountered as in the great cave temples of north China where certain Buddhist figures are seated on thrones with a lion at either side. The practice developed of depicting small guardian lions with the figure of the Buddha, and two very fierce lions can be seen below the feet of the Buddha preaching on the Vulture Peak in a large embroidery (fig. 86a) from Dunhuang.[3] During the Tang period ambassadors sent gifts of lions which were kept in imperial zoos. According to the *Xin Tang shu*,[4] in the section on the western regions, the emperor Taizong, who had received a lion from Samarkand in 635, treasured very highly such animals and ordered his secretary Yu Shinan to compose a poem about them.[5] The poet describes the majesty of the lions in terms that are probably also intended as flattery of the emperor himself:

It glares its eyes — and lightning flashes,
It vents its voice — and thunder echoes.
It drags away the tiger,
Swallows down the bear,
Splits the rhinoceros,
Cleaves the elephant…[6]

In the Buddhist religion lions are considered defenders of the faith and of the Buddhist law. For this reason they are often found guarding the entrances to Buddhist temples. Buddha was seen as a lion amongst men and Mañjuśrī, the bodhisattva associated with wisdom and a popular figure

in Chinese Buddhist art, was shown mounted on a lion. The prowling feline so popular in the Han dynasty gradually came to be replaced by Buddhist-inspired lion door guardians of the type that can be seen, dating from the fifth century, in the Yungang Buddhist grottoes near Datong in Shanxi province.

The lion dance, which is associated with many Chinese festivals, also seems to have come to China from Western Asia some time in the Tang dynasty, introduced to China by Xiliang performers.[7]

On early examples of silverware lions are portrayed singly or in pairs without any other ornament, but they gradually came to be surrounded with flowers or grasses, as on this bowl. Like the lotus, the lion became assimilated into Chinese ideology but it never replaced the tiger as a symbol of the highest authority: imperial seals were carved with dragons and tigers but not with lions.

Published: *Wenwu* 1972.1, p. 30; Hejiacun 1972, p. 40, no. 22; Beijing 1972b, p. 55; Rawson 1982, no. 10; Osaka 1987, no. 107; Wang Renbo 1990, p.167, no. 3; White 1995, p. 118; Shanghai 1996, p. 108, no. 65.

1 Eberhard 1986, pp. 164–5.
2 Rawson 1984b, pp. 110–14.
3 Whitfield and Farrer 1990, p. 113, fig. 88a.
4 For this work see Wilkinson 1998, p. 786.
5 *Xin Tang shu*, Zhonghua shuju, 1975,

87

juan 221, p. 6244. Tribute lions were also depicted in contemporary paintings by painters such as Yan Liben. Schafer 1963, p. 86.
6 As translated and quoted in Schafer 1963, p. 85.
7 Zou Zongxu 1991, p. 136.

87 Bowl

Tang dynasty (AD 618–906)
Gold
Height 5.5 cm; diameter (of mouth) 13.7 cm, (of foot) 6.7 cm; weight 391.5 g
Excavated 1970, Hejiacun, southern suburbs of Xi'an, Shaanxi province
Shaanxi History Museum

This is a particularly magnificent example of Tang dynasty goldware. The bowl has a flared lip and a trumpet-shaped foot with beaded rim. The body is beaten into shape, with two interlocking rows of repoussé lotus petals against a ring-punched background. The upper layer of petals and the shapes between them are decorated with animals such as foxes, deer, roebuck and rabbits and birds such as geese, wagtails, ducks, parrots and mandarin ducks against a background of plants and lotus blossoms suggesting these creatures' natural habitat. The lower layer of petals is filled with honeysuckle scrolls. There is even a flying duck and scrolling leaves engraved on the base of the foot and a rhomboid design above the beaded footrim. The interior of the bowl is decorated with rosette medallions. Three Chinese characters are inscribed in black on the inside cavetto of the bowl, which record the weight of the bowl as 9.3 *liang* (approximately 370 grams). These show how closely the production of gold and silver wares of the Tang dynasty was supervised.

Fig. 87a Details of the decoration.

The shape of the bowl and its petal whorls have been described as Indian in inspiration.[1] The formal layout and symmetrical motifs suggest Near Eastern influences but the freer displacement of the animals amongst the stylized plant elements is more Chinese and shows how foreign decorative motifs had been sinicized by the Tang dynasty.

Published: *Wenwu* 1972.1, p. 30; Hejiacun 1972, p. 42, no. 34; Beijing 1972b, p. 44; W Watson 1973, no. 305; Melbourne 1977, no. 185; Qian, Chen and Ru, no. 247; Tokyo 1981, no. 180; Rawson 1982, no. 12; Han and Lu 1985, no. 50; Yang Boda 1981, no. 53; Wang Renbo 1990, p. 167, no. 1; Xi'an 1992, p. 139; Hong Kong 1993, no. 35; Berger 1994, no. 43; Han Wei 1994a, no. 1; Xi'an 1995, p. 5; Shanghai 1996, p.106, no. 58; Xi'an 1997, p. 42; *Daito Bunmei ten* 1998, no. 18.

1 Gyllensvärd 1957, pp. 77–8; but a Chinese inspiration has also been suggested in the carved stone pillar base of the tomb of Sima Jinlong at Shijiazhai near Datong in Shanxi province, dating from AD 484 of the Northern Wei period (Rawson 1982, pl. 34 and pp. 10–14).

88 Cup

Tang dynasty (AD 618–906)
Silver
Height 5.1 cm; diameter (of mouth) 9.1 cm, (of foot) 3.8 cm; weight 209 g
Excavated 1970, Hejiacun, southern suburbs of Xi'an, Shaanxi province
Shaanxi History Museum

This lobed cup appears to be supported by the eight lotus petals opening out from its base. The lobes have alternate scenes of women and hunting, separated by strings of willow leaves. The cup is finished at the rim, the edge of the foot and on the curve of the handle with beading. On top of the round handle is a disc or small plate and underneath it a curved tail. The disc is in the shape of a *ruyi* cloud (see cat. no. 43) and the central motif is a horned deer (fig. 88a).

Deer appear frequently on Tang silver,

88

Fig. 88a *Detail of the decoration.*

possibly due to the influence of Sasanian and provincial Iranian silver which portrayed lions and deer prominently.[1] However, deer had been assimilated as one of the range of powerful animals by the Han dynasty and they appear, for example, on Han dynasty coffin decoration, along with other auspicious animals. Han emperors hunted deer and they were sacrificed in ceremonies. Fantastical, composite animals with deer-like features were also popular, such as the *qilin,* a kind of unicorn, and the *tianlu,* literally heavenly deer or sacred deer.[2]

The lobes depicting women portray four different activities: going on a spring outing, playing with children, getting dressed and putting on makeup, and playing music. The other panels follow a hunt: the hunters

search out the animals and birds, then run after them, shoot at them and finally kill them. The background to each scene is ring-punched, with decoration of birds, flowers and trees. The supporting eight lotus leaves in the lower section of the body have an acanthus pattern inside each and the ring foot is engraved with curling grasses. At the base of the inside of the cup is a wave design with an elephant's head and three small fish surrounded by lotus leaves (fig. 88a).

This cup is a popular Sogdian[3] and Sasanian shape. As is typical of the gold and silver wares of this relatively early period of the Tang dynasty, it combines a foreign shape with Chinese decorative motifs.

The ring handle makes its first appearance in China in the Tang period, having come originally from the West: Luristan bronze and late Sasanian cups had ring handles.[4] The many ceramic examples are probably copies of the silver prototype. However, the ring handle was a short-lived phenomenon, having disappeared by the Song dynasty and not returning until the eighteenth century when there were further great waves of Western influence.

Gold and silver ware of the Tang dynasty found in Xi'an and its surroundings is generally assumed to have associations with the royal court. Hunting was a popular pastime at court and hunting scenes are a common theme in Tang wall murals,[5] silverware[6] and ceramic models (cat. no. 46).[7] Emperor Taizong counted it as one of the greatest pleasures of his life and although initially a very successful and energetic ruler, his love of expensive hunting trips gradually led him to neglect state affairs. Hunting was an aristocratic privilege restricted to court nobility and forbidden to artisans and merchants by an edict of 667. We do not know, however, how strictly such regulations were followed. [8]

Published: *Wenwu* 1972.1, p. 31; Hejiacun 1972, p. 39, no. 17; Beijing 1972b, p. 52; Yang Boda 1987, no. 52; Han Wei 1989, plates p. 4; Song Yanyan 1991, no. 11; Han Wei 1994a, no. 2; Yin Shengping 1994; Xi'an 1995, p. 9; Shanghai 1996, p. 102, no. 49.

1 Hayashi 1975, figs 4 and 12.
2 Rawson 1984b, pp. 107–10. For references to *tianlu* see cat. nos 20, 21.
3 Sogdians were a people who occupied the region of Central Asia around modern Samarkand. Because of their strategic position on the main East–West trade routes, they were an important link in the chain of cultural exchange. Sogdiana remained a prosperous centre until the Mongol invasions.
4 Willetts 1965, p. 272.
5 Boston 1976, p. 91.
6 See British Museum silver cup, Rawson 1992, fig. 197, p. 267, OA 1968.4-22.10.
7 Numerous examples of three-colour pottery figurines of hunters were found in the tomb of Crown Prince Yide (Li Zhongrun) and there is a detailed mural of forty hunters in the tomb of Prince Zhanghuai (Li Xian). See Boston 1976, figs 108–12; Tang Changdong 1996, figs 24–30, pp. 27–30.
8 Schafer 1963, p. 59.

89 Cup

Tang dynasty (AD 618–906)
Gold
Height 5.9 cm; diameter (of mouth) 6.8 cm, (of foot) 3.5 cm; weight 230 g
Excavated 1970, Hejiacun, southern suburbs of Xi'an, Shaanxi province
Shaanxi History Museum

This cylindrical cup has a flaring lip and a slightly concave body silhouette, a ring handle with a volute thumb piece, and a rounded base to which is soldered an everted footrim. The ring handle has been

89

soldered to an escutcheon which has then been riveted to the cup. There are four six-petalled, stylized flower medallions formed from gold wires soldered on to the body, evenly spaced around it, and the outer limits of the flowers are delineated by small gold dots in granulation technique. In between the medallions of flowers, at top and bottom, are gold filigree cloud designs. Between the top of the foot and the main part of the cup are further half medallions. There are indications that some of the filigree medallions were originally inlaid with pearls and precious stones as, though only sparse remains of a greyish-white substance survive, there are clear signs of the roughened ground. This technique may be a forerunner of the later cloisonné technology as the cup could be said to show all the stages of cloisonné preparation apart from the enamels melted into the cloisons. [1]

This cup illustrates a variety of goldsmithing techniques such as casting, cutting, polishing, soldering, riveting and filigree work and is a very good example of the high level of sophistication reached by the early Tang metalworkers. The style of the flower medallion shows Persian or Sasanian

influence but the cloud or *ruyi* design is of Chinese origin, dating back to the Han dynasty (see cat. no. 43).

Published: *Wenwu* 1972.1, p. 31; Hejiacun 1972, p. 40, no. 26; Beijing 1972b, p. 51; Brinker and Goepper 1980, no. 89; Han and Lu 1985, no. 60; Yang Boda 1987, no. 55; Wang Renbo 1990, p. 169, no.7; Kuhn 1993, no. 56; Yin Shengping 1994; Shaanxi 1995, p. 9; Shanghai 1996, p. 99, no. 44; *Daito Bunmei ten* 1998, no. 20.

1 H Brinker and A Lutz, *Chinese Cloisonné: The Pierre Uldry Collection*, New York 1989, pp. 65–70.

90

90 Cup

Tang dynasty (AD 618–906)
Gilded bronze with an iron core
Height 6.5 cm; diameter (of mouth) 7 cm,
(of foot) 4.3 cm; weight 379 g
Excavated 1970, Hejiacun, southern suburbs of
Xi'an, Shaanxi province
Shaanxi History Museum

The Hejiacun hoard contained two octagonal cups decorated with foreign entertainers. This ring-handled cup has a wide flared mouth, arched body and a trumpet-shaped ring foot. The footrim is outlined with a ring of dotted pearl design. The mouthrim is slightly damaged and a little rusty. The cup was cast into shape and the body is divided into eight decorative panels with beaded frames.[1]

Each decorative panel contains a figure in high relief. There are seven musicians dressed in foreign clothing and holding foreign musical instruments. The eighth figure is bald and wears only a loin cloth, suggesting that he was some kind of acrobatic performer or a servant. The musicians wear short jackets, baggy trousers, pointed hats with upturned brims and shoes with upturned toes. Their

instruments include clappers, a *konghou* (ancient plucked stringed instrument), a conch, a *pipa* (type of lute), a flute, and a *bibi* (trumpet-like instrument). Foreign musicians, dancers and all kinds of other entertainers came to perform at the Chinese capital Chang'an; many are depicted in ceramic form (see cat. no. 39). The oldest indigenous instruments in China include chimes, large zithers and mouth organs. Most of the plucked and bowed

Fig. 90a *Detail of the roundel depicting the heads of two foreigners.*

instruments, such as the lutes, were imported over the centuries from Central Asia.[2] The clothing worn by the musicians shows the kind of fashions imitated by many Tang ladies. It was therefore not always possible to identify a foreigner from the clothing alone. However, the combination here of foreign dress and foreign musical instruments leaves no doubt that this is a foreign troupe, typical of the time.

The ring handle is made up of twelve beads. Lying flat over the top of the handle are the relief profiles of two foreigners, joined at the hair (fig. 90a). These are probably Persians, elderly men with deep-set eyes, large noses and long beards. Persians outnumbered the other foreigners in cosmopolitan Chang'an and were certainly amongst the most important and wealthiest. Most were traders, although some were artisans and designers influential in the introduction of new metalworking techniques to the Chinese.

The Near Eastern or Sasanian shape of this cup and the decoration of foreigners makes this an item that shows little sinicization.

Published: *Wenwu* 1972.1, p. 31; Hejiacun 1972, p. 40, no. 27; Beijing 1972b, p. 52; W Watson 1973, no. 306; Brinker and Goepper 1980, no. 94; Qian, Chen and Ru 1981, no. 253; Tokyo 1981, no. 182; Han and Lu 1985, no. 62; Montreal 1986, no. 103; Yang Boda 1987, no. 48; Han Wei 1989, plates p. 1; Wang Renbo 1990, p. 169, no. 6; Beijing 1992a, no. 275; Kuhn 1993, no. 55; Berger 1994, no. 41; Yin Shengping 1994; Xi'an 1995, p. 14; White 1995, p. 117; Shanghai 1996, p. 99, no. 45; Xi'an 1997, p. 42.

1 This technique is reminiscent of that used on a ceramic rhyton with moulded decoration, dating to the seventh century, in the British Museum, OA 1968.4-22.21. For further information on the use of beading on ceramics and metalwork and the transmission of foreign decorative motifs into China generally, see Rawson 1977, 1982, 1984b, 1991.

2 For information on Chinese music see *Cambridge Encyclopaedia of China*, ed. Brian Hook, Cambridge 1982, pp. 376–8 and L Picken *et al*, *Music from the Tang Court*, Oxford 1981–98, vols 1–6.

1 Imaginary idealized lotus-like floral design associated with Buddhism.
2 Rawson 1992, p. 32, no. 10.
3 Michaelson 1992. See British Museum, Hotung Gallery, case 14, OA 1955.10-24.1.

91

92 Two coins

Tang dynasty (AD 618–906)
Silver
Diameter 2.5 cm; weights 6 g and 5.8 g
Excavated 1970, Hejiacun, southern suburbs of Xi'an, Shaanxi province
Shaanxi History Museum

91 Cup

Tang dynasty (AD 618–906)
Silver with gilding
Height 3 cm; diameter (of mouth) 10.5, (of foot) 7.6 cm; weight 144 g
Excavated 1970, Hejiacun, southern suburbs of Xi'an, Shaanxi province
Shaanxi History Museum

This oval cup has an everted rim, a flat base and two rectangular handles or ears soldered to it, one at the centre of each of the two long sides of the oval. It has been hammered into shape and has spectacular decoration of gilded flowers, beasts and birds against a silver ring-punched background. In the centre of the base, both on the inner and outer surfaces of the cup, is an oval *baoxianghua* design.[1] Around the inside of the cup (fig. 91a) are four floral

Fig. 91a Detail of the interior baoxianghua *design.*

sprays, between which are scrolling clouds. The two 'ears' are decorated with parts of floral sprays. On the outer surface of the cup, among intertwining tendrils and flowers, are stylized lotus flowers on which stand mandarin ducks, some with wings open, some closed. As Chinese mandarin ducks always live in pairs they are symbols of marital bliss and were often incorporated into the designs of utensils of the Tang dynasty.

This cup is similar in shape to the so-called eared lacquered and jade cups of the Qin and Han periods (see cat. no. 70). This was a popular shape for drinking both wine and broth and of all the lacquered pieces excavated from the Qin and Han period over one third are eared cups. The British Museum has an example of an inscribed lacquered eared cup which well illustrates the mass-production techniques used then to make such vessels;[2] it was made in the equivalent year of AD 4 and an inscription on it lists the names of the six craftsmen who participated in the various processes of making it and those of the seven product inspectors who inspected it at every turn.[3] However, silver eared cups are rare, and the workmanship of this cup is particularly fine.

Published: *Wenwu* 1972.1, p. 32; Beijing 1972b, p. 50; W Watson 1973, no. 309; Rawson 1982, no. 11; Han and Lu 1986, no. 68; Wang Renbo 1990, p. 155, no. 4; Han Wei 1994a, no. 3; Shanghai 1996, p. 105, no. 55.

Four hundred and twenty-one silver *Kaiyuan tongbao* coins were found in the Hejiacun hoard, of which one is illustrated here. *Kaiyuan tongbao* coins were first issued by the Tang dynasty in the fourth year of its Wude period, AD 621. Bronze *Kaiyuan tongbao* coins then became the major currency of China for several hundred years. They are round coins with a square hole in the centre and have four Chinese characters: *kai yuan tong bao* (circulating treasure of the opening of the dynasty) written on the obverse in *lishu*, or clerical script. The first issue in 621 used the calligraphy of the renowned calligrapher Ouyang Xun. There are no characters on the reverse. Alongside the regular bronze issues, gold and silver *Kaiyuan tongbao* were made, but these did not function as currency. They were made as presentation coins to be given as imperial gifts and rewards.

92 obverse

In one of the histories of the Tang dynasty, the *Jiu Tang shu*, in the biography of Xuanzong, it is recorded that the emperor Xuanzong held a banquet in Chen Tian Gate to entertain the nobles and courtiers, and he asked his servants to throw gold and silver coins from the upper part of the building. The secretaries above the fifth grade and other officials above the third grade were allowed to compete to pick them up, to show the intimate relationship between the emperor and his officials and his munificence to them.[1]

The Tang dynasty court was normally filled with as many as 3000 concubines, though many passed their entire lives there without even seeing the emperor. There are many moving poems and stories about these concubines. To keep themselves busy they undertook tasks such as making clothes for soldiers. One such soldier, when examining his new uniform, discovered some characters written on its inner lining:

Those who fight on the frontier
Can hardly sleep through the cold nights.
I have made this battle gown,
But know not to whom it will belong.
Carefully I have sewn it with thread
And added cotton along with my love.
In this life I have missed the chance,
So I pray for our union in the next.[2]

He reported this to his officer who then had the gown returned to the court. The emperor finally saw it and, after investigation, met the beautiful young concubine who had sewn it; he thereupon released her from the harem (a very unusual occurrence) and she was married to the soldier.

Every spring Xuanzong played a gold coin throwing game with a few of his most beautiful concubines, who would toss coins to see whose turn it was to attend on the emperor. Such coins were also used as celebratory gifts when concubines gave birth.

Published: *Wenwu* 1972.1, p. 33.

1   The *Jiu Tang shu* (Old Standard History of the Tang) was written by Liu Xu (887–964) *et al* and covers the years 618–906 (see *Jiu Tang shu*, Zhonghua shuju edn, 1975, juan 8, p. 171; Wilkinson 1998, p. 785.
2   Quoted in Shang Xizhi (ed.) (trans. Liang Liangxing), *Tales of Empresses and Imperial Consorts in China*, Hong Kong 1994, pp. 137–8.

93 Unworked block of jade

Tang dynasty (AD 618–906)
Jade
Length 11 cm; width 9.5 cm; weight 2.35 kg
Excavated 1970, Hejiacun, southern suburbs of Xi'an, Shaanxi province
Shaanxi History Museum

This is a rectangular block of pale green jade with yellow inclusions, possibly from the Manchurian area of China. On one side is a black cloud-shaped marking. It has been polished and is ready for processing, possibly into a seal, or perhaps a wrist rest or pulse pillow which were commonly made in ceramic and sometimes in silver.

During the Tang period the empire was as large in extent as it would be until the last imperial dynasty, the Qing. This meant that access to sources of jade was relatively easy, at least until 845 when religious persecutions began and trade routes from the jade-producing regions appear to have suffered disruption.

93

The main sources of jade at this time were Khotan and Yarkand in present-day Xinjiang province. Although large amounts seem to have been imported, relatively few carved jades have been securely dated to the Tang period. By this time they tended not to be buried in tombs and so few can be dated according to an archaeological context. It is possible also that jade was now in competition with items of gold and silver and there was less demand for it.[1] However, jade had been for so long held in such high esteem by the Chinese that demand for items in jade did not die out completely: personal ornaments such as hairpins and combs for women, and belts for men, continued to be made in considerable numbers, although the use of jade for belts was regulated by sumptuary laws (see cat. no. 42).

Jade was still considered of great value. At the time of the burial of the Hejiacun hoard this block of jade may just have been acquired to be worked by a jade craftsman and was therefore hoarded in the hope that the commission would be fulfilled when the owners came to retrieve their treasures, as they clearly assumed or hoped they would.

Another possibility is that the jade was destined for use as a drug. According to the imperial pharmacopoeia jade was supposed to have the power to lighten the body and therefore somehow extend its life. It was often made into a liquid according to alchemical recipes or it was swallowed in the form of powder or grains.[2]

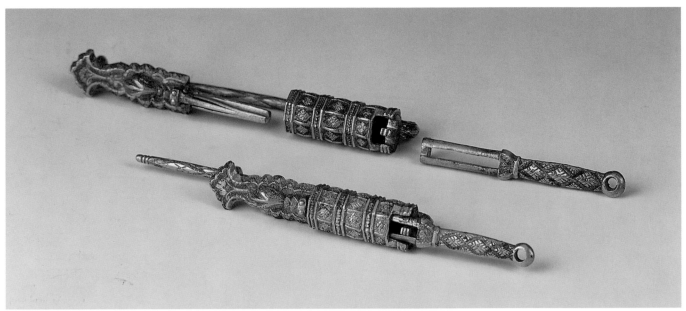

94

Published: *Wenwu* 1972.1, p. 33.

1 Forsyth and McElney 1994, pp. 272–3.
2 See Needham 1976, p. 43 and the *Bencao gangmu* (Compendium of *materia medica*) by Li Shizhen (1518–93), published in 1602, the most famous of the Chinese *materia medica*. It contains 1892 varieties, 11,096 prescriptions and 1110 illustrations (*Bencao gangmu,* 4 vols, Renmin weisheng 1977).

94 Padlock

Tang dynasty (AD 618–906)
Silver with gilding
Length of each part 13.5 cm; weights 36 g, 28 g
Excavated 1970, Hejiacun, southern suburbs of Xi'an, Shaanxi province
Shaanxi History Museum

Seventeen padlocks like this one, in silver with gilding, and a further six in silver were excavated at Hejiacun. Their shape and decoration are almost identical, but they differ slightly in size.

The padlock is made up of three parts: the pin with a spring, the socket and the key. The spring was the second innovation in the locksmith's art (tumblers being the first), introduced into China, probably from the West, some time before the Tang dynasty. When the pin or bolt is fully home, the spring which it bears expands and prevents its removal. To undo the padlock the key is inserted from the other end and, by compressing the springs close to the bolt, allows its removal.[1] Such a barrel or barb-bolt padlock was also known to the Romans and has been found on Romano-British sites.[2]

The lock is cast and hammered into a hexagonal shape. The barrel is engraved with flowers, rhomboids and dotted pearls which are all gilded. Such attention to detail on what was essentially a utilitarian item is typical of the meticulous care taken by the Tang metalworker.

Such clasp-like padlocks were commonly used in Tang times to lock chests and boxes, as can be evidenced from those seen on the miniature chests found in tombs. There are a number of similar locks in collections in the United States and Europe.[3]

Published: *Wenwu* 1972.1, p. 32; Hejiacun 1972, p. 42, no. 39; Xi'an 1992, p. 25.

1 Needham 1965, vol. 4:2, pp. 236–46.
2 W H Manning, *Catalogue of the Romano-British Iron Tools, Fittings and Weapons in the British Museum,* London 1922, p. 95.
3 Gyllensvärd 1957, p. 51; Fontein and Wu 1973, cat. no. 92.

Buddhist Temples and Crypts

This last section focuses on finds from Buddhist crypts, specifically those found in the Qingshan and Famen[1] temples,[2] two important archaeological discoveries of the late 1980s.[3]

Buddhism was founded in northern India by the prince Gautama Śākyamuni (*c.* 563–483 BC). Distressed by scenes of suffering, illness, old age and death, he left his family, wife and newborn son to become a religious mendicant. After years of searching for the right path to follow, he attained Enlightenment, and during meditation under the *bodhi* tree became a Buddha, an 'Enlightened One'. He wanted to save man from an endless cycle of rebirth and he taught that suffering was caused by the desire for attachment to material possessions. He claimed that this suffering was unnecessary as material things are an illusion and if people realized this they would be free from suffering. If desire could be extinguished, the cause of rebirth, *karma*, one's actions, would no longer be generated, karmic debt would be repaid and the endless cycle of rebirth would cease. The individual would then achieve supreme Enlightenment or Nirvāṇa and his individuality would end. Early Buddhism taught that this could be achieved through withdrawal into a monastery where one would follow the Noble Eightfold Path, the Buddha's rules for right living, right speech and right action. Once the Buddha had achieved this understanding he travelled and lectured on this doctrine for the rest of his life.

Buddhism first spread throughout India, then to Pakistan, Afghanistan and Southeast Asia. It also travelled along the Silk Routes to China, Korea, Japan and Tibet. Buddhism arrived in China in the Han dynasty but did not gain widespread popularity until after the fall of that dynasty in AD 220. This was a period when China was fragmented, in political turmoil, and in this precarious and turbulent political climate Buddhism, a doctrine of personal salvation, was particularly popular. Also at this time the north of China was ruled by non-Chinese rulers who were themselves Buddhists and they inaugurated vast building programmes, particularly of Buddhist cave shrines. The success of Buddhism in China was in large part due to its tolerance of other religious practices and its willingness to adopt and adapt to Daoism and Confucianism. Buddhism was at the peak of its popularity in the Tang dynasty when it was supported by all levels of society, the imperial household, nobility, great and wealthy families and the common people. Buddhist temples served as places of entertainment for the urban crowds and Buddhist festivals provided entertainment and diversions to the masses in the villages and cities. Religious lectures and vegetarian feasts were attended by many pious laymen, and monasteries acted as banks, pawnbrokers, medical centres, places of study and the focus for quasi-religious clubs. However, after the severe persecution of Buddhism in the mid-ninth century, Buddhism's power and influence began to wane, although China remained a Buddhist country until the modern era.

Early Buddhism, called Theravada or the Doctrine of the Elders, stressed the individual's independent quest for Enlightenment but alternative methods of salvation developed later which were termed Mahāyāna, or Greater Vehicle (of salvation), by their followers. Theravada was then called Hinayāna, or Lesser Vehicle. The essential difference between these two schools was that Mahāyāna held that Buddhahood was available to all, and not just to a few monks. Whereas the enlightened monk, the *arhat* or *luohan*, is representative of Hinayāna, the bodhisattva is representative of Mahāyāna. The bodhisattva is a being on the point of Enlightenment who chooses to remain in the world of illusion – *samsāra* – until all other beings reach the same stage. Mahāyāna iconography is distinguished by its many Buddhas and many paradises in which these Buddhas were worshipped along with the numerous bodhisattvas who, somewhat like Catholic saints, served intercessory roles.

Hinayāna Buddhism, asserting that Enlightenment comes only through one's own efforts, was most popular in Southeast Asia whereas the Mahāyāna form and a later tradition of Esoteric Buddhism were transmitted to East Asia.[4] However, for a long time, both schools existed side by side and, even after Mahāyāna became dominant along most of the Silk Route, some regions, such as the city-state of Kucha, were known for their Hinayāna tradition. Many different sects developed under the umbrella of Mahāyāna, including the Pure Land School with its appeal to the multitude of the promise of the Western Paradise of Amitābha Buddha. Rebirth in this 'Pure Land' was attainable simply through the repeated invocation of Amitābha's name. Amitābha Buddha was aided by the most popular bodhisattva in East Asia (he was also popular in India, Nepal, Tibet, Korea and Japan), Avalokiteśvara, or Guanyin, originally a male deity who, over centuries, evolved into the goddess of mercy (see cat. no. 97) in China. He or she was everywhere, delivering people from suffering, granting children to the childless and saving the faithful from peril, the textual authority for the tradition coming from chapter 25 of the *Lotus Sūtra*. Guanyin was capable of assuming any form or shape and in the Esoteric tradition is depicted with several heads, or with a thousand eyes and arms, symbol of the multiplicity of his powers of compassion.

Another branch of Buddhism that also gained in popularity in Tang China was Chan (or Zen in Japan). It lays stress on lay practice, claiming that the Buddha nature is immanent in all and can be achieved without recourse to endless study (although the Chan sect soon built up a considerable body of texts). It had its origin in *dhyāna* (meditation), the religious discipline that aims at tranquillizing the mind in order to look inward at one's consciousness. In practice this meant intense meditation, and the founder of the Chan school, Bodhidharma, meditated in front of a cliff for nine years. This non-verbal and non-analytical approach to the ultimate reality had a profound influence over the Chinese for more than a thousand years.

A further important major doctrinal division in Buddhism in China was Esoteric Buddhism, also called Tantric or Vajrayāna (Diamond Vehicle) Buddhism. Like Chan (Zen), Vajrayāna Buddhism taught that Enlightenment could be achieved in one lifetime. In Chinese this was translated as *mijiao* (secret teachings) or *mizong*. This form of Buddhism received official recognition and active encouragement during Xuanzong's reign (see cat. nos 95 and 97). It had already reached Tibet independently and became dominant there. Vajrayāna introduced into Chinese Buddhist practice the use of *mandalas* (diagrams of the sacred universe and maps of consciousness) and *mantras* (sounds or syllables that embodied the spiritual energy of a god).

Many of the most distinguished translators of the Buddhist texts were important influences in China. One early missionary and translator was a Parthian prince, whose Chinese name was An Shigao, who arrived in Luoyang in AD 148. Kumarajiva, an aristocrat turned monk (344–c. 410), was another influential monk who learnt Chinese during enforced captivity in what is now Gansu province but arrived in Chang'an in 402 and organized many translations of sacred Buddhist scriptures. One of the best known Chinese monks (fig. 25) is Xuanzang (c. 596–664),[5] who began a journey to India in 629 without official sanction. He went to collect Buddhist texts from India to seek answers to his own personal unresolved doubts and he crossed Central Asia, sailed down the Ganges and saw the *bodhi* tree under which it is said the Buddha attained Enlightenment. He became famous throughout India and eventually returned home through Central Asia, arriving in April 645 and receiving a warm

Fig. 25 Travelling monk, ink and colours on paper, Tang dynasty (618–906).
Height 41 cm.

welcome from the emperor Taizong who offered support
for his project to translate the Indian texts. By his death
Xuanzang had completed the translation of seventy-three
sūtras out of the 657 he had brought from India. His book
about the western regions gave the Tang court first-hand
knowledge of Central Asia and India and his travels became
the subject of a legendary novel which is still read and
enjoyed today: *Journey to the West* (or *Monkey* in a partial
translation by Arthur Waley).[6]

Chang'an (see fig. 7, p. 32) was a cosmopolitan city in
the Tang dynasty. As early as 635 Emperor Taizong received
a Nestorian monk and allowed this branch of Christianity
to be preached freely throughout the empire. In the second
half of the seventh century the Zoroastrian religion was
practised by Persians fleeing the Arabs; and Sogdians, who
converted to Manichaeism, converted Uighurs who had

come to help the Tang Chinese fight the rebels in the 750s.
There were also Muslim and Jewish communities in China.
At times, depending on the religious persuasion of the
ruler, Buddhism had to compete with Daoism and
Confucianism, but despite this Buddhism remained a
prominent force.

Empress Wu Zetian (see fig. 14, p. 60) became a devoted
adherent of Buddhism, partly through the influence of her
parents and partly through expedience. At her behest,
from 672 to 675, the great Buddha of the Rocks, the
Cosmic Buddha Vairocana, was carved out in the grottoes
of Longmen, near Luoyang in Henan, together with the
surrounding company of bodhisattvas and guardians of the
world.[7] She donated 20,000 cash for the commission
(from her cosmetics fund),[8] and some scholars have
claimed (although this is very contentious) that the statue's
features are based on those of the empress (fig. 26). After
the death of her husband Gaozong, she took over the
reins of government and exiled the legitimate emperor.
Although sixty at the time, she embarked on an affair with
a licentious peddler, Feng Xiaobao, who subsequently
became a monk in order to facilitate his entry into the
imperial palace and then became the abbot of the famous
White Horse temple outside Luoyang.[9] In order to explain
her usurpation of the imperial throne, which was not
permitted to women under the Confucian system, Wu
Zetian sought justification in Buddhist literature. The *Da
Yun jing* (Great Cloud Sūtra), which contains within it the
prediction that seven hundred years after his Nirvāṇa the
Buddha would be reborn in a small country in south India
where a pious woman would become ruler of a worldwide
empire to which all others would submit, seemed very
appropriate. The abbot and others implied that Empress
Wu was the incarnation of Maitreya (the Buddha of the
future) on earth and so qualified to rule as successor to the
Tang emperors. The empress had the *Da Yun jing* circulated
throughout the empire and in 690 seized the throne and
founded her new dynasty, which she named Zhou.
Buddhism flourished under her imperial patronage,

Fig. 26 *Image of the Vairocana Buddha in the Fengxian temple at the Longmen caves, 7th century AD. The statue's features are said to be based on those of Empress Wu Zetian.*

architectural forms were adapted to a Buddhist purpose when the Chinese adopted the Indian practice of enshrining relics (*śarīra, sheli* in Chinese) beneath a stūpa. The stūpa, which originated in India and predated Buddhism, consisted of a large hemispherical mound with a central mast topped with canopies or *chattras*. Instead of stūpas, the Chinese built multi-storeyed towers known as pagodas. Many early Chinese secular and Buddhist buildings were built of wood and so often burned down. When a Buddhist structure was rebuilt, the relics were often added to and subsequently resealed in the new building.

According to ancient tradition the Buddha was cremated after attaining his final Nirvāṇa and the *śarīra* were the pure crystallized grains resulting from the cremation. These remains were divided among eight stūpas, seven of which were opened in the third century BC by India's first Buddhist ruler, King Aśoka of the Mauryan empire, who dispersed the *śarīra* to 84,000 stūpas throughout his kingdom. Tradition says that these were subsequently divided again and again, and since *śarīra* came to mean the remains of Buddhist saints and patriarchs generally, rather than just those of the historical Buddha, there evolved an almost inexhaustible supply of them. The figure 84,000 refers to the number of atoms in the Buddha's corpus as well as to the corpus of his sacred words. The possession of 'authentic' relics supposedly ensured the possessor an elevated place both in the ecclesiastical hierarchy and in society in general and at the same time stimulated donations from the faithful which guaranteed economic independence.[10]

Many deposits of Buddhist relics have been discovered over the past decades, from Liaoning in the northeast of China to Yunnan in the southwest. Most have been found within pagodas, usually in sealed crypts, but also in other parts of the building, such as at the base of the mast on the top of the pagoda. Two of the most important recent discoveries have been at the monasteries of Qingshan and Famen in Shaanxi province.

particularly from 685 to 705. In 705 Empress Wu abdicated and, with the accession of Xuanzong in 712, Daoism regained imperial favour and took precedence over Buddhism. However, this was not a time of great repression, rather more a curtailing of some of the worst extravagances.

The magnificent festivals of the Buddhist calendar, such as the festival of the lanterns, the feast of the dead, the procession of the Buddha images and the reception of the Buddha's relics into the imperial palace, were dazzling spectacles in which all classes of society participated. Many of these festivals and ceremonies were associated with the wealthy monasteries, of which Qingshan and Famen were two of the best known.

The Chinese multi-storeyed tower probably had its origins in the Han dynasty watch-towers which were built along the Great Wall for defence purposes. However, such

Qingshan monastery in Lintong county is four kilometres to the northeast of the mausoleum of the First Emperor of China, Qin Shi Huangdi, and about forty kilometres from the ancient city of Chang'an, present-day Xi'an. It was one of the forty-eight monasteries built in the Sui and Tang dynasties in the metropolitan area. Not much remains of the monastery today but in 1985, in the ruins of the basement, a small monument was unearthed. A five-hundred-word inscription gives the story of the monastery, relating how the original building was blown down by a strong wind and that the rebuilding was completed in 741. In the middle of the main room was found the square pavilion-shaped Buddhist shrine (cat. no. 99) together with its associated inner coffins and glass reliquary holder. Besides the shrine and its inner caskets, there were about a hundred other sacrificial articles made of gold, silver, bronze, pottery and glass. There were incense burners, a gold cup, silver spoons and chopsticks and many alms bowls. Decoration on the reliquary-shaped coffins reproduced the Central Asian forms seen on pre-Tang silverware and ceramics.[11] Similar reliquaries have come from Jingchuan in Gansu province and the Ganlu temple at Zhenjiang, Jiangsu province.[12] Around the brick walls of the main hall were frescoes showing Chinese and foreign monks, as well as performances by singers and dancers.[13]

The Famen temple (Famensi) is situated about 110

Fig. 27 Famen temple, Fufeng county, Shaanxi province.

kilometres to the west of Xi'an (fig. 27). It has a long history going back at least to the Northern Wei dynasty. In 558, in the Northern Zhou period, the base of the pagoda was opened and inside was placed a relic, a finger bone of the Buddha, supposedly presented by King Aśoka of India in 272 BC. The Famen temple was renowned in its time as one of only four Buddhist temples in China to contain such a true relic (or śarīra) of the Buddha.[14]

Due to its geographical proximity to Chang'an the Famen temple maintained its importance and came to serve as the principal place of worship for the imperial family. The relics of the Buddha were periodically brought from the Famen temple to the palace where they were worshipped by the royal family. Under Taizong the crypt of the temple was opened and the finger bone worshipped. From then onwards various emperors and the empress Wu Zetian worshipped at the temple and the empress commissioned gold and silver caskets to encase the finger bone. The relic continued to be worshipped until Emperor Xizong's time. In 873 Xizong was the last to bring the Buddha's finger bone relic back to the imperial palace in Chang'an. On its return to the Famen temple it, along with other treasures, was sealed within the crypt where they remained hidden for 1114 years until 1987. They were rediscovered by chance during renovations of the foundations of the temple which had collapsed in 1981. The crypt, containing 121 pieces of gold and silver, precious ceramics and glass, as well as about one thousand pieces of silk fabric (fig. 28), was an immensely important discovery. The extensive documentary records[15] which were found with it led, for example, to the identification of the hitherto unauthenticated *mise* ware (see cat. no. 116). These deposited treasures and their preservation have been vital to an understanding of Chinese Buddhist practices in the Tang dynasty.

There were four sets of caskets (fig. 29) for holding śarīra in the temple (see cat. no. 117).[16] It is argued that the reason there were four sets was that three acted as decoys while the fourth, the one that contained the

Fig. 28 *Gold embroidered, red short-sleeved coat, possibly made for the bodhisattva (cat. no. 104). Excavated in 1987 from the Famen temple, Fufeng county, Shaanxi province.*

genuine *śarīra*, was kept in the hidden niche to prevent anything happening to it in times of persecution.

Of all the various Buddhist festivals that attracted the crowds in Chang'an, the several connected with the worship of the Buddha's relics were the most popular. At least four other temples claimed to have a tooth of the Buddha. These four teeth were put on annual display by the temples for a limited period, and all the offerings were placed on public display. During the heyday of the Famen temple, the great procession of its Buddhist relics was one of the highlights in the Buddhist calendar. The relic, decorated with gold, jade, silk and jewellery, would be transported in luxury, in imperial carriages, with streamers, from the temple to the palaces in Chang'an or Luoyang for worship.

The Buddha's finger bone relic from the Famen temple is immortalized by the famous memorial of 819 presented by Han Yu, an influential Confucian and official in the Tang government. In it he protested vigorously against the imperial practice of welcoming the Buddha's finger bone into the royal palace. It appears that the imperial reception of this relic was not an annual affair. The first such reception took place in 660 and thereafter in 790, 819 and 873. The relic was kept in the palace for three days before being taken to one of the Buddhist temples in the city for public viewing. There was patently a great deal of religious frenzy and in 819 Han Yu charged that the multitudes burned their heads and roasted their fingers, threw away their clothes and scattered their money, and that old and young rushed about abandoning their work and disregarding their place in society. Other sources spoke of officials and noble families donating great sums to the monasteries, while the common people vied with one another in making offerings to the Buddha, giving up their earnings of a lifetime.[17] Gold and jade decorated piles of earth built to form incense posts along the route. The extravagance of such displays and feasts is recorded by Ennin, a Japanese monk who visited China. He described the festival of the ghosts as he observed it in 844:

On the fifteenth day of the seventh moon the various monasteries of the city made offerings. The monasteries made flowery candles,

Fig. 29 *Set of seven caskets for holding the Buddha's finger bone, Tang dynasty (618–906). Excavated in 1987 from beneath the Famen temple, Fufeng county, Shaanxi province.*

flowery cakes, artificial flowers, fruit trees, and the like, vying with one another in their rarities. Customarily they spread them all out as offerings in front of the Buddha halls, and [people of] the whole city go around to the monasteries and perform adoration. It is a most flourishing festival.[18]

One feast at Wutaishan described by Ennin was sponsored by a private individual and attended by 750 clerics and secular guests, both male and female.[19]

The growth of anti-Buddhist sentiment was a complex and subtle process. From the earliest entry of Buddhism into China, critics had stressed the foreignness of the religion and therefore its inappropriateness for the Chinese. They pointed out that the monastic system violated traditional Confucian views that family duties, including having children and paying respect to one's ancestors, were fundamental. But their views had little influence at first. The state also had reasons to be critical of Buddhism. Temple lands were tax-exempt, as were the clergy; in times of economic hardship this became an important issue. The vast treasures in the temples in the form of gold, copper and bronze images meant that wealth was withdrawn from circulation at a time when hard metals were scarce. In fact, growing political instability and economic uncertainty led the Chinese in the latter part of the Tang to reject their earlier openness towards things foreign and to reconsider their own traditions. This culminated in the rise of neo-Confucianism a century later, but, despite this, Buddhism continued to flourish.

Han Yu was the leader of the important literary movement in the Tang dynasty which argued for the revival of the classical prose style. His own writing harked back to that of the Zhou and Han dynasties and ran counter to the flowery, rhymed prose style more popular in the early part of the Tang. He set out to weaken the influence of Buddhism and to promote Confucianism to its former position of preeminence in the minds of the people. He was xenophobic as far as Buddhism was concerned and asserted that its unsuitableness to the Chinese was proved by the fact that dynasties which supported Buddhism were short-lived (although, as his critics pointed out, this was factually incorrect).

Now the Buddha was of barbarian origin. His language differed from Chinese speech; his clothes were of a different cut; his mouth did not pronounce the prescribed words of the Former Kings, his body was not clad in the garments prescribed by the Former Kings. He did not recognize the relationship between prince and subject, nor the sentiments of father and son. …now that he has long been dead, is it fitting that his decayed and rotten bones, his ill-omened and filthy remains, should be allowed to enter in the forbidden precincts of the Palace? Confucius said, 'Respect ghosts and spirits, but keep away from them. … I pray that Your Majesty will turn this bone over to the officials that it may be cast into water or fire, cutting off for all time the root and so dispelling the suspicions of the empire and preventing the befuddlement of later generations'.[20]

The emperor Xianzong was enraged, particularly as a supporter of Buddhism himself, by the assertion that all dynasties which supported Buddhism were short-lived. He ordered the death of Han Yu but was persuaded to retract by his ministers who confirmed that only Han Yu's great loyalty motivated him into making such a declaration. Han Yu was demoted and sent another memorial to the emperor in appreciation of the fact that his life had been spared.

Nothing was done at the time to suppress Buddhism but twenty years later the emperor Wuzong, having massacred thousands of Uighur refugees on the northern borders of China, set in motion an anti-foreign purge that was to result in the suppression of Buddhism. It started in 842 with the suppression of Manichaeism, the religion of the Uighurs. Manichaean priests – who did not shave and who wore white – were forced to dress as Buddhist monks, with shaven heads and dark robes. Manichaean temples both in Chang'an and Taiyuan were destroyed and books burned.

In 845 Wuzong instigated a suppression of Buddhism,

although it is uncertain whether or not this was in response to Han Yu's memorial or if he had even read it. In 845 there was an order from the office of the Imperial Grand Secretariat ordering bells and bronze Buddhist images to be surrendered to the Salt and Iron Commissioner to be melted into coins, while images of gold, silver and jade were to be handed in to the Bureau of Public Revenue. Only clay, wood and stone images could remain within the temple.

Ennin, the Japanese monk, wrote about this disaster as follows:

What limit was there to the bronze, iron, and gold Buddhas of the land? And yet, in accordance with the imperial edict, all have been destroyed and have been turned into trash.[21]

Undoubtedly the loss of revenue to the state, brought about by the large number of tax-exempt individuals and the tax-exempt land possessed by the monasteries, was another economic factor that forced the emperor to take drastic action. From a census specially prepared in 845 we know that there were 260,000 monks and nuns, 4600 temples and 40,000 shrines. This persecution of Buddhism in 845 was undoubtedly the most widespread of its kind ever in China and the majority of the monks and nuns were returned to lay life and were therefore again taxable. It was a pivotal point marking the end of the apogee reached by Buddhism in the Tang. The suppression itself though was of short duration. Within a year Wuzong died, probably as a result of the Daoist immortality potions he had been taking, and Xuanzong, who succeeded to the throne, retracted the anti-Buddhist measures. Although Buddhism remained the main religion in China, it never again enjoyed the momentum and popularity it had under the Tang.[22]

1 In this catalogue we use the term Famen temple which is often written Famensi, *si* in Chinese meaning temple.

2 For information on the Famen temple finds see (in Chinese) *Wenwu* 1988.10, pp. 1–43; (in English) Whitfield 1990; Zhu Qixin 1990.

3 For information on the entries that make up this section I am immensely grateful to Professor John Huntington of Ohio State University for his help and advice.

4 Esoteric or Tantric Buddhism flourished for some time in Cambodia and Indonesia but ultimately gave way to Theravada Buddhism and later, in Indonesia, to Islam.

5 Ch'en 1964, pp. 235–40.

6 A Waley, *Monkey*, London 1943; Wu Cheng'en (trans. A Yu), *Journey to the West*, 3 vols, Chicago 1977.

7 Clunas 1997, p. 105, who also mentions that the Longmen temples were built to bring supernatural aid to the Tang armies who had been unsuccessful in Central Asia against the Tibetans.

8 Willetts 1965, figs 149–50. Worth approximately forty bolts of silk in AD 729 (I am grateful to Helen Wang for this information).

9 Jiu Tang shu, Zhonghua shuju edn, 1975, juan 183, pp. 4741–3. Feng Xiaobao was also known as Xue Huaiyi.

10 Helmut Brinker, 'Transfiguring Divinities', in Guggenheim 1997, p.149.

11 *Wenbo* 1985.5, pp. 12–37, colour pl. 4.

12 Han and Lu 1985, nos 110–13 and 157–62.

13 For a brief description of this monastery see An Keren, in Zuo Boyang 1995, pp. 41–4.

14 Generally only the Buddha's relics are referred to as *śarīra* but it has been estimated that after Śākyamuni's achieving Nirvāṇa there were 384,000 relics or *śarīra* in existence.

15 In order to record the transactional details of the ceremony when Emperor Yizong had the relics transported to Chang'an and then returned to the Famen temple augmented by a large quantity of precious objects donated by him, he had an inventory stele, termed the 'Yiwu Stele', which runs to more than 1700 characters, erected in the temple. For details of this see *Wenbo* 1996.1, pp. 58–85.

16 For the cultural connotations of *śarīra* containers see *Dongnan wenhua* 1997.2, pp. 64–75.

17 For an example of the phenomenal prices paid for Buddhist relics and the reverence shown to relics of the saints and masters of Buddhism, see Schafer 1963, pp. 266–7.

18 Reischauer 1955, p. 131.

19 Ch'en 1964, p. 284.

20 Quoted from Ch'en 1964, pp. 225–6. Also see Shih Shun Liu, *Chinese Classical Prose: The Eight Masters of the T'ang-Sung Period*, Renditions, Hong Kong 1979.

21 Reischauer 1955, p. 268.

22 Ch'en 1964, pp. 232–3.

95

95 Aparājitā Vidyārajā

Tang dynasty (AD 618–906)
Marble
Height 71 cm
Excavated 1959, Anguo Temple site, Shaanxi province
Beilin Museum

This Buddhist figure represents a type of deity known in Sanskrit as a *vidyārajā*, or in Chinese Ming Wang, King of Wisdom. His naked muscular torso thrusts to the right as he wields the remains of a single-pointed

vajra and his left arm is raised and bent, the hand broken off. His face is set in an angry grimace, with bared teeth, long fangs and protruding eyes. His hair, which was once bright red, is swept back with a tiara which was formerly jewel-encrusted and gilded. His jewellery was also once gilded. A swirling shawl is draped over his arms and a *dhoti*[1] covers his lower body.

This deity is one of a series of eight *vidyārajās*[2] that were introduced into China as part of the Zhenyan (true word or *mantra*) tradition of Buddhism. Originally he must have been part of a *mandala* of all eight that was centred on the *vidyārajā* form of

Vairocana Buddha Acala (the Immovable One). All eight *vidyārajās* are manifestations of the Buddhas and great bodhisattvas who appear in a fearsome form in order to 'convert those who are hard to convert'. Most, if not all, violent angry deities are manifestations of the power of compassion and benevolence that may be shown to man. At a more esoteric level there are specific meditations wherein the meditator visualizes himself as the fearsome deity and takes on his powers to help humanity.

Aparājitā's attribute is the single-pointed *vajra*, often simplistically translated as diamond or thunderbolt. In the most ancient of the Indian texts, the *Vedas*,[3] it is the powerful weapon of Indra, which, in Buddhism, is transformed into the symbol of the adamantine reality; the single-pointed version is directed specifically at the purification of unfortunate actions, and at the removal of negative forces from sacred spaces.

This *vidyārajā* belongs to a branch of Buddhism known as Esoteric or Tantric Buddhism which, with its distinctive cult and rites, suffered severely under the Buddhist proscription of 845. The importance of this piece is that it is one of the few Chinese statues relating to Esoteric Buddhism to have survived the persecution. Having developed in the last decades of the seventh century, Tantric or Esoteric Buddhism flourished for only a brief period, in the eighth and early ninth century, probably co-existing, even within the same temple, with other schools of Chinese Buddhism. Today Esoteric Buddhism is followed in Tibet, Nepal and Japan.

The Anguo temple (literally Monastery for National Peace or Tranquillity) was founded in 710 and its Buddha Hall is said to have been the bed-chamber of the emperor Xuanzong, although this was dismantled and transferred to the temple grounds by imperial decree in 713.[4] The temple became a well known centre for Esoteric Buddhism, its rites administered by a politically powerful monk under the patronage of three emperors, Xuanzong, Suzong and Daizong.[5] It was therefore an obvious target in the 845 persecution.

In 1959 workmen excavating a water conduit system in the area accidentally discovered ten statues, some heavily damaged. Eight have been attributed to the pantheon of Esoteric Buddhism and one is Trailokyavijaya (Victor over the Three Worlds, past, present and future). Eight of the statues were of white marble and two of bluish limestone, the marble statues bearing traces of gilt and polychrome. Because the statues were discovered in a spot verified by historical sources as the location of the famous Anguo temple, they are assumed to have belonged to the temple. The sculptural quality of all the Anguo temple statuary is exceptional, well illustrating the technical and artistic skills of the artisans who made

it. They possess a forceful expressiveness and sensitivity and must have been commanding icons in their time, especially with their original polychromy and gilding.[6]

Published: Brinker and Goepper 1980, fig. 47; Guggenheim 1997, no. 170; Ghose 1998, p. 123.

1 The *dhoti* is one of the two Indian costumes worn by men on the lower body. It is made of a single piece of woven but unsewn cloth which is wrapped around the waist as well as between the legs, thus allowing freedom of movement. There are many ways of wearing a *dhoti*, but one of the commonest is completed with a cascade of pleats at the middle of the back.

2 The *vidyārajā* is mentioned in the *Jin guang ming jing* (*Sūtra* of Gold, Light and Brightness). I am grateful to Dr Susan Whitfield for identification of this *sūtra*. For some background information see Zhao Yide, 'The Secrets of the Empress associated with the Grotto of the Mother of Buddha Stūpa at Yungang', *Dunhuang Yanjiu* 1996.1, pp. 1–10, and translated in *China Archaeology and Art*

Digest, vol. 1, no. 2, Hong Kong, April–June 1996, pp. 77–9.

3 The *Vedas* are the earliest surviving texts from India, composed some time in the second millennium BC, but not written down until much later. They are today regarded by Hindus as the basis for their religion.

4 Acker 1954, pp. 271–3; A Soper, 'A Vacation Glimpse of the T'ang Temples of Ch'ang-an', *Artibus Asiae* 23, 1960, pp. 22–3; *Wenwu* 1961.7, pp. 61–3.

5 Katherine Tsiang, 'Images of the Dharma: Regional Formations and National Revisualizations', *Orientations*, February 1998, p. 81.

6 For the entries on this and the following three Buddhist statues, I have relied very heavily on information, help and references given to me by Professor John Huntington of Ohio State University, to whom I am extremely grateful. I am also very grateful for the help given me by Dr Stephen Little of The Art Institute of Chicago, Dr Frances Wood and Dr Susan Whitfield of the British Library, Messrs Richard Blurton and Victor Harris of the British Museum and Professor Helmut Brinker, University of Zurich.

96

96 Lokapāla

Tang dynasty (AD 618–906)
Stone
Height 100 cm
Collected 1949
Beilin Museum

This damaged figure is one of a group of four guardian kings known as the Si Tianwang or Four Heavenly Kings in Chinese (Sanskrit Lokapāla, World Protector). In the Indian context such figures are considered as kings, whereas in China they were transformed into dynamic idealized generals modelled on the great warriors of China, especially the field commanders of the Tang dynasty.

Each of the Four Heavenly, or Guardian, Kings has a specific iconography, which, although it may vary, usually allows us to identify a particular king in context. However, because this figure is missing its left arm, both hands and its head, no such identification is possible. The figure is wearing a magnificent suit of armour, with long tassels and with protective plates on the breast and stomach, in the shape of medallions, from which hangs a decorative chain. Across both his chest and stomach there are belts made up of fifteen plaques.[1] Loose fabric is looped around the body, fastened at the waist and left to drape down on to the base of the statue. Under the armour he wears a warrior's skirt, its lower part skimming the ground. The bottoms of his trouser legs are tied up and over these he wears warrior's boots. His upper body leans to the left and he stands with one foot at right angles to the other. Despite the heavy damage to the figure, there is a sense of confidence in his striking pose, and great naturalism in the carving of the armour and drapery, suggesting a sculptor of considerable skill.

The Lokapāla were originally warrior protectors of the Buddhist law, residing on the fourth terrace of Mount Meru.[2] Four were responsible for looking after the Buddha and his Law, the sanctuary and Buddhist congregations, and they had control over all of the animistic spirits of the Buddhist realms. Among these spirits are the *yakṣas*, in charge of wealth, a negative force that had to be reckoned with. Lokapāla are especially important in Buddhist temples where they are controllers of negative forces and protect the upper realms of Mount Meru from unfortunate incidents. Their presence at the gates of a monastery serves as a reminder to a mortal that he is making a spiritual entrance to the sacred ground at the top of Mount Meru or one of the heavenly worlds beyond.

As Buddhist ideas were absorbed into Chinese culture, the Lokapāla assumed a more secular role as guardians of the country and its people, capable of averting disasters. As such they were frequently made in ceramic and placed as guardians in tombs to protect both the tomb and its occupant.[3]

Published: Guggenheim 1997, no. 167.

1 See cat. nos 42–44 for more information on belt plaques.
2 Mount Meru is the centre of the universe in Buddhist – indeed Indian – cosmology.
3 See those in the British Museum, OA 1936.10-12.222–3, Hotung Gallery. Also see J Baker, 'Sui and Early Tang Period Images of the Heavenly King in Tombs and Temples', *Orientations*, April 1999, pp. 53–7.

97 Vajradharma Avalokiteśvara or Guanyin

Tang dynasty (AD 618–906)
Stone
Height 71.5 cm; width 33.5; weight 66.7 kg
Excavated 1952, Jinlong pond, Dongguan, Xi'an (Tang dynasty Xingqing Palace site)
Beilin Museum

This white stone figure of the bodhisattva Avalokiteśvara is sitting cross-legged on a lotus base that is itself positioned on top of a pedestal in the form of Mount Meru, the cosmic mountain of Buddhist teaching. He is easily identified by the position of his right hand which pulls gently at a petal of the lotus bud in his left hand, a gesture which probably refers to the transcendent insight to be gained by the meditator.

As far as is known there is no independent cult of Vajradharma Avalokiteśvara in China or Japan where it might have survived from a lost Chinese tradition. We must therefore assume that some sort of *maṇḍala* was made that included this image, whether a full *maṇḍala* with all thirty-seven deities, or some sort of abbreviation such as survives at the Kūkai's Kyō-ō Gokokuji in Japan. Further excavations in the area may reveal figures that will confirm the existence of a full *maṇḍala*.

This image, along with the two others from this group (cat. nos 95, 96), provides great insight into the rich imperial patronage lavished on the esoteric teachings introduced into China by the eighty-year-old Indian monk Subhakarasimha and his successors, the Javanese monk Vajrabodhi and Ceylonese Amoghavajra. In 726 Xuan Zong invited Vajrabodhi to perform Tantric rites to avert drought. Although dismissed by the imperial historians as 'Rainmaking monks', they actually brought a profound and ancient tradition of Esoteric Buddhism which flourished briefly in China and Korea and continues to do so in Japan today. At the height of its power there were several temples dedicated to the Zhenyan tradition, one of which, the Famen temple, has

97

recently been excavated, revealing a dedication deposit, a finger bone of the Buddha, housed in a lavish reliquary that contained a complete iconography of the dual *maṇḍalas* of the Zhenyan tradition[1] (cat. nos 117–120).

The first mention of Guanyin occurs in chapter 25 of the *Lotus Sūtra* (*Miaofa lianhua jing*) which was transmitted to China in AD 286. It describes how Guanyin vows to rescue all those in danger of murder, shipwreck or some other disaster, and it became a popular text, often copied separately from the rest of the *sūtra* in portable booklets and soon referred to as 'the Guanyin *sūtra*'. Many of the booklets were illustrated and the scenes described became popular subjects for Buddhist murals in cave temples, such as those at Kizil and Dunhuang. During the social unrest of the Six Dynasties period in China, from the third to the sixth century, a cult devoted to Guanyin grew appreciably because of the bodhisattva's supposed powers to save people from peril generally. Another facet of Guanyin's appeal for the Chinese was that, according to the *Lotus Sūtra*, the Bodhisattva of Compassion possessed the power of bestowing male progeny, a very important consideration in any Chinese family, and gradually women came to regard Guanyin as their special protector. Another sacred text, the *Pure Land Sūtra*, described Guanyin as an emanation of the Buddha Amitābha, Lord of the Western Paradise, an emissary of the Buddha of Infinite Light. The image of the Buddha Amitābha in the headdress of a Guanyin, as in this statue, is one of the identifying characteristics of this Buddhist figure.

Although the earliest Chinese figures of Guanyin conformed closely to Indian prototypes they were gradually sinicized. Between the sixth and ninth century the most popular form of Guanyin was as the Compassionate Saviour, depicted sitting or standing and usually holding a bottle of

heavenly dew, to cure all illnesses, and a willow sprig with which to dispense it. There are many images of such a figure in the Dunhuang cave paintings.[2] Chinese sculpture of the seventh and early eighth century saw renewed Indian influences such as an emphasis on the solidity of the body, enhanced by full and sensuous plastic modelling as in this statue. The plumpness of the figure is however also related to the Tang predilection for plump females (cat. no. 38), and the freer rendition of ornamental features is typical of Chinese decoration of the period. During the flourishing of Esoteric Buddhism in China Guanyin assumes a distinctive form, multi-armed and multi-headed.

In Indian Buddhism bodhisattvas were always represented as male, but in the early Tang period sculptors depicted Guanyin with both masculine and feminine characteristics because the bodhisattva was considered to have transcended the illusory notion of self, which includes that of gender. In China the Guanyin deity gradually evolved to become female,[3] a transformation that was more or less complete by the Song dynasty.

Published: Brinker and Goepper 1980, fig. 140; Beijing 1992a, no. 47; *Empress Wu* 1998, no. 19.

1 Patricia Berger, 'Preserving the Nation: The Political Uses of Tantric Art in China', in Weidner 1994, pp. 90–3.
2 Whitfield and Farrer 1990, cat. no. 57, p. 76 and illustration p. 79.
3 Chun-fang Yu, 'Guanyin: The Chinese Transformation of Avalokiteshvara', in Weidner 1994, pp. 151–81.

98 Figure of the Buddha, perhaps Amitābha

Tang dynasty (AD 618–906)
Stone
Height 79 cm; width 24 cm
Excavated 1973, Shahutuo village, Xi'an city, Shaanxi province
Beilin Museum

This figure stood originally on a base which has broken off. His face is plump and smooth, his eyes are slightly open and his large ears have pendulous lobes which reach nearly to his shoulders. His hair is shown in snail-shell curls, characteristic of many East Asian images of this period. The image has been decapitated at some time, probably during the great persecutions of 845, but it has been restored. The figure wears a *kāṣāya*, the mendicant's robe, draped over both shoulders and hanging in regular U-shaped folds across the chest and down both legs. His left arm is slightly bent with his palm facing outwards and fingers downwards, the fingertips broken. His right arm bends slightly upwards and the hand is missing. The formal gestures and upright posture make this a most majestic and dignified figure.

The tight waist accentuates the pectoral muscles and hips, and the thin drapery highlights the body beneath, an indication of Indian influence. Chinese traits are also evident: the manner in which the light, thin robe falls in parallel pleats over the legs is typical of mid-Tang dynasty sculpture.

The Buddha's gesture is one of welcoming a devotee to the Pure Land.[1] Most Buddha images make the gesture of reassurance (*abhayamudrā*) with the right hand and bestowal (*varada*) with the left, a combination known to the Chinese as *laiying*, meaning welcome. This is one of the best known gestures in lay or popular Buddhism in China, and may be made by any manifestation of the Buddha as he welcomes a being to his Pure Land.[2] For example, Amitābha may make the gesture as he welcomes the soul of the departed into his land of Bliss (Sukhāvatī). Because of the popularity of Amitābha during the Tang, it is possible that the present statue represents this Buddha.

Published: Hong Kong 1993, no. 98; *Empress Wu* 1998, no. 18.

1 The Pure Land school was the one that flourished longest and survived most obviously in later popular Buddhism. It stressed meritorious deeds and devotion to Amitābha who presides over the Pure Land (Sukhāvatī) of the West.
2 Maitreya Buddha may display the same gesture as he invites beings into his worldly paradise of Ketumatī, and Bhaiṣajyaguru may show it upon welcoming the deceased into the land of Lapis Lazuli (Vaidūryavati).

98

99 Stone reliquary

Tang dynasty (AD 618–906)
Limestone, gold and bronze
Height (of total) 102 cm, (of flower) 41–9 cm,
(of lotus) 39 cm; width of base 83.5 cm
Excavated 1985, Qingshan temple site, Xinfeng
town, Lintong county, Shaanxi province
Shaanxi Lintong Museum

This Buddhist reliquary, made of limestone,
was excavated from the main room in the
underground crypt of the pagoda of
Qingshan monastery. The pavilion-shaped
shrine was used not only for housing the
relics themselves but also as protection for
the reliquary vessels placed inside it, the
silver and gold caskets and glass bottle
(cat. nos 100–102). Because of the shrine's
size it would have been seen as a
magnificently generous expression of the
devotion of the donor, who in turn would
have earned great merit from the gift. This is
the largest casket set ever excavated which
makes it a particularly interesting discovery.

The main body of the casket is square
with a two-tiered roof. Each of the four
faces of the body is engraved with a story
from the life of Śākyamuni, the historical

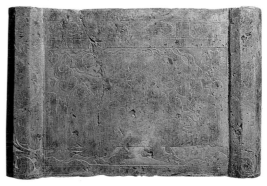

Fig 99a The Buddha lies supine on a straw mattress,
surrounded by standing or kneeling monks in great
sorrow.

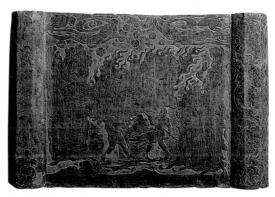

Fig 99b Two monks, each carrying torches, are
lighting firewood to incinerate Śākyamuni's remains.

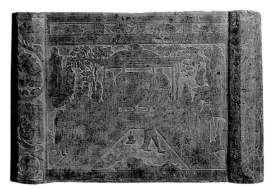

Fig 99c A coffin contains the Buddha's relics in a Chinese-
style stūpa, in front of which a monk holds an alms bowl with
food which he is distributing to the kneeling monks.

99

Buddha.[1] Chronologically these are: the
Buddha preaching the Buddhist law, with
one hand in his lap and the other gesturing
to his followers; his death, the Pari-nirvāṇa
scene, with the Buddha's entry into Nirvāṇa
(fig. 99a); his cremation, with *apsaras* above

his body and flowers falling around him (fig. 99b); and the scene of the veneration of his relics, where these can be seen covered with material and ready for worship (fig. 99c).

Below the eaves are carved peony flowers, grasses and flying *apsaras*. Some of the *apsaras*[2] are scattering flowers to the world below, some are holding fruit, some are blowing a wind pipe instrument, and others are playing stringed *pipa* instruments.

The lid or roof is made up of two tiers crowned by a lotus pearl sitting on three layers of lotus petals. Four gilded bronze *bodhi* trees with flowers have been inserted into the corners of the lower tier. Beneath, in the centre of the front, are eight Chinese characters[3] stating that this is a Buddhist reliquary shrine. These characters have first been engraved and then inlaid with gold and on each side of the inscription are *kalavinka* birds.[4]

The pedestal of the shrine consists of two rows of lotus petals resting on a stepped base with two bands of flower design and, in three of its corners, gilded bronze lotus flowers have been inserted. Altogether, considering the size and the workmanship involved in making this shrine, it is a particularly impressive monument to Buddhist piety.

One of the earliest references to coffin-shaped *śarīra* caskets in China is dated to 660 when, during the reign of Gaozong, the relics from the Famen temple were removed to the eastern capital, Luoyang, and the empress Wu Zetian donated a thousand bolts of silk from her funerary wardrobe account to make nine gold and silver inner and outer coffins to house the *śarīra*. These have never been found. The oldest set to be discovered by archaeologists is a set of five, one nesting inside the other, from the foundations of Dayunsi, a monastery in Gansu province. These were buried in 694.[5] The workmanship of the *śarīra* caskets found in the foundations of the Qingshan monastery, buried in the mid-eighth century, was much

superior.[6] After the An Lushan rebellion of 755 the practice of burying Buddhist *śarīra* in gold and silver reliquaries continued and amongst the most notable are those buried in the pagoda at Ganlusi in Zhenjiang, Jiangsu province, which are dated to 829.[7] After Wuzong's persecution of Buddhism in 845 the practice continued for a time, as witnessed by the Famen temple caskets, donated to the monastery by Emperor Yizong (cat. nos 117–120).

Published: *Wenbo* 1985.5, pp. 12–37; *Oriental Art*, vol. XXXIII.2, Summer 1987, pp. 208–11; *Empress Wu* 1998, no. 37; *Daito Bunmei ten* 1998, no. 66.

1 Typical of these stories are sermons, the Nirvāṇa and the cremation, to be distinguished from stories of the Buddha and his previous incarnations, the *Jātaka*.
2 *Apsaras* are Buddhist heavenly beings which were extensively depicted in the Tang dynasty. (Outside of a Buddhist context Jessica Rawson has suggested they could equally well be Daoist Jade Maidens, Rawson 1995a, pp. 332–3.) The representation of *apsaras* is influenced by Central Asian forms and many examples of these can be seen in cave 285 at Dunhuang, Gansu province, dated to the sixth century. The style of the figures on this casket is somewhat different to that found in the Dunhuang murals.
3 *Shi jia ru lai she li bao zhang*, meaning Buddhist reliquary casket.
4 There are numerous references in Buddhist literature to *kalavinka* birds and their beautiful singing voices. They sometimes represented the Buddha himself and also signified generally the suffering and impermanence of the physical world. See Schafer 1963, pp. 103–4; Soothill and Hodous 1975, p. 317.
5 Han and Lu 1985, nos 110–13 and *Wenwu* 1966.3, pp. 8–15. For general information on sets of *śarīra* caskets see 'A silver casket from a Dulan sacrificial horse trench', *Zhongguo Lishi Bowuguan guankan* 1995.1, translated in *China Archaeology and Art Digest*, vol. 1, no. 3, Hong Kong, July–September 1996, pp. 37–49.
6 As above.
7 *Kaogu* 1961.6, pp. 302–15; Han and Lu 1985, nos 157–62.

100 and 101
Coffin-shaped reliquaries

Tang dynasty (AD 618–906)
Silver, gold, bronze, precious stones
100 Height (of total) 18.5 cm, (of reliquary) 11–14.5 cm; length 21 cm; width 7.5–13 cm
101 Height 6.5–9.5cm; length 14.5 cm; width 4.5–7.4 cm
Weight (of two reliquaries together) 1.8 kg
Excavated 1985, Qingshan temple site, Xinfeng town, Lintong county, Shaanxi province
Shaanxi Lintong Museum

These two coffin-shaped reliquaries were originally placed inside the stone casket (cat. no. 99). The reliquaries comprise a silver outer coffin, which sits on a gilded Buddhist *sumeru* platform, and a gold coffin. The gold coffin was fitted inside the silver coffin, and the glass bottle (cat. no. 102) and one other bottle were found inside the gold coffin.

The silver coffin has an arc-shaped lid, resembling a Chinese roof tile, and its centre is decorated with lotus flowers with gilded petals, and stamens and pistils of white jade and agate. Thick silver wires swirl up from the agate on the lid, and around the large flower on the lid are four small posies of flowers with stamens of pearls and pistils of thick spiralling silver wires. The edges of the lid are decorated with pearls in the shape of plum flowers. The front of the silver reliquary has two doors, above which is a monster head with a ring suspended from its mouth. On each door are gilded bodhisattvas in relief with flaming haloes around their heads. Between the two bodhisattvas is a gilded relief carving representing the soles of the Buddha's feet.[1] The back is decorated with gilded *maṇi* pearls.[2] Both sides of the reliquary are decorated with five *luohan* in relief, either sitting or standing; they are mourning the passing of the Śākyamuni Buddha. The base, on which the coffin stands, is rectangular and stepped, made of copper with a hollow-

100 (left)   **101 (above)**

cut balustrade. The various levels are decorated with pearls.

The gold coffin, which was placed inside the silver coffin, has a rectangular base and arc-shaped lid, in the centre of which are intertwining *baoxiang*[3] blossoms. The lid is decorated with festoons of trailing decoration and both the lid and back of the coffin are decorated with pearls. The front is adorned with garlands of flowers made of pearl clusters. A pair of lions in relief appear as protective devices on the front of the reliquary.[4] The gold coffin was lined with silk to protect the two green glass bottles inside (see cat. no. 102).

The earliest containers for *śarīra*, or corporeal relics of the Buddha, have been found in the Indian subcontinent and were placed in structures known as stūpas which were worshipped as part of the cult of relics. In India there was an extensive cult of relics[5] and the notion of pilgrimage to honour them is set forth in the *Mahāparinirvāṇasūtra* in which the dying Buddha tells his followers that the monks should not concern themselves with the relics of the Buddha but that the lay followers should venerate (perform *pūjā* at) the place of his birth, his Enlightenment, his first sermon and his death.

Indian *śarīra* containers were generally jar-like in shape[6] and have been found to

contain burned bones, pearls, crystal, gold foil, precious stones, precious metal items and coins. As Buddhism spread from India the belief in *śarīra* developed in different ways and the shape of *śarīra* containers changed. In Central Asia the practice of placing the bones of the deceased in a special container had its origins in the distant past and was adopted by the Sogdians. Sogdian *śarīra* containers[7] absorbed influences from a type of Zoroastrian reliquary for holding bones as the Sogdians believed that flesh and bone should be separated: to prevent the flesh from polluting the earth, the body was exposed to allow the flesh to be eaten by birds. The Sogdian rectangular box-shaped receptacles for bones influenced the containers used by Sogdian Buddhists and it is possible that such containers in turn influenced the Chinese. In ancient China it was customary to bury corpses in double coffins and it is possible that the idea in medieval China of using several reliquary holders, nesting one inside the other in the shape of coffins, is related to this practice.

100 Published: *Wenbo* 1985.5, pp. 12–37; Yang Boda 1987, nos 75–7; Han Wei 1989, plates, p. 2; Wang Renbo 1990, p. 276, no. 6; Kuhn 1993, no. 92.1; Xi'an 1995, pp. 10–11; Shanghai 1996, p. 127, no. 118; *Empress Wu* 1998, no. 38-2; *Daito Bunmei ten* 1998, no. 65-1; *Famous Capital*, p. 147, no. 2; *Oriental Art*, vol. XXXIII–2, Summer 1987, pp. 208–11.

101 Published: *Wenbo* 1985.5, pp. 12–37; Yang Boda 1987, nos 75–7; Wang Renbo 1990, p. 275, no. 5; Kuhn 1993, no. 92.1; Xi'an 1995, p.10; Shanghai 1996, p. 127, no. 118; *Empress Wu* 1998, no. 38-1; *Daito Bunmei ten* 1998, no. 65-3; *Oriental Art*, vol. XXXIII–2, Summer 1987, pp. 208–11.

1 The earliest representation of the Buddha was in symbolic form only, such as his footprints or the *bodhi* tree. The earliest known representation of the Buddha in human form is that on the gold and jewelled Buddhist reliquary from Bimaran in Afghanistan. This dates to *c.* AD 60 and is in the British Museum, Hotung Gallery.

2 The pearl or jewel in the fortieth of the thousand hands of Guanyin, towards which worship is paid in case of fevers (see Soothill and Hodous 1975, p. 157). Also as a jewel, such as a crystal or a pearl, it came to be a symbol of purity and therefore the Buddha and his doctrine (Soothill and Hodous 1975, pp. 191, 435).

3 Imaginary, idealized lotus-like flower associated with Buddhism.

4 Pairs of lions are often seen as guardians of temples. In such pairings, the right lion is a male and has an ornamental ball under his left paw, the left lion is a female with a cub under her right paw (Eberhard 1986, pp. 164–5). The Buddha was also born into the Śākya (lion) clan; Śākyamuni means 'sage of the Śākyas'.

5 Three classes of relic were recognized: the *śarīra* or bodily relic, the *pariboghika* or relic of a place of activity of the Buddha, and the *uddeśika* or relic of the Buddha's teachings.

6 Zhu Qixin 1990, p. 77.

7 'A silver casket from a Dulan sacrificial horse trench', *Zhongguo Lishi Bowuguan guankan* 1995.1, translated in *China Archaeology and Art Digest*, vol. 1, no. 3, Hong Kong, July–September 1996, p. 47.

102

102 Bottle

Tang dynasty (AD 618–906)
Glass, bronze and crystal
Height 5.3 cm
Excavated 1985, Qingshan temple site, Xinfeng
town, Lintong county, Shaanxi province
Shaanxi Lintong Museum

This glass bottle was placed inside the gold coffin-shaped reliquary (cat. no. 101) and contained crystal representations of the Buddha's incinerated bones. The crystals are transparent and the size of butter beans. (There were originally two glass bottles inside the gold casket; the other was half the size of this one.) The bottle is made of a deep green glass and has a slender neck and globular body. The glass is very thin and the mouth is damaged. The base of the bottle is made up of gilded bronze lotus petals.

The glass has not been analysed so it is not known whether this bottle was made locally or whether it was imported, like cat. no.115.[1] As is explained in that entry the Chinese did not have a strong tradition of glass making, and foreign glass, particularly that imported before the Tang, was considerably less fragile than the native Chinese product which contained a high percentage of barium and lead. Even in the Tang dynasty utensils of fine clear glass from abroad were still considered exotic treasures: 'It is a jewel of Western countries, and is akin to jade and other stones. It is born within the earth, and some say that it is water transformed after a thousand years; still this is not necessarily so'.[2] Others thought it was petrified ice, like rock crystal. This implies that foreign glass was seen as an exotic import and would probably have been considered more appropriate for housing the Buddha's relics than a glass of Chinese manufacture, though it was during the Tang dynasty that the Chinese appear to have begun making soda and potash glasses in place of their lead glass. Enthusiasm for glass vessels seems to have been expressed most in Buddhist religious art with monks both importing foreign glass from the West and encouraging local glass manufacturers to make the Buddhist reliquaries and liturgical vessels they needed for their ceremonies.[3]

Other glass reliquary bottles which have been found include that at the Jingchuan pagoda in Gansu province, dated to 694. It contained fourteen reliquary grains and was placed in a stone coffer within nesting containers of gold, silver, bronze and stone. Another thin-bodied glass bottle was discovered in the eastern suburbs of Xi'an in a gilded bronze box in a reliquary pagoda dated to 719 and a third example in a reliquary casket in Heilongjiang province. All three may well have been of local Chinese manufacture.[4]

The possession of a 'true' *śarīra* relic and its placement in a stūpa or pagoda sanctified the site with the actual presence of the Buddha and was believed to have great talismanic effect for the state as well as for individual practitioners.[5] In parts of the Buddhist world, *śarīra* had to be substituted with other materials.[6] In China, *śarīra* (*sheli* in Chinese), while understood to be bones or teeth, etc, also refers to the pure crystallized grains believed to have come from the cremation process. That is clearly what is present in this relic container. This is not meant to be a deception. On the contrary, through a process of consecration such objects become the relics of the Buddha and become 'real' or a 'functional reality' that serves the faithful every bit as well as if they were the actual bones of Śākyamuni.

From an early date, great teachers were also accorded the honour of having a stūpa built to hold their relics, or in many cases simply to commemorate their attainments. This practice continues in parts of the Buddhist world to the present day.

The Tang dynasty poet Bai Juyi (unlike Han Yu, as mentioned on pp. 135–6) rhapsodized over the presentation of the Buddha's relics:

In twin vases of pallid tourmaline
(Their colour colder than the waters of an autumn
stream)
The calcined relics of Buddha's Body rest —
Rounded pebbles, smooth as the Specular Stone.[7]

Published: *Wenbo* 1985.5, pp. 12–37; Yang Boda 1987, nos 75–7; Kuhn 1993, no. 92.2; *Empress Wu* 1998, no. 39; *Daito Bunmei ten* 1998, no. 65-2.

1 An Jiayao, *Early Chinese Glassware*, trans. M Henderson, Oriental Ceramic Society Translations 12, London 1987, pp. 24–5 for characteristics and uses of early Chinese glassware; Moore 1998, pp. 78–84.
2 Quoted in Schafer 1963, p. 236.
3 Moore 1998, p. 80.
4 An Jiayao, *Early Chinese Glassware*, trans. M Henderson, Oriental Ceramic Society Translations 12, London 1987, pp. 19–20.
5 According to the *Mahāparinirvāṇasūtra*, the Buddha was cremated after attaining his final Nirvāṇa. The *śarīra* (body relics) are the crystallized grains resulting from the cremation fires. These remains were divided by the Brahman Drona into eight subsets and were placed in stūpas in each of eight minor kingdoms of the time. In about 250 BC, the emperor Aśoka of the Mauryan dynasty opened seven of these stūpas and redistributed the relics to many sites throughout his empire. Possible bone relics of the Buddha have been found at several locations in India including Piprawa, Sanchi and Nagarjunakonda. The Aśoka Avadana states that Aśoka created 84,000 stūpas, a

number that has been variously interpreted throughout the Buddhist world but which, in context, simply means 'many' and is used in exact parallel to the Chinese use of 10,000 as an adjective for many or all.

6 Because of the popularity of the cult of relics, there was always a demand for authentic examples.

7 Translated by A Waley, *The Temple and Other Poems*, London 1923, p. 106.

103 Jug

Tang dynasty (AD 618–906)
Bronze
Height 29.5 cm
Excavated 1985, Qingshan temple site, Xinfeng town, Lintong county, Shaanxi province
Shaanxi Lintong Museum

This extraordinary bronze jug was found with the limestone casket and other treasures (cat. nos 99–102) in the ruins of the Qingshan monastery crypt. When it was excavated, the footring and the body of the jug had become separated and the bottom of the jug has several repair marks. It has a long

Fig. 103a *Ivory figure of a girl looking in a mirror, from Brahminabad, Sind, 8th century* AD.

103

slender neck with three raised rings halfway up. The mouth is shaped like a phoenix head and there is a sinuous 'dragon' handle on one side. The jug has a spreading foot and the body is composed of human heads in high relief. Their faces are round, with large eyes and curved eyebrows that lead into long, straight, high-bridged noses protruding over small mouths. The loops of the centrally parted hairstyles link the heads, with small buns in between each. All features are strongly suggestive of Indian faces, which are rarely found on Chinese objects.[1]

These faces, together with the very un-Chinese shape of the jug, suggest that it

was one of the many imports from the West, possibly from Central Asia, Persia or India, that were so popular in the Tang dynasty. The shape has affinities with a traditional Sasanian shape of the period, examples of which can be found in the Shōsō-in in Nara, Japan, and in many other museums.[2] The faces are similar to those on ivory figures dating to the eighth century from Brahminabad, Sind, examples of which (fig. 103a) can be found in the British Museum.[3]

Xuanzang is probably the best known Chinese to have travelled to India (see pp. 131–2), embarking in 629. He travelled as far as the Indus valley, sailed down the Ganges and saw the *bodhi* tree under which the Buddha is said to have attained Enlightenment. However, he was only one of the many Buddhist pilgrims and travellers (see fig. 25, p. 132) journeying in both directions. Some of these travellers would have brought imports from India, considered particularly appropriate as India was the birthplace of Buddhism.

Published: *Wenbo* 1985.5, pp. 12–37; Kuhn 1993, no. 93; Xi'an 1997, p. 81; *Empress Wu* 1998, no. 42.

1 A stone head of a Buddha with five faces, dating to the Song or Yuan dynasty, belonging to the Tsui Museum collection, is published in Ghose 1998, no. 117. The faces on it look more Chinese than those on the Qingshan jug.

2 British Museum, Addis Islamic Gallery, OA 1959.10-23.1.

3 BM OA 1857.11-18.1,4,6. I am grateful to Michael Willis of the Department of Oriental Antiquities, British Museum, for pointing me to this reference.

104

104 Bodhisattva

Tang dynasty (AD 618–906)
Silver with gilding
Height 38.5 cm; weight 1.9 kg
Excavated 1987, from the crypt of Famen
temple, Fufeng county, Shaanxi province
Famen Temple Museum

This bodhisattva, identifiable as
Avalokiteśvara or Guanyin by the image of
Amitābha in his crown, is one of the most

notable offerings found in the crypt of the
Famen temple. It was specially made as
tribute for the Tang emperor Yizong to hold
the Buddha's finger bone *śarīra* for worship
and it is the only Tang dynasty silver vessel
inscribed with the emperor's titles. It is
made up of two parts: the bodhisattva and
the lotus throne.

The bodhisattva is cast into shape, his
hair piled up in a high bun, and he wears a
headdress with flower scrolls, festooned
with pearls. He has a plump face, elongated
eyes, high-bridged straight nose, wide
mouth and ears with lobes which hang to his
shoulders. The upper part of his body is
naked and there is a long scarf draped over
his shoulder. He wears a long skirt to his
feet and his arms are decorated with
bracelets. He kneels on one knee, on a lotus
petal throne, and the body has more than
two hundred seawater pearls from the
Persian Gulf draped around it.[1]

In his two arms he holds aloft a lotus-
leaf-shaped tray containing a plaque. This
plaque is rectangular and the front cover is
gilded all over and the edge decorated with
a circle of lotus petals. A hollowed-out,
trident-shaped protective cover is
connected by chains to the plaque. Before
this plaque was discovered it was not known
how the relic of the Buddha was displayed
for the royal family to worship in the palace
in Chang'an. This figure provided the
answer: the relic was placed on the lotus leaf
plate in the hands of this bodhisattva. On the
plate is a gilded silver plaque inscribed with
a special imperial prayer, written in eleven
lines and comprising sixty-five characters:

*For His Majesty being the far-sighted, cultured
marshal, virtuous, most benevolent, great holy and
pious emperor, I reverently made this bodhisattva to
hold the true body for worship forever. My humble wish
is that the holy life span be ten thousand springs, the
holy one's branches have ten thousand leaves, the eight
barbarians come to submit, the four seas have no
turbulence. Recorded on the fourteenth day of the
eleventh lunar month, the twelfth year of Xiantong to
congratulate the emperor on his birthday.[2]*

The bodhisattva was made as a tribute by
Dengyi, an eminent monk, for the thirty-
ninth birthday of Tang Yizong in 871.[3]

The lotus throne has a very complex
iconography that has been recently
published in Chinese.[4] Around the base are
the eight *vidyārajās* (see cat. no. 95 for a
marble sculpture of one of these), known as
Ming Wang in Chinese, Kings of Wisdom
(having the Esoteric Buddhist techniques of
conversion). Immediately above them are
the Sanskrit *bīja* mantras,[5] or seed syllables,
of the four directional Buddhas and their
respective bodhisattvas. Above that, on the
narrow central portion of the base, are the
four Lokapāla or guardian kings. On the
upper lotus there are sixteen offering deities
and bodhisattvas.

A number of textiles were also buried in
the crypt. These appear to have been
specially made, some possibly for this
bodhisattva. However, the atmospheric
conditions had caused most of the silk fabric
to carbonize or stick together; only the silks
in tightly sealed containers had retained
their original colour and texture. Some of
the textiles were donated by the royal family
or nobility and included gold-brocaded and
embroidered clothing, and an exceptional
piece, a miniature robe embroidered in
gold-wrapped thread and red silk (see
fig. 28, p. 135). Other textiles were for
wrapping objects such as the gold and silver.

Yizong in his later years was a fervent
worshipper of Buddhism, cutting military
costs and raising special taxes in order to
build Buddhist temples. He is reputed to
have said that having seen this precious and

beautiful figure he could happily die. Within two years of its manufacture, and shortly after the relics arrived in the capital, Yizong did indeed die.

Published: *Wenwu* 1988.10, p. 18; Shi Xingbang 1988, no. 25; Beijing 1992a, no. 287; Xi'an 1992, p. 28; *Famensi* 1994, no. 2; Xi'an 1994, p. 94; Shanghai 1996, p. 132, no. 128; Hong Kong 1997, no. 86; *Famous Capital*, p. 144, no. 3.

1 See Zhu Qixin 1990 for a general account in English of this Buddhist treasure.
2 Quoted and adapted from Beijing 1992a, p. 312.
3 Louis 1999, p. 152.
4 Wu and Han 1998. I am indebted to Professor John Huntington of Ohio State University for the information on the iconography of the lotus throne and for this bibliographical reference.
5 For information on *vajras* and *mandalas* see Whitfield 1990, p. 85; Zhu Qixin 1990, p. 81.

105 Incense burner

Tang dynasty, dated by inscription to 869
Gilded silver
Height 29.5 cm; weight 6.4 kg
Excavated 1987, from the crypt of Famen temple, Fufeng county, Shaanxi province
Famen Temple Museum

This incense burner is one of the masterpieces of the metalsmith's art. It was found in the crypt of the Famen temple in the innermost chamber, its prominent position indicating its importance.[1] Made in 869 by the Wensi yuan royal workshop, which supplied gold and silver wares for the royal family and was famous in its time for its technical skills, it was consecrated by the emperor Yizong. This information is contained in a chased, forty-nine-character inscription on the base of the body (fig. 105a) detailing and describing its height, weight and hanging rings. It names the craftsmen as Chen Jingfu, the administrative assistant, Wu Hongque[2] and the commissioner Neng Shun. The censer

105

was listed on the inventory found in the monastery as the first item of the 122 objects dedicated by the emperor in 873.

It is composed of a body and a lid. The centre of the domed lid culminates in a lotus bud emerging from two layers of lotus petals. The bud is pierced to allow the smoke of the incense to escape.[3] The purity of the lotus flower, which grows out of muddy roots, made it an appropriate symbol for the Buddha who, despite having lived in the material world, retained his purity. The lower section of the lid has five lotus flowers on each of which lies a tortoise with its head turned backwards and with auspicious herbs in its mouth.

The deep body, with its wide, slanting rim and flat base, is decorated with cloud patterns suggesting wreaths of incense smoke. Riveted to the body are five legs, the tops of which have heads resembling those of unicorns. The legs terminate in four-

Fig. 105a *Detail of the inscription on the base.*

taloned paws. In between the animals' feet hang ornaments, knotted festoons, which are suspended from rings nailed into the body.

The burner stands on a silver plate with a chased design of phoenixes. The five feet of the plate and the hanging appendages are similar to those of the burner itself. When it was excavated it was found together with an incense scoop and there was still some incense inside the burner. This set with its matching appendages is unique and is therefore considered to be one of the great Buddhist treasures of the Tang dynasty. It is one of the largest known and is considerably bigger than the one found in the Qingshan monastery in 1985.

The combination of iconographical detail – the Buddhist lotus flower and the Chinese tortoise and phoenix – is an interesting one. In ancient China the tortoise and the phoenix are two of the four spirits, the *si ling*. The tortoise has connotations of longevity[4] and phoenixes came to represent the empress.

Published: *Wenwu* 1988.10, pp. 14–16; Shi Xingbang 1988, no. 14; Wang Renbo 1990, p. 274, no. 3; Beijing 1992a, no. 291; *Famensi* 1994, no. 64; Xi'an 1994, p. 95; Shanghai 1996, p. 131, no. 126; Hong Kong 1997, no. 87; *Famous Capital*, p. 146, no. 1.

1 For Chinese report see *Wenwu* 1988.10, pp. 1–28.
2 Wu Hongque was the Assistant Administrator of the Wensi yuan in 869 and the Commissioner from 872. Louis 1999, p. 159.
3 Further information on incense and incense burners can be found in cat. nos 18, 72 and 73.
4 See cat. nos 25 and 26.

106 Five-ringed incense burner

Tang dynasty (AD 618–906)
Gilded silver
Height 15 cm; diameter (of mouth) 24.5 cm; weight 1.3 kg
Excavated 1987, from the crypt of Famen temple, Fufeng county, Shaanxi province
Famen Temple Museum

This incense burner dish has a wide mouth with slanting rim, flat base and gilded decoration. Indentations on the dish of the burner divide it into five sections, each of which has a lion-like face riveted to it with a

106

ring suspended from its mouth. On either side of each ridge are symmetrical honeysuckle designs.

The lower part of the burner, which is almost a mirror image of the dish, is riveted to the dish. On its shoulder is a ring of moulded lotus leaves, above five hollowed-out openings in the shape of *ruyi* with inserted trefoils or lotus buds inside. Between each hollow is a flying goose surrounded by trailing plants and grasses against a ring-punched ground. The exterior of the base of the dish is inscribed: '50 *liang* [approx. 2 kilograms] given by Minister Zhang Zongli' (fig. 106a).

Fig. 106a
Detail of the inscription.

This incense burner is a combination of traditional Chinese motifs, such as the animal-headed escutcheons with rings, and innovative elements such as the polylobed bowl which was probably the result of Tang contact with Indian and Near Eastern metal prototypes. The burner is similar to one found at Hejiacun (cat. no. 72) and to others in museums and private collections. [1]

Published: *Wenwu* 1988.10, p. 16; *Kaogu yu wenwu* 1988.2, p. 100; Shi Xingbang 1988, no. 15; *Famensi* 1994, no. 63.

1 Kelley 1984, cat. no. 75, p. 106, an altar dish in the Asian Art Museum, San Francisco, The Avery Brundage Collection.

107 Box

Tang dynasty (AD 618–906)
Silver with gilding
Height 12 cm; diameter 17.3 x 16.8 cm; height (of footrim) 2.4 cm; weight 799 g
Excavated 1987, from the crypt of Famen temple, Fufeng county, Shaanxi province
Famen Temple Museum

This approximately square box on a trumpet-shaped ring foot has a tight-fitting base and lid of similar depth, with vertical undulating sides. It has been hammered and decorated with gilded designs. The domed lid is engraved with leaping winged lions (fig. 107a), flowers and entwining vines within a lozenge frame of dotted beads. On the edge of the lid is a band of shell design and at each corner there are chrysanthemum flowers, the whole set against a ring-punched ground. The sides of the box are decorated with leaves and entwining vines.

The ring foot and the bottom of the box are soldered together and the ring foot is

107

Fig. 107a *Detail of leaping lion decoration.*

decorated with a narrow band of simplified lotus petal design. On the base of the box is a thirty-two-character inscription in four lines from which we can tell that the box was made for Emperor Yizong to celebrate his birthday. The weight is recorded as twenty *liang* (approx. 800 grams) and the box was presented by Mr Li, a surveillance commissioner for military training.[1]

We cannot tell what this box was used for but it may well have been for medicine as were many of the silver boxes in the Hejiacun hoard (cat. nos 76, 79). Alternatively, as it was in the imperial

collection it may have been used in some imperial Buddhist ceremony.

Published: *Wenwu* 1988.10, p.14; Shi Xingbang 1988, no. 4; *Famensi* 1994, no. 44.

1 Title translated from Hucker 1985, p. 549, no. 7386. According to Louis this refers to Li Zhi, who was based in Jiangnan-West (Louis 1999, p. 158).

108 Box

Tang dynasty (AD 618–906)
Silver
Height 10 cm; diameter 18.4 cm; weight 816 g
Excavated 1987, from the crypt of Famen temple, Fufeng county, Shaanxi province
Famen Temple Museum

There is something very chaste about this smooth, undecorated, round silver box. The lid curves upward into a shallow dome and the foot curves outward. The box has been made by a combination of metalworking

techniques: hammering, soldering and turning on a lathe, the use of a lathe indicated by concentric scars on both lid and base, with the centre point well demarcated.

It was possibly used for medicines (see cat. nos 76, 79) or for sweetmeats in a Buddhist ceremony.

Published: *Wenwu* 1988.10, p. 8; Shi Xingbang 1988, no. 6; *Famensi* 1994, no. 72.

109 Ewer

Tang dynasty (AD 618–906)
Silver with gilding
Height 19.8 cm; diameter (of body) 13 cm, (of mouth) 7.5 cm; weight 659 g
Excavated 1987, from the crypt of Famen temple, Fufeng county, Shaanxi province
Famen Temple Museum

This ewer[1] has a generally symmetrical appearance, its narrow neck and flat mouth reflecting the trumpet-shaped ring foot. The body is round, with a curved spout. On the shoulder is a decoration of *ruyi* lappets and on the body are four *viśvavajra* (crossed *vajra)* medallions, each with four tridents or three-pronged *vajras.*[2] The medallions are connected by two bands of bow string pattern. Under the belly are eight upward-facing lotus petals interspersed with eight three-pronged *vajras.* The basic shape of the ewer is based on the ancient Indian *kuṇḍikā,* a drinking bottle used by monks.[3]

The ring foot is welded on to the body. On the upper part is a ring of persimmon-fruit-shaped decoration. On the ring foot is a circle of inverted lotus petals from which stem three-pronged *vajras.* The edge of the ring foot is decorated with a wave design. On the inside of the ringed foot are inscribed in black the characters 'nan bei' (south, north). The *vajras* point in all directions of the compass, symbolizing the unlimited power of the law and its ability to conquer all evil. They also signify the

108

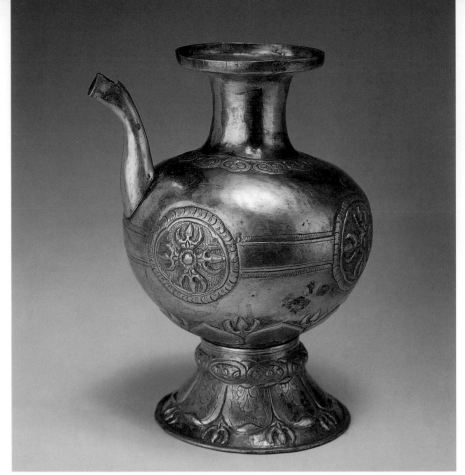

109

indestructibility of the Buddhist law.

3 Coomaraswamy and Kershaw 1928, p. 123.

4 See cat. nos 117–120. For a picture of other sets of caskets in the Famen temple, see Shi Xingbang 1988, no. 41; Zhu Qixin 1990, p. 78; *Famous Capital*, p.103.

5 A *maṇḍala* is a circle, globe, wheel, ring or diagram, a round or square altar on which Buddhas and bodhisattvas are placed. The purpose of a *maṇḍala* is to gather together the spiritual powers in order to promote the effective operation of the *dharma* or law. The term is commonly applied to magic circles, subdivided into circles or squares, in which are painted Buddhist divinities and symbols (Soothill and Hodous 1975, p. 352).

110 Five dishes

Tang dynasty (AD 618–906)
Silver with gilding
Diameters 11.1–11.4 cm; weights 113.7–125 g
Excavated 1987, from the crypt of Famen temple, Fufeng county, Shaanxi province
Famen Temple Museum

These five dishes are part of a set of twenty found in the Famen temple. They are hammered, flat-bottomed and two have a footring; three do not. The designs are engraved and the decoration is gilded. Each dish is in the shape of a five-lobed sunflower with raised ridges extending from the rim to the central point of the dish. In between the lobes are engraved five flowers in a cross shape. In the centre of the cavity is one flower with broad leaves. Along the rim is a lotus petal design. The fact that there were twenty dishes suggests that they were probably used for holding the materials to be consumed in fire-offering rituals in Buddhist ceremonies at the Famen temple.[1]

The shape of these dishes, the manufacturing technique and the decorative designs all reflect the popular style of gold and silver metalwork of the mid-Tang dynasty. The five-lobed shape is Central Asian and the sunflower decoration is Chinese. During the sixth and seventh centuries Sogdian silver bowls and dishes were often lobed or flower shaped.

adamantine nature and purity of the vessel and its contents.

Four of these ewers were found in the Famen temple, one in each of the four corners of the underground rear chamber. The inscription on this ewer may suggest that it was placed either in the south or north of the chamber. Three of the four ewers were marked with the characters for east, south or north; none was marked west. The combination of the *vajra* symbol and the iconography of the nesting sets of caskets reflects the influence of the Esoteric sect of Buddhism, known as Vajrayāna, which flourished briefly in China at about this period. It would seem that these ewers, therefore, combined with the relics in the sets of caskets,[4] formed part of a *maṇḍala*[5] as used in the Buddhist ritual. Such ewers normally held clean, scented water which is used by the priest to purify the sacred space of the *maṇḍala*. In rituals still in practice today the priest will mark out a space by pouring water in a circle, the inside of

which is then considered to be the heavenly realm of Mount Meru where a Buddha exists.

This vessel would have been used by the royal family in their worship of the Buddha and in ceremonies in which the emperor prayed for long life for himself and for his family as well as for peace, prosperity and security for his empire. Any such object had to be an example of the best technology available and had to be aesthetically pleasing.

Published: *Wenwu* 1988.10, p. 20; Shi Xingbang 1988, no. 39; Zhu Qixin 1990, p. 81; *Famensi* 1994, no. 25; Xi'an 1994, p. 103; *Empress Wu* 1998, no. 116.

1 The Sanskrit word for this type of ewer is *arghya* (Soothill and Hodous 1975, p. 285).

2 A *vajra*, thunderbolt or diamond sceptre, is a one-, three-, five- or nine-pronged sceptre of gold, silver, iron or copper and also a weapon used by Indian soldiers. It was employed by the esoteric sects of Buddhism as a symbol of the indestructible teaching of the Buddha and as an implement of Mahāyāna Buddhist worship to conquer enemies. The diamond, because of its hardness, was a symbol of the

110

However, the decoration on Central Asian wares tended to incorporate auspicious animals as the main motif whereas Chinese wares more often had flower designs.

Published: *Wenwu* 1988.10, p. 14; Shi Xingbang 1988, no. 13; Kuhn 1993, no. 66; *Famensi* 1994, no. 56; Xi'an 1994, pp. 106–7; Yin Shengping 1994; Shanghai 1996, p. 114, no. 80; *Daito Bunmei ten*, no. 69.

1 I am grateful to Professor John Huntington of Ohio State University for this information.

111 Box

Tang dynasty (AD 618–906)
Silver with gilding
Height 9.5 cm; circumference 21.5 cm;
weight 1.58 kg
Excavated 1987, from the crypt of Famen temple, Fufeng county, Shaanxi province
Famen Temple Museum

This flat, square box has straight sides, a shallow foot and symmetrical lid and body which fit tightly together. It has been hammered into shape and the decoration gilded. The edge of the domed lid is decorated with a ring of lotus petals and the centre with two flying phoenixes holding ribbons in their mouths. In the four corners of the lid are knots of flowers.

111

The rim of the lid and the body of the box are engraved with posies of flowers. The bottom of the box is soldered to a shallow foot rim and on the base of the box is an engraved inscription stating that the box was contributed by Li Fu, minister of the works department and of salt and iron. On the centre of the lid, inside the posy of flowers, is a further inscription, in black ink, stating that the box was presented by the emperor. From these two inscriptions it has been deduced that the box was a gift from Li Fu to the emperor who then presented it to the Famen temple.[1]

This box was used as an everyday utensil in the late Tang court and may have held food, incense or medicine. As the decoration on it is of phoenixes, symbol of the empress, it is possible that it was used by one of the emperor's wives.[2] As the histories state, in the tenth year of the Xiantong period, 874, the Yizong emperor welcomed the Buddha relics into the court and worshipped them with a number of gold and silver wares which he then presented to the Famen temple. The black ink characters on this box indicate that it was one of those presentation pieces.

The shape of this box is quite different from the Western-style boxes of the high

Tang period, such as those excavated at Hejiacun. The body of this box is deeper, the lid is more domed and it has a sloping ring foot. This indicates that by the late Tang period silverware had developed from its initial imitation of Central Asian and Western styles and was now imbued with a Chinese character.

Published: *Wenwu* 1988.10, p.13; Shi Xingbang 1988, no. 2; *Famensi* 1994, no. 48; Xi'an 1994, p. 100; Shanghai 1996, p. 125, no. 111; *Famous Capital*, p.140.

1 According to the *Jiu Tang shu*, Zhonghua shuju edn, 1975, juan 14, p. 4487, Li Fu was a brother of Li Shi, a prime minister, and was a minister in the works department. In 758 a monopoly on the marketing of salt was introduced and a special commissioner appointed to be in charge (as there had been in the Han dynasty when iron was also a state monopoly). Within a few years of its establishment the salt monopoly provided over 50 per cent of total imperial cash revenue (Twitchett and Fairbank 1979, p. 575).
2 Louis 1999, p. 158.

112 Tea sieve

Tang dynasty (AD 618–906)
Silver with gilding
Height 9.8 cm; length 14.9 cm; weight 1.47 kg
Excavated 1987, from the crypt of Famen temple, Fufeng county, Shaanxi province
Famen Temple Museum

Amongst the Famen temple finds were many items connected with tea.[1] The present item is a container for a sieve which was used to sieve the leaves from tea cakes before use. 'If the sieve is fine, the tea will float, if the sieve is coarse, the water will float'.[2] Therefore the sieve controlled the fineness of the tea powder. The sieve is contained within a covered box with a drawer, standing on a base. The rectangular lid has indented edges and is decorated with gilded flying *apsaras*, floating clouds and lotus petals. Gilded decoration also adorns the body of the sieve: immortals holding banners, riding on cranes against a

background of mountains in a mist, and two cranes in the clouds. The base has ten cloud-shaped openings. The sieve fits into the base and is formed by a double frame that holds a piece of silk fabric in position through which the tea is sieved. The drawer under the sieve, which was for collecting the sieved tea, is decorated with floating clouds and lotus petals. There is an inscription on the base (fig. 112a) stating that the sieve was made in the equivalent of 869 for the emperor Yizong by the Wensi yuan[3] and giving the names of the artisans and inspectors who were in charge of its manufacture.

The other components of the tea set were a grinder to crush the tea leaves, a container in the form of a silver tortoise, a tripod salt stand (salt was one of the ingredients added to tea at this time), a basket made of gold and silver 'chain-mail' and another, with holes, in which tea cakes were kept. There were also containers for the tea and for the spices added to tea (cat. nos 113, 114).[4] All of these items are particularly beautiful examples of the metalsmith's art.

Tea, like silk, is one of China's major contributions to the world. The plant grew wild in China and the Chinese were the first people to cultivate it for culinary and medicinal use. According to Chinese legend it was discovered by Shen Nong, the sage who taught agricultural skills to the Chinese, but it is more likely that it was found by farmers in their search for edible crops. According to the Chinese chronicles, the custom of drinking tea began in southern China in Sichuan province, around the time of the Han dynasty, when it was made more like a soup. It had spread northwards by the Tang dynasty and would appear to have been widely drunk by that time. It is mentioned by the Japanese Buddhist monk Ennin, who wrote a book describing his travels in the ninth century.[5] Even today tea is part of the fabric of everyday life in China.

There are many hundred varieties of Chinese tea, the flavours of which differ according to where the plants are grown and the time of day and season when the leaves are picked. The method of processing and brewing the tea leaves also makes a difference to the final taste. Chinese tea is classified into three main types: unfermented green, fermented black and semi-fermented red. Traditionally tea was formed into cakes from which pieces were broken off and thrown into boiling water but it was also compressed into powder or left as loose leaves. Many ingredients could be added. The traditional method of preparation inherited from pre-Tang times involved cooking the tea with onion, ginger, dates, orange peel, dogwood fruit and mint.[6] Sometimes just salt was added, or spices, and these were possibly what the storage jars (cat. nos 113 and 114) were used for. By the Tang dynasty tea was produced in many parts of southern China including the provinces of Hubei, Anhui, Zhejiang, Jiangsu, Guangdong and Guizhou.

Many Chinese are connoisseurs of tea and are very concerned with its colour, fragrance and flavour, its place of origin, the way it is stored and the source of the water with which it is brewed. Poets of the Tang dynasty such as Bai Juyi (772–846) wrote in

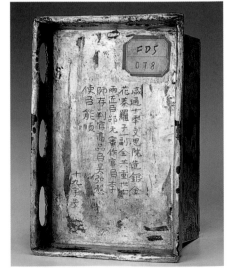

Fig. 112a *Detail of inscription inside the tea sieve.*

112

his poem entitled 'Lord Xiao sent me a dose of fresh Sichuan tea':

The tea was surprisingly fresh when it arrived from Sichuan
Its delicious taste was realized when brewed with water from the River Wei .[7]

The Chinese believe that tea drinking provides many health benefits, such as stimulating the nervous system and aiding digestion. As early as the Han dynasty it was mentioned in the *Shennong baicao jing* that tea drinking calmed people down and brought longevity. Tea was offered to the ancestors in ritual offerings from the period of the Southern and Northern Dynasties in the fifth and sixth centuries but tea drinking received its greatest boost in the Tang dynasty from Buddhist monks who found that tea helped to keep them awake during long hours of meditation. Gradually tea drinking spread to people of all walks of life and Feng Yan in his *Fengshi wenjian ji* (Records of Feng's travels), around the end of the eighth century, wrote:

Tea houses and tea shops in provincial cities are as numerous as those in the capital. Tea drinks are sold to people from all walks of life. People just put down the money and take the drink. Tea comes from regions along the Yangzi river and the Huai river both by boat and cart, piling sky high at stops en route. There is great variety in kind as well as in grade.[8]

The fashion for tea drinking spread to non-Chinese living in China during the Tang dynasty and it was reported that Uighur visitors to Chang'an went first to drink tea before doing anything else.[9] The government soon realized the popularity of tea drinking and in 780 the emperor Dezong levied taxes and imposed measures to ensure the imperial court received tribute of the best quality.

Secular use of tea included gatherings where people could share their appreciation of fine teas and tea utensils. Lu Yu, the eighth-century tea master, wrote the influential *Chajing* (Classic of Tea)[10] which promoted tea drinking to an aesthetic experience for the leisured and well-to-do of society. He particularly recommended

green wares (see cat. no.116) as suitable for tea, as the colour enhanced the green of green teas. Tea was valued both for its practical uses (quenching the thirst, counteracting over-indulgence in alcoholic drinks, calming the mind) and for its medicinal uses.[11] However, as has been pointed out, despite the early association of tea with Buddhism, China developed a social tea culture centred on teahouses, but not the equivalent ritual of the Japanese tea ceremony.[12]

The process of tea making was depicted by the famous Tang painter Yan Liben in his painting *Xiao Yi obtaining the Lanting manuscript by trickery*, which is now in the National Palace Museum, Taiwan.[13]

Published: *Wenwu* 1988.10, p. 16; Shi Xingbang 1988, no. 18; Xi'an 1992, p. 40; Wang Renbo 1990, p. 205, no. 20; *Famensi* 1994, no. 49; Xi'an 1994, pp. 114–15; Hong Kong 1997, no. 91.

1 Han Wei 1988. For general information on tea, see the various publications by the Flagstaff Museum of Tea, Hong Kong; Lu Yu 1974; the chapter on tea in Beijing 1983b, pp. 329–36; and Sun Ji 1996, pp. 62–9.
2 Hong Kong 1997, p. 236.

3 The royal workshop that produced many gold and silver items for the imperial family.

4 A group of items in gold and silver for tea was excavated in 1991 from the tomb of the Taifuren of the Qi state in Yinchuan and reported in *Wenbo* 1997.4, pp. 51–2. This included twenty-one gold and silver objects typologically similar to those tea utensils from the Famen temple: a silver stand, cage and rods for roasting tea, a tea grinder, a silver pot, gold cups and silver saucers and platters for holding sweets eaten after drinking tea.

5 Reischauer 1955, p. 110.

6 Quoted in Flagstaff 1984, part 1, p. 20 and verified by this author who enjoyed several cups of such tea in October and December 1998 at the staff restaurant at Lintong, Museum of the Terracotta Warriors.

7 Flagstaff 1984, part 2, p. 14.

8 This book contains observations made in the second half of the eighth century on such things as lives of the famous, customs, court life and local sights. See Wilkinson 1998,

p. 791. English quote from Flagstaff 1984, part 1, p. 21.

9 Schafer 1963, p. 20.

10 Lu Yu 1974; Blofeld 1985.

11 The English phrase 'a cup of char', meaning a cup of tea, derives from the Chinese word for tea, *cha*.

12 Sun Ji 1996.

13 Reproduced in Flagstaff 1984, part 1, pl. 1.

113 Jar with musicians and entertainers

Tang dynasty (AD 618–906)
Silver with gilding
Height 11.7 cm; diameter of mouth 5.4 cm; weight 149.5 g
Excavated 1987, from the crypt of Famen temple, Fufeng county, Shaanxi province
Famen Temple Museum

This Tang dynasty tea utensil resembles a modern Chinese tea cup. It belonged to the Tang dynasty imperial palace and was presented to the Famen temple for worship during Buddhist relics ceremonies. Its purpose was probably similar to that of the jar in catalogue no. 114, that is as a container for the tea ceremony, used either for storing the tea itself or the salt and spices to go with it.

The jar has a domed lid with a broad band round the edge and a knob in the shape of a lotus pearl. The lid and rim of the jar are decorated with lotus leaves and a pattern of entwining vines against a ring-punched background.

Sinuous foliage also creates a background on the deep waisted body, against which stand out three gilded musicians and dancers. The first figure is a musician with his hands on the *qin* (a traditional Chinese zither, a stringed instrument) which is one of the most refined musical instruments in China. His left leg is raised and his right foot taps the ground. The second figure has the

palms of his hands clasped together on the top of his head. He has a naked upper body and feet, and his left leg raised, and looks very confident.[1] The third figure has his two legs spread apart and his hands hold the flute he is playing, his cheeks bulging with the effort.

The lower part of the body bulges to balance the rim of the lid and has two rows of moulded lotus leaves with ears of wheat in repoussé. The elegance of the splayed foot is enhanced by fine fluting which flows out to leaves at the edge. Music played an important part in Chinese life and rituals from very early times.[2] A Han dynasty commentary on the *Shijing* (Book of Odes) states: 'Governing the state is comparable to playing the *qin*. If the large strings are too tight, the small strings break', and music was already included among the six genres of classical learning in the Han dynasty.[3]

Published: *Wenwu* 1988.10, p.12; Shi Xingbang 1988, no. 11.

1 In the model of a bronze house with musicians playing the zither (*qin*) and mouth organ (*sheng*) from the Eastern Zhou period, fifth century BC, found at Shaoxing, Zhejiang, illustrated in Rawson 1996a, cat. no. 70, none of the musicians is wearing any clothing. Rawson suggests that this may indicate either the low social status of the musicians or the warm climate of the region.

2 See, for example, the *Liji*, a ritualist's anthology of ancient usages, prescriptions, definitions and anecdotes. Many sections are purported to be connected with Confucius but the text is very diverse in style and was compiled over a long period of time, during the Warring States period, and its date is contentious (Loewe 1993, pp. 293–7). Legge 1967, vol. 2, pp. 92–131 has a translation of the section on music and the *qin*: 'The stringed instruments give out a melancholy sound, which produces the thought of purity and fidelity, and awakens the determination of the mind'.

3 See K J DeWoskin, *A Song for One or Two: Music and the Concept of Art in Early China*, Ann Arbor, Michigan 1982, pp. 7, 99. I am grateful to Dr Stephen Little for referring me to this book.

113

114

114 Jar with figures in landscapes

Tang dynasty (AD 618–906)
Silver with gilding
Height 24.7 cm; diameter (of mouth) 12.3 cm;
weight 903 g
Excavated 1987, from the crypt of Famen
temple, Fufeng county, Shaanxi province
Famen Temple Museum

This jar has a deep body and a raised ring
foot which is similar in outline to the lid and
has been soldered on to the body. The knob
on the lid is shaped like a lotus pearl and the
lid is decorated with gilded deer chasing
each other among trailing vines. The foot has
gilded decoration of birds, waves and sea-
creatures.

But it is the four cartouches adorning the
body of the jar which are of principal
interest as they portray both human and
animal themes.[1] One shows a man in a short
robe sitting under a tree and looking at a
man with a bundle on his back.

Another scene shows two old men
playing Chinese chess, while an onlooker
sits behind. There are several chess pieces on
the table, a tea bowl in the foreground and
in the distance tree trunks and scattered
grasses.[2]

A third depicts a youth, sitting under a
broad-leaved tree, by water, with a curved
stick or cane in his hand. A bundle is slung
over the extended branch of the tree and far
away in the distance is a whale jumping up
from the waves.

The fourth picture shows a man with
headscarf and short jacket and a hoe on his

Figs 114a, b, c Details of the scenes in the
cartouches.

shoulders. His head is turned back towards
two men in long-sleeved robes, bowing with
their palms folded respectfully in front of
them.

These scenes have been given a Buddhist
explanation as the jar was found in a
Buddhist temple. For example, it has been
suggested that the whale in fig. 114b is the
reincarnation of a bodhisattva and that the
man in fig. 114c is being told not to kill
animals, which was a Buddhist precept.

However, Daoism and Confucian precepts also played important roles in Chinese life at this time, so these cartouches may equally well depict either Daoist tales[3] or stories about the paragons of filial piety related to Confucianism. Their exact meaning is not certain.

These four cartouches are offset against a background of intertwining grasses on a ring-punched ground. The scenes are typical of the late Tang dynasty, depicting traditional Chinese figures rather than foreigners.

This jar was used for storage and is one of many such silverware objects presented to the Famen temple by the emperors Yizong and Xizong for use in Buddhist ceremonies. It forms part of the series of tea utensils; there are two jars of identical shape with similar decoration.[4] This is the only complete set of tea utensils belonging to the Tang dynasty royal family discovered so far and, as such, is of extraordinary historical value. Although very few containers of this shape have been found, many are illustrated in paintings in Dunhuang[5] so it may be assumed they were in common use during the Tang period.

Published: *Wenwu* 1988.10, pp.17–18; Shi Xingbang 1988, no. 10; Wang Renbo 1990, p. 205, no. 20; Xi'an 1992, p. 35; *Famensi* 1994, no. 68; Xi'an 1994, pp. 116–19; Guggenheim 1997, no. 65; *Empress Wu* 1998, no. 113.

1 All the descriptions of the scenes in the cartouches have been provided by the staff of the Administrative Bureau of Museums and Archaeological Data of Shaanxi Province.
2 The modern version of Chinese chess or *xiangqi* was developed in the late Tang dynasty but was probably played in some form long before then. The object of *xiangqi* is to checkmate one's opponent's king and as this is the same as Western chess it is presumed that they have a common origin. It is possible that it was first played in India but several scholars now think that China had a version of chess before India. See R Keene, 'Mind Sports', *Spectator*, 17 July 1999, for further information and diagrams of the game.
3 Dr Stephen Little of the Art Institute of Chicago has suggested, for instance, that the scene of the two gentlemen playing chess is similar to many later Ming dynasty scenes of

the woodcutter Wang Zhi of the Han dynasty, who stumbles on two Daoist immortals playing the game.
4 Han Wei 1988, p. 53, says this is a container for salt for use in tea.
5 See, for example, Whitfield 1982–3, vol. 2, pl. 67, from the Buddha Preaching the Law, a frontispiece of a booklet of the *Diamond Sūtra* (the earliest extant dated complete printed book, dated to 868, found by Aurel Stein in cave 17, Dunhuang, Gansu province, in 1907, now exhibited in the British Library). The Buddhist paintings, textiles and manuscripts walled up in cave 17 are very important for the history of Buddhism as Dunhuang was under Tibetan occupation between 781 and 848 and escaped destruction in the Buddhist persecution of 845.

115 Plate

Tang dynasty (AD 618–906)
Glass
Height 2.1 cm; diameter 15.8 cm
Excavated 1987, from the crypt of Famen temple, Fufeng county, Shaanxi province
Famen Temple Museum

This flat-bottomed blue glass dish was one of thirteen glass items bestowed on the Famen temple by the emperor Yizong in 874. The decoration is both incised and gilded. The centre of the dish is slightly domed and decorated with plantain leaves which are composed of double petals, the insides with slanting or wavy lines which are incised and gilded, in a technique of cold working.[1] Around the flower patterns are

ripples with gold infill. The glass is quite transparent and there are several places on the surface where the decoration is worn away. Many of the plates have the greyish remains of what was probably the size to which the gold leaf was stuck. The centre of the base of the plate shows the marks left by the glassmaker's pontil.[2]

Along the lines of the engraved patterns are inconsistencies, irregularities and line-breaks, showing a freehand use of the graver tool. Generally Chinese wares were more carefully engraved, suggesting that this glass plate is of foreign origin. There are several places where such gold-incised blue plates could have been made. Nishapur in Iran or the Mediterranean area, where there was an early Islamic tradition, are possibilities.[3] Similar incised blue glass has been found at Samarra in Iraq, another possible source for this piece. Whatever their origin, the plates illustrate the trade that existed along the Silk Routes.

China was so steeped in a tradition of ceramics and was so skilled at this that there was no great need to develop a separate glassmaking tradition. The Chinese may have imported glass as early as the late Western Zhou period, possibly in the form of eye beads, and they had definitely begun making their own glass during the Eastern Zhou period.[4] Chinese glass is easily identifiable because of its peculiar chemical composition: it contains significant amounts

115

of lead and barium. This tended to make the glass somewhat brittle, hence relatively little remains, and it was opaque rather than translucent like the glass made in the West. A quite considerable amount of Chinese-made glass was coloured pale green, particularly during the Han dynasty, because its opacity made it resemble jade, for which it was used as a substitute on occasions when sumptuary laws prohibited the use of jade, or when a cheaper and quicker substitute for jade was required.[5] However, there seems no doubt that translucent glass from the West continued to be imported into the Tang dynasty and was regarded as something both exotic and unusual.

Excavations in China this century have revealed a published total of thirty-six Islamic vessels or fragments from twelve different sites over half of which were Buddhist monasteries.[6] The richest discovery of Islamic glass at a dated religious site is that at the Famen temple. Glass vessels were a prominent import item for use by monks for reliquaries, dishes for liturgical offerings and alms bowls. Various images exist of bodhisattvas, such as Guanyin (Avalokiteśvara), holding a faceted glass.[7] Wealthy lay Buddhists also owned glass vessels such as beakers, bird-shaped flasks and foreign glass vessels which were used as relic holders (cat. no. 102). Faceted glass bowls were made in Iran and were imported into the Far East. The Shōsō-in storehouse at the Tōdaiji temple in Nara, Japan, also has a good collection of such glassware which has not survived to the same extent in China. This Japanese temple is very important as it contains a carefully recorded treasury of luxury goods, many of which have a Chinese origin, belonging to the Japanese emperor Shōmu. After the principal donation by the empress in AD 756 few other pieces were added so the treasury represents a unique source of datable material contemporary with the Tang.

Published: *Wenwu* 1988.10, p. 24; Shi Xingbang 1988, no. 50.

1 Cold working: an all-embracing term for the various techniques such as engraving, grinding, carving, cutting etc. carried out when the glass is cold.
2 Zhu Qixin 1990, p. 83. A pontil is a solid metal rod used to hold the hot glass during the final reheating and shaping operations. The hot glass is attached to the pontil just before it is separated from, or cracked off, the blowpipe.
3 Jens Kröger, 'Painting on Glass Before the Mamluk Period', in R Ward (ed.), *Gilded and Enamelled Glass from the Middle East,* London 1998, p. 10; An Jiayao, 'Dated Islamic Glass in China', *Bulletin of the Asia Institute*, New Series 5, pp. 123–37; R H Brill and P M Fenn, 'Some thoughts on the Famen Temple Glass Finds' (private correspondence).
4 R H Brill, 'Glass and Glassmaking in Ancient China, and some other things from other places', The Toledo Conference, The Glass Art Society, 1993, pp. 56–69.
5 C Michaelson, 'Han Dynasty Glass', *Transactions of the Oriental Ceramic Society*, vol. 63 (forthcoming).
6 Moore 1998, pp. 78–84. R H Brill and P M Fenn, 'Some Thoughts on the Famen Temple Glass Finds' (private correspondence); R H Brill and P M Fenn, 'Glasswares in Famen Temple', Selected papers from the First International Symposium on the History and Cultures of the Famen Temple, 1992, pp. 254–8; P M Fenn, R H Brill and Shi Meiguang, 'Addendum to Chapter 4', in R H Brill and J H Martin, *Scientific Research in Chinese Glass*, Corning, NY, The Corning Museum of Glass 1991, pp. 59–64. I am extremely grateful to Dr Brill for advice on this entry and for his bibliographical references.
7 Rawson 1992, fig.198, p. 268: OA 1919.1-1.0139.

116 *Mise* bowl

Tang dynasty (AD 618–906)
Ceramic
Height 9.2 cm; diameter (of mouth) 21.4 cm; weight 610 g
Excavated 1987, from the crypt of Famen temple, Fufeng county, Shaanxi province
Famen Temple Museum

This five-lobed bowl was one of fourteen *mise* (secret colour) Yue[1] ware bowls, plates and vases unearthed in the Famen temple. When it was found it was wrapped in material which has left traces on the surface of the bowl.[2] The glaze on *mise* wares is particularly fine, as is the potting, and many of the pieces are of imposing size.

This dish has a splayed mouth with a five-lobed rim resembling petals and a flat base with a circular footring. The clay body is very pure and is covered with an even layer of lustrous yellowish green glaze.

Various texts of the Tang and Five Dynasties periods mention *mise* porcelain and say that it was strictly reserved for imperial use. During the eighth century the popularity of white wares was challenged by that of green wares, particularly those made in the southeast of China, at the Yue kilns of Zhejiang. One reason for this was the emergence of tea as a fashionable drink and connoisseurs such as Lu Yu (733–804), who wrote an essay discussing the relative merits of different tea bowls, concluding that Yue ware bowls were best. He noted that such green-glazed porcelains enhanced the colour of the green tea and he likened Yue

116

117–120

ware to jade. *Mise* Yue ware was praised for its jade-like appearance by Tang poets, Song connoisseurs and Ming historians. However, its identity was a matter of conjecture. Only in 1987 when the Famen temple discoveries were made was identification possible as, along with the treasures themselves, there was a detailed inventory, the *yiwuzhang,* which listed 'secret colour' wares and identified them as fourteen *mise* wares used by the emperor Yizong to hold Śākyamuni's cremated finger bones.

The archaeological find not only identified this mysterious ware but it also highlighted the changed status of ceramic which only in the Tang dynasty began to rival bronze, gold and silver as a prized material. Yue ware's similarity in colour to jade was obviously one factor in its promotion to a high-status material since the Chinese had always revered jade as one of the most precious materials in their hierarchy of valued materials. This bowl also shows the influence of silverware on Tang and later ceramics as its shape is similar to that of many Tang silver bowls.[3]

Published: *Wenwu* 1988.10, pp. 23–4; Wang Renbo 1990, p. 260, no. 7; *Famensi* 1994, no. 78; Xi'an 1994, p. 79; Hong Kong 1997, no. 94; *Empress Wu* 1998, no. 117; *Famous Capital*, p. 151, no. 4.

1 For information on Yue ware and *mise* porcelain see particularly Kamei 1996, p. 51 and

Vainker 1996, pp. 70–2; for a summary of research on *mise* ware see Wang Liying and Wang Xingping, *Gugong Bowuguan yuankan* 1996.1, pp. 53–61 (abbreviated version in English in *China Archaeology and Art Digest*, vol. 1, no.1, Hong Kong, January–March 1996, pp. 109–11).
2 *Wenwu* 1988.10, p. 23, pls 7–2, 3 and colour pl. 2–2.
3 Rawson 1991, p. 150.

117 Casket

Tang dynasty (AD 618–906)
Iron
Height 22 cm; body 22 x 22 cm
Excavated 1987, from the crypt of Famen temple, Fufeng county, Shaanxi province
Famen Temple Museum

This is the outer layer of the five-layered casket set made specifically for the worship of one of the Buddha's relics, a finger bone. Three of the inner caskets, of gilded silver, crystal and jade respectively, are discussed in the following three entries (cat. nos 118–120). The fifth casket, which fitted between the gilded silver and the crystal casket, is of sandalwood, its corners overlaid with silver. Unfortunately it could not be sent from China because of its fragile condition.

Altogether there were four such sets of caskets in the Famen temple. This one was excavated from the hidden niche, in the

back room of the underground chamber of the temple. It is thought that the other three casket sets were merely decoys for this set which, according to Zhao Puchu, chairman of the Chinese Buddhist Association, was the true holder of the genuine *śarīra*. The other sets are said to have contained 'shadow bones' in a ploy to protect the genuine relic in the case of persecution.[1] This is not the most sumptuous of the casket sets, the intention probably being to divert attention from it. In fact the most resplendent of the casket sets, a set of eight, also contained a *śarīra* of bone, but this is thought not to be the 'true' bone.[2]

This iron casket is cube shaped and the lid has a square ring on it. The silk covering, which has now disintegrated, has left visible marks of warp and weft threads over the iron.

Several willow-leaf-shaped gold flowers decorate the outside of the casket and on one side is a lock and key with a chain. When the casket was excavated the lock was so seriously corroded that it could no longer be used. Once the casket was opened, the archaeologists discovered inside, fitting one inside the other, the caskets of gilded silver, of sandalwood, of crystal, and finally the jade casket which held the 'true' finger bone.

The three other casket sets found in the

118

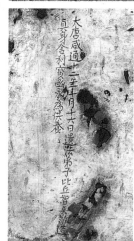

underground chambers of the Famen
temple also contained *śarīra*. A *śarīra* of a
bony material was found in the
antechamber, inside a gilded silver coffin-
shaped reliquary which itself was inside a
bronze stūpa and then this was placed inside
the white marble 'Aśoka' stūpa (as it was
referred to in an inscription).[3] A *śarīra* was
discovered in the middle chamber placed
inside a silver coffin then an iron casket. The
śarīra found in the rear chamber was of bone
and was preserved inside the set of eight
caskets mentioned above. These caskets
were originally protected in an embroidered
red bag. The largest of the eight, which has
disintegrated, was of sandalwood with silver
fittings, then there were three caskets of
silver (one plain and two gilded), a
bejewelled marble casket and finally three
gold caskets. The *śarīra* was inside the
smallest of the gold caskets, which is stūpa
shaped (see fig. 29, p. 135).

Published: *Wenwu* 1988.10, p. 7.

1 Zhao Puchu called these decoys merely
  'shadows' – like the reflection of the moon in
  water, but still possessing significant power.
  See Wang Zhaolin and Xiong Lei, 'Report
  from China: Discovery of Rare Buddhist
  Relics', *Oriental Art*, Spring 1989, pp. 61–5.
2 For general information on the sets of *śarīra*
  caskets, see Zhu Qixin 1990, pp. 79–80, and
  Shi Xingbang 1988. (An interesting
  comparison can be made to Shakespeare's *The*

Merchant of Venice when Bassanio has to
choose between three caskets, lead, gold and
silver, in order to win Portia.)
3 Zhu Qixin 1990, p.78. King Aśoka, Ayuwang
  in Chinese, is also called 'the Great'. He
  reigned from 274 to 232 BC as the Mauryan
  emperor and was a great patron of
  Buddhism.

118 Casket

Tang dynasty (AD 618–906)
Gilded silver
Height 17 cm; box 17.5 x 17.5 cm;
weight 1.61 kg
Excavated 1987, from the crypt of Famen
temple, Fufeng county, Shaanxi province
Famen Temple Museum

This is the gilded silver cube-shaped casket
of the five-layered casket set described in
cat. no. 117. This casket nestled between the
iron casket and the sandalwood one. It has
been hammered into shape and the Buddhist
images are engraved and gilded; it is a
particularly beautiful and accomplished
example of the Tang metalworker's art.

The subject matter of the images on this

and another metal casket found at Famen
temple has been the subject of an extensive
study in Chinese.[1] Based on the details of
that study it is impossible to overestimate
the historical importance of these caskets.
They fully document the presence of the
mizong or Esoteric sect in China and the
imperial patronage of the sect during the
third quarter of the ninth century. The
figures on the caskets (figs 118a–c) are the
Buddhas, Pāramitā goddesses, bodhisattvas,
offering goddesses and *vidyārajās* from the
Vajradhātu maṇḍala of the *Sarva-Tathagata-
Tattva-samgraha Sūtra*. While this text is
known from literary evidence to have
existed in China and to have been taken to
Japan from China by Japanese in the early
ninth century, no full representation of the
maṇḍalas had come to light in China prior to
the discovery of these two caskets.

The lid connects tightly with the body of
the casket and the side panels of the body
are rectangular in shape. Between the
figures there is a decoration of intertwining
vines and grasses. The edges of the panels
are decorated with either three- or four-

pronged *vajras*, posies of flowers and flame designs. All of the figures sit on lotus flowers, with a variety of objects in their hands – snakes, the wheel of the law supported in the palms of their hands, swords, Buddhist staffs, ribbons, three-pronged *vajras,* lotus flowers, utensils in the shape of the figure 'nine' or alms bowls.

The front of the casket is engraved with characters stating that 'this casket is made respectfully for the emperor, to worship the Buddha's relic'. On the base is another inscription (fig. 118d): 'The great Tang dynasty, Xiantong reign, twelfth year [AD 871], sixteenth day of the tenth month, the monk Zhiying respectfully made the Buddha's relic precious reliquary casket for the purpose of worshipping it for evermore'. Zhiying was a high-ranking monk of one of the temples in Chang'an.[2]

Published: *Wenwu* 1988.10, p. 7.

1 Wu and Han 1998. In this exceptionally valuable work, every figure is identified in detail as to name and position.
2 Information supplied by the Administrative Bureau of Museums and Archaeological Data of Shaanxi Province.

119 Casket

Tang dynasty (AD 618–906)
Crystal
Height 7 cm; length 10.5 cm; front width 5 cm; back width 4.5 cm; weight 437 g
Excavated 1987, from the crypt of Famen temple, Fufeng county, Shaanxi province
Famen Temple Museum

This casket is one of the set of five described in cat. no. 117. It was inside the sandalwood casket (not exhibited). The lid is arc-shaped and the front is wider than the back. The front and the back of the lid are each decorated with sapphires and topazes which are transparent and lustrous. These yellow stones are extremely large and rare.

The front of the casket, decorated with gold pomegranate-leaf-shaped flowers, is

119

wide and high, whilst the back is short and narrow. The base is short and connected to the body by a mortice and tenon joint. When it was excavated the jade casket (cat. no. 120) was found inside this crystal casket.

Published: *Wenwu* 1988.10, p. 7; *Famensi* 1994, no.19.

120 Casket

Tang dynasty (AD 618–906)
Jade
Height: 4.8 cm; length 6.5 cm; front width 3.5 cm; back width 2.7 cm; weight 95 g
Excavated 1987, from the crypt of Famen temple, Fufeng county, Shaanxi province
Famen Temple Museum

This is the innermost casket of the set of five described in catalogue no. 117. It contained the 'genuine' Buddha's finger bone relic.

This discovery was confirmed by Zhao Puchu, chairman of the Chinese Buddhist Association, who wrote a poem about it in 1987.[1]

The casket is made of white jade and is similar in shape to the crystal casket which contained it. The lid is in the shape of an arc and the front is wider than the back. On both sides of the body are three openings and the lid and the body are fastened by grooves. Inside the casket is a platform and the Buddha's finger bone – the true relic – was placed on it. When the casket was excavated its lid bore traces of gold-lined embroidered silk with which it had obviously once been wrapped.

Published: *Wenwu* 1988.10, p. 7; *Famensi* 1994, no. 18.

1 See Xi'an 1994, pp. 8–9.

120

Acker 1954, 1974 Acker, William PB. *Some T'ang and Pre-T'ang Texts on Chinese Painting*, London, vol. 1, 1954; vol. 2, 1974

Allen 1950 Allen, MR. 'Early Chinese Lamps', *Oriental Art*, 1950.4, pp. 133–41

Ariadne 1998 Ariadne Galleries. *Treasures of the Eurasian Steppes: Animal Art from 800 BC to 200 AD*, New York 1998

Bagley 1993 Bagley, Robert W. 'Replication Techniques in Eastern Zhou Bronze Casting' in Lubar, Steven and W. David Kingery (eds). *History from Things: Essays on Material Culture*, Washington, DC and London 1993

Bagley 1995 Bagley, Robert W. 'What the Bronzes at Hunyuan Tell Us about the Foundry at Houma', *Orientations*, January 1995, pp. 46–54

Bagley 1996 Bagley, Robert W. (ed.). *Art of the Houma Foundry*, Princeton 1996

Ball 1927 Ball, Katherine M. *Decorative Motives in Oriental Art*, London and New York 1927

Bao Quan 1982 Bao Quan. 'Xianshi wenguanhui shouzang de jijian Tangdai jinyin qi', *Kaogu yu Wenwu* 1982.1, pp. 54–8

Baoji 1993 Baoji Excavation Report. *Wenwu* 1993.10, pp. 1–4

Beal 1885 Beal, Samuel. *Si-yu-ki: Buddhist Records of the Western World Translated from the Chinese of Hiuen Stiang (A.D. 629)*, 2 vols, Boston 1885

Beck 1990 Beck, BJ Mansvelt. *The Treatises of the Later Han: Their Authors, Sources, Contents and Place in Chinese Historiography*, Leiden 1990

Beijing 1954 *Chu wenwu zhanlan tulu*, Beijing, 1954

Beijing 1956 *Shou Xian Cai Hou mu chutu yiwu*, Beijing 1956

Beijing 1959a *Luoyang Shaogou Han mu*, Beijing 1959

Beijing 1959b *Luoyang Zhongzhoulu*, Beijing 1959

Beijing 1961 *Xin Zhongguo di kaogu shouhuo*, Beijing 1961

Beijing 1963 *Nei Menggu chutu wenwu xuanji*, Beijing 1963

Beijing 1972a *Xin Zhongguo chutu wenwu*, Beijing 1972

Beijing 1972b *Wenhua da geming qijian chutu wenwu, di yi ji*, Beijing 1972

Beijing 1973a *Zhongguo Renmin Gongheguo chutu wenwu, zhanlan zhanpin xuanji*, Beijing 1973

Beijing 1973b *Changsha Mawangdui yi hao Han mu*, 2 vols, Beijing 1973

Beijing 1974a *Gugong Bowuyuan cang gongyi pinxuan*, Beijing 1974

Beijing 1974b *New Archaeological Finds in China: Discoveries During the Cultural Revolution*, Beijing 1974

Beijing 1976 *Zhonghua Renmin Gongheguo chutu wenwu xuan*, Beijing 1976

Beijing 1979 *Wenwu kaogu gongzuo sanshi nian 1949–1979*, Beijing 1979

Beijing 1980a *Yinxu Fuhao mu*, Beijing 1980

Beijing 1980b *Sui Xian Zeng HouYi mu*, Beijing 1980

Beijing 1980c *Zhongguo Kaogu Xuehui de yici nianhui lunwen ji 1979*, Beijing 1980

Beijing 1980d *Mancheng Han mu fajue baogao*, 2 vols, Beijing 1980

Beijing 1980e *Bang Chang'an chengjiao Sui Tang mu*, Beijing 1980

Beijing 1983a *Baoji Baishouling*, Beijing 1983

Beijing 1983b Institute of History of Natural Sciences, Chinese Academy of Sciences. *Ancient China's Technology and Science*, Beijing 1983

Beijing 1984a *Xin Zhongguo de kaogu faxian he yanjiu*, Beijing 1984

Beijing 1984b *Zhongguo kaoguxue nianjian, 1984*, Beijing 1984

Beijing 1985 *Zhongguo meishu quanji: Diaosu bian 2, Qin Han diaosu*, Beijing 1985

Beijing 1986a *E'erduosi shi qingtongqi*, Beijing 1986

Beijing 1986b *Xinyang Chu mu*, Beijing 1986

Beijing 1986c Shanghai Institute of Ceramics, Academica Sinica. *Scientific and Technological Insights on Ancient China, Pottery and Porcelain: Proceedings of the International Conference on Ancient Chinese Pottery and Porcelain*, Beijing 1986, pp. 129–33

Beijing 1987 Culture Department, Cultural Relics Bureau and Gugong Museum. *Quanguo chutu wenwu zhenpinxuan, 1976–84*, Beijing 1987

Beijing 1989 *Zeng Hou Yi mu*, 2 vols, Beijing 1989

Beijing 1990 Editorial Committee of 'Gems of China's Cultural Relics'. *Gems of China's Cultural Relics (Zhongguo wenwu jinghua)*, English and Chinese texts, Beijing 1990

Beijing 1991a *Xi Han Nan Yue Wang mu*, Beijing 1991

Beijing 1991b Editorial Committee of 'Gems of China's Cultural Relics'. *Gems of China's Cultural Relics (Zhongguo wenwu jinghua)*, English and Chinese texts, Beijing 1991

Beijing 1992a China Cultural Relics Promotion Center (eds). *Treasures: 300 Best Excavated Antiques from China*, Beijing 1992

Beijing 1992b Editorial Committee of 'Gems of China's Cultural Relics.' *Gems of China's Cultural Relics (Zhongguo wenwu jinghua)*, English and Chinese texts, Beijing 1992

Beijing 1992c *Xi'an, Legacies of Ancient Chinese Civilization*, Beijing 1992

Beijing 1993a Editorial Committee of 'Gems of China's Cultural Relics'. *Gems of China's Cultural Relics (Zhongguo wenwu jinghua)*, English and Chinese texts, Beijing 1993

Beijing 1993b *Kaogu jinghua*, Beijing 1993

Beijing 1997 Editorial Committee of 'Gems of China's Cultural Relics'. *Gems of China's Cultural Relics (Zhongguo wenwu jinghua)*, English and Chinese texts, Beijing 1997

Beijing 1998 Department of Archaeology, Beijing University (ed.). *Proceedings of the International Conference on 'Chinese Archaeology Enters the Twenty-first Century'*, Beijing 1998

Berger 1987 Berger, Patricia. *Ancestral Dwellings: Furnishing the Han Tomb*, San Francisco 1987

Berger 1994 Berger, Patricia (ed.). *Tomb Treasures from Ancient China: The Buried Art of Ancient Xi'an*, Fort Worth and San Francisco 1994

Beurdeley 1985 Beurdeley, Cécile. *Sur les Routes de la Soie: Le grand voyage des objets d'art*, Fribourg, Switzerland 1985

Bingham 1941 Bingham, Woodbridge. *The Founding of the T'ang Dynasty: The Fall of Sui and Rise of T'ang*, Baltimore 1941

Birrell 1982 Birrell, Anne. *New Songs from a Jade Terrace*, London 1982

Birrell 1988 Birrell, Anne. *Popular Songs and Ballads of Han China*, London, Sydney and Wellington 1988

Birrell 1993 Birrell, Anne. *Chinese Mythology: An Introduction*, Baltimore and London 1993

Birrell 1999 Birrell, Anne (trans.). *The Classic of Mountains and Seas*, London 1999

Blofeld 1985 Blofeld, John. *The Chinese Art of Tea*, London 1985

Bodde 1961 Bodde, Derk. 'Myths of Ancient China' in Samuel Noah Kramer (ed.), *Mythologies of the Ancient World*, New York 1961, pp. 367–408

Bodde 1975 Bodde, Derk. *Festivals in Classical China: New Year and Other Annual Observances during the Han dynasty, 206 BC–AD 220*, Princeton and Hong Kong 1975

Bodde 1991 Bodde, Derk. *Chinese Thought, Society, and Science: The Intellectual and Social Background of Science and Technology in Pre-modern China*, Honolulu 1991

Boltz 1994 Boltz, William G. *The Origin and Early Development of the Chinese Writing System*, New Haven 1994

Boston 1976 *Han and T'ang Murals Discovered in Tombs in the People's Republic of China and Copied by Contemporary Chinese Artists*, Boston 1976

Boulnois 1966 Boulnois, L. (trans. D. Chamberlin). *The Silk Road*, London 1963

Bower 1993 Bower, Virginia. 'Two Masterworks of Tang Ceramic Sculpture', *Orientations*, June 1993, pp. 72–7

Brinker 1979 Brinker, Helmut. *Zauber des Chinesischen Fächers*, exhibition catalogue, Zurich 1979

Brinker 1981 Brinker, Helmut. *Kunstschätze aus China*, exhibition catalogue, Zurich 1981

Brinker and Goepper 1980 Brinker, Helmut and Goepper, Roger. *Kunstschätze aus China, 5000 v. Chr. bis 900 n. Chr., Neuere archäologische Funde aus der Volksrepublik China*, Zurich 1980

Brussels 1982 Palais des Beaux Arts. *Trésors d'art de la Chine*, Brussels 1982

Bulling and Drew 1971 Bulling, A. Gutkind and Drew, Isabella. 'The Dating of Chinese Bronze Mirrors', *Archives of Asian Art*, vol. 25, 1971–2, pp. 36–57

Bunker 1978 Bunker, Emma C. 'The Anecdotal Plaques of the Eastern Steppe Region', in Philip Denwood (ed.). *Arts of the Eurasian Steppe Lands*, Colloquies on Art and Archaeology in Asia, no. 7, London 1978

Bunker 1993 Bunker, Emma C. 'Gold in the Ancient Chinese World: A Cultural Puzzle', *Artibus Asiae* LIII, 1993, pp. 27–50

Bunker 1994 Bunker, Emma C. 'The Enigmatic Role of Silver in China', *Orientations*, November 1994, pp. 73–8

Bunker 1997 Bunker, Emma C. et al. *Ancient Bronzes of the Eastern Eurasian Steppes, from the Arthur M. Sackler Collection*, New York 1997

Burkhardt 1958 Burkhardt, VR. *Chinese Creeds and Customs*, 3 vols, Hong Kong 1958

Cahill 1977 Cahill, James. *Chinese Painting*, New York 1977

Cahill 1993 Cahill, Suzanne E. *Transcendence and Divine Passion: The Queen Mother of the West in Medieval China*, Stanford, California 1993

Cammann 1946 Cammann, Schuyler. 'A Rare T'ang

Mirror', *The Art Quarterly*, vol. 9, no. 2, Spring 1946, pp. 93–8

Cammann 1953 Cammann, Schuyler. 'The Lion and Grape Patterns on Chinese Bronze Mirrors', *Artibus Asiae*, vol. XVI, no. 4, 1953, pp. 265–91

Capon 1982 Capon, Edmund. *Qin Shihuang Terracotta Warriors and Horses* (2nd edn), Clayton, Victoria 1982

Capon 1992 Capon, Edmund *et al. Imperial China: The Living Past*, Sydney 1992

Capon and Foreman 1989 Capon, Edmund and Forman, Werner. *Tang China: Vision and Splendour of a Golden Age*, London 1989

Carter 1955 Carter, Thomas F. *The Invention of Printing in China and Its Spread Westward* (2nd edn, rev. by LC. Goodrich), New York 1955

Chang Kwang-chih 1977 Chang Kwang-chih. *Food in Chinese Culture*, New Haven and London 1977

Chang Kwang-chih 1983 Chang Kwang-chih. *Art, Myth, and Ritual: The Path to Political Authority in Ancient China*, Cambridge, Mass. and London 1983

Chang Kwang-chih 1986 Chang Kwang-chih. *The Archaeology of Ancient China* (4th edn), New Haven and London 1986

Chase and Franklin 1979 Chase, WT. and Franklin, Ursula Martius. 'Early Chinese Black Mirrors and Pattern-Etched Weapons,' *Ars Orientalis*, vol. 11, 1979, pp. 215–58

Chavannes 1969 Chavannes, E. *Les Mémoires historiques de Se-Ma Ts'ien*, 5 vols, Paris 1969

Ch'en 1956 Ch'en, Kenneth KS. 'The Economic Background of the Hui-ch'ang Suppression of Buddhism', *Harvard Journal of Asiatic Studies*, vol. 19, nos 1–2, 1956, pp. 67–105

Ch'en 1964 Ch'en, Kenneth KS. *Buddhism in China: A Historical Survey*, Princeton 1964

Ch'en 1973 Ch'en, Kenneth KS. *The Chinese Transformation of Buddhism*, Princeton 1973

Cheng Te-k'un 1954 Cheng Te-k'un. 'Tang and Ming Jades', *Transactions of the Oriental Ceramic Society*, vol. 28, London 1953–4, pp. 23–35

Cheng Te-k'un 1963 Cheng Te-k'un. *Archaeology in China, Volume III, Chou China*, Cambridge 1963

Chiu 1990 Chiu, Simon S. 'Tea Drinking in China', in Urban Council of Hong Kong, *The Art of the Yixing Potter: The K.S. Lo Collection in the Flagstaff Museum of Tea Ware*, Hong Kong 1990, pp. 22–33

Chung Wah-Pui 1996 Chung Wah-Pui (ed.). *Chinese Jade Animals*, Hong Kong 1996

Clunas 1997 Clunas, Craig. *Art in China*, Oxford 1997

Collon 1997 Collon, Dominique (ed.). *7000 Years of Seals*, London 1997

Coomaraswamy and Kershaw 1928 Coomaraswamy, Ananda K. and Kershaw, Francis Stewart. 'A Chinese Buddhist Water Vessel and Its Indian Prototype', *Artibus Asiae*, vol. III, nos 2/3, 1928, pp. 122–41

Cooper 1973 Cooper, Arthur (ed. and trans.). *Li Po and Tu Fu*, Harmondsworth 1973

Cooper 1978 Cooper, Jean Campbell. *Illustrated Encyclopaedia of Traditional Symbols*, London 1978

Cotterell 1981 Cotterell, Arthur. *The First Emperor of China*, London and Basingstoke 1981

Crump 1970 Crump, JI., Jr (trans.). *Chan-Kuo T'se*, Oxford 1970

Dai and Sun 1983 Dai Yingxin and Sun Jiaxiang. 'Shaanxi shenmu xian chutu Xiongnu wenwu', *Wenwu* 1983.12, pp. 23–30 and plate 5.4

Daito Bunmei ten 1998 Sensaishōten jumbi inkai (ed.). *Daito bunmei ten* (Art of the Great Tang), exhibition catalogue, Kagawa Prefecture, Shikoku 1998

Deydier 1994 Deydier, Christian. *Qin Gold*, London 1994

Dien 1981–2 Dien, Albert. 'A Study of Early Chinese Armour', *Artibus Asiae*, vol. XLIII, nos 1/2, 1981–2, pp. 5–67

Dubs 1944 Dubs, HH. *The History of the Former Han Dynasty by Pan Ku*, 3 vols, Baltimore 1944

Dudbridge 1995 Dudbridge, Glen. *Religious Experience and Lay Society in T'ang China, a Reading of Tai Fu's Kuang-I chi*, Cambridge 1995

Dunhuang 1981 Dunhuang Institute of Cultural Relics. *The Art Treasures of Dunhuang: Ten Centuries of Chinese Art from the Mogao Grottoes*, Hong Kong and New York 1981

Eberhard 1986 Eberhard, Wolfram. *A Dictionary of Chinese Symbols: Hidden Symbols in Chinese Life and Thought*, London 1986

Edinburgh 1996 *Gateway to the Silk Road: Relics from the Han to the Tang Dynasties from Xi'an, China*, exhibition catalogue, Edinburgh 1996

Edwards 1937–8 Edwards, ED. *Chinese Prose Literature of the T'ang Period, A.D. 618–906*, London, vol. 1, 1937, vol. 2, 1938

Empress Wu 1998 Tokyo National Museum. *The Glory of the Court: Tang Dynasty Empress Wu and Her Times*, exhibition catalogue, Tokyo 1998

Erickson 1992 Erickson, Susan N. 'Boshanlu – Mountain Censers of the Western Han Period: A Typological and Iconographic Analysis, *Archives of Asian Art*, vol. XLV, 1992, pp. 6–28

Erickson 1994a Erickson, Susan N. 'Twirling Their Long Sleeves, They Dance Again and Again … Jade Plaque Sleeve Dancers of the Western Han Dynasty', *Ars Orientalis*, vol. XXIV, 1994, pp. 39–63

Erickson 1994b Erickson, Susan N. 'Money Trees of the Eastern Han Dynasty', *Bulletin of the Museum of Far Eastern Antiquities*, no. 66, 1994, pp. 5–115

Erkes 1944 Erkes, E. 'Der Hund im alten China', *T'oung Pao*, no. 37, 1944, pp. 186–225

Falkenhausen 1990 Falkenhausen, Lothar von. 'Ahnenkult und Grabkult im Staat Qin' in Ledderose and Schlombs 1990, pp. 35–48

Falkenhausen 1994 Falkenhausen, Lothar von. 'Sources of Taoism: Reflections on Archaeological Indicators of Religious Change in Eastern Chou China', *Taoist Resources*, vol. 5, no. 2, 1994, pp. 1–12

Famensi Symposium 1992 Zhang Qizhi and Han Jinke (eds). *Shoujie guoji Famensi lishi xueshu yan tao hui*, Xi'an 1992

Famensi 1994 Cultural Relics Publishing House and Kwang Fu Book Enterprises Co. Ltd. *Zhongguo kaogu wenwu zhi mei, vol. 10: Famen mibao da Tang yi zhen, Shaanxi Fufeng Famensi digong*, Beijing and Taipei 1994

Famous Capital Xi'an Tourist Affairs Bureau. *The Famous Capital of China: Xi'an*, Xi'an, n.d.

Fan Weiyue 1982 Fan Weiyue and the Lantian Cultural Centre. 'Shaanxi Lantian faxian yipi Tangdai jin yin qi', *Kaogu yu Wenwu*, 1982.1, pp. 46–51

Finsterbusch 1952 Finsterbusch, Käte. *Das Verhältnis des Schan-hai-djing zur bildenden Kunst*, Berlin 1952

Finsterbusch 1971 Finsterbusch, Käte. *Verzeichnis und Motivindex der Han-Darstellungen*, vol. 2, Wiesbaden 1971

Fitzgerald 1933 Fitzgerald, CP. *Son of Heaven: A Biography of Li Shih-min Founder of the T'ang Dynasty*, Cambridge 1933

Fitzgerald 1947 Fitzgerald, CP. 'The Consequences of the Rebellion of An Lu-shan upon the Population of the T'ang Dynasty', *Philobiblon*, vol. 2, no. 1, September 1947, pp. 4–11

Fitzgerald 1965 Fitzgerald, CP. *China: A Short Cultural History*, London 1965 (1st edn, 1935)

Fitzgerald 1968 Fitzgerald, CP. *The Empress Wu*, London and Vancouver 1968 (2nd edn)

Flagstaff 1984 Urban Council of Hong Kong. *The K.S. Lo Collection in the Flagstaff Museum of Tea Ware*, 2 parts, Hong Kong 1984

Fong 1994 Fong, Grace S. 'The Early Literary Traditions' in Murowchick 1994, pp. 81–9

Fong 1991 Fong, HM. 'Tomb Guardian Figurines: Their Evolution and Iconography' in Kuwayama 1991

Fong 1973 Fong, Mary H. 'Four Chinese Royal Tombs of the Early Eighth Century', *Artibus Asiae*, vol. LXIII, no.1/2, 1973

Fontein and Wu 1973 Fontein, Jan and Wu Tung. *Unearthing China's Past*, Boston 1973

Forsyth and McElney 1994 Forsyth, Angus and McElney, Brian. *Jades from China*, Bath 1994

Franklin 1983a Franklin, Ursula Martius. 'The Beginnings of Metallurgy in China: A Comparative Approach' in Kuwayama 1991, pp. 94–9

Franklin 1983b Franklin, Ursula Martius. 'On Bronze and Other Metals in Early China' in Keightley 1983, pp. 279–96

Fu Tianchou 1985 Fu Tianchou (ed.). *The Underground Terracotta Army of Emperor Qin Shi Huangdi*, Beijing 1985

Fung 1994 Fung, Christopher. 'The Beginnings of Settled Life' in Murowchick 1994, pp. 50–8

Gao and Gao 1997 Gao Wei and Gao Haiyan. 'Cong Yinwan Han mu chutu de mu zhi wenwu tan guren de shumu guan', *Shixue yuekan*, 1997:5, pp. 118–119

Gernet 1987 Gernet, Jacques (trans. JR. Foster). *A History of Chinese Civilization*, Cambridge 1987 (1st edn, 1982, trans. of *Le Monde chinois*, Paris 1972)

Ghose 1998 Ghose Rajeshwari *et al. In the Footsteps of the Buddha: An Iconic Journey from India to China*, Hong Kong 1998

Giles 1932 Giles, Lionel. 'A Chinese Geographical Text of the Ninth Century', *Bulletin of the School of Oriental and African Studies*, vol. 6, 1935, pp. 1–26

Giles 1935 Giles, Lionel. 'Dated Chinese Manuscripts in the Stein Collection: II, Seventh Century A.D.', *Bulletin of the School of Oriental and African Studies*, vol. 8, 1935, pp. 1–26

Giles 1937 Giles, Lionel. 'Dated Chinese Manuscripts in the Stein Collection: III, Eighth Century A.D.', *Bulletin of the School of Oriental and African Studies*, vol. 9, 1937, pp. 1–25

Goepper 1995 Goepper, Roger (ed.). *Das Alte China: Menschen und Götter im Reich der mitte*, Munich 1995

Golas 1999 Golas, Peter J. *Joseph Needham, Science and Civilization in China, Vol. 5: Chemistry and Chemical Technology, Part XIII: Mining*, Cambridge 1999

Gray 1959 Gray, Basil. *Buddhist Cave Paintings at Tunhuang*, with photographs by JB. Vincent, London 1959

Guang Qing 1993 Guang Qing. 'Xi'an faxian Tangdai yuewu yu daikua', *Wenbo, yuqi yanjiu zhuan kan* 1993, pp. 78–81

Guggenheim 1997 Rogers, Howard (ed.). *China 5000 Years: Innovation and Transformation in the Arts*, New York 1997

Guimet Girard-Geslan, Maud. *Un Cheval Exceptionnel* (avec l'autorisation du collectioneur), Paris, nd

Guisso 1978 Guisso, RWL. *Wu Tse-T'ien and the Politics of Legitimation in T'ang China* (Occasional papers: Program of East Asian Studies, Western Washington University, vol. 11), Bellingham 1978

Güntsch 1988 Güntsch, G. *Das Shen-hsien chuan und das Erscheinungs bild eines Hsien*, Frankfurt, Bern, New York and Paris 1988

Gyllensvärd 1953 Gyllensvärd, Bo. *Chinese Gold and Silver in the Carl Kempe Collection,* Stockholm 1953

Gyllensvärd 1957 Gyllensvärd, Bo. 'Tang Gold and Silver', *Bulletin of the Museum of Far Eastern Antiquities*, no. 29, 1957, pp. 1–230

Gyllensvärd 1971 Gyllensvärd, Bo. *Chinese Gold, Silver and Porcelain: the Kempe Collection,* New York 1971

Han and Lu 1985 Han Wei and Lu Jiugao. *Tangdai jin yin qi*, Beijing 1985

Han Wei 1982 Han Wei. 'Tang Chang'an chengnei faxian de shouzhen yin xun qiu', *Kaogu yu Wenwu* 1982.1, pp. 59–63

Han Wei 1987 Han Wei. 'In Splendour Laid,' *China Pictorial*, 1987.4, pp. 14–17

Han Wei 1988 Han Wei. 'Cong yincha fengshang kan Famensi deng di chutu de Tangdai jinyin cha ju,' *Wenwu* 1988.10, pp. 44–56

Han Wei 1989 Han Wei. *Hai nei wai Tangdai jin yin qi huapian*, Xi'an 1989

Han Wei 1993 Han Wei. 'Tang Dynasty Tea Utensils and Tea Culture: Recent Discoveries' (trans. Zane Ferry), *Chanoyu Quarterly*, no. 74, 1993, pp. 38–58

Han Wei 1994a Han Wei. 'Gold and Silver Vessels of the Tang Period', *Orientations*, July 1994, pp. 31–5

Han Wei 1994b Han Wei. 'An Important Cultural Discovery: Pure Gold Decorative Plaques from Li County, Gansu Province' in Deydier 1994, pp. 21–32

Harper 1985 Harper, Donald. 'A Chinese Demonography of the Third Century B.C.', *Harvard Journal of Asiatic Studies*, vol. 45, 1985, pp. 459–98

Harper 1994 Harper, Donald. 'Resurrection in Warring States Popular Religion', *Taoist Resources*, vol. 5, no. 2, 1994, pp. 13–29

Haskins 1952 Haskins, John F. 'Northern Origins of "Sasanian" Metalwork', *Artibus Asiae*, vol. XV, no. 3, 1952, pp. 241–67, 324–47

Hawkes 1985 Hawkes, David. *Ch'u Tz'u: The Songs of the South*, Harmondsworth 1985 (1st edn Oxford 1959)

Hay 1973 Hay, John. *Ancient China*, New York 1973

Hayashi 1975 Hayashi Ryoichi. *The Silk Road and the Shōsō-in* (trans. Robert Ricketts), *The Heibonsha Survey of Japanese Art*, vol. 6, New York and Tokyo 1975

Hearn 1980 Hearn, Maxwell K. 'The Terracotta Army of the First Emperor of Qin (221–206 B.C.)', in New York 1980, pp. 353–73

Hebei 1988 The Hebei Provincial Institute of Cultural Relics and the Baoding Municipal Office of Cultural Relics. *Wang Chuzhi's Tomb of the Five Dynasties Period*, Beijing 1988

Hebei 1991–3 *Zhongguo yuqi quanji*, 1991–3: vol. 1 (Neolithic), 1992; vol. 2 (Shang and Western Zhou), 1993; vol. 3 (Spring and Autumn, Warring States Period), 1993; vol. 4 (Qin, Han and Six Dynasties),

1993; vol. 5 (Sui, Tang and Ming), 1993; vol. 6 (Qing), 1991, Shijiahuang 1991–3

Hejiacun 1972 Hejiacun Excavation Report, *Wenwu* 1972, no. 1, pp. 30–42

Herdan 1973 Herdan, Innes (trans.). *300 T'ang Poems*, New York 1973

Herm 1995 Herm Christoph *et al.* 'Analysis of Painting Materials of the Polychrome Terracotta Army of the First Emperor Qin Shi Huang' in Vincenzini 1995, pp. 675–84

Herman 1910 Herman, A. *Die Alten Seidenstrassen zwischen China und Syrien*, Berlin 1910

Hirth 1975 Hirth, F. *China and the Roman Orient*, Chicago 1975

Hobson 1926 Hobson, RL. 'A T'ang Silver Hoard', *British Museum Quarterly*, vol. 1, no. 1, May 1926, pp. 18–21

Hodges 1970 Hodges, HWM. 'Interaction between Metalworking and Ceramic Technologies in the T'ang Period, in Watson, William (ed.), *Pottery and Metalwork in T'ang China: Their chronology and external relations*, Colloquies on Art and Archaeology in Asia, no. 1, London 1970, pp. 64–7

Hong Kong 1992 *Zhongguo Han Yangling caiyong*, Hong Kong 1992

Hong Kong 1993 Hong Kong Museum of Art (ed.). *Treasures of Chang'an: Capital of the Silk Road*, Hong Kong 1993

Hong Kong 1994a Tang Chung (ed.). *Nan Zhongguo ji linjin diqu gu wenhua yanjiu*, Hong Kong 1994

Hong Kong 1994b Centre for Chinese Archaeology and Art, ICS and the Chinese University of Hong Kong (eds), *Ancient Cultures of South China and Neighbouring Regions*, Hong Kong 1994

Hong Kong 1997 Hong Kong Museum of Art. *National Treasures – Gems of China's Cultural Relics*, Hong Kong 1997

Hong Kong and Shaanxi 1993 Regional Council, Hong Kong and Shaanxi Archaeological Overseas Exhibition Corporation. *Daily Life of Aristocrats in Tang China*, Hong Kong 1993

Hopkirk 1984 Hopkirk, Peter. *Foreign Devils on the Silk Road: The Search for the Lost Cities and Treasures of Chinese Central Asia*, Oxford 1984

Hsia Nai 1983 Hsia Nai. *Jade and Silk of Han China: The Franklin and Murphy Lectures III*, Lawrence, Kansas 1983

Hsu and Linduff 1988 Hsu Cho-yun and Linduff, Kathryn M. *Western Zhou Civilization*, New Haven and London 1988

Huang Xuanpei 1988 Huang Xuanpei. *Ritual and Power: Jades of Ancient China,* New York 1988

Hucker 1985 Hucker, Charles O. *A Dictionary of Official Titles in Imperial China,* London 1985

Imperial China 1992 *Imperial China: The Living Past*, exhibition catalogue, Sydney 1992

Ishida and Wada 1954 Ishida Mosaku and Wada Gunichi. *The Shōsōin: An Eighth-Century Treasure House*, English résumé by Harada Jiro, Tokyo, Osaka and Moji 1954

Jan 1977 Jan Yunhua. 'The Silk Manuscripts on Taoism', *T'oung Pao*, vol. LXIII, 1997, pp. 65–84

Jenyns and Watson 1980 Jenyns, Soame R. and Watson, William. *Chinese Art*, Preface and Revisions to the Second edition by William Watson, vol. 2: *Gold, Silver, Later Bronzes, Cloisonné, Cantonese Enamel, Lacquer, Furniture, Wood*, New York 1980

Jiangsu 1982 Dantuxian wenjiaoju and Zhenjiang Museum, 'Jiangsu Dantu Dingmaoqiao chutu Tangdai yinqi yaozang', *Wenwu* 1982.10, pp. 15–27

Jin Weinuo 1986 Jin Weinuo (ed.). *Zhongguo meishu quanji – Diaosu bian*, 1, Beijing 1986

Joseph, Moss and Fleming 1970 Joseph, Adrian M., Moss, Hugh M. and Fleming, SJ. *Chinese Pottery Burial Objects of the Sui and T'ang Dynasties*, London 1970

Juliano 1975 Juliano, Annette L. *Art of the Six Dynasties: Centuries of Change and Innovation*, New York 1975

Kamei 1996 Kamei Meitoku. 'The Term of Yue Ware "Mi Ce Ci" Mentioned in Japanese Ancient Historical Documents' in Wang Qingzheng 1996, pp. 51–2

Keightley 1983 Keightley, David N. (ed.). *The Origins of Chinese Civilization*, Berkeley, Los Angeles and London 1983

Kelley and Wilson 1928 Kelley, CF. and Wilson, DK. 'Chinese Silver in the Buckingham Collection', *Bulletin of the Art Institute of Chicago*, vol. 22, no. 7, October 1928, pp. 88–91

Kelley 1984 Kelley, Clarence W. *Tang Dynasty Chinese Gold and Silver in American Collections*, Dayton 1984

Kerr 1990 Kerr, Rose. *Later Chinese Bronzes*, London 1990

Kerr 1991 Kerr, Rose. *Chinese Art and Design,* London 1991

Kerr 1999 Kerr, Rose. 'Celestial Creatures: Chinese Tiles in the Victoria and Albert Museum', *Apollo*, March 1999, pp. 15–21

Kesner 1991 Kesner, Ladislav. 'Portrait Aspects and Social Functions of Chinese Tomb Sculpture', *Orientations*, August 1991, pp. 33–42

Kesner 1995 Kesner, Ladislav. 'Likeness of No One: (Re)presenting the First Emperor's Army', *Art Bulletin*, vol. LXXVII, 1995, pp. 115–32

Knechtges 1982, 1987, 1996 Knechtges, David R. (trans. with annotations). *Wen Xuan or Selections of Refined Literature*, 3 vols, Princeton 1982, 1987, 1996

Koch 1995 Koch, Alexander. *Der Goldschatz des Famensi Prunk et Pietät in chinesischen der Tang-Zeit*, Mainz, Germany 1995

Kohn 1992 Kohn, Livia. *Early Chinese Mysticism: Philosophy and Soteriology in the Taoist Religion*, Princeton 1992

Krahl 1987 Krahl, Regina. 'Plant Motifs of Chinese Porcelain: Examples from the Topkapi Saray Identified through the *Bencao Gangmu*', Parts I and II, *Orientations*, May 1987, pp. 52–65, and June 1987, pp. 24–37

Kuhn 1993 Kuhn, Dieter (ed.). *Chinas Goldenes Zeitalter: Die Tang-Dynastie (618–907 n.Chr.) und das kulturelle Erbe der Seidenstrasse*, Heidelberg 1993

Kuwayama 1991 Kuwayama, George (ed). *Ancient Mortuary Traditions of China: Papers on Chinese Ceramic Funerary Sculpture*, Los Angeles 1991

Kwan Pui Ching 1987 Kwan Pui Ching. *Qiannian gudu Xi'an*, Hong Kong 1987

Lally 1998 Lally, JJ. *Arts of the Han Dynasty,* New York 1998

Lau 1991 Lau, Eileen (ed.). *Spirit of Han: Ceramics for the After-Life,* Singapore 1991

Laufer 1913 Laufer, Berthold. *Notes on Turquoise in the Far East*, Museum of Natural History, Publication 169, Anthropological Series, vol. 13, no. 1, Chicago 1913

Laufer 1914 Laufer, Berthold. *Chinese Clay Figures*, Chicago 1914

Laufer 1962 Laufer, Berthold. *Chinese Pottery of the Han Dynasty*, Tokyo 1962

Lawton 1973 Lawton, Thomas. *Chinese Figure Painting*, vol. II of Freer Gallery of Art, Fiftieth Anniversary Exhibition, Washington, DC 1973

Lawton 1982 Lawton, Thomas. *Chinese Art of the Warring States Period: Change and Continuity, 480–222 BC*, Washington, DC 1982

Lawton 1987 Lawton Thomas (ed.). *Asian Art in the Arthur M. Sackler Gallery: The Inaugural Gift*, Washington, DC 1987

Ledderose 1992 Ledderose, Lothar. 'Module and Mass Production' in *International Colloquium on Chinese Art History, 1991, Proceedings, Antiquities, Part I*, Taipei 1992, pp. 826–47

Ledderose and Schlombs 1990 Ledderose, Lothar and Schlombs, Adele. *Jenseits der Grossen Mauer: Der Erste Kaiser von China und Seine Terrakotta-Armee*, Munich 1990

Legge 1967 Legge, J. (ed.). *Li Chi, Book of Rites: An Encyclopedia of Ancient Ceremonial Usages, Religious Creeds, and Social Institutions*, 2 vols, New York 1967

Leslie and Gardner 1982 Leslie, DD. and Gardiner, KHJ. 'Chinese Knowledge of Western Asia During the Han', *T'oung Pao*, vol. LXVIII, nos 4–5, 1982, pp. 244–308

Levy 1957a Levy, Howard S. 'The Career of Yang Kuei-fei', *T'oung Pao*, vol. XLV (1957), pp. 451–89

Levy 1957b Levy, Howard S. 'The Family Background of Yang Kuei-fei', *Sinologica* 5.2, 1957, pp. 101–18

Levy 1958 Levy, Howard S. *Harem Favorites of an Illustrious Celestial*, Taichung 1958

Levy 1962 Levy, Howard S. *Lament Everlasting: The Death of Yang Kuei-fei*, Tokyo 1962

Levy 1970–8 Levy, Howard S. (ed. and trans.). *Translations from Po Chü-I's Collected Works*, 4 vols, New York 1970–8

Li and Wang 1997 Li Sucheng and Wang Xiaomou. 'Xianyang chutu zhenpin yilan', *Connoisseur* no. 5, March 1997, pp. 26–32

Li Jian 1998 Li Jian. *Eternal China: Splendors from the First Dynasties*, Dayton 1998

Li Xiyu 1994 Li Xiyu (ed.). *Huangdi ling yu long wenhua*, Shanghai 1994

Li Yinde 1990 Li Yinde. 'The "Underground Palace" of a Chu Prince at Beidongshan', *Orientations*, October 1990, pp. 57–61

Liaoning 1977 Kalaqinqi Culture Bureau. 'Liaoning zhaomeng kalaqinqi faxian Tangdai liu jin yin qi', *Kaogu*, 1977.5, pp. 327–34

Lim 1987 Lim, Lucy (ed.). *Stories from China's Past: Han Dynasty Pictorial Tomb Reliefs and Archaeological Objects from Sichuan Province, People's Republic of China*, San Francisco 1987

Lindqvist 1989 Lindqvist, Cecilia. *China – Empire of Living Symbols* (trans. Joan Tate), Reading, Mass. 1989

Lintong 1978 Lintong Excavation Report, *Wenwu* 1978.5, pp. 1–19

Lion-Goldschmidt and Moreau-Gobard 1980 Lion-Goldschmidt, Daisy and Moreau-Gobard, Jean-Claude, with Foreword by George Savage. *Chinese Art* (English revised edn), vol. 1: *Bronzes, Jade, Sculpture, Ceramics*, New York 1980

Liu and Liu 1982 Liu Jiugao and Liu Jianguo. 'Dantu Dingmaoqiao chutu Tangdai yinqi shixi, *Wenwu* 1982.11, pp. 28–33, 41

Liu Liang-yu 1996 Liu Liang-yu. 'Preface', in Wang, Wellington 1996

Liu Xinru 1988 Liu Xinru. *Ancient India and Ancient China: Trade and Religious Exchanges AD 1–600*, Delhi 1988

Liu Yonghua 1993 Liu Yonghua. *Zhongguo gudai junwu kuijia*, Shanghai 1993

Loehr 1967–8 Loehr, Max. 'The Fate of the Ornament in Chinese Art', *Archives of Asian Art*, vol. XXI, 1967–8, pp. 8–19

Loehr 1980 Loehr, Max. *The Great Painters of China*, Oxford 1980

Loewe 1974 Loewe, Michael. *Crisis and Conflict in Han China, 104 BC to AD 9*, London 1974

Loewe 1977 Loewe, Michael. 'Manuscripts Found Recently in China: A Preliminary Survey', *T'oung Pao*, vol. LXIII, 1977, pp. 98–136

Loewe 1979 Loewe, Michael. *Ways to Paradise: The Chinese Quest for Immortality*, London 1979

Loewe 1982 Loewe, Michael. *Chinese Ideas of Life and Death: Faith, Myth and Reason in the Han Period*, London 1982

Loewe 1985 Loewe, Michael. 'Royal Tombs of Zhong-shan', *Arts Asiatiques*, vol. XL, 1985, pp. 130–4

Loewe 1993 Loewe, Michael (ed.). *Early Chinese Texts: A Bibliographical Guide*, Berkeley 1993

Loewe 1994 Loewe, Michael. 'China's Growing Strength: The Han Dynasty' in Murowchick 1994, pp. 113–23

London 1935 *Catalogue of the International Exhibition of Chinese Art 1935–6*, London 1935

London 1955 The Oriental Ceramic Society, London. *The Arts of the T'ang Dynasty*, London 1955

Los Angeles 1957 Los Angeles County Museum. *The Arts of the T'ang Dynasty*, exhibition catalogue, Los Angeles 1957

Los Angeles 1987 *The Quest for Eternity: Chinese Ceramic Sculptures from the People's Republic of China*, Los Angeles and San Francisco 1987

Louis 1999 Louis, François. *Die Goldschmiede der Tang-und Song-Zeit*, Bern 1999

Lu Delin 1986 Lu Delin (ed.). *Luoyang Handai caihua*, Luoyang 1986

Lu Liancheng 1993 Lu Liancheng. 'Chariot and Horse Burials in Ancient China', *Antiquity*, vol. 67, 1993, pp. 824–38

Lu Yu 1974 Lu Yu. *The Classic of Tea* (trans. Francis Ross Carpenter), Boston and Toronto 1974

Luo Zongzhen 1997 Luo Zongzhen. 'Yuqi jin yin de zhen mian mao', *Connoisseur*, no. 5, March 1997, pp. 60–9

Luoyang 1990 Luoyang Wenwu Gongzuodui (ed.). *Ancient Treasures of Luoyang 1990*, Beijing 1990

Mahler 1959 Mahler, Jane Gaston. *The Westerners among the Figurines of the T'ang Dynasty of China*, Rome 1959

Major 1993 Major, JS. *Heaven and Earth in Early Han Thought: Chapters Three, Four and Five of the Huainanzi*, New York 1993

Marschak 1986 Marschak, Boris. *Silberschätze des Orients: Metallkunst des 3.–13. Jahrhunderts und ihre Kontinuität*, Leipzig 1986

Maspero 1953 Maspero, H. *Les documents chinois de la troisième expédition de Sir Aurel Stein en Asie Centrale*, London 1953

Mathieu 1983 Mathieu, Rémi. *Étude sur la mythologie et l'ethnologie de la Chine ancienne. Traduction annotée du Shanghai jing*, 2 vols, Paris 1983

Medley 1955 Medley, Margaret. 'The T'ang Dynasty: A Chinese Renaissance, A.D. 618–906', *History Today*, vol. 5, no. 4, April 1955, pp. 263–71

Medley 1970 Medley, Margaret. 'T'ang Gold and Silver', in Watson, W. 1970, pp. 19–26

Medley 1972 Medley, Margaret. *Metalwork and Chinese Ceramics*, Percival David Monograph Series No. 2, London 1972

Medley 1981 Medley, Margaret. *T'ang Pottery and Porcelain*, London 1981

Meishu Quanji 1987 Gongyi meishu (ed.). *Zhongguo meishu quanji: (vol. 10) Jin yin boli falang*, Beijing 1987

Melbourne 1977 Australian Art Exhibitions Corporation. *The Chinese Exhibition*, Melbourne 1977

Melikian-Chirvani 1979 Melikian-Chirvani, Asudullah Souren. 'Iranian Silver and its Influence in T'ang China', in Watson, W. 1970, pp. 12–18

Mizuno and Nagahiro 1941 Mizuno Seiichi and Nagahiro Toshio. *A Study of the Buddhist Cave Temples at Lung-men, Honan*, Tokyo 1941

Montreal 1986 Montreal Palais de la Civilisation, *Chine: Tresors et Splendeurs*, Montreal 1986

Moore 1998 Moore, Oliver. 'Islamic Glass at Buddhist Sites in Medieval China', in Ward, Rachel (ed.), *Gilded and Enamelled Glass from the Middle East*, London 1998

Mote 1971 Mote, Frederick W. *Intellectual Foundations of China*, New York 1971

Mou Lingsheng 1992 Mou Lingsheng. *Zhongguo Han Yangling caiyong*, Xi'an 1992

Mou Yongkang 1989 Mou Yongkang. 'Liangzhu yuqi shang shen congbai de tansuo', in *Qingzhu Su Bingqi kaogu wushinian lunwenji*, Beijing, 1989

Munakata 1990 Munakata Kiyohiko (ed.). *Sacred Mountains in Chinese Art*, Champaign-Urbana 1990

Munsterberg 1948 Munsterberg, Hugo. 'Chinese Buddhist Bronzes of the T'ang Period', *Artibus Asiae*, vol. XI, nos 1/2, 1948, pp. 27–45

Munsterberg 1967 Munsterberg, Hugo. *Chinese Buddhist Bronzes*, Rutland and Tokyo 1967

Munsterberg 1972 Munsterberg, Hugo. *Dragons in Chinese Art*, exhibition catalogue, New York 1972

Murowchick 1994 Murowchick, Robert E. (ed.). *China: Ancient Culture, Modern Land*, Norman, Oklahoma 1994

Needham 1959 Needham, Joseph. *Science and Civilization in China, Vol. 3: Mathematics and the Sciences of the Heavens and the Earth*, Cambridge 1959 (reprinted 1970)

Needham 1962 Needham, Joseph. *Science and Civilization in China, Vol. 4: Physics and Physical Technology, Part I: Physics*, Cambridge 1962

Needham 1965 Needham, Joseph. *Science and Civilization in China, Vol. 4: Physics and Physical Technology, Part II: Mechanical Engineering*, Cambridge 1965

Needham 1974 Needham, Joseph. *Science and Civilization in China, Vol. 5: Chemistry and Chemical Technology, Part II, Spagyrical Discovery and Invention: Magisteries of Gold and Immortality*, Cambridge 1974

Needham 1976 Needham, Joseph. *Science and Civilization in China, Vol. 5: Chemistry and Chemical Technology, Part III: Spagyrical Discovery and Invention: Historical Survey, from Cinnabar Elixirs to Synthetic Insulin*, Cambridge 1976

Needham and Yates 1994 Needham, Joseph and Yates, Robin DS. *Science and Civilization in China, Vol. 5: Chemistry and Chemical Technology: Military Technology, Part VI: Missiles and Sieges*, Cambridge 1994

Nelson 1995 Nelson, Sarah Milledge (ed.). *The Archaeology of Northeast China beyond the Great Wall*, London 1995

New York 1980 Fong, Wen (ed.). *The Great Bronze Age of China: An Exhibition from the People's Republic of China*, New York 1980

Nienhauser 1986 Nienhauser, William H., Jr (ed.). *The*

Indiana Companion to Traditional Chinese Literature, Bloomington 1986

Ong 1993 Ong Hean-Tatt. *Chinese Animal Symbolisms*, Selangor Darul Ehsan 1993

Osaka 1987 Osaka Fine Arts Museum. *Kinryu-Kimba to Dokubutsu Kokuhōten*, exhibition catalogue, Osaka 1987

Owen 1986 Owen, Stephen. *Remembrances: The Experience of the Past in Classical Chinese Literature*, Cambridge, Mass. 1986

Paludan 1991 Paludan, Ann. *The Chinese Spirit Road: The Classical Tradition of Stone Tomb Statuary*, New Haven 1991

Paludan 1994 Paludan, Ann. *Chinese Tomb Figurines*, Hong Kong 1994

Paludan 1998 Paludan, Ann. *Chronicle of the Chinese Emperors*, London 1998

Paris 1984 *Zhongshan: Tombes des Rois Oubliés – Exposition archéologique chinoise du Royaume de Zhongshan*, Paris 1984

Paris 1994 Musée national des Arts asiatiques-Guimet. *Chine des Origines*, Paris 1994

Paris 1996 Musée national des Arts asiatiques-Guimet. *Chine des cheveaux et des hommes: Donation Jacques Polain*, Paris 1996

Picken 1981–98 Picken, Laurence (ed.). *Music from the Tang Court*, 6 vols, London 1981–98

Pirazzoli-t'Serstevens 1982 Pirazzoli-t'Serstevens, Michèle. *The Han Dynasty*, New York 1982

Pirazzoli-t'Serstevens 1991 Pirazzoli-t'Serstevens, Michèle. 'The Art of Dining in the Han Period: Food Vessels from Tomb no. 1 at Mawangdui', *Food and Foodways*, 1991, vol. 4 (3 & 4), pp. 209–19

Pirazzoli-t'Serstevens 1994 Pirazzoli-t'Serstevens, Michèle. 'Pour une archéologie des échanges. Apports étrangers en Chine – transmission, réception, assimilation', *Arts Asiatiques*, vol. XLIX, 1994, pp. 21–33

Poo 1998 Poo, Mu-chou. *In Search of Personal Welfare: A View of Ancient Chinese Religion*, Albany, NY 1998

Powers 1987 Powers, MJ. 'Social Values and Aesthetic Choices in Han Dynasty Sichuan', in Lim 1987, pp. 54–63

Priest 1944 Priest, Alan. *Chinese Jewellery: A Picture Book*, New York 1944

Prodan 1960 Prodan, Mario. *The Art of the T'ang Potter*, London 1960

Pulleyblank 1955 Pulleyblank, EG. *The Background of the Rebellion of An Lu-shan*, London Oriental Series, vol. 4, London, New York and Toronto 1955

Pulleyblank 1960 Pulleyblank, EG. 'Neo-Confucianism and Neo-Legalism in T'ang Intellectual Life, 755–805', in Wright 1960, pp. 77–114

Qian, Chen and Ru 1981 Qian Hao, Chen Heyi and Ru Suichu. *Out of China's Earth: Archaeological Discoveries in the People's Republic of China*, London and Beijing 1981

Qin Shi Huang Museum 1989 The Museum of Qin Shi Huang's Terracotta Army. *Bronze Chariots and Horses in Qin Shi Huang's Mausoleum*, Hong Kong 1989

Ran Wanli 1975 Ran Wanli. 'Shilun Tangdai beifang qin yin qi de faxian ji tezheng', *Wenbo* 1975.5, pp. 56–60

Rao Zongyi 1953 Rao Zongyi. *Chinese Tomb Pottery Figurines*, Hong Kong 1953

Rawson 1977 Rawson, Jessica M. 'Chinese Silver and its Western Origins', *Connoisseur*, September 1997, pp. 36–43

Rawson 1978 Rawson, Jessica M. 'The Transformation and Abstraction of Animal Motifs on Bronzes from Inner Mongolia and Northern China', in Philip Denwood (ed.), *Arts of the Eurasian Steppelands*, Colloquies on Art and Archaeology in Asia, no. 7, London 1978, pp. 52–73

Rawson 1980 Rawson, Jessica M. *Ancient China: Art and Archaeology*, London 1980

Rawson 1982 Rawson, Jessica M. 'The Ornament of Chinese Silver of the Tang Dynasty', British Museum Occasional Paper, no. 40, London 1982

Rawson 1984a Rawson, Jessica M. 'Song Silver and its Connections with Ceramics', *Apollo*, July 1984, pp. 18–23

Rawson 1984b Rawson, Jessica M. *Chinese Ornament: The Lotus and the Dragon*, London 1984

Rawson 1985 Rawson, Jessica M. 'The Dragon and the Phoenix', *The Antique Collector*, April 1985, pp. 80–3

Rawson 1986a Rawson, Jessica M. 'Silver Decoration on a Chinese Lacquered Box', *Arts of Asia*, May–June 1986, pp. 91–8

Rawson 1986b Rawson, Jessica M. 'Tombs or Hoards: The Survival of Chinese Silver of the Tang and Song Periods, Seventh to Thirteenth Centuries AD', in Michael Vickers (ed.), *Pots and Pans*, Oxford 1986, pp. 31–56

Rawson 1989a Rawson, Jessica M. 'Chinese Silver and its Influence in Porcelain Development', in PE. McGovern (ed.), *Ceramics and Civilization*, vol. IV, *Cross-craft and Cross-cultural Interactions in Ceramics*, Westerville 1989, pp. 253–73

Rawson 1989b Rawson, Jessica M. 'Chu Influences on the Development of the Han bronze vessels', *Arts Asiatiques*, vol. XLVIV, 1989, pp. 84–99

Rawson 1991 Rawson, Jessica M. 'Central Asian Silver and its Influence on Chinese Ceramics', paper presented to the Second European Seminar on Central Asian Studies, University of London (SOAS), 7–10 April 1987, *Bulletin of the Asia Institute*, vol. 5, 1991, pp. 139–51

Rawson 1992 Rawson, Jessica M. (ed.). *The British Museum Book of Chinese Art*, London 1992

Rawson 1995a Rawson, Jessica M. *Chinese Jade from the Neolithic to the Qing*, London 1995

Rawson 1995b Rawson, Jessica M. 'Jade and Gold: Some Sources of Ancient Jade Design', *Orientations*, June 1995, pp. 26–37

Rawson 1996a Rawson, Jessica M. *Mysteries of Ancient China: New Discoveries from the Early Dynasties*, London 1996

Rawson 1996b Rawson, Jessica M. 'Chinese Views of the Spirit World', *China Review*, no. 5, Autumn/Winter 1996, pp. 38–41

Rawson 1996c Rawson, Jessica M. 'Changes in Representation of Life and the Afterlife as Illustrated by the Contents of the Tombs of the T'ang and Sung Periods', in Maxwell K. Hearn and Judith G. Smith (eds), *Arts of the Sung and Yuan*, New York 1996, pp. 23–44

Rawson 1998 Rawson, Jessica M. 'Thinking in Pictures: Tomb figures in the Chinese view of the afterlife', *Transactions of the Oriental Ceramics Society*, vol. 61, 1996–7, pp. 19–37

Rawson forthcoming Rawson, Jessica M. 'The External Palaces of the Western Han: A New View of the Universe', *Artibus Asiae*, forthcoming

Rawson and Ayers 1975 Rawson, Jessica M. and Ayers, John. *Chinese Jade Throughout the Ages*, London 1975

Rawson and Bunker 1990 Rawson, Jessica M. and Bunker, Emma C. *Ancient Chinese and Ordos Bronzes*, Hong Kong 1990

Reischauer 1940 Reischauer, EO. 'Notes on T'ang Dynasty Sea Routes', *Harvard Journal of Asiatic Studies*, vol. 5, no. 2, June 1940, pp. 142–64

Reischauer 1955 Reischauer, EO. *Ennin's Travels in T'ang China*, New York 1955

Reischauer and Fairbank 1958 and 1960 Reischauer, EO and Fairbank, John K. *East Asia: The Great Tradition*, Boston 1958 and 1960

Rietburg 1996 Liang-Lee, Yeajen and Louis, Francois. *An Index of Gold and Silver Artifacts Unearthed in the People's Republic of China*, Zurich 1996

Ronan 1978–94 Ronan, Colin. *The Shorter Science and Civilization in China*, 4 vols, Cambridge 1978, 1981, 1986, 1994

des Rotours 1947 des Rotours, R. *Traité des fonctionnaires et traité de l'armée; traduits de la nouvelle histoire des T'ang*, vol. 1, Leiden 1947

des Rotours 1948 des Rotours, R. *Traité des fonctionnaires et traité de l'armée*, vol. 2, Leiden 1948

des Rotours 1952 des Rotours, R. 'Les insignes en deux parties (fou) sous la dynastie des T'ang (618–907)', *T'oung Pao*, vol. 41, 1952, pp. 1–148

des Rotours 1968 des Rotours, R. (ed. and trans.). *Courtesans chinoises à la Fin des T'ang, entre circa 789 et le 8 janvier 881: Pei-li Tche (Anecdotes du quartier du Nord) par Souen K'i*, Paris 1968

des Rotours 1981 des Rotours, R. (ed. and trans.). *Le Règne de L'Empereur Hiuan-Tsong (713–756) par M. Lin Lu-tche*, Paris 1981

Rowland 1963 Rowland, Benjamin. *The Evolution of the Buddha Image*, exhibition catalogue, New York 1963

Rudolph 1959 Rudolph, RC. 'Chinese Medical Stelae', *Bulletin of the Institute of History and Philology, Academia Sinica*, vol. 30, 1959, pp. 681–8

Salmony 1954 Salmony, Alfred. *Antler and Tongue: An Essay on Ancient Chinese Symbolism and its Implications*, Ascona, Switzerland 1954

Sawyer 1993 Sawyer, Ralph D. (trans.). *Wu ching ch'i shu* (The seven military classics of ancient China), Boulder and Oxford 1993

Sawyer 1995 Sawyer, Ralph D. (trans.). *Sun Pin, Military Methods*, Boulder, San Francisco and Oxford 1995

San Francisco 1975 *The Chinese Exhibition: A Pictorial Review of the Exhibition of Archaeological Finds of the People's Republic of China*, San Francisco 1975

Schafer 1950 Schafer, Edward H. 'The Camel in China Down to the Mongol Dynasty', *Sinologica*, vol. 2, 1950, pp. 165–94, 263–90

Schafer 1951 Schafer, Edward H. 'Iranian Merchants in T'ang Dynasty Tales', *Semitic and Oriental Studies Presented to William Popper*, University of California Publications in Semitic Philology, vol. XI, 1951, pp. 403–22

Schafer 1955 Schafer, Edward H. 'Orpiment and Realgar in Chinese Technology and Tradition', *Journal of the American Oriental Society*, vol. 75, 1955, pp. 73–89

Schafer 1956a Schafer, Edward H. 'The Development of Bathing Customs in Ancient and Medieval China and the History of the Floriate Clear Palace', *Journal of the American Oriental Society*, vol. 76, 1956, pp. 57–82

Schafer 1956b Schafer, Edward H. 'The Early History of Lead Pigments and Cosmetics in China', *T'oung Pao*, vol. 44, 1956, pp. 413–38

Schafer 1956c Schafer, Edward H. 'Cultural History of the Elaphure', *Sinologica*, vol. 4, 1956, pp. 250–74

Schafer 1957a Schafer, Edward H. 'Rosewood,

Dragon's Blood and Lac', *Journal of the American Oriental Society*, vol. 77, 1957, pp. 129–36

Schafer 1957b Schafer, Edward H. 'War Elephants in Ancient and Medieval China', *Oriens*, vol. 10, 1957, pp. 289–91

Schafer 1959a Schafer, Edward H. 'Falconry in T'ang Times', *T'oung Pao*, vol. 46, 1959, pp. 293–338

Schafer 1959b Schafer, Edward H. 'Parrots in Medieval China', *Studia Serica Bernhard Karlgren Dedicata*, Copenhagen 1959

Schafer 1961 Schafer, Edward H. *Tu Wan's Stone Catalogue of Cloudy Forest: A Commentary and Synopsis*, Berkeley and Los Angeles 1961

Schafer 1963 Schafer, Edward H. *The Golden Peaches of Samarkand: A Study of T'ang Exotics*, Berkeley and Los Angeles 1963

Schafer 1967 Schafer, Edward H. *The Vermilion Bird*, Berkeley 1967

Schafer and Krieger 1967 Schafer, Edward H. and Krieger, Leonard. *Ancient China*, New York 1967

Schafer and Wallacker 1961 Schafer, Edward H. and Wallacker, BE. 'Local Tribute Products of the T'ang Dynasty', *Journal of Oriental Studies*, vol. 4, 1957–8, pp. 213–48

Schiffler 1978 Schiffler, John W. *The Legendary Creatures of the Shan Hai Ching*, San Francisco 1978

Schipper 1965 Schipper, Kristopher M. *L'empereur Wou des Han dans la légende taoiste: Han Wou-ti Nei-tchouan*, Paris 1965

Schipper 1978 Schipper, Kristopher M. 'The Taoist Body', *History of Religions*, vol. 17, 1978, pp. 355–86

Schlombs 1990 Schlombs, A. 'Die Herstellung der Terrakotta-Armee', in Ledderose and Schlombs 1990, pp. 88–97

Schloss 1969 Schloss, Ezekiel. *Foreigners in Ancient Chinese Art*, New York 1969

Schloss 1975 Schloss, Ezekiel. *Ming-ch'i: Clay Figures Reflecting Life in Ancient China*, Katonah, New York 1975

Schloss 1977 Schloss, Ezekiel. *Ancient Chinese Ceramic Sculpture: From Han through T'ang*, 2 vols, Stamford, Conn. 1977

Schloss 1979 Schloss, Ezekiel. *Art of the Han*, New York 1979

Schmidt-Glintzer 1990 Schmidt-Glintzer, H. 'Qin Shihuangdi. Der Erste Gottkaiser von China', in Ledderose and Schlombs 1990, pp. 58–65

Scott 1966 Scott, Hugh. *The Golden Age of Chinese Art: The Lively T'ang Dynasty*, Rutland and Tokyo 1966

Scott and Hutt 1987 Scott, Rosemary E. and Hutt, Graham (eds). *Style in the East Asian Tradition*, Colloquies on Art and Archaeology in Asia, no. 14, London 1987

Seidel 1982 Seidel, Anna. 'Tokens of Immortality in Han Graves' (with appendix by Marc Kalinowski), *Numen*, vol. XXIX, fasc. 1, July 1982, pp. 79–122

Seidel 1983 Seidel, Anna. 'Treasures and Taoist Sacraments: Taoist roots in the Apocrypha', in Strickmann 1983, pp. 291–371

Seidel 1984 Seidel, Anna. 'Taoist Messianism', *Numen*, vol. XXXI, fasc. 2, December 1984, pp. 161–98

Seidel 1987 Seidel, Anna. 'Traces of Han Religion in Funerary Texts Found in Tombs', in Akizuki Kan'ei (ed.), *Dōkyō to shūkyō bunka*, Tokyo 1987, pp. 678–714

Shaanxi 1964 Shaanxi sheng wenwu guanli weiyuan hui. 'Tang Yongtai gongzhu mu fajue jian bao', *Wenwu* 1964.1, pp. 7–33

Shaanxi 1966 Shaanxi sheng bowuguan. 'Shaanxi sheng

Yaoxian Liulin Beiyincun chu tu yipi Tangdai yin qi, *Wenwu* 1966.1, pp. 33, 46–7

Shaanxi 1972a Shaanxi sheng bowuguan. Tang Chang'an Xinghua fang zhi zhan tongjian bao', *Wenwu* 1972.1, pp. 43–6

Shaanxi 1986 The Museum of Qin Shi Huang's Terracotta Army. *Qin Shihuang bingmayong*, Beijing 1986

Shaanxi 1990 Shaanxi sheng bowuguan (ed.). *Han Tang sichou zhi lu wenwu jinghua*, Hong Kong 1990

Shaanxi 1993 Museum of Qin Shi Huang's Terracotta Army. *A Wonder of the World, Treasures of the Nation: Terracotta Army of Emperor Qin Shihuang*, Hong Kong 1993

Shaanxi 1998a Qin Shihuang bing ma yong bowuguan, Shaanxi sheng kaogu yanjiusuo. *Qin shihuang ling tongche ma fajue baogao*, Beijing 1998

Shaanxi 1998b Qin Shihuang bing ma yong bowuguan. *Qin shihuang ling tongche ma xiufu baogao*, Beijing 1998

Shanghai 1996 Zhongguo wenwu ju. *Zhongguo wenwu jinghua da cidian: jin yin yu shi juan*, Shanghai 1996

Shanxi 1994a Shanxi sheng kaogu yanjiusuo (ed.). *San Jin kaogu*, vol. 1, Taiyuan 1994

Shanxi 1994b Shanxi sheng kaogu yanjiusuo (ed.). *Shanxi kaogu sishinian*, Taiyuan 1994

Shaughnessy 1988 Shaughnessy, Edward L. 'Historical Perspectives on the Introduction of the Chariot into China', *Harvard Journal of Asiatic Studies*, vol. 48, 1988, pp. 189–237

Shi Xingbang 1988 Shi Xingbang (ed.). *The Precious Cultural Relics in the Crypt of Famensi Temple* (text in English and Chinese), Xi'an 1988

Sickman and Soper 1968 Sickman, Laurence and Soper, Alexander. *The Art and Architecture of China* (3rd edn), Harmondsworth 1968

Sima Qian 1959 Sima Qian. *Shiji*, Beijing 1959

Singapore 1990 Empress Place (ed.). *Treasures from the Han*, exhibition catalogue, Singapore 1990

Singapore 1991 Empress Place (ed.). *The Silk Road: Treasures of Tang China*, exhibition catalogue, Singapore 1991

Singapore 1993 Empress Place (ed.). *War and Ritual: Treasures from the Warring States 475–221 BC*, exhibition catalogue, Singapore 1993

Singer 1972 Singer, Paul. *Early Chinese Gold and Silver*, New York 1972

Sirén 1925 Sirén, Osvald. *Chinese Sculpture from the Fifth to the Fourteenth Centuries*, 4 vols, London 1925

Sirén 1938 Sirén, Osvald et al. *Studies in Chinese Art and Some Indian Influences*, London 1938

Sirén 1940 Sirén, Osvald. 'Chinese Marble Sculptures of the Transition Period', *Bulletin of the Museum of Far Eastern Antiquities*, no. 12, 1949, pp. 473–96

Sirén 1956–8 Sirén, Osvald. *Chinese Painting: Leading Masters and Principles*, 7 vols, New York 1956–8

Sirén 1963 Sirén, Osvald. *The Chinese on the Art of Painting*, New York and Hong Kong 1963

Skorupski 1989 Skorupski, Tadeusz (ed.). *Buddhica Britannica Series Continua I: The Buddhist Heritage*, Papers delivered at the Symposium convened at the School of Oriental and African Studies, University of London, November 1985, Tring 1989

Snellgrove 1978 Snellgrove, David L. (ed.). *The Image of the Buddha*, Tokyo 1978

Song Boyin 1984 Song Boyin. 'Tea drinking, tea ware and purple clay ware', in Flagstaff 1984, pp. 14–25

Song Yanyan 1991 Song Yanyan (ed.). *Tangdai yishu*, Xi'an 1991

Soothill and Hodous 1975 Soothill, WE. and Hodous, L. *A Dictionary of Chinese Buddhist Terms, with Sanskrit and English Equivalents and a Sanskrit-Pali Index*, Taipei 1975 (originally published London 1937)

Soper 1958 Soper, Alexander. 'T'ang ch'ao ming hua lu: Celebrated Painters of the T'ang Dynasty, by Chu Ching-hsüan of T'ang', *Artibus Asiae*, vol. 21, 1958, pp. 204–30

Sowerby 1937 Sowerby, A de C. 'The Horse and Other Beasts of Burden in China', *China Journal*, vol. 26, 1937, pp. 282–7

Stein 1907 Stein, Aurel. *Ancient Khotan: Detailed Report of Archaeological Explorations in Chinese Turkestan*, Oxford 1907

Stein 1921 Stein, Aurel. *Serindia: A Detailed Report of Explorations in Central Asia and Westernmost China*, Oxford 1921

Stein 1925 Stein, Aurel. 'Innermost Asia: Its Geography as a Factor in History', *Geographical Journal*, vol. 65, 1925, pp. 377–403, 473–501

Stein 1928 Stein, Aurel. *Innermost Asia: Detailed Report on Explorations in Central Asia, Kan-su and Eastern Iran*, Oxford 1928

Stein 1933 Stein, Aurel. *On Ancient Central Asian Tracks: Brief Narrative of Three Expeditions in Innermost Asia and North-western China*, London 1933 (reprinted Chicago and London 1964)

Steinhardt 1990 Steinhardt, Nancy Shatzman. *Chinese Imperial City Planning*, Honolulu 1990

Strickmann 1977 Strickmann, Michel. 'The Mao Shan Revelations: Taoism and the Aristocracy', *T'oung Pao*, no. 63, 1977, pp. 1–64

Strickmann 1983 Strickmann, Michel (ed.) *Tantric and Taoist Studies in Honour of R. A. Stein, vol. 2, Mélanges Chinois et Bouddhiques*, vol. XXI, Brussels 1983

Sturman 1988 Sturman, Peter C. 'Celestial Journey: Meditations on (and in) Han dynasty Painted Pots at the Metropolitan Museum of Art', *Orientations*, May 1988, pp. 54–67

Sullivan 1962 Sullivan, Michael. *The Birth of Landscape Painting in China*, London 1962

Sullivan 1980 Sullivan, Michael. *Chinese Landscape Painting of the Sui and T'ang Dynasties*, Berkeley, Los Angeles and London 1980

Sun Ji 1986 Sun Ji. 'Woguo gudai de gedai', *Wenwu yu kaogu lunji*, Beijing 1986

Sun Ji 1991 Sun Ji. *Handai wuzhi wenhua ziliao tushuo*, Beijing 1991

Sun Ji 1994 Sun Ji. 'Xian Qin, Han, Jin yaodai jinyin dai kou', *Wenwu* 1994.1, pp. 50–64

Sun Ji 1996 Sun Ji. 'Zhongguo cha wenhua yu riben chadao', *Zhongguo lishi bowuguan guankan* 1996.1, pp. 62–6, translated in *China Art and Archaeology Digest*, vol. 1, no. 3, July–September 1996, pp. 102–4

Swann 1963 Swann, Peter. *Chinese Monumental Art*, New York, 1963

Swart and Till 1984 Swart, Paula and Till, Barry. 'Bronze Carriages from the Tomb of China's First Emperor', *Archaeology*, vol. 37, no. 6, 1984

Taipei 1967 National Palace Museum (ed.). *Chinese Cultural Art Treasures 1967*, 4th edn, Taipei 1967

Taipei 1992a *International Colloquium on Chinese Art History, 1991, Proceedings*, 2 vols, Taipei 1992

Taipei 1992b Wenwu Jiaoliu Zhongxin and Zhanwang Wenjiao Jijinhui (eds). *Dalu guwu zhenbaozhan*, Taipei 1992

Taipei 1995 National Palace Museum, *Auspicious Ju-i Scepters of China*, Taipei 1995

Tait 1976 Tait, Hugh. *Jewellery Through 7000 Years*, London 1976

Tan 1996 Tan, Rita C. 'Influence of Yue Ware on Shapes and Decorative Styles of Other Wares', in Wang Qingzheng 1996, pp. 28–33

Tang Chengdong 1996 Tang Chengdong. *Magnificent Frescoes from the Great Tang Dynasty* (text in English and Chinese), Xi'an 1996

Tang Jinyu 1959 Tang Jinyu. 'Xi'an xijiao Sui Li Jingxun mu fajue jianbao', *Kaogu* 1959.9, pp. 471–2

Teggart 1939 Teggart, Frederick J. *Rome and China: A Study of Correlation in Historical Events*, Berkeley 1939

Temple 1991 Temple, Robert. *The Genius of China*, London 1991

Thieme 1995 Thieme, Cristina *et al.* 'Research on Paint Materials, Paint Techniques and Conservation Experiments on the Polychrome Terracotta Army of the First Emperor Qin Shi Huang', in Vincenzini 1995, pp. 591–601

Thompson 1967 Thompson, Nancy. 'The Evolution of the T'ang Lion and Grapevine Mirror', *Artibus Asiae*, vol. XXVIIII, no. 1, 1967, pp. 25–40

Thorp 1982 Thorp, Robert L. 'The Date of Tomb 5 at Yinxu, Anyang', *Artibus Asiae*, vol. XLIII, no. 3, 1982, pp. 239–46

Thorp 1988a Thorp, Robert L. *Son of Heaven, Imperial Arts of China*, Seattle 1988

Thorp 1988b Thorp, Robert L. 'The Archaeology of Style at Anyang: Tomb 5 in Context', *Archives of Ancient Art*, vol. XLI, 1988, pp. 47–69

Thorp 1991 Thorp, Robert. 'Mountain Tombs and Jade Burial Suits: Preparations for Eternity in the Western Han', in Kuwayama 1991, pp. 26–39

Thote 1993 Thote, Alain. 'Aspects of the Serpent on Eastern Zhou Bronzes and Lacquerware', in Whitfield, R. 1993, pp. 150–60

Thote 1995 Thote, Alain. 'De quelques décors au serpent sur les bronzes rituels du royaume de Chu', in Diény, Jean-Pierre (ed.), *Hommage à Kwong Hing Foon: études d'histoire culturelle de la Chine*, Paris 1995

Till 1980 Till, Barry. 'Some Observations on Stone Winged Chimeras at Ancient Chinese Tomb Sites', *Artibus Asiae*, vol. XL, no. 4, 1980, pp. 261–81

Till and Swart 1988 Till, Barry and Swart, Paula, *Images from the Tomb: Chinese Burial Figurines*, Victoria 1988

Tokyo 1973 Tokyo National Museum and Asahi Shimbun (eds). *Archaeological Treasures Excavated in the People's Republic of China*, exhibition catalogue, Tokyo 1973

Tokyo 1981 Wenwu Publications and Kodansha (eds). *Senseisho Hakubutsukan (Shaanxi Provincial Museum)*, Tokyo 1981

Tokyo 1992 Tokyo National Museum. *Tomb of Yi, the Marquis of Zeng*, exhibition catalogue (text in Japanese), Tokyo 1992

Toronto 1992 Royal Ontario Museum. *Homage to Heaven, Homage to Earth: Chinese Treasures from the Royal Ontario Museum*, Toronto 1992

Trubner 1957 Trubner, Henry. *The Arts of the T'ang Dynasty: A Loan Exhibition Organized by the Los Angeles County Museum from Collections in America, the Orient and Europe, January 8–February 17, 1957*, Los Angeles 1957

Trubner 1959 Trubner, Henry. 'The Arts of the T'ang Dynasty', *Ars Orientalis*, vol. III, 1959, pp. 147–52

Tsao 1997 Tsao Hsingyuan. 'From Hair to Ear: Head Ornaments Represented in Chinese Art as Signs of Cultural Identity', *Orientations*, March 1997, pp. 79–87

Twitchett 1979 Twitchett, Denis (ed.). *The Cambridge History of China: Vol. 3: Sui and T'ang China*, part 1, Cambridge 1979

Twitchett and Loewe 1986 Twitchett, Denis and Loewe, Michael (eds). *The Cambridge History of China: Vol. 1: The Ch'in and Han Empires, 221 B.C.–A.D. 220*, Cambridge 1986

Unesco 1984 The Institute of Archaeology, Academy of Social Sciences, People's Republic of China. *Recent Archaeological Discoveries in the People's Republic of China*, Tokyo 1984

Vainker 1991 Vainker, SJ. *Chinese Pottery and Porcelain*, London 1991

Vainker 1996 Vainker, SJ. 'Identification of "Secret Colour" Yue Ware Amongst the Greenwares in the Ashmoleum Museum, Oxford', in Wang Qingzheng 1996, pp. 57–9

Venice 1983 *7000 Years of Chinese Civilisation: Chinese art and archaeology from the Neolithic Period to the Han Dynasty*, exhibition catalogue, Milan 1983

Venice 1986 Museum of Chinese History in Beijing, Seminar of Chinese Language and Literature of the University of Venice and the Italian Institute for the Middle and Far East. *China in Venice*, Milan 1986

Vienna 1974 Österreichisches Museum für Angewandte Kunst (ed.). *Archäologische Funde der Volksrepublik China*, Vienna 1974

Vincenzini 1995 Vincenzini, P. (ed.). *The Ceramics Cultural Heritage: Proceedings of the International Symposium of the 8th CIMTEC–World Ceramics Congress and Forum on New Materials, Florence, Italy, June 28–July 2, 1994*, Faenza 1995

Wagner 1997 Wagner, Lothar. 'Chinese Seals', in Collon 1997, pp. 205–22

Wagner 1994 Wagner, M. 'Jade – Der edel Stein für die Elite', in Eggebrecht 1994, pp. 96–104

Waley 1923 Waley, Arthur. 'T'ai Tsung's Six Chargers', *Burlington Magazine*, vol. 43, September 1923, pp. 117–18

Waley 1927 Waley, Arthur. 'Foreign Fashions: Po Chü-I (772–846)', *Forum*, vol. 78, July 1927, p. 3

Waley 1931 Waley, Arthur. *A Catalogue of Paintings Recovered from Tun-huang by Sir Aurel Stein, K.C.I.E., Preserved in the Sub-Department of Oriental Prints and Drawings in the British Museum, and in the Museum of Central Asian Antiquities, Delhi*, London 1931

Waley 1941 Waley, Arthur. *Translations from the Chinese*, New York 1941

Waley 1952 Waley, Arthur. *The Real Tripitaka and Other Pieces*, London 1952

Waley 1954 Waley, Arthur. *The Book of Songs*, London 1954

Waley 1955 Waley, Arthur. 'The Heavenly Horses of Ferghana: A New View', *History Today*, vol. 5, 1955, pp. 95–103

Waley 1960 Waley, Arthur. *Ballads and Stories from Tunhuang: An Anthology*, London 1960

Waley 1961 Waley, Arthur. *Chinese Poems* (new edn), London 1961

Wang Kai 1990 Wang Kai. 'The Han Terra-cotta Army in Xuzhou', *Orientations*, October 1990, pp. 62–6

Wang Qingzheng 1996 Wang Qingzheng (ed). *Yue Ware Miseci Porcelain*, Shanghai 1996

Wang Renbo 1990 Wang Renbo (ed.). *Sui Tang wenhua*, Hong Kong 1990

Wang, Wellington 1996 Wang, Wellington. *Belt Ornaments Through the Ages*, Taipei 1996

Wang Wenqing 1994 Wang Wenqing. *Ten Major Museums of Shaanxi*, Hong Kong 1994

Wang Xueli 1992 Wang Xueli (ed.). *Zhongguo Han Yangling caiyong*, Hong Kong 1992

Wang Zhongshu 1982 Wang Zhongshu. *Han Civilization*, New Haven 1982

Watson 1961 Watson, Burton. *Records of the Grand Historian of China, translated from the Shih chi of Ssu-ma Ch'ien*, vol. 1, *Early Years of the Han Dynasty, 109 to 141 BC*; vol. 2, *The Age of Emperor Wu, 140–c. 100 BC*, New York and London 1961

Watson 1993 Watson, Burton (trans.). *Records of the Grand Historian: Qin Dynasty*, Hong Kong 1993

Watson 1970 Watson, William (ed.). *Pottery and Metalwork in T'ang China: Their Chronology and External Relations*, Colloquies on Art and Archaeology in Asia, no. 1, London 1970

Watson 1971 Watson, William. *Cultural Frontiers in Ancient East Asia*, Edinburgh 1971

Watson 1973 Watson, William. *The Genius of China: An Exhibition of Archaeological Finds of the People's Republic of China*, London 1973

Watson 1974 Watson, William. *Style in the Arts of China*, Harmondsworth 1974

Watson 1984 Watson, William. *Tang and Liao Ceramics*, London 1984

Watson 1991 Watson, William. *Pre-Tang Ceramics of China: Chinese Pottery from 4000 BC–600 AD*, London and Boston 1991

Watt 1980 Watt, James CY. *Chinese Jades from Han to Ch'ing*, New York 1980

Watt 1990 Watt, James CY. *The Arts of Ancient China: The Metropolitan Museum of Art Bulletin, Summer 1990*

Wei Zhengjin 1993 Wei Zhengjin. 'Yingpanshan guwenhua yizhi', in *Jinling shengyi daquan*, Nanjing 1993, pp. 169–72

Weidner 1994 Weidner, Marsha (ed.). *Latter Days of the Law: Images of Chinese Buddhism 850–1850*, Lawrence, Kansas 1994

Welch and Seidel 1979 Welch, Holmes and Seidel, Anna (eds). *Facets of Taoism*, New Haven 1979

Werner 1961 Werner, ETC. *A Dictionary of Chinese Mythology*, New York 1961

Weschler 1974 Weschler, Howard J. *Mirror to the Son of Heaven: Wei Cheng at the Court of T'ai-tsung*, New Haven and London 1974

White 1934 White, W. *Tombs of Old Lo-yang*, Shanghai 1934

White 1995 White, Garrett (ed.). *Imperial Tombs of China*, Memphis 1995

White and Bunker 1994 White, Julia and Bunker, Emma C. *Adornment for Eternity: Status and Rank in Chinese Ornament*, Denver and Hong Kong 1994

Whitfield 1982–3 Whitfield, Roderick. *The Art of Central Asia: The Stein Collection in the British Museum*, 2 vols, Tokyo 1982–3

Whitfield 1990 Whitfield, Roderick. 'The Significance of the Famensi Deposit', *Orientations*, May 1990, pp. 84–5

Whitfield 1993 Whitfield, Roderick (ed.). *The Problem of Meaning in Early Chinese Ritual Bronzes*, Colloquies on Art and Archaeology in Asia, no. 15, London 1993

Whitfield and Farrer 1990 Whitfield, Roderick and Farrer, Anne. *Caves of the Thousand Buddhas: Chinese Art from the Silk Route*, London 1990

Whitfield 1999 Whitfield, Susan. *Life Along the Silk Road*, London 1999

Wilkinson 1998 Wilkinson, Endymion. *Chinese History: A Manual*, Cambridge, Mass. and London 1998

Willetts 1965 Willetts, William. *Foundations of Chinese Art from Neolithic Pottery to Modern Architecture*, London 1965

Williams 1976 Williams, CAS. *Outlines of Chinese Symbolism and Art Motives: An Alphabetical Compendium of Antique Legends and Beliefs, As Reflected in the Manners and Customs of the Chinese*, New York, 1976 (3rd revised edn)

Wirgin 1985 Wirgin, Jan, *The Emperor's Warriors*, exhibition catalogue, Edinburgh 1985

Wong Yanchong 1988 Wong Yanchong 1988. 'Bronze Mirror Art of the Han Dynasty, *Orientations*, December 1988, pp. 42–53

Wright 1957 Wright, Arthur F. 'Buddhism and Chinese Culture: Phases of Interaction', *Journal of Asian Studies*, vol. 17, 1957, pp. 17–42

Wright 1959 Wright, Arthur F. *Buddhism in Chinese History*, Stanford 1959

Wright 1960 Wright, Arthur F (ed.). *The Confucian Persuasion*, Stanford 1960

Wright and Twitchett 1973 Wright, Arthur F. and Twitchett, Denis (eds). *Perspectives on the T'ang*, New Haven and London 1973

Wu and Han 1998 Wu Limin and Han Jinke. *Famensi digong Tang mi Mantuluo zhi yanjiu* (Research on Tang period Esoteric mandalas from the Famensi crypt), Hong Kong 1998

Wu Hung 1987 Wu Hung. 'Myths and Legends in Han Funerary Art', in Lim 1987, pp. 72–82

Wu Hung 1988 Wu Hung. 'From Temple to Tomb: Ancient Chinese Art and Religion in Transition', *Early China*, vol. 13, 1988, pp. 78–115

Wu Hung 1989 Wu Hung. *The Wu Liang Shrine: The Ideology of Early Chinese Pictorial Art*, Stanford 1989

Wu Hung 1994 Wu Hung. 'Beyond the "Great Boundary": Funerary Narratives in the Cangshan Tomb', in John Hay (ed.), *Boundaries in China*, London 1994

Xi'an 1964 Xi'an shi wenwu guanli weiyuan hui. 'Xi'an shi dongnanbiao Shapocun chu tu yipi Tangdai yin qi', *Wenwu* 1964.6, pp. 30–2

Xi'an 1986 Museum of Qin Shi Huang's Terra-cotta Army (ed.). *Terra-cotta Figures and Bronze Chariots and Horses at Qin Mausoleum*, Xi'an 1986

Xi'an 1992 Shaanxi Provincial Museum, *The Gems of the Cultural Relics*, Xi'an 1992

Xi'an 1994 Famen Temple Museum. *Famen Temple*, Xi'an 1994

Xi'an 1995 Shaanxi History Museum. *Gold and Silver Treasures of the Tang Dynasty*, Xi'an 1995

Xi'an 1996 *China Xianyang 3000 Western Han Painted Terra-Cotta Figurines of Warriors and Horses*, Xi'an 1996

Xi'an 1997 Administrative Bureau of Museums and Archaeological Data of Shaanxi Province. *Past Revealed and Antiquity Revisited*, Xi'an 1997

Xiao Kangda 1992 Xiao Kangda. *Handai lewu baixi yishu yanjiu*, Beijing 1992

Xing and Tang 1984 Xing Runchuan and Tang Yunming. 'Archaeological Evidence for Ancient Wine Making', in *Recent Discoveries in Chinese Archaeology*, Beijing 1984, pp. 56–8

Xiong and Laing 1991 Xiong Victor Cunrui and Laing, Ellen Johnston. 'Foreign Jewellery in Ancient China', *Bulletin of the Asia Institute*, no. 5, 1991, pp. 163–73

Yang Boda 1986 Yang Boda (ed.). *Zhongguo meishu quanji – gongyi meishu bian 9: yuqi*, Beijing 1986

Yang Boda 1987 Yang Boda (ed.). *Zhongguo meishu quanji – gongyi meishu bian 10 : Jin yin boli falang*, Beijing 1987

Yang Boda 1993 Yang Boda (ed.). *Zhongguo yuqi quanji – bian 5: Sui, Tang–Ming*, Beijing 1993

Yang Hong 1992 Yang Hong. *Weapons in Ancient China*, New York and Beijing 1992

Yang and Yang 1979 Yang Hsien-yi and Yang, Gladys. *Selections from the Records of the Historian, by Sima Qian*, Beijing 1979

Yang Jianfang 1987 Yang Jianfang. *Jade Carving in Chinese Archaeology*, vol. 1, Hong Kong 1987

Yao 1983 Yao, Esther S. Lee. *Chinese Women: Past & Present*, Mesquite, Texas 1983

Yao Qinde 1991 Yao Qinde (intro. Hsiao-Yen Shih, trans. Vivian Ho). 'Spring and Autumn Period Jades from the State of Wu', *Orientations*, October 1991, pp. 47–52

Yates 1994 Yates, Robin DS. 'Philosophers and Statemen', in Murowchick 1994, pp. 91–9

Yen Lei 1959 Yen Lei. 'Xian chutu de Tangdai jinyin qi', *Wenwu* 1959.8, pp. 34–5

Yetts 1930 Yetts, WP. *The Catalogue of the George Eumorfopoulos Collection of Chinese and Corean Bronzes, Sculptures, Jades, Jewellery and Miscellaneous Objects*, London 1930

Yetts 1934 Yetts, WP. 'A Chinese Silver Vessel', *Burlington Magazine*, vol. LXIIII, April 1934, pp. 176–81

Yin and Li 1992 Yin Shengping and Li Xixing (eds). *Shaanxi History Museum: Selected Treasures*, Hong Kong 1992

Yin Shengping 1994 Yin Shengping (ed.). *Shaanxi History Museum*, Hong Kong 1994

Yü Yingshih 1964–5 Yü Yingshih. 'Life and Immortality in the Mind of Han China', *Harvard Journal of Asiatic Studies*, vol. 25, 1964–5, pp. 80–122

Yü Yingshih 1987 Yü Yingshih. 'O Soul, Come Back! A Study in the Changing Conceptions of the Soul and Afterlife in Pre-Buddhist China', *Harvard Journal of Asiatic Studies*, vol. 47, no. 2, December 1987, pp. 363–95

Yuan Ke 1991 Yuan Ke (ed.). *Shanhaijing quanyi*, Guizhou 1991

Yuan Zhongyi 1990 Yuan Zhongyi. *Qin Shihuang ling bing ma yong yanjiu*, Beijing 1990

Zhang Hongxiu 1995 Zhang Hongxiu. *A Collection of Tang Dynasty Frescoes* (text in English and Chinese), Xi'an 1995

Zhang Wenli 1996 Zhang Wenli. *The Qin Terracotta Army: Treasures of Lintong*, London 1996

Zhang Xiying 1994 Zhang Xiying. 'Zhongguo zongjiao yishu suyuan', *Bowuguan yanjiu* 1994.2

Zhang Zhengming 1987 Zhang Zhengming. *Chu wenhuashi*, Shanghai 1987

Zhang Zibo 1979 Zhang Zibo. 'Xianyang shi Xinzhuang chutu de si jian Handai yu diao qi', *Wenwu* 1979.2, p. 60

Zhao Chao 1994 Zhao Chao. 'Luetan Tangdai jin yin qi yanjiu zhong de fenqi wenti', in CASS, Institute of Archaeology (ed.), *Han Tang yu bianjiang kaogu yanjiu*, vol. 1, Beijing 1994

Zhejiang 1982 Zhangxing xian bowuguan and Xia Xingnan. 'Zhejiang Zhangxing xian faxian yipi Tangdai yin', *Wenwu* 1982.11, pp. 38–42

Zhejiang 1984 'Shao xing 306 hao zhanguo mu fajue jian bao', *Wenwu* 1984.1, pp. 10–26

Zhou and Gao 1987 Zhou Xun and Gao Chunming. *5000 Years of Chinese Costumes*, San Francisco 1987

Zhou and Gao 1991 Zhou Xun and Gao Chunming. *Zhongguo lidai funü zhuangshi*, Shanghai 1991

Zhou Xibao 1984 Zhou Xibao. *Zhongguo gudai fushishi*, Beijing 1984

Zhu Bao 1981 Zhu Bao. 'Tang ruan niao shou di wen jin yin ping tuo tong jing', *Kaogu yu Wenwu* 1981.3, pp. 107, 127

Zhu, Li and Liu 1982 Zhu Jieyuan, Li Guozhen and Liu Xiangqun. 'Xi'an xijiao chutu Tang "xuan hui jiu fang" yin jiu zhu', *Kaogu yu Wenwu* 1982.1, pp. 51–2

Zhu Qixin 1990 Zhu Qixin. 'Buddhist Treasures from Famensi', *Orientations*, May 1990, pp. 77–83

Zou Zongxu 1991 Zou Zongxu (trans. Susan Whitfield). *The Land Within the Passes: A History of Xian*, New York and London 1991

Zuo Boyang 1984 Zuo Boyang (trans.). *Recent Discoveries in Chinese Archaeology*, Beijing 1984

Zuo Boyang 1995 Zuo Boyang (trans.). *The Discovery of a Missing King's Tomb – Selections of Chinese Relics and Archaeology*, Beijing 1995

Zürcher 1972 Zürcher, E. *The Buddhist Conquest of China*, 2 vols, Leiden 1972

Zwalf 1985 Zwalf, W (ed.). *Buddhism: Art and Faith*, London 1985

CHRONOLOGY

EARLY DYNASTIES

Shang	c.1500–1050 BC
Western Zhou	1050–771 BC
Eastern Zhou	
Spring and Autumn	770–475 BC
Warring States	475–221 BC

IMPERIAL CHINA

Qin	221–207 BC
Han	
Western Han	206 BC–AD 9
Xin	AD 9–25
Eastern Han	AD 25–220
Three Kingdoms	
Shu (Han)	221–263
Wei	220–265
Wu	222–280

Southern dynasties (Six Dynasties)

Western Jin	265–316
Eastern Jin	317–420
Liu Song	420–479
Southern Qi	479–502

Liang	502–557
Chen	557–589
Northern dynasties	
Northern Wei	386–535
Eastern Wei	534–550
Western Wei	535–557
Northern Qi	550–577
Northern Zhou	557–581
Sui	589–618
Tang	618–906
Five Dynasties	907–960
Liao	907–1125
Song	
Northern Song	960–1126
Southern Song	1127–1279
Jin	1115–1234
Yuan	1279–1368
Ming	1368–1644
Qing	1644–1911

REPUBLICAN CHINA

Republic	1912–49
People's Republic	1949–

TANG DYNASTY RULERS

EMPEROR	TEMPLE NAME	REIGN DATES	PRINCIPAL WIFE/CONSORT
Li Yuan	Gaozu	618–626 (abdicated)	Empress Dou
Li Shimin	Taizong	626–649	Empress Wende
Li Zhi	Gaozong	649–683	Empress Wang (demoted)
Li Zhe	Zhongzong	684 (deposed)	Empress Wei
Li Dan	Ruizong	684–690 (deposed)	
Wu Zhao	Empress Wu Zetian	690–705	Gaozong (husband)
Li Zhe	Zhongzong	705–710	Empress Wei
Li Dan	Ruizong	710–712 (abdicated)	
Li Longji	Xuanzong (Ming Huang)	712–756 (abdicated)	Consort Yang Guifei
Li Yu	Suzong	756–762	
Li Yu	Daizong	762–779	
Li Shi	Dezong	779–805	
Li Song	Shunzong	805 (abdicated)	
Li Chun	Xianzong	805–820	
Li Heng	Muzong	820–824	
Li Zhan	Jingzong	824–827	
Li Ang	Wenzong	827–840	
Li Yan	Wuzong	840–846	
Li Chen	Xuanzong	846–859	Zhao (not Empress)
Li Wen	Yizong	859–873	
Li Yan	Xizong	873–888	
Li Jie	Zhaozong	888–904	
Li Zhu	Aidi (Zhaoxuan)	904–907 (deposed)	

The Han empire and its neighbours.

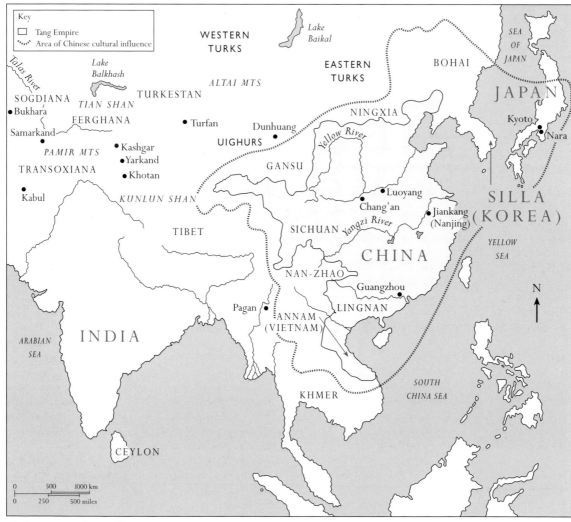

The Tang empire and its neighbours.

INDEX

18, 20–3; seals 54, 55–6; tombs and hoards 14, 59–129

Tang Huiyao (documents) 85, 113

Tang Shi lu 75

tea 154–5, 159; tea ceremony 102; tea sieve, silver 22, 154–6, *155*; tea storage jars, silver 154, 156, 157–8; tea warming vessels 117

terracotta army 14, 24, 35–6, *35*, 39–42, *45*; charioteer 37

textiles 20, 59, 74; in Buddhist temple 134, *135*, 148; on figures in tombs 45, 70; incense sachets 112; *see also* silk

Tianma Qucun, tombs 74

Tibet (Tibetans) 16, 59, 61, 62, 80, 81

tigers, as objects and motif 25, 53, 95, 123; gold 27, *27*; seal handles 54

tombs 13–14, 21, 24–58; lion guardian figures 122; Tang dynasty 59–129 *passim*; spirit way to 51, 58

tortoises 100, 149, 150, 154; on seals, gold 54–5, and silver 55–6, *55*

trees, gold 94–5, *94*; *see also* lamp trees; money trees

Turkestan: gold 16; tomb figurines 70

Turkey 59, 84

Turks 60, 61, 80, 116, 118–19

Uighurs 48, 59, 62, 80, *83*, 132, 136, 155

unicorns 56, 149; inlays 95

Vedas (Indian texts) 138, 139

vermilion 67, 93

vidyārajās see under Buddhism

Vietnam 44, 59, 84

Wang Jian, poet 113

Wang Wei, poet 13, 14

Warring States period 16, 17, 31, 33, 41, 47, 64, 156; armour 45; belt plaques 74; bronze technique 46; currency 56; gold 19–20, 24, *24*, 25, 26

weapons 37, 39, 41–2, *42*, 45, *45*, 46

Wei, empress 59, 61, 68, 76 ·

Wei family 68, 101; tomb 76, 77

Wei kingdom 80

Wei Xun, tomb 76, *76*, 100–1, *101*

Wei Ying Wu, poet 65–6

Wei Zheng, minister 15

Weiling, jades 50–3

Wensi yuan royal workshop 149, 154

Western Han *see* Han dynasty

Western Zhou 18, 19, 29, 91, 102, 158

wine 85, 99, 110; wine cups 21, 63, 84, 127; wine drinking vessels 99; wine flask, silver 118–19, *118*; wine vessels 18, 100; wine warmer, gold 116–17, *117*

women: amber as protection 53; on cup 124; facial ornament 67, *67*; fashions 70–1, 84; foot binding 15, 60; freedom of 59–60, 71, 72–3; hairstyles 64, 66, 71; makeup 67, *67*, 68–9; status denoted by jewellery 104

Wu Daozi, painter 120

Wu kingdom 80

Wu Zetian, empress 59, 60, *60*, 68, 73, 76, 120, *133*; and Buddhism 132–3, 134, 144; tomb 81, *81*, 92, *93*

Wudi, Han emperor 43, 44, 48, 49, 50, 56, 79, 91, 93, 94; Maoling tomb 48, *91*, *98*

Wuling, King of Zhao 28, 29

Wuzong, emperor 110, 136–7, 144

Xi'an *see* Chang'an

Xianyang *32*, 33, 44; ewer and cover, gold 99–100, *100*

Xiao, King of Liang 19

Xichuan Xiasi, jade handle 28

Xijing zaji 94, 95

Xin Tang shu (new Tang history) 75, 77, 98, 122

Xinzhuang village, jade animals 50–3

Xiongnu nomads 26, 44, 47, 48, 52, 79, 80; tombs 26

Xizong, emperor 134, 158

Xuanzang, Buddhist monk 44, 104, 131–2, 147

Xuanzong (Minghuang, the Brilliant Emperor) 61, 62, 64–5, 66, 73, 81, 83, 106, 112, 116, 118, 120, 128, 131, 137, 138, 139, 140

Yan Liben, painter 155

Yang Guifei, concubine 59, 61–2, *61*, 64–5, 66, 70, 71, 72, 96, 99, 106, 112, 120

Yang Guozhong 61–2

Yang Xiong 55

Yangjiawan, earthenware miniature soldiers 44–5, *45*, 46, *46*

Yangling Mausoleum of Emperor Jing 45

Yangxin, Princess 48, 49

Yaoxian, silverware 23

Yarkand, jade source 128

Yellow Emperor 49, 103

Yi of Zeng, Marquis, tomb 18, 19, 24, *24*, 28, 39, 47, 72

Yide (Li Zhongrun), Prince, tomb 60, 61, *61*, 87, 125

Yijing (text) 91

Yimen village: belt hooks, gold 27–8, *27*; harness ornaments 29–30, *30*; sword and hilt 19, 30–1, *31*

Ying Shao, writer 26

Yizong, emperor 144, 148–9, 151, 153, 154, 158, 160

Yongcheng, horse decoration 29, *29*

Yongtai, Princess, tomb 60, 86–7, *86*

Yu Shinan, poet 122

Yuan dynasty, wine vessels 100

Yuandi, emperor 50

Yuanzitou village, inlay decorations 95–6, *95*, *96*

Yuezhi, the 79

Yungang Buddhist grottoes *83*, 123

Yutian, jade from 105

Zhang E, poet 113

Zhang Jianfeng 73

Zhang Qian, general 44, 48, 79, 99, 110

Zhang Shigui, tomb 119

Zhang Yue, poet 113, 118

Zhanghuai (Li Xian), Prince, tomb 60, 61, *61*, 73, 81, *81*, 87, 125

Zhanguo ce (text) 19

Zheng, King *see* Qin Shi Huangdi

Zheng Rentai, tomb of 71–2

Zhenjiang, reliquary 22, 134, 144

Zhi Shi Fengjie, tomb 84

Zhongpu village, pottery female figure 70, *70*

Zhongshan, King of, silver wares in tomb 16

Zhongshan tombs 19, 28

Zhongzong, emperor 60, 61, 68, 76, 118

Zhou Bo, general, tomb 44

Zhou Yafu, tomb 44

Zhouli (Rites of Zhou) 26

zodiacal animals, pottery 102–3, *103*

Zuo Zhuan (text) 102